THEORY AND PRACTICE IN THE EIGHTEENTH CENTURY: WRITING BETWEEN PHILOSOPHY AND LITERATURE

THEORY AND PRACTICE IN THE EIGHTEENTH CENTURY: WRITING BETWEEN PHILOSOPHY AND LITERATURE

EDITED BY

Alexander Dick
AND
Christina Lupton

LONDON
PICKERING & CHATTO
2008

Published by Pickering & Chatto (Publishers) Limited
21 Bloomsbury Way, London WC1A 2TH

2252 Ridge Road, Brookfield, Vermont 05036-9704, USA

www.pickeringchatto.com

BRITISH LIBRARY CATALOGUING IN PUBLICATION DATA
Theory and practice in the eighteenth century: writing between philosophy and
literature
1. Philosophy, British – 18th century
I. Dick, Alex II. Lupton, Christina
192

ISBN-13: 9781851969388

This publication is printed on acid-free paper that conforms to the American
National Standard for the Permanence of Paper for Printed Library Materials.

Typeset by Pickering & Chatto (Publishers) Limited
Printed in the United Kingdom at the University Press, Cambridge

CONTENTS

NOTES ON CONTRIBUTORS

Mark Blackwell is Associate Professor and Chair of English at the University of Hartford. His most recent essays – on Austen, Locke, Radcliffe, and Burke – have appeared in *Eighteenth-Century Fiction, Studies in Eighteenth-Century Culture, Modern Philology, Philological Quarterly*, and *A Concise Companion to the Restoration and Eighteenth Century* (ed. Cynthia Wall). His article on live-tooth transplantation, published in *Eighteenth-Century Life*, won the 2004–5 James L. Clifford Prize. He is also the editor of *The Secret Life of Things: Animals, Objects, and It-Narratives in Eighteenth-Century England* (2007).

Adam Budd is a Lecturer in the Graduate School of Literatures, Languages, and Cultures at the University of Edinburgh. He has published articles on the eighteenth-century novel and print culture in such journals as *Eighteenth-Century Life* and *Review of English Studies*. He is the editor of *The Modern Historiography Reader: Western Sources*.

Joseph Chaves is an Assistant Professor of English at the University of Northern Colorado specializing in early American literature. He is currently working on a book titled *Polite Converse: Civility and Intimacy, 1711–1782*.

Eva M. Dadlez, Professor of Philosophy at the University of Central Oklahoma, is the author of *What's Hecuba to Him? Fictional Events and Actual Emotions* (1997). Her work on aesthetics and the philosophy of literature has appeared in *Hume Studies*, the *British Journal of Aesthetics*, the *Journal of Aesthetics and Art Criticism, Philosophy and Literature, Film and Philosophy* and other philosophical and interdisciplinary journals. She is now completing a book on the ethical and intellectual continuities between David Hume and Jane Austen.

Alexander Dick is Assistant Professor of English at the University of British Columbia. He has published articles and chapters on Wordsworth, Coleridge, Shelley, Charlotte Smith, Jane Austen and British Romantic Drama in such journals as *Studies in Romanticism* and *European Romantic Review*. He is also the co-editor (with Angela Esterhammer) of *Spheres of Action: Speech and Performance in Romantic Culture* (2008).

Maureen Harkin is Associate Professor of English and Humanities at Reed College. She is the editor of Mackenzie's *The Man of Feeling* (2004) and the author of a number of articles on Scottish Enlightenment philosophy, aesthetics and fiction in such journals as *ELH, Eighteenth Century Fiction* and *Studies in Eighteenth-Century Culture*.

Nicholas Hudson, Professor of English at the University of British Columbia, is author of *Samuel Johnson and Eighteenth-Century Thought* (1988), *Writing and European Thought, 1600–1830* (1994), *Samuel Johnson and the Making of Modern England* (2003) and of numerous essays on eighteenth-century literature, culture and philosophy. He is currently editing a volume of essays entitled *Swift's Travels: Eighteenth-Century British Satire and its Legacy*.

Jonathan Brody Kramnick is Associate Professor of English at Rutgers University. He is the author of *Making the English Canon: Print Capitalism and the Cultural Past, 1700–1770* (1990) as well as articles in *Eighteenth-Century Studies, ELH, Yale Journal of Criticism* and elsewhere. He is currently completing a book entitled *Uneasiness: Problems of Action from Rochester to Richardson*.

Christina Lupton is Assistant Professor of English at the University of British Columbia. She has published articles on Sterne, Goethe, Franklin, Dickens and critical theory in such journals as *Eighteenth Century Studies, ELH* and *New German Critique*. She is currently completing a book entitled *Knowing Books: Self-Conscious Writing in Eighteenth-Century Britain*.

Brian Michael Norton is completing his dissertation, 'The Art of Life: Ethics, Happiness, and the Philosophical Novel in Eighteenth Century Britain and France' in Comparative Literature at New York University. His article 'The Moral of Phutatorius' Breeches: Tristram Shandy and the Limits of Stoic Ethics' appears in *Eighteenth Century Fiction* (2006).

Adam Potkay, Professor of English at the College of William and Mary, is the author of *The Fate of Eloquence in the Age of Hume* (1994), *The Passion for Happiness: Samuel Johnson and David Hume* (2000) and *The Story of Joy from the Bible to Late Romanticism* (2007); he is also co-editor of *Black Atlantic Writers of the Eighteenth Century* (1995). He has written dozens of articles and reviews for journals including *PMLA, Raritan, Eighteenth-Century Studies, Wordsworth Circle* and *Studies in Early Modern Philosophy*.

John Richetti is A. M. Rosenthal Professor of English at the University of Pennsylvania. His books include *Popular Fiction before Richardson: Narrative Patterns 1700–1739* (1969), *Defoe's Narratives: Situations and Structures* (1975), *Philosophical Writing: Locke, Berkeley, Hume* (1983), *The English Novel in History, 1700–1780* (1999) and *The Life of Daniel Defoe* (2005). He has edited *The*

Cambridge Companion to the Eighteenth-Century Novel (1996), *The Columbia History of the British Novel* (1994) and (with Paula Backscheider) *Popular Fiction by Women: 1660–1740* (1996). He is also the editor of the Restoration and Eighteenth-Century volume of the *New Cambridge History of English Literature* (2005).

Jonathan Sadow completed his PhD in English at the University of Massachusetts, Amherst and is now Adjunct Professor at Concordia University in Montreal where he teaches courses on eighteenth-century fiction and aesthetics.

Nancy Yousef is Associate Professor of English at the City University of New York, Graduate Center and Baruch College. She is the author of *Isolated Cases: The Anxieties of Autonomy in Enlightenment Philosophy and Romantic Literature* (2004). Her current book project is 'Intimacy: Sympathetic Endeavor in Ethics, Narrative, and Psychoanalysis', an interdisciplinary study of the challenge of intersubjectivity as imagined in three related cultural manifestations: eighteenth-century ethical hypotheses of natural affections, nineteenth-century narratives representing the unstable ground between psychic privacy and exposure, and twentieth-century psychoanalytic efforts to theorize the possibilities and constraints of empathy.

INTRODUCTION

Christina Lupton and Alexander Dick

When, in the first book of *A Treatise of Human Nature*, Hume wants to exemplify the kind of belief allowing one to make sense of the most everyday experience, he offers an example that has become well known: hearing the door creak downstairs and seeing a porter arrive in his room a few minutes later, he must assume that the man has arrived by way of the stairs. But this example carries on, as the porter delivers a letter

> which upon opening it I perceive by the hand-writing and subscription to have come from a friend, who says he is two hundred leagues distant. 'Tis evident I can never account for this phenomenon, comfortable to my experience in other instances, without spreading out in my mind the whole sea and continent between us, and supposing the effects and continu'd existence of posts and ferries, according to my memory and observation.[1]

The example of the letter in Hume's hands as an object indecipherable by rational means is one of several moments when the *Treatise* calls attention to the written word in its tactile form, physically encountered by readers even at the moments when they are asked to suspect material forms of evidence. In order to read a letter, Hume suggests, one must actively make sense of something that is not actually perceptible: forgetting the distance it has travelled (for how could one verify that the posts and ferries still ran, or observe every step of its way?) and the contingencies that inevitably haunt its claims (so much time has passed since they were made), one must handle the letter irrationally in order to make sense of its words on paper. If a text is to be functional and pleasurable, the reader must accept the fiction of the distant friend's presence in writing.

This illustration calls up by inference the task of reading any book, produced, as Hume was well aware, as the result of frequent shuffling across oceans, between publishers and editors, printing, correcting and reprinting. In order to read the *Treatise*, Hume's example of the letter suggests, one must imagine Hume's unmediated voice in the room, and thus engage with reading as one of the sociable practices that makes up for the kinds of doubt that Hume expresses about all rational perceptions – and which are now connected, through the example of the letter, to the case of all writing in its physicality. In the end, Hume will suggest, the letter is more reliable as a common fiction than it is as a piece of physical evidence. And yet the example of the letter also calls attention to the way in which the reader holds the *Treatise* at the moment when he or she reaches the page that contains this example. The sheer reflexivity of the device, juxtaposing the prickly sensation of the real page and Hume's presentation of the fictional page as the most imaginatively constructed of all surfaces, brings writing into the argument as a case that must complicate, even as it is employed to confirm, Hume's suggestion that writing can only serve as a fictional, and never as an ontological, point of access to the material world.

As this example suggests, there are two kinds of 'practice' described by this word in our title. One is the practice of writing in its sheer materiality – a materiality that was particularly tactile and, as Clifford Siskin has argued in the *Work of Writing: Literature and Social Change in Britain 1700–1830*, quantitatively overwhelming in the eighteenth century. This proliferation of writing itself – understood here as a nexus of writing, print and silent reading – gave rise, Siskin argues, to the categories in which we now understand texts to originate: disciplinarity, professionalism and literature.[2] For our case, the terms of this reversal in our thinking about the relation between medium and content are crucial, for they suggest the possibility that the practice of writing came before its theory and help to explain what Mark Blackwell describes as the 'preposterous' logic pertaining to eighteenth-century philosophical texts.

The other practice implied by our title is the social practice that writing is understood to be by eighteenth-century writers who use genre, rhetoric and sensation as powerful tools in the construction – rather than just the representation – of the reality their texts describe. Practice may involve, as in the case of Hume or Reid, a belief in the positive power of language as a fiction that compensates for the doubts that an argument raises at the level of content. It might also involve, as in the case of experimental novelists like Diderot, Rousseau, Johnson and Sterne, the stretching of the categories of philosophy and literature themselves into new and compelling conjunctions. The essays in this collection share a sense of the way that one or both of the practical dimensions of writing mattered to the theoretical arguments they expressed. Thus, in the case of Hume described above, the *Treatise*, well-known for its audaciously sceptical epistemology, actually begins to look much more constructive once we take account of the way in which it performs the fictions of reality to which Hume ultimately refers, and of the way in which its material composition as a work of writing (its sequence, its various editions, its format) introduces a material dimension to experience that much of its argument denies. These kinds of practice can obviously intersect and inflect the theories expressed by eighteenth-century philosophers at the same time. But for the purposes of this introduction, and in the arrangement of our chapters, we have chosen to treat them individually.

Writing Philosophy

In the third Book of his *Essay Concerning Human Understanding* (1690), John Locke asserts that words stand, not for the reality of things, but only for ideas in the mind that uses them: 'It is a perverting use of Words and brings unavoidable Obscurity and Confusion into their Signification whenever we make them stand for anything but those *Ideas* we have in our own Minds'.[3] His account of the fully human origin of language, and of the subjective link between words and ideas, was a corrective both to the Cartesian account of innate ideas and to the view that language involved a divine correspondence between words and the things they named. Locke's position went on to influence the view of language of philosophers from Shaftesbury to Addison, Berkeley, Rousseau, Johnson and Kant. Fifty years later, David Hume would describe languages as 'gradually establish'd by human conventions' and stress their necessary but arbitrary value, analogous to the value assigned to gold and silver as a measure of exchange linked by convention alone to the objects they come to represent.[4] With these unsettling assertions in mind, the eighteenth century be can described as a period when language became a focus of anxiety as much because of the limited access to a stable reality that it seemed to promise as because of the sources of confusion and false responses that new genres of fiction might provoke.

In this respect it now seems obvious that many eighteenth-century theories of language resonate with those of the second part of the twentieth century, with the 'literary turns' taken in both periods exposing the extent to which language shapes, obscures and redefines the reality it claims to describe. As Nicholas Hudson puts it in the opening chapter of this collection, the empiricists' insistence 'that all human approaches to experience are mediated through signs ... *sounds* a lot like the implications of deconstruction' (below, p. 12). The fact that the writing of Locke, Hume, Berkeley and Reid has become the province of literary critics during the last decades reflects this affinity. Several strong literary studies of the 1980s and 1990s to which this collection is indebted explicitly use the licence of poststructuralism to unfold the operation of eighteenth-century philosophical texts, not just as theoretical statements about the subjective nature of language, but as discourses that put rhetoric to work in the service of reality. Rather than seeing empiricist writing as an expression of philosophical problems that had to be solved elsewhere, in the realms of society and science, John Richetti, Jerome Christensen, Leo Damrosh and Fred Parker all point out that the rhetorical performance of empiricism is part of the condition described and can, on occasion, make doubt itself reassuring. As Fred Parker has claimed, all 'sceptical thinking involves ... an essential tension or doubleness: a power of affir-mation that emerges from, without denying or transcending, the inadequacy of intellect to master the fluidity and variousness of things'.[5]

Just as Parker's willingness to concede to the 'fluidity and variousness of things' points to a realm of understanding beyond eighteenth-century rhetoric, these studies are all generally informed by the emphasis, common to at least one version of eighteenth-century empiricism and twentieth-century poststructur-alism, that it is language that shapes the way we experience the world. In this perspective, the popular version of poststructuralism suggests, an epistemology of language will always present itself as alternative to ontological certainty rather than a path to its recovery. Such a comparison of empiricism and poststructural-ism as semiotic projects leaves aside, however, the *a priori* concern with writing that philosophers in both traditions have maintained despite their attacks on metaphysics and their subsequent reputations as 'deconstructive'. Hudson argues that Derrida in fact conceded neither the ontological or material dimension of philosophy to a realm beyond his jurisdiction: his version of poststructuralism was deeply concerned with the materiality of writing as something that could be known and experienced apart from its status as language, and without the sur-render of *a priori* categories, and it was on this basis that he refused to recognize empiricism as philosophy.

Yet, from the perspective of many of the essays in the first part of this collec-tion, the same ontological dimension can be reclaimed for empiricist philosophy *as writing*. Jonathan Kramnick points to the importance of words on a page, sug-gesting that it is the mediation of absence and presence that occurs with writing that makes sense of Locke's fluctuating versions of desire as something that comes before and after the object. When Joseph Chaves argues that Shaftesbury's *Char-acteristics* is positioned at the intersection of polite and philosophical worlds so as to bend the distinctions it upholds at the level of content, he is reading for a possible give-and-take between the written text and the conversations into which it enters. This directs us, similarly, beyond rhetorical postures to the text as something that anticipates its physical immersion in the world of readers and responses. And just as Thomas Reid complains in his attacks on Humean scepti-cism that the reason why Hume's system does not work is because it reveals too much of its own technical foundation in writing, so Alexander Dick argues that Reid's own preference for a naturally visual over an artificially scriptural media-tion hides his own frequently admitted position that writing for all its artifice is the fundamental medium through which we know and experience the world. Such readings produce a new angle from which to associate empirical and post-structuralist thinking; not only as kindred descriptions of radical slippage and constructivism, but as linguistic performances in which ontological concerns make their way back into the picture via the materiality of language – literally, as words upon the page and more generally as an occasion for contact with the material word. Isobel Armstrong writes of Derrida and de Man, they '*unthink* the aesthetic and *have* it'; their deconstruction of aesthetics takes place in 'flagrantly aesthetic texts'.[6] In the first section of the collection we see analogous cases made for Locke, Hume, Shaftesbury, and Reid: while they may unthink the *a priori*, as writers they also have it.

Reading Hume

Hume's letter shows how the physical certainty of the book and its media upstage the contingencies of human consciousness, but it also signifies the logical problems that haunt sociable communication and make it an entirely human construction. Indeed, Hume is a central figure in our collection for precisely this reason. He was throughout his career consumed by the ambiguities that writing entailed both for the epistemology that he inherited from Locke and for the fate of philosophy in the future. His divided and troubled career can be tracked, as the essays in this section suggest, largely as a conscious exploration of genre and the different forms of audience that philosophy, essays, history and dialogue could generate. But it can also be tracked, as Adam Budd and Mark Blackwell show, through Hume's particular attention to the medium of the book in its successive editions and physical structure. Hume was a meticulous proofreader of his own work and his letters to his publisher William Strahan record him worrying over font, errata and paper long after his texts were in press.[7] Hume's concern with the medium of writing and the problems of genre go a long way to explain his status as the Scottish Enlightenment's most widely read representative and the self-proclaimed controversialist of its academic traditions.

Hume's sense of the performative power of his own rhetoric has already been a major topic for scholars interested in the literary aspects of eighteenth-century philosophy. In *Practicing Enlightenment*, for instance, Christensen argues, 'In Hume, rhetoric is both the sign of logical contradiction or inconsistency and the device for putting inconsistency to work. It is because of the inexorable failure of rationality either to work on its own terms or to account satisfactorily for the behavior of humans in society that rhetoric becomes inevitable, not merely as the expression of the failure of rationality, but as the remedy for its lapse.'[8] In emphasizing the subtle ways that Hume's literary practice overcomes the form of crisis it articulates, Christensen elaborates upon John Richetti's argument, which shares Christensen's emphasis on the fact that for Hume, 'writing is the ultimate and sure relation, providing almost in spite of his relations as a thinker a persuasive tendency to stabilize or at least to ground in relationships the unruly perceptual relationships his thought so intensely explores'.[9] Adding to this sense of Hume as an author for whom writing can be both the venue for sceptical thought and a practical forum for more conservative endeavours, Leo Damrosch included Hume in a group of writers that he (more than Richetti and Christensen) asserts consciously explored the 'fertile tension' between writing as something necessarily fictive, and writing as a way of recreating reality.[10]

But the four chapters on Hume included here push this productive realm of rhetorical analysis in directions that take account of writing as technology as well as style, and of genre as a fundamental condition of thought. For Mark Blackwell, whose close reading of the *Treatise on Human Nature* opens the second section of this collection, the anti-sequential arrangement of Hume's argument plays with its written form as linear narrative. The architecture of Hume's thought is thus a physical as well as rhetorical condition. Such an argument differs from the ones that literary critics have made about Hume to date because it shifts the emphasis from rhetoric as a supplementary dimension of meaning making to writing in particular as a field of real encounter structuring the arrangement of thought. Adam Budd also uses the history of the *Treatise* as text to rethink not only its philosophical trajectory but also its usefulness as the basis for critical method. Using several early essays and sections of the *Treatise* that were both moved within and removed from the published version, Budd suggests that Hume did not in fact argue that literary works (poetry and fiction) could be the basis for sympathetic understanding but rather claimed that our sympathetic responses to literature are of an order below the real sympathy we feel for actually occurring incidents of pain or pleasure. The larger implication of this is that, contrary to now standard assumptions, Hume may have been trying to prevent the very transference of his sentimental thesis to literary aesthetics.

Whatever Hume's intentions for the *Treatise* might have been, reading and writing became critical points of consideration both in the development of his own philosophy and in the way it was read by other writers. If writing is the essential philosophical problem of the *Treatise*, how might philosophical argument – which after all exists first and foremost as writing – overcome it? One answer, provided here by Eva Dadlez, is that it does not have to. Literature for Hume and later for Jane Austen provides thought experiments for moral reasoning. Another possibility, entertained by John Richetti, is that Hume turned to genres outside philosophy proper, such as history and – in Richetti's study – the theological dialogue, to advance a connection between narrative process and philosophical reasoning. Contesting the view that the dialogue form embodies indeterminability, Richetti argues that Hume's manipulation of the rhetorical positions of his speakers through the dramatic conversation in *Dialogues on Natural Religion* demonstrates a willingness to use the genre toward a determinable position, one that is only evident through the experience of reading it fully and critically. While the *Treatise* stands, even for Hume himself, as a test case for the combination of certainties and anxieties that eighteenth-century philosophers were beginning to feel while holding onto their books, Hume's experiments with other genres such as the essay and the dialogue show how important literary experience was to the development of his thought.

Thinking Literature

Hume was not, of course, the only philosopher in the period to sense that the traditional authority that philosophy had always assumed over other forms of knowledge was being challenged, on one hand, by its inability to encompass rationally the different and varied experiences that commerce and science were bringing home to Britain and, on the other hand, by the increasing popularity of new genres like history and the novel that seemed better able to manage this plethora of objects and feelings. Consider for instance Francis Hutcheson's remarks in the Preface to his *Inquiry Concerning Beauty, Order, Harmony and Design*. Why, he asks would anyone read philosophy at all? 'Philosophy', Hutcheson worries, 'has become so ungainly a Form, that a Gentleman cannot easily bring himself to like it; and those who are strangers to it, can scarcely bear to hear out our Description of it'.[11] Later in the same essay, Hutcheson makes the case that it is not information merely that makes the reading of important books rewarding. 'Everyone knows', he writes,

> how dull it is to read over a collection of Gazettes. which shall perhaps relate all the same Events with the Historian: The superior Pleasure then of History must arise, like that of Poetry, from the Manners; as when we see a Character well drawn, wherein we find the secret Causes of a great Diversity of seemingly inconsistent Actions; or an interest of State laid open, or an artful View nicely unfolded, the execution of which influences very different and opposite Actions, as the circumstances may alter.[12]

For Hutcheson, history and poetry are more significant forms of writing than newspapers because they give us the opportunity to reflect on the ambivalence of life and the necessity of change, reflections that he insists are a 'pleasure'. Hutcheson thereby turns the aesthetic experience of mixing and blending styles and genres into a form of compensation for the anxieties that empiricism had accrued.

For poststructuralist readings of empiricism, the mixing of philosophy and literature is a mark, as Paul de Man notably contended regarding Locke, of the seemingly insufferable collapse of philosophical logic into its literary other: metaphor. Viewing the issue from the somewhat broader perspective of the 'generic murkiness' of the philosophical novels of Marivaux, Diderot, Fielding and Sterne, Jonathan Sadow suggests that what de Man saw as the limit of empiricism's pretensions to truth became the starting point for European culture's consciousness of its own modernity *as* the constant flow of generic invention. 'Genre', as Sadow defines it 'represents neither metaphysical objects nor collections of features, but a form of ongoing cultural discourse and production inextricable from questions surrounding the classification and understanding of knowledge and language' (below, p. 162). As Sadow concludes, eighteenth-century writers anticipated twentieth-century critics in recognizing that no genre could be absolutely pure or distinct. But they also differed from their present-day peers in regarding mixed modes as an opportunity for the production of and pleasure in culture rather than as a point of individual rational anxiety.

Maureen Harkin makes a similar case for the mixed modality of Adam Smith's reflections on history. Though he never completed a book about history (as he sometimes projected), Smith has been long supposed to have been an adherent of the stadial theory popularized by William Robertson and Adam Ferguson: human civilization grew in distinct stages from the near anarchy of primitive hunter-gatherers, to the constantly threatened pastoral societies of shepherds and then farmers and finally to the success and equanimity of commercial states. But Smith also suggested that early human societies had a dignity and restraint that modern commercial societies no longer have. As a result, in Smith, history can no longer be seen as a linear narrative or 'rise', but rather as a narrative that looks in two directions at once. As Harkin states, Smith was both a 'believer in history as progress towards commercial civilization *and* [a] Rousseavian elegist of a lost social harmony' (below, p. 184). The importance of this ambiguity lies in the fact that it persisted into the nineteenth century long after the stadial theory itself had played out its usefulness; it is evident in William Godwin's unpublished essay 'On History and Romance' for instance and in many of Walter Scott's novels.

As the example of Smith's history attests, what was pulling eighteenth-century writers away from the rationality of philosophy and toward a new sense of their historical moment as a moment of culture was feeling, the sentiments, passions and affections that from Hume on became the central focus of the empirical conversation and, to a great extent, account for its fragmentation into the genres and disciplines that make up the humanities and social sciences today. But, as the final three essays in our collection make clear, this move toward sentiment was also an attempt to refashion philosophy, as in fact Hume had originally believed it might, by allowing literature to rescue it from the scepticism produced by and in writing. Such an effort implies, indeed demands, that the process be something of a challenge, becoming in turn the stuff of literary adventure rather than sociable conversation. Thus in Nancy Yousef's reading of Rousseau, marriage becomes the basis for an ideal contract not because marriage embodies the absolute transparency of self to other, but on the contrary, because in the form of Rousseauvian romance the mysterious anxieties surrounding commitment and betrayal that haunt all marriages appear as narrative. Similarly, Brian Michael Norton finds in the eighteenth-century novel a venue for unfolding the peculiarly ambiguous dynamics of human happiness – an obsession of eighteenth-century ethics – 'on the level of the particular' case (below, p. 213) rather than on the level of general maxims suited to the form of the treatise.

Finally, rounding out the volume, Adam Potkay argues that William Words-worth's poetic experiments with 'the still sad music of humanity' were an attempt to recast the kind of obedient conscience promoted in eighteenth-century ser-mons as a sense or feeling of harmony and bliss such as one finds while listening to music. This final turn in the volume toward Romanticism marks perhaps the final transformation of what had been the pre-eminent problem of Lockean philosophy, that of representation, into the foundation for a new cultural epis-teme. Nevertheless, as Potkay notes, Wordsworth's return to conscience in his later verse suggests further that the problematics of ethical determination and epistemological clarity were in no way resolved by the late eighteenth century's discovery of literature. They were merely reshaped into a new set of dialectical conflicts, ones that are, to a great extent, still with us today.

Whether or not literature could be said to have replaced philosophy as the principle discipline of critical thinking is, to be sure, a question best answered in a history of the canon and the disciplines. We acknowledge the work of Clif-ford Siskin, Jonathan Kramnick and John Guillory, who have pursued precisely this historical question. Nevertheless, the present collection proposes that liter-ary practice – its technologies, genres and responses – was a crucial and indeed constant preoccupation of eighteenth-century philosophy. And eighteenth-century writing – poetry, history, fiction – became a vital force in European culture because it insistently posed and reposed the epistemological and ethical questions it inherited from philosophy. The point, we submit, is not simply that philosophy and literature were on friendly terms during the eighteenth century but rather that the questions posed by each were the condition of possibility for the other. Whatever tensions this friendship might have provoked were ulti-mately productive ones. They are, to return to our opening observation from Hume, the posts and ferries by which we cross the seas and continents of self understanding.

In the spirit of Enlightenment sociability, this volume has been from the start very much a collaborative venture. Our contributors have all been delightfully punctual and patient and for that we are very grateful. Many of the contribu-tors participated in an intensive exploratory workshop held in May 2007 and funded by the Peter Wall Institute for Advance Study at the University of Brit-ish Columbia. The editors would like to thank Diane Newell, Olav Slaymaker and Markus Pickartz from the Peter Wall Institute for their advice, assistance and support as well as our colleagues from the Departments of English and Phi-losophy at UBC and elsewhere who participated in the workshop but did not contribute to the volume. This volume was completed in part with funding from the UBC Humanities and Social Sciences Granting programme. We would like especially to thank our research assistant and editor, Monica Brown, for her diligence and good humour throughout the process of putting together both the workshop and the volume.

1 PHILOSOPHY/NON-PHILOSOPHY AND DERRIDA'S (NON) RELATIONS WITH EIGHTEENTH-CENTURY EMPIRICISM

Nicholas Hudson

Perhaps only the glamour shed by the name Jacques Derrida could explain recent claims about his 'lifetime engagement with the eighteenth-century archives'.[1] For the body of his writing devoted to this century is in fact very small. Besides scattered references to Kant, Sade and some others, there are the long and famous chapters in *De la grammatologie* devoted to an unpublished work by Rousseau; a little discussed book on a largely neglected French philosopher, Condillac; a largely ignored essay about the origins of writing according to an eighteenth-century Anglican apologist, William Warburton. But even this meagre corpus does not fully measure Derrida's neglect of one of the most robust periods in Western philosophy, particularly in France. The most telling lacuna in Derrida's supposed 'lifetime engagement' with the eighteenth century lies in his almost entire failure to deal with this era's reigning philosophical tradition, empiricism. Even in the works mentioned above, Derrida has virtually nothing to say about empiricism itself. The pre-eminent empiricist philosophers of this age – Locke, Berkeley, Hume, just to start – all merit hardly a mention in the entire corpus of Jacques Derrida.

This neglect is not surprising. It is a repeated and imperative assertion in Derrida's writing that empiricism is not in fact 'philosophy' at all: 'empiricism always has been determined by philosophy, from Plato to Husserl, as *nonphiliosophy*: as the philosophical pretension to nonphilosophy, the inability to justify oneself, to come to one's own aid as speech'.[2] That this very statement draws a kind of institutional plasma from empiricism (consider: 'from Plato to Husserl') is just the point: Derrida's deconstructive career drove an invasive, contraband journey along the border of a territory he called 'non-philosophy', the outland of empiricism. A philosopher who built his career on evidence gathered from archival texts across history clearly had links to this country, as little as he liked to admit this affinity. In other ways, as well, he sometimes sounded, suspiciously, like an empiricist. Empiricists have historically denied the relevance of ontology, and the reality of 'being' as anything except a verbal abstraction. Particularly during the eighteenth century, empiricists insisted that human consciousness is fundamentally semiotic, and that all human approaches to experience are mediated through signs.

While this position *sounds* a lot like the implications of deconstruction, Derrida was unremitting in his ejection of empiricism from the canon of 'philosophy': 'the true name of this inclination of thought to the Other, of this resigned acceptance of incoherent incoherence inspired by a truth more profound than the "logic" of philosophical discourse, the true name of this renunciation of the concept, of the a prioris and transcendental horizons of language, is *empiricism*. For the latter, at bottom, has ever committed but one fault: the fault of presenting itself as a philosophy.'[3] This passage derives from 'Violence and Metaphysics', an essay that relegates his contemporary Emmanuel Levinas to the region of 'non-philosophy'. The reasons he gives for this exile illuminate the reasons for Derrida's disdain for empiricism and his failure to engage in any sustained or direct way with the major philosophical tradition of the eighteenth century. We will see that his exclusion of empiricism from the category of philosophy is linked with his insistence that philosophy *properly* concerned itself with 'the a prioris and transcendental horizons of language' – with questions of ontology. Particularly given Derrida's deconstruction of the 'proper', however, we need to consider whether he succeeded in distinguishing his own methods and conclusions from this empiricist *Ausland*, this territory which Derrida visited only at its outskirts, not wanting to be mistaken as a citizen.

Levinas and 'Violence and Metaphysics'

In an essay published in 1986, Jeffrey Barnouw weighed similar ironies in an examination of Derrida's unacknowledged affinities with Charles Peirce. According to Barnouw, Derrida travelled a long way down the road paved by Peirce's empiricism, with its insistence on the essentially semiological nature of cognition. In Derrida's own words, in *Of Grammatology*, 'Peirce goes very far in the direction that I have called the de-construction of the transcendental signified.'[4] At the critical moment, however, Derrida reasserts the irrefragable claims of ontology. Here is a passage from *Speech and Phenomena*, Derrida's deconstruction of Edmund Husserl:

> In affirming that *perception does not exist* or that what is perception is not primordial, that somehow everything 'begins' by 're-presentation' (a proposition which can only be maintained by the elimination of these last two concepts ...) and by reintroducing the difference in involved in 'signs' at the core of what is 'primordial,' we do not retreat from the level of transcendental phenomenology toward either an 'empiricism' or a 'Kantian' critique of the claim of having a primordial intuition.[5]

Husserl had proclaimed, in Derrida's terms, 'The certitude of inner existence',[6] the undifferentiated presence of phenomena. By inserting the sign, difference, into these phenomena, argues Barnouw, Derrida brought himself into alignment with Peirce. In the above passage, however, Derrida indicates his desire to marginalize Peirce and empiricism from his own philosophy, which holds fast to the principle that the very being of *Dasein* is precisely to bestow 'being'. For this reason, he subordinates a philosophy like Peirce's that begins by regarding being and presence as themselves fundamentally semiotic.[7]

The same structure underlies Derrida's examination of Emmanuel Levinas in 'Violence and Metaphysics', which we must present here in a highly truncated form. In *Totality and Infinity*, Levinas associates the Western preoccupation with ontology with a 'violence' that seeks to absorb and subordinate the Other under the category of being. Thinking particularly of Heidegger's *Being and Time*, Levinas claims that the idea of being denies the individuality and freedom of the Other, implying that the Other is fully knowable through totalizing truths abstracted from lived experience, and ultimately seeking to make the Other an extension of the ego's needs and enjoyment. This 'ontological imperialism' therefore implies an 'egology',[8] a violent assertion of the ego's freedom and enjoyment against the Other, who is subordinated to the category of being. In real experience, however, the Other is never fully knowable, and is entirely exterior to the ego. The Other is encountered as a 'Face', a mysterious sign of infinite and non-totalizable possibilities. The Same comes to know the Other primarily through language, which is offered between speakers as 'gift' or 'revelation' of one's private world, a self-revelation that nonetheless falls endlessly short of completion. It is through the communal experience of dialogue that the Same and the Other construct a shared world, an unfolding agreement on 'the generality of the Object',[9] which remains infinite, ongoing and driven by 'desire' rather than 'need'. 'Ontology' is therefore secondary to relations that Levinas denominates 'ethical'.

Particularly notable about this vision of experience is its areas of similarity to deconstruction. Levinas denies the existence of absolute truths; he regards language as constitutive of human experience, though infinitely deferred; the 'Face', as Derrida observes, is a 'trace', a signifier unanchored by some fixed or transcendent signified.[10] Derrida compares the unclosable dialogue of the Same and Other to *écriture*, wondering why Levinas privileges spoken dialogue over writing.[11] As in his discussion of Peirce, however, Derrida wishes to maintain the supposedly apodictic claims of ontology as well as 'the irreducibly egoic essence of experience'.[12] Derrida's notion of being is carefully situated beyond Plato: ardently defending Heidegger, Derrida denies that being exists apart from a particular existent. 'Being is but the *Being-of* this existent, and does not exist outside of it as a foreign power.'[13] Without assuming the being of the Other, there can be no language and no ethics, for both these activities dictate '*respect* for the other *as what it is*: other'.[14] All human relations, moreover, must begin with 'egoity', the determination of the self, ipseity, as the precondition for identifying the Other as other. It is on the basis of this critique that Derrida ends up charging Levinas with being an 'empiricist':

> By radicalizing the theme of the infinite exteriority of the other, Levinas thereby assumes the aim which has more or less secretly animated all the philosophical gestures which have been called empiricisms in the history of philosophy ...But can one speak of an *experience* of the other or of difference? Has not the concept of experience always been determined by the metaphysics of presence? Is not experience always an encountering of an irreducible presence, the perception of a phenomenality?[15]

Clearly this is a heavy charge. And this is not just because Derrida implies that Levinas has not actually written 'philosophy'. Empiricism, by Derrida's account, is incoherent, self-deluding and even disingenuous. It rejects ontology, yet 'more or less secretly' relies on ideas of being; it dismisses being as a metaphor, but refuses to weigh the ontological status of metaphors themselves: 'As Hegel says somewhere, empiricism always forgets, at the very least, that it employs the words to be. Empiricism is thinking *by* metaphor without thinking the metaphor *as such*.'[16]

To what extent has Derrida succeeded in deconstructing the arguments of Levinas? Derrida claims that 'violence', by Levinas's own account, must inhabit all discourse and all human relations – for these relations are inevitably grounded in egoity and ontology. In Levinas's defence, however, he does not regard egoity, the sanctity and self-sufficiency of the self, as itself 'violent'. The ego itself, at 'home' with its private needs and enjoyments, is entirely innocent. 'Violence' emerges only in so far as the ego attempts to subordinate the Other through a concept of being that denies the mutual independence and exteriority of the Other. This 'violence' is not only an ethical fault, an 'injustice', but also a philosophical error. The mediation of the relation between self and Other through being forgets that being is itself bound up in the endless process of language – that even the verb 'to be' is *itself* a trace, a signifier projected through time by the infinite play of Desire.

This certainly sounds a lot like 'deconstruction'. Yet faced with what he calls the 'non-philosophy' of empiricism, Derrida draws back towards an ontology that reaffirms the 'a prioris and transcendental horizons of language' in a way that Levinas does not. Derrida would doubtless deny that 'being' or the ego can be separated from the play of signification. On the other hand, he endows these concepts with an a priori and transcendent status that conditions language in a way that can never be denied or avoided. Moreover, while he satirizes empiricism as a 'resigned acceptance of incoherent incoherence', his own alterative to Levinas's ethics imagines 'philosophy' is itself resigned. Unable to jettison incoherent concepts of being and ego, philosophy can only helpless subject itself to endless criticism. Philosophy 'can only *let itself be questioned*'.[17]

'Empiricism'. Levelled by Derrida, this word sounds like an exclusion from the whole discipline that Derrida professed, and must surely cause us to recheck the credentials of Levinas, or for that matter of Locke, Berkeley and Hume. Levinas, we should note, carefully distanced himself from empiricism, as he understood it. For him, empiricism embodied a finite, egoistic and instrumental understanding of reality. As we have already suggested, however, Derrida seems right to connect Levinas with empiricism's denial that either 'presence' or 'being' can be experienced in a form unmediated by language. Whether this denial is incoherent and self-deceiving, or whether Derrida does justice to the empiricist tradition, are nonetheless questions that we need to re-evaluate.

Eighteenth-Century Empiricism and Language

Derrida's reading of the eighteenth century, as exemplified by *Of Grammatology*, takes off from a history of linguistic thought during this era that is profoundly problematic, especially in the light of recent research.[18] He was aware of schemes in the seventeenth century to invent a philosophical script, a 'real character' – by Mersenne, Wilkins, Beck, Dalgarno, Leibniz and many others – that would ideally *replace* speech with a more correct and truthful writing.[19] But he regarded the era which followed as an organized 'defense of phonocentrism and of logocentrism', an effort to reassert the pre-eminence of speech and its unmediated expression of 'presence' though 'auto-affection, only through the *voice*'. His only evidence for these sweeping claims are Descartes, who disliked Mersenne's writing schemes and 'had driven out the sign', and Rousseau, whose position in eighteenth-century thought we shall later consider.[20] In fact, empiricist philosophy moved quickly and decisively towards the view that language does not merely reflect but *constitutes* reason. Language does not merely mirror reality; what we call 'reality' is *made* of words. So far from expelling the 'sign' from consciousness, eighteenth-century empiricism approached a semiotic notion of consciousness comparable in many ways to that of Peirce and Levinas.

A major inspiration for these developments was the empiricism of John Locke, who nonetheless remained linked to an older tradition of realism. Ideas, he wrote, are 'real' to the extent that they have a 'Foundation in Nature ... [a] Conformity with that reality of Being, to which they are tacitly referr'd, as to their Archetypes'.[21] Words are deceptive, he insists, when they fail to refer to distinct ideas, becoming the source of virtually all the errors of philosophy. While never fully integrating language into the human understanding, however, Locke ended up creating a semiotics of the mind in which ideas behaved like words, and indeed seemed inseparable from the very act of naming. All general knowledge about 'Nature', he admits, concerns species and genera, classes of objects rather than individuals or simple perceptions. Yet it was an error of the 'Schools' (an error paradoxically induced by the habit of *naming*) to believe that each class was differentiated by a 'real Essence'. In fact, our 'general Ideas' of species and genera are mental signs which group together individuals which 'are, in their internal Constitution, as different one from another, as several of those which are ranked under different specifick Names'.[22] As this passage indicates, individuals are classed as members of a species *not* because (as far we can tell) they share some 'real Essence' in common but because they are given a common *name*. They share only a 'nominal Essence'. The inherently arbitrary nature of this naming and classifying is proved by our irresolvable disputes about whether, for example, a fœtus, changling or drill is really a 'man'. It is language, not 'Nature', that really constitutes 'general Knowledge': 'the sorting of Things by us, or the making of determinate *Species*, being in order to naming and comprehending them with general terms, I cannot see how it can be properly said, that Nature sets the Boundaries of the *Species* of Things'.[23] In other words, having begun by castigating the Schools for confusing names with real essences, language with 'Nature', Locke ends up (however inconsistently and even unwillingly) acknowledging that 'we sort and name Substances by their nominal, and not by their real Essences ... 'tis evident they are made by the mind, and not by Nature'.[24]

In the empiricism of Locke, we begin to see ontology supplanted by semiotics. Contrary to the impression left by Derrida in 'Violence and Metaphysics', the empiricist Locke did not nefariously fail to face up to the ontology implicit in his own language, his own use of the verb 'to be'. Firstly, he was pushed very reluctantly away from his original intention to protect scientific 'truth' from the deceptions of language. Secondly, and more importantly, Locke continued to meditate hard on the persistence of a language of 'being' in all our ways of thinking and (what is inseparable) talking about the world. As he wrote, we make 'a secret Supposition' that things possess some 'real Essence'.[25] Similarly, we inevitably use the word 'I' to refer to 'Spirit' or some 'real Essence' in ourselves, though we have no clear or distinct idea of selfhood. Personal identity consists entirely in what we remember about ourselves, which means that we 'are' what we *name* our selves: 'every one is to himself that which he calls *self*'.[26]

Authors who built on Locke's philosophy were less concerned to protect even the vestige of a realist conception of nature, more fully integrating language and signs into consciousness. Most famously, George Berkeley denied the possibility of 'general ideas'. What Locke called a 'general idea' could only be a particular idea – a word or some mental image – which is made into a 'sign' of a whole group of objects. As Berkeley writes: 'an idea, which considered in itself is particular, becomes general, by being made to represent or stand for all other particular ideas of the same sort'.[27] 'Nature', as Berkeley argued at length in *A New*

Theory of Vision, is a system of signs, a 'Language' as arbitrary as 'languages and signs of human appointment'.[28] Not unlike Husserl, Berkeley conceived of mental phenomena as a semiotic field without a transcendental signified. Experience is only 'an habitual connexion',[29] a system of references spread across a semiotic network ungrounded by any assurance of order besides the will of God. Even this assurance is provisional, for Berkeley's God is not a 'presence' but rather a 'notion', an inherently unfathomable absence. In no ordinary way can we say that God 'exists', for 'the existence of an idea, consists in being perceived'.[30] Similarly, *mind, spirit, soul,* or *myself* is not an 'idea' or a 'presence', but only a 'notion', a being that we habitually infer as the unperceived recipient of perceptions.[31] In what way, then, is Berkeley 'more or less secretly' avoiding the 'metaphysics of presence'? Like Derrida, Berkeley affirms that we *must* bestow the concepts of being and the self on experience, even if this experience consists entirely of a play of signs. And in what manner does Berkeley's philosophy confirm the 'auto-affection' of the unmediated presence of the voice that, according to Derrida, presides over the entirety of the 'Age of Rousseau'?

Remove even the 'notion' of God and the self, and we have a form of empiricism submerged even more deeply in the abyss of unknowability. Berkeley's admirers made precisely this leap. Hume had no time for either the self or God. The self and being ('substance') were 'fictions' used by the mind to evade the 'interruption' of believing that our impressions were entirely disconnected and lacked any semiotic coherence whatsoever.[32] These concepts belonged, *pace* Heidegger and Derrida, not to some ontic realm that underpinned the being of *Dasein*, but to 'custom', an entirely habitual realm of experience that revealed nothing at all about ourselves or the world. The language of philosophy, 'abstract ideas', were not merely *like* signifiers arbitrarily instituted by human beings; they *were* arbitrary signs made by humans: 'all general ideas are nothing but particular ones, annexed to a certain term, which gives them a more extensive signification, and makes them recall upon occasion other individuals, which are similar to them'.[33] Hume wrongly, or modestly, attributed this insight to Berkeley. But it is in fact a further deepening of human language into human consciousness. The entire identity of language and thought was consummated by, among others, Berkeley's French admirer, Pierre-Louis Moreau de Maupertuis. The self and being were for Maupertuis entirely 'economical' inventions designed to facilitate the operations of language. In making languages, humans are faced with the problem that the memory is not capacious enough to hold a separate word for every individual perception, as would be ideally the case. Instead, we separate out qualities that objects have in common: a certain shape, for example, justified the word 'tree' used to denominate a class of tall, branchy objects.[34] Similarly, we separate out the term 'I see' as an abbreviation linking objects that we encounter personally.[35] Terms denoting existence shorten and organize our perceptions: the phrase 'there is' ('il y a') classifies objects that did not merely occur in dreams, and to which we can theoretically return.[36] Central to de Maupertuis's thesis is that this process of naming lays that foundation of knowledge and all science, and that it could have occurred in an entirely different form: 'Ce que nous appelons nos sciences dépend si intiment des manières dont on s'est servi pour designer les perceptions, qu'il me semble que les questions & les propositions seroit toutes différentes si l'on avoit établi d'autres expressions des premiers perceptions'.[37]

For these writers, in short, all experience, and all ideas of being and the self, are mediated through language. This conclusion was generally shared, with variations, by philosophers in the empiricist tradition including, as we will later consider, Condillac. Locke, Berkeley, Hume, Maupertuis, Diderot, Burke, Smith and Condillac did not anchor their semiotics in some *logos* or being abstracted from a linguistically mediated experience.[38] While they by no means ignored problems of egoity or ontology, they regarded both the self and being as linguistic constructs. Where they differed from Derrida (and also, it seems, Husserl and Heidegger) was in their refusal to extrapolate the words 'I' and 'to be' into ontological conclusions about what constrains and conditions experience. Their difference, that is, lies in their total rejection of a metaphysical tradition that Derrida presents as the only 'proper' philosophy. Evidently determined to affirm his own legitimacy in the metaphysical tradition, Derrida excludes those empiricist thinkers that, very often, sound most like himself.

Condillac and Derrida's *Archeology of the Frivolous*

The writer conspicuously excluded from the above list of empirical philosophers is Jean-Jacques Rousseau, for Rousseau stands as something of an exception in 'the Age of Rousseau', as we will consider. Excluding Rousseau, the one eighteenth-century philosopher engaged at any length by Derrida is the Abbé de Condillac. Derrida himself characterizes Condillac's major work, *Essay on the Origin of Human Knowledge* (1746), as 'through and through a semiotics',[39] an early and highly-influential attempt to prove the entire dependence of thinking on signs. How, then, can such a work be embraced in Derrida's thesis concerning the reigning 'phonocentricism' of this century? His deconstruction of Condillac, *The Archeology of the Frivolous*, turns in part on this philosopher's deferred and inconsistent attempts to establish a 'method' for the discovery of 'truth'. We should nonetheless consider whether Condillac truly belongs to the 'logocentric' tradition of Western metaphysics, and whether Derrida is correct in reading his thought through a filter of deconstructive concepts – origin, presence, nature, writing and so forth.

While affirming the semiological basis of Condillac's thought, *The Archeology of the Frivolous* conveys the impression that he feared and resisted the intrusion of the 'arbitrary sign' into the origin of reason, and that he remained protectively insistent on the basis of reason in unmediated 'nature' and 'presence'. 'In going back to the presemiotic stratum of practical need', writes Derrida, 'he wants to institute or restore all scientific languages, all theoretical discourses'.[40] Against Condillac's own wishes, however, 'He had *always already* said that the sign as such was *always already* destined for the arbitrary, with its whole system of associated values'.[41] This familiar deconstructive language culminates a line of analysis inaugurated in the opening pages of *Archeology of the Frivolous* and sporadically continued through many detours and interruptions to the end of the book. Its premise dictates that the *Essay* begins by positing two versions of 'imagination', an imagination of 'instinct' and an imagination of 'reason', the first concerned with 'practical' knowledge and the second with 'theoretical' knowledge. Derrida would seem to imply that Condillac wishes to secure the verity of theoretical knowledge, made possible with arbitrary signs, through an appeal to its unbroken connection with the 'presence' of instinctual and presemiotic knowledge. According to this analysis, Condillac cannot avoid acknowledging, against his wishes, that the 'sign' always already mediates knowledge even at its dawning stages.

Let us go back to what Condillac actually argues. As Derrida correctly affirms, de Condillac defines 'imagination' as that which '*retraces*' and which 'produces as reproduction the lost object of perception'.[42] At the stage before the introduction of language, this retracing of lost perceptions is haphazard and (though Condillac does not deploy this term in this context) arbitrary. The sight of a certain dangerous object, for example, might revive an emotion of fear; the sight of a certain tree might prompt a sensation of hunger for its fruit. It is only at the stage when 'arbitrary' signs are instituted that the individual gains 'mastery' over the imagination, using a vocal perception to revive voluntarily the perception of the dangerous object or fruitful tree. At the beginning of Part II of the *Essay*, Condillac conjectures about how these arbitrary signs might have been invented, imagining that the spontaneous and 'natural' cries and gestures of some Adamic couple might eventually have been converted into voluntary signs. Gradually, over many centuries, this original language might have evolved into the languages of the present day. Condillac admits that this 'conjectural history' (as Dugald Stewart later called this method)[43] represented a fiction contradicted, in fact, by the evidence of the Bible. His purpose is not to write a 'history'; it is rather to create a heuristic model to analyse the principles of the human understanding.

Contrary to what Derrida implies, the original 'instinctual' stage of the imagination permits knowledge, 'presence', and even consciousness only in the most fleeting and attenuated form. Condillac does maintain that we are 'conscious' of perceptions even when they belong to the rushed and chaotic manifold of mental phenomena, though he notes that this opinion was not universally shared.[44] But it is only through 'memory' and 'reflection', operations impossible without instituted signs, that we gain all but the most elemental and tenuous awareness of 'self' or the 'being' of objects. Without language and reflection, a person's 'perceptions could be very few; and as he had no remembrance of those which had preceded, followed, and interrupted them, he would never have recollected the succession of the parts over time. The consequence of this must have been, that he never would have suspected it to have had any beginning, and yet he would have considered it only as an instant.'[45] A true notion of 'self' begins only with the insertion of the arbitrary sign, which (curiously like Levinas) is learned only though dialogue – by hearing *another* speak. And what the sign makes possible is not the 'auto-affection' of unmediated 'presence', but precisely an idea of self mediated through language, a personal being fabricated through a temporal sequence of absent perceptions re-evoked by communal signs. As for 'being', Condillac is like other empiricists in his time in regarding terms like 'being', 'essence' and 'substance' as philosophical abstractions without meaning. Developing Locke's ideas, however, he does indicate that the mind attributes 'being' to both the self and to abstract ideas as the 'necessary' condition of considering them at all. 'For we can perceive nothing within us', as he writes, 'but we consider it as belonging to ourselves, as belonging to our being, or as our very being that exists in such or such a manner'.[46] Similarly, when perceptions are abstracted into general concepts, they 'become objects of the mind' only 'by continuing to consider them as beings'.[47] Condillac makes clear that while this attribution of being is a *fiction*, it is such a necessary and embedded fiction that metaphysicians have mistaken such abstractions as realities.

As Derrida points out, Condillac insists that the difference between imagination of 'instinct' and imagination of 'reason', 'practical' knowledge and 'theoretical' knowledge, is one of 'degree'; indeed, as instituted signs open up new possibilities of error (as in the creation of philosophical abstractions like 'being'), reason should continue to consult its original basis in 'analogies' formed through instinct and 'nature'.[48] But Derrida's reading of Condillac is misleading to the extent that he presents the primitive, instinctual levels of consciousness as logocentric, or as capable of furnishing the mind with any access to truth or unmediated 'presence'. Indeed, while Condillac sometimes reserves the word 'signs' for instituted signs, instinctual knowledge is not really 'presemiotic': its 'signs' are 'natural' rather than 'arbitrary' in the sense that random perceptions (a fearful object, a fruitful tree) recall absent perceptions. Beyond these kinds of passing traces and reflexive judgments (mental operations also experienced by animals), all knowledge and reasoning for Condillac is mediated through arbitrary signs. Theoretical reasoning on beings or on the self relies on signs, and a sign evokes an absent perception only '*as if* it were really present' (emphasis added).[49]

Derrida's reading hence obscures the ways in which Condillac's philoso-phy openly acknowledges semiotic *différance*, the play of presence and absence, inherent in phenomenological experience. The important word is 'openly', for Condillac by no means flinches from acknowledgements that Derrida instead wants to find covert, guilty, constrained by philosophical language itself. Condil-lac's philosophy of mind in fact leaves Derrida little to deconstruct. Nevertheless, Condillac sounds more characteristic of the logocentric tradition in Western philosophy in those places, predominantly in the latter parts of the *Essai*, and even more fully in later works such as his *Logic* and *Art of Writing*, where he dwells on the 'method' necessary for the discovery of 'truth'. This method decrees the refinement of 'analysis' in which complex ideas are systematically reduced to their component simple ideas without the inaccuracies and superadditions often sanctioned by language. Condillac's reasoning in these sections is unclear and inconsistent in a number of ways. First, Condillac makes clear that 'ideas' should not be confused with 'things'. He is sharply aware of profound individual vari-ations in the way every person experiences the world and articulates that world in language: 'every man according to his passions has a particular [language] of his own'.[50] And these variations are repeated at the level of entire nations, each of which creates a language reflective of 'national genius' and the particular climatic and political conditions that governed its creation.[51] How then can he speak coherently of a 'truth' which supersedes all individual and national differences? While he does indeed suggest that such a language is theoretically possible, broader indications point to his concern for clear *communication* within any lan-guage group, particularly through the elimination of philosophical abstractions which convert fictional or convenient notions into 'things'.

A second problem inherent in Condillac's reasoning on 'method' arises from his indications that the refinement of language towards greater philosophical accuracy is not in every sense 'progressive'. Philosophy has given language greater 'precision and perspicuity'. But it has also 'damped' the 'fire of the imagination',[52] undermining the expressive power of language and the arts, the subject of a long section in the middle of the *Essay* that Derrida ignores. Imagination and analysis, vivid expression and precision, represent contrary and irreconcilable forces in the creation of language. The most 'perfect' language would not, by this reasoning, be the most methodical or truthful, but 'should take possession of the middle' between these two operations.[53] In thus representing the history of language as process of both gain and loss, Condillac differed from a writer he strongly influenced, Jean-Jacques Rousseau. And Rousseau, of course, is a main subject of Derrida's most famous exposition of the West's alleged prejudice against *écriture*, *Of Grammatology*.

Theories of Writing: Warburton and Rousseau

According to Derrida, 'the Age of Rouseau' marked the point where 'a certain set of problems about writing came to the fore in an original way',[54] for *écriture* allegedly posed an unprecedented threat to the primacy of the voice and 'presence'. Yet a superficial review of the century's literature does little to create an impression of anxiety. With the virtual demise of projects to institute a 'universal character' after the seventeenth century, authors generally relegated writing to a minor role in their discussions of language. Most students of language seemed satisfied that the supposed evolution of writing from pictograms to alphabetical characters had been adequately traced in a single chapter in a theological work, William Warburton's *Divine Legation of Moses* (1738–41). Condillac himself, as Derrida himself notes, essentially rehearsed Warburton's account in the one brief chapter of *An Essay on the Origin of Human Knowledge* that discusses written language.[55] Derrida nonetheless deploys this chapter in his essay 'Signature, Event, Context' as an instance of the 'classical' understanding of writing unopposed by 'a single counterexample' in 'the entire history of philosophy'.[56] As overstatements in Derrida's writing go, this is a fairly large one: Warburton's thesis that hieroglyphics represented an abstract form of pictographs, without phonemic value, was refuted by Jean-François Champollion in the 1820s, and the subsequent history of grammatology (the coinage of archeologist I. C. Gelb) has determined that even the earliest forms of writing, like cuneiform, corresponded to sounds, not things or ideas. It may be objected that Derrida's assertion about the typical status of the Warburton/Condillac thesis refers to the belief that only writing functions in the absence of speaker or writer, and therefore in the absence of a conscious intention. But John Searle, in his well-known response to 'Signature, Event, Context', notes (among other objections) that twentieth-century linguistics no longer makes conscious intention the source of meaning for either speech or writing.[57] Derrida's linguistic thought seems strangely entrenched in a model of signifiers and signifieds, vocal marks referring to preformed ideas, persuasive only to readers who have failed to absorb Wittgenstein, Whorf and Austin. This model was already under pressure, as we have considered, in the work of Condillac. For Condillac regarded 'ideas' of a fully conscious kind as merely extensions of arbitrary signs. So far from believing that 'absence' was the exclusive characteristic of writing, he insisted that the role of signs was precisely to trigger the mental trace of an absent sensation. And writing, in his view, played precisely the same role as speech, though with the advantage of facilitating transmission over a greater distance.

Given that Condillac gave only brief and second-hand attention to the history of writing, it would seem gratuitous for Derrida to conclude that this philosopher deemed writing 'the root of evil'.[58] Indeed, where Condillac considered the role of written language in his work on grammar and logic, he judged that it exemplified 'les langues formées et perfectionnés'.[59] For Condillac, good writing, particularly good philosophical writing, represented language in its most analytical and precise form. As we have seen, Condillac's allegiance to this ideal of precision and accuracy was not consistent or uncomplicated. The most perfect language, he wrote elsewhere, should combine such precision with 'the fire of the imagination'. As such expressive qualities derived from national idioms constructed through a process of social dialogue and public performance (such as the dances and songs of ancient drama), he advised the philosopher aiming purely at accuracy and precision to separate himself from the national language. He should 'not to enter into any conversation'.[60] His model in this case was mathematics, particularly calculus and geometry, obviously written forms: 'It is with languages as with geometrical signs; they give a new insight into things, and dilate the mind in proportion as they are more perfect.'[61] In this respect Condillac was still influenced by creators of a 'real character' such as Wilkins and Leibniz, whom Derrida (as previously mentioned) placed in the tradition supposedly rejected by the eighteenth century.

Condillac's debt to what we might call a *grammacentric* tradition of the seventeenth century, when writing often became a template for the reform of speech, indeed makes much of his logic (as opposed to his influential 'conjectural history' or his rhetoric) seem dated in the eighteenth century. For Derrida is right to identify a 'phonocentric' tendency in eighteenth-century thought to the following extent: philosophers, and also novelists and poets, became increasingly attuned to communicative resources of tone and gesture not readily duplicated in writing, a trend exemplified by Condillac's more famous conjectures on the invention of speech. But this enriched understanding of oral communication did not entail a fearful determination to fend off or denigrate writing as some kind of threat or intruder, an argument that I have made elsewhere at book-length. Many authors of 'conjectural histories' speculated that writing came *before* speech, and that in the beginning 'Sound would be the name of the Mark', as David Hartley put it.[62] Furthermore, there was wide consensus that alphabetical writing marked the superiority of the West, the progress of society from 'barbarism' to civilization, and the primary boundary between the illiterate herd and a literate elite.[63] This powerful link between the idea of Western superiority and the invention of writing remains with us today, a pride strengthened by print and later digital permutations of the *gramme*. Pride and confidence in *écriture*, moreover, found support in empiricism. Empiricism regarded speech as itself arbitrary and linked in no privileged way to 'presence' or 'being'. To cite Condillac again, 'l'art de parler, l'art d'écrire, l'art de raisonner et l'art de penser ne sont, dans le fond, qu'un seul et même art'.[64] While interchangeable with speech as arbitrary signs, writing (and, especially, print) made language more stable and durable. The supplementation of writing was not 'dangerous', but rather beneficial.

All these observations are corroborated by the work that Derrida makes the centrepiece of his thesis regarding the prejudice against writing in the 'classical age', *Divine Legation of Moses* (1738–41). The fame of Warburton's chapter on the history of writing, which was enthusiastically received in France after its translation by Léonard des Malpeines (1744), seems curious given that Warburton's goals in this work were theological and not philosophical. He was indeed an empiricist, but of a very crude sort. (Warburton had little to say about the nature of cognition, assuming that all mental impressions derived unmediated from outward material objects.) His primary target was the seventeenth-century Jesuit philosopher Anthansius Kircher who, engrossed by the *'Fanatic-Philosophy'* of *'Platonists and Pythogorians'*,[65] mistook the Egyptian hieroglyphics as the repositories of ancient wisdom, philosophical anticipations of even the mysteries of Christianity. In fact, Warburton argued, the hieroglyphics derived from the crude efforts of primitive humans to express their conceptions of the world. Like Condillac, Warburton imagined the first languages as extremely elementary and imperfect: 'LANGUAGE, as appears from both the Record of Antiquity and the Nature of the Thing, was at first extremely rude, narrow, and equivocal; so that Men would be perpetually at a loss, on any new Conception, or uncommon Adventure to explain themselves.' This language would therefore have been supplemented 'by apt and significant *Signs*'.[66] Early language was filled with visual metaphors, often modelled on gestures, and these metaphors in turn became the basis for the first written marks, pictographs and hieroglyphics of increasing abstruseness and complexity as civilization evolved and people's conceptions multiplied. Against Kircher's Platonic conception of writing, therefore, Warburton offers an empiricist alternative.

Derrida's deconstruction of Warburton, 'Scribble (Writing-Power)', pays little attention to the empiricist epistemology underlying this chapter on writing. Rather, as in his account of Condillac, Derrida makes Warburton sound phonocentric, committed to privileging some pure, original voice: 'If the deficiency of the human voice in its finitude, is immediately supplied by action language and by the marks of writing, the "voice of nature" everywhere and ceaselessly supplies its own deficiencies in metaphors, properly, of itself.'[67] Derrida is equivocating here on the word 'voice' used in two senses – the literal voice of speech (which, in its imperfect form, comes first) and Warburton's conventional metaphor of the 'voice of nature'. While half-acknowledging that Warburton always sees literal speech as deficient, and in need of supplementation by writing, Derrida notes that these corrections are directed by 'nature', which Warburton sometimes calls a 'voice'. Of particular interest to Derrida is that the increasing abstractness of writing, leading to the invention of the alphabet, was finally utilized by those in power, particularly priests, to secret their knowledge from the public. Again, that is, writing is again the root of evil – 'dissimulation, ruse, and perfidy of writing, reversal of places and of history, again a catastrophe of tristes tropiques'.[68] And, by Warburton's account, it is precisely the 'voice of nature' that led to this corruption. The good bishop, we are to understand, finds himself ensnared in the immemorial deconstructive trap.

The problems that afflict this reading can only be summarized briefly. Despite what Derrida claims, writing itself is not responsible for the priests' corruptions. (They indeed developed a secret *speech* as well.)[69] Rather, they exploited, for their own purposes, developments in script spurred forward not by the desire for secrecy but in order to abbreviate marks and expand their denotative range. The creation of secret scripts was by no means 'necessary and inevitable'.[70] As Warburton makes clear, this deceitful use of writing happened only among the Egyptians, and not, for example, among the Chinese. The creation of a secret writing in a long-dead civilization marked no 'catastrophe' for Warburton; he followed the conventional thinking of his time in believing ancient Egypt to be particularly corrupt and priest-laden. A priest himself, Warburton had no objections to priestly castes, or even the enlightened use of priestly power. But the Egyptian priests do implicitly evoke Warburton's religious enemies – free-thinking 'enthusiasts' (who imagine all kinds of mystery in the Bible) and Jesuitical Papists like Kircher. In contrast with Kircher, Warburton regarded himself a stolid representative of the most world's rational faith, the Church of England, which he spent his career defending. In this written exposition, *The Divine Legation of Moses*, he presents the public with a clear and rational account of Biblical history free from nefarious Popery and the 'fanatic' speculations of 'metaphysicians'. Empiricism, in his view, defined a demystified and level-headed understanding of religion and history.

The problems of reading in 'Scribble', like those in *The Archeology of the Frivolous*, arise precisely because Derrida sets out to impose a deconstructive grid of concepts – presence, phonocentrism, *écriture* and so forth – that apply problematically, at best, to eighteenth-century empiricism. In making this observation, I am of course setting Condillac and Warburton in historical context, and everyone knows that Derrida did not believe in 'history'.[71] Yet in *Of Grammatology*, to which we now turn, Derrida himself admits that 'the *departure*' of his methodology is 'radically empiricist'. He promises, however, that his conclusions will arrive at some validity that surpasses the *a posteriori* uncertainties of empirical evidence: 'we shall see that this abyss is not a happy or unhappy accident. An entire theory of the structural necessity of the abyss will be gradually constituted in our reading'.[72] How can this 'structural necessity' (common, evidently, to the entire 'Age of Rousseau') possibly be established? However we answer this question, we are reminded of his insistence against Levinas on 'the a prioris and transcendental horizons of language'. Derrida resists, strenuously, the suggestion that he is advancing merely empiricist claims, for 'the opposition of philosophy and non-philosophy is another name for empiricism'.[73] Underlying *Of Grammatology* is the anxiety to convince us that this is a work of 'philosophy' in its deployment of apodictic, non-historical truths about the 'structures' of discourse itself.

Hence, Derrida repeatedly asserts that the supposed 'contradictions' in Rousseau in fact represent 'the unity of intention and the necessity of a constraint'.[74] But to what extent do the 'necessities' of Rousseau's discourse reflect 'the Age of Rousseau'? In 'Scribble', Derrida claims (empirically) that Warburton's chapter on writing (1741) is 'precisely contemporaneous' with 'Rousseau's *Discourses*' (1750 and 1754).[75] In fact, the decade that separated these works is of considerable importance. Rousseau had absorbed the ideas of Condillac's *Essay on the Origin of Human Knowledge* (1746). While professedly influenced by Condillac, Rousseau pushed strongly against the sceptical current of that work and of empiricist language theories in his own time. He may well have been particularly prone to the methods of deconstruction not because he was representative of his time, but precisely because he was so aggressively non-conformist.

While the main subject of Derrida's analysis is a small, unpublished work, *Essay on the Origin of Languages*, he marshals evidence that this work is contemporaneous with the more famous *Discourse on the Origin of Inequality* and that it presents an identical understanding of language. In the second *Discourse*, Rousseau develops Condillac's insights into the dependence of all thinking on language: 'Let it be remembered how many ideas we owe to the use of language; how much grammar exercises and facilitates the operations of the mind.'[76] Indeed, he goes further than Condillac in arguing that reason is so dependent on language that the very invention of language presents an insoluble paradox: 'if men needed speech in order to learn to think, they needed still more to know how to think in order to discover the art of speech'.[77] He rejects Condillac's thesis on the initial creation of instituted signs through spontaneous cries and gestures because he finds no basis for believing that individuals in the state of nature would have had any social contact. Rousseau regards individuals at this primitive level as totally self-sufficient, following the directions of 'instinct' in order to fulfil their desires for food and sex. In this respect, Rousseau is less sceptical than Condillac: for Condillac, the primitive and speechless human is driven by instinct in an entirely random way, and is bereft of memory or really any notion of 'self' at all. But Rousseau's primitive human has free will, memory and the capacity to make comparisons even without language. This is hardly surprising. An historical paradigm of self-absorption, Rousseau considers the self, egotity, innate to humans, a doctrine which makes him a ready target for Derrida's deconstructive arsenal of 'presence' and 'supplementarity'.

For all of human history after the (inexplicable) invention of language constitutes, according to Rousseau, the history of supplementation and the erosion of presence. The self is drawn into comparison with other humans, the source of pride, deceit, subjection and social inequality; language and reason transform the instinctive impulses of pity and compassion into abstract rules of justice and virtue which in fact justify the suppression of instinctive goodness. Hence, Rousseau starts then from an empiricist understanding of mind professedly indebted to Condillac. But Condillac had characterized the movement of the mind from instinct to reason, from mute perception to language, as a process of both gain and loss, of expressive power increasingly supplanted by clarity and precision. Rousseau presents the same process as a history of pure loss – the progressive supplementation of selfhood and spontaneous virtue. According to Rousseau, any shift away from the pure presence of the self acting instinctively towards sensible impressions marks the beginning of humankind's inevitable decline towards the injustice, inequality and alienation of modern civilization.

Ironically, then, Rousseau attacks the empiricist orthodoxies of his day by being the purest empiricist of them all. In *Essay on the Origin of Language,* Rousseau fixates on precisely this claim: everything beyond sensation, either from the senses or from 'feeling', contains the seeds of evil. As Derrida himself observes of his attack on Rameau's theories of harmony, Rousseau excoriates 'false empiricism, empiricism falsifying *the immediate givens of experience*' (emphasis added).[78] Harmony depends on the abstract combinations of pure sounds. Melody on the other hand 'imitates and expresses',[79] presenting an unmediated picture of the soul's feelings and the sounds of the world. 'In all kinds of imitation', he writes in the *Essay,* 'some form of discourse must substitute for the voice of nature'.[80] This substitution was faithful only in the song-like language of the primitive humans, whose 'root words would be imitative sounds or accents of passions'.[81] Again following Condillac, Rousseau presents 'ideas' not as spontaneous 'imitations' but as complex abstractions made possible through the conversion of natural cries and gestures into arbitrary signs. But for Rousseau, unlike Condillac or other eighteenth-century empiricists, ideas are therefore bad. The perfect primitive speech, consisting of melodic expressions of feeling, 'would represent without reasoning'.[82] Similarly with writing: Rousseau agrees with Condillac in regarding writing as the ultimate achievement of precision and clarity in language, the culmination of a linguistic process towards abstraction, reason and analysis. Indeed, he may well be thinking of Condillac's 'method' when he compares writing to 'algebra'.[83] But, for that very reason, writing *is* for Rousseau 'the root of evil'. The evil of writing is that it represents the ultimate distancing of human language and experience from pure sensation and feeling: 'Feelings are expressed in speaking, ideas in writing'.[84]

Derrida's reading of Rousseau in *Of Grammatology* is therefore essentially correct. Moreover, he is probably correct that Rousseau's account of language courts, by its very nature, 'the catastrophe of supplementarity'.[85] Rousseau cannot possibly describe a melodic first language unsullied by the articulations that make writing possible; accepting no language but that of imitation and re-presentation, he cannot, in his *Essay* or *The Confessions*, sustain the 'myth of consciousness' as 'immediacy'.[86] But, curiously, both of these observations were widely confirmed by the empiricist tradition that surrounded Rousseau, and which he assailed even in drawing from many of its premises. It is certainly *not* true of Condillac – or of Locke, Berkeley, Maupertuis, or Hume – that they relied on a myth of unmediated consciousness. For these authors, consciousness consists of signs, a play of presence and absence, and they by no means yearned for a return to a state of pure sensation and unmediated feelings. It is unclear, in short, how Derrida's deconstruction of *Essay on the Origin of Languages* can demonstrate 'an entire theory of the structural necessity of the abyss'. Empirically tested, his reading reveals little about the so-called 'Age of Rousseau', much less Western philosophical discourse.

Conclusions

Was Derrida, by his own terms, a 'philosopher'? It is his unique justification that the very indefinability of his position with regard to the binary of philosophy/non-philosophy confirms his own deconstructive method. However we approach this problem, the term 'non-philosophy' is inexorably connected in his own vocabulary with empiricism. He seems, on the other hand, to share a great deal with this tradition. From Locke, to Condillac, to Peirce, to Levinas (if we agree with Derrida in placing him there), empiricists have developed a deeply semiotic understanding of consciousness, and have held up metaphysical concepts of being, presence and selfhood to scepticism. Where Derrida maintains his status of 'philosopher' is in his resistance to full scepticism on these very questions. As revealed in his critique of Levinas, he held jealously to the position that these terms constituted the intransigent and irreducible essence of any truly 'philosophical' language. But he then, over the course of his career, subjected these concepts to a broadly *empiricist* critique. From this perspective, this method seems an ingenious hybrid of traditional metaphysics and the traditional critique of that metaphysics.

Derrida's special contribution, therefore, may lie ultimately in his deconstruction, and perhaps his transcendence, of his own identity as a 'philosopher'. He is not what he claims to be; he is not doing what he claims he does. Like the texts of the philosophers whom he deconstructs, Derrida's text thrusts to the margins that abyss of ephemeral sensation, the abyss of empiricism, that would nullify the rationale for philosophy, an institution and an education that he defended with great energy. For Derrida saw rightly and clearly that empiricism can ultimately do without 'philosophy' in the traditional sense that Heidegger wished to revive: having reached an ontological edge that it considers unknowable or fictional, empiricism ceases to ask anymore, and proceeds in Humean fashion with quotidian 'facts'. The engineer or the scientist – or for that matter the reader of books by 'Jacques Derrida' (for reading is an *empirical* activity) – simply does not ask about the ontological status of his or her objects. Hence, during what we call the 'Enlightenment', the most sceptical empiricists like Hume, Berkeley or Maupertuis could get on, unperturbed, with writing history books, performing experiments, or playing billiards. 'Jacques Derrida' went down the same path of scepticism and the erasure of his own identity as a 'philosopher'. In both mimicking and ejecting empiricism, however, he attempted to make this erasure an endless process, placing his text in irreducible suspension.

2 LOCKE'S DESIRE

Jonathan Brody Kramnick

Among the categories examined by the Enlightenment, few were so elusive as desire. Then as now, the term lent itself to an equal balance of meanings and vagaries. What did seventeenth- and eighteenth-century writers intend when they sought to demarcate the nature of motivation and name the experience of wanting? One answer is that they endeavored to bring sexuality into a new culture of expertise. 'Desire' became one of several areas of knowledge laid bare for the separate disciplines of moral philosophy and experimental science. But Enlightenment theorists also summoned the category to help explain institutions that dwelled outside the realm of the personal, such as the market, civil society and the aesthetic. The erotic seemed to have this special feature: it accounted for one's habits of mind and gave form to the grand systems of a secular culture often at the same time. Witness Bernard Mandeville's *Search into the Nature of Society* (1723): the 'sociableness of man', he there argues, 'arises from these two things, viz. the multiplicity of desires and the continual opposition he meets with in his endeavours to gratify them'.[1] The social order initiates a longing from which it also takes shape, hence the 'search' turns from the realm of public life to the inner world of the self: 'I beg of my serious reader that he would for a while abate a little of his gravity and suffer me to examine these people separately, as to their inside and the different motives they act from'.[2]

In the lair of feeling lies the map of society, and in the form of society reside the springs of affection. But that is not to say that the Enlightenment found it easy to navigate between the two. One way that we can get a sense of the effort that went into desire and to tracking it within the new, secular institutions of market and culture is to follow closely the changing meaning of the term. The following pages thus attempt something like a comparative philology of the erotic at the close of the British seventeenth century; they place the word 'desire' in what was arguably its most significant array of philosophical use and speculative meaning. Lexical shifts create a pattern that is intelligible within some of the leading tensions of the age. We may state these briefly as follows. According to many, the modernity of modern society lay in the differentiation of its parts: politics from commerce, art from science, religion from reason.[3] Each was a separate discipline of thought or an independent domain of value. No single system of faith inhibited the cultivation of knowledge or the accumulation of capital. Yet the advent of modern, disciplinary culture cast a certain shadow. The same sharpness of focus that provided new levels of expertise appeared to estrange intellectual concerns from the habits and language of daily living.[4] The imagined fluidity of public or intimate life unmoored from tradition entailed new varieties of risk. The resulting strain placed on the concept of 'desire' was unique: it criss-crossed the subjective and the social, the personal and the disciplinary, at their most sensitive points of contact and so became inseparable, as we shall see, from a certain 'uneasiness'.[5]

This configuration will become clearer by turning now to our example. Few writers bring into bolder relief the contrary aspirations of their period than John Locke. A philosopher of mind and political theorist, medical doctor and economist, Locke shows by his example the Enlightenment's ambivalent regard to the very disciplines it cultivated.[6] Nowhere is this more evident than in his effort to name desire and calculate its provenance. In the first edition of the *Essay Concerning Human Understanding* (1690), Locke describes an inner drive toward the good, a direction of the will by the moral sense. The second edition (1694) has a more forbidding cast. When we desire something, Locke there argues, we anxiously covet its presence. Between the first and second editions, Locke engages in a fervent correspondence with the Irish scientist William Molyneux. Their letters often reach a peak of tonal intensity – with resonant declarations of convivial emotion – precisely when they discuss the limits of the will and the nature of wanting. Looking at the letters alongside the revisions, I hope to show how the naming of desire (absent as a term in the first edition), and the separation of it from the domain of religion or ethics, raised to philosophical abstraction the conditions of affect first encountered in the new cultures of expertise. It is a familiar tactic of modern philosophy to speculate from experience. For this reason, we should not be surprised to find that Locke's final theory of desire is similar in shape and bearing to the feelings first evoked by the letters and that both reflect the new discipline's peculiar mixture of anomie and intimacy.

Locke's theory of desire is spelled out in the twenty-first chapter of Book II of the *Essay*, entitled 'Of Power'. This chapter was evidently important to Locke. He revised it more than any other part of the *Essay* (almost doubling its length in the process) and discussed it obsessively in his correspondence. 'Of Power' introduces a number of significant themes: free will versus determinism, the psychology of motives and action, and the ethics of human conduct.[7] In the first edition, the argument ran something like this: moral agents are drawn toward the greater good, but they sometimes mistake present pleasure for later happiness and so, freely, act against their long-term interest. Locke begins with the novel claim to have put to rest 'that long agitated and, I think, unreasonable, because unintelligible, question *viz. whether man's will be free or no*.[8] The question misunderstands the nature of willing as an action. It is 'as insignificant to ask, whether man's will be free, as to ask, whether his sleep be swift, or his virtue square'.[9] With this droll assertion, Locke means to argue that liberty is not an attribute of the will but a condition of the agent. People are free or confined to the degree to which they can exercise their wills, but the will itself cannot be free because it cannot act alone. Locke calls this exercise 'volition ... the actual choosing, or preferring forbearance to the doing, or doing to the forbearance, of any particular action in our power, that we think on'.[10] 'And what is the will', he continues, 'but the faculty to do this?'[11] The will enacts our choices. It is here that the idea of free will is, on Locke's reckoning, demonstrably antithetical. Agency enslaves the will. Freedom entails that the will always serves one's choice to do or forbear from doing: 'The will ... is determined by something without itself'.[12] Put this way, Locke's concerns may seem far from what we would recognize as the erotic. Up to a point this is so, and we will want to watch how the chapter takes up the question of desire over the years of revision. But it is important to see this process underway already in the first edition, where Locke is concerned to delimit the aleatory field of wants and passions.

Reading these pages, Locke's friend William Molyneux described the thread of the argument as 'wonderfully fine spun', and it is not hard to see why. Locke appears to accept the spirit of the argument for free will (agents are not predetermined in their thoughts and actions) while splitting hairs on its terms. The principal incentive behind the unusual separation of agency from willing is apparently to move the discussion from simple freedom to 'actual choosing' and so to dwell at greater length on affective and emotional complexity. Consciousness takes form out of an ambivalent tissue of preferences: 'it is the mind, or the man, that operates, and exerts these powers; that does the action, he has the power, or is able to do. *That which has the power or not the power to operate, is that alone, which is, or is not free*; and not the power itself'.[13] Willing is not as interesting a topic, Locke seems to say, as the variable thoughts that cause people to do or not to do something. The question ought not to be is the will free, but rather, given freedom to choose, what shapes our motives? What causes moral agents to select one action over another, to do or forbear doing, when faced with multiple options? Locke's answer in the first edition is plain: '*Good*, then, *the greater good is that alone which determines the will*'.[14] In this simple inducement lies an important thesis about the nature of motivation; 'pleasure and pain are produced in us, by the operation of certain objects, either on our minds, or our bodies; and in different degrees: therefore what has an aptness to produce pleasure in us, is that we labour for, and is that we call *good*'.[15] Locke's notion of the object will undergo significant revision in the second edition. We might simply note here that 'labour' for the good is not yet termed desire. Locke uses that word only once in the first edition, in a dismissive (if revealing) aside. Explaining that 'preference' is a better word for his purposes than 'choice', he writes that the latter is of 'a more doubtful signification, and bordering more upon desire, and so is referred to things remote'.[16] Desire resides only in what is doubly murky, remote and doubtful in turns. It confounds rather than expresses our preferences among the objects we confront.

Contemplating one's options, the mind is drawn toward the object that appears to present the greatest pleasure. Locke spends the rest of the chapter attempting to demonstrate that on this basis we are ethical beings: 'This is not an imperfection in Man, it is highest perfection of intellectual natures' because goodness, in the last instance, is always defined in terms of the 'future state' of our souls.[17] The recourse to the doctrine of the 'future state' situates Locke's argument, at this stage, well within the parameters of normative Anglicanism. 'Future state' was the increasingly prominent term, in late-seventeenth-century discourse, for the condition of our souls after we die, when our past conduct is judged and our eternal condition sealed.[18] Locke's version of the argument was both typical and bland:

> To him, I say, who hath a prospect of the different state of perfect happiness, or misery that attends all men after this life, depending on their behaviour here, the measures of good and evil that govern his choice, are mightily changed. For since nothing of pleasure and pain in this life, can bear any proportion to endless happiness or exquisite misery of an immortal soul hereafter, actions in his power will have their preference, not according to the transient pleasure, or pain that accompanies, or follows them here; but as they serve to secure that perfect durable happiness hereafter.[19]

The flat style of these sentences is oddly matched with their distended content: hellfire in plain language. Yet the moderation of tone reveals an important point. Locke wants to argue that all reasonable people calmly incline toward the good. A turbulent psychology of preferences gives way to a rational calculation of benefits. Accordingly, wrongdoing is a fault not of the will but of the understanding; 'when we compare present pleasure or pain with future, we often make wrong judgments of them'.[20] The will passively follows the misperception of the understanding; we are defeated by 'the weak and narrow constitutions of our minds'.[21] In the switch from passions to the intellect, Locke absolves the will of any guilt in the pursuit of this-worldly pleasures, as he had earlier denied the will any capacity for freedom. We are always only after what we think will give us maximum delight; our failure to see what will bring us long-term pleasure is a failure of rationality and not of feeling.

The argument that we are drawn insuperably toward the good is radically revised in the second edition. One reason may lie in the unexpected company the early argument kept. In the conventional history of the Enlightenment,

Locke's epistemology seeks to break with its metaphysical forbears, devotees of Platonic essences and innate ideas alike.[22] The initial version of 'Of Power' demonstrates that this break is as yet incomplete. Compare Locke's language to that of the great 'Cambridge Platonist' himself, Henry More, as the latter describes the nature of desire in his influential work *The Immortality of the Soul* (1659). Here is a precursor vision of the 'greater good' conceived in a rather different form:

> There is nothing more certain than that the love of God and our neighbour is the greatest happiness that we can arrive unto, either in this life or that which is to come. And whatever things are there described, are either the causes, effects or concomitants of that noble and divine passion. Neither are the external incitements thereto, which I there mention, rightly to be deemed sensual, but intellectual: For even such is the sensible beauty, whether it show itself in feature, musick or whatever graceful deportments or comely actions. And those things that are not properly intellectual, suppose odours and vapours, yet such a spirit may be transfused into the vehicles of these aerial inhabitants thereby, that may more than ordinarily raise up into their intellectual faculties.[23]

The contrast to the tranquillity of Locke's prose registers a larger split between the two systems of thought. On More's vivid account of things, bodies pulse with the motion of 'incorporeal substance'.[24] An 'intellectual' and 'sensual' blend daubs the ashen world of extension with the ethereal pleasures of the good. 'Spirits do act really upon the senses, by acting upon matter that affects the senses'; they produce what More calls 'desire', a 'harmless and momentary ablegation of the soul from the body' in which 'the power of fancy may carry the soul to the place intended'.[25] The distance of this animated tableau from Locke's becalmed portrait is instructive. We are enspiralled in the 'diversity of impulsions from objects'; our desire for these objects is an imaginative and ecstatic 'ablegation' (casting out or dispatching) that eludes the calm interdiction of judgment.[26] Even in its early form, the *Essay*'s sober balance of preference and forbearance is far from this lurid portrait, but the subdued account of moral judgment does bear a certain resemblance: we are drawn to the goodness of certain objects.

Locke's halting evocation of the 'greater good' betrays a residual affinity to a tradition of thinking with which he is otherwise uncomfortable.[27] Closer even than More is John Norris's *The Theory and Regulation of Love* (1688). A fellow of All-Souls College, Norris was an important interlocutor of Locke's throughout the 1690s.[28] His 'theory' was that all ethics could be reduced to the question of love, which he defines as 'a motion of the soul towards good':[29] 'This moral gravity of the soul will be its connaturality to all good, or good in general, that is God as its primary and adequate object, and to particular goods only so far as they have something of the common nature of good, something of God in them'.[30] By 'object' Norris means both goal and thing. God is the direction toward which all desire leans and the reality that lies under all substance; he is the 'great and supreme magnet'.[31] As it searches out this magnetism, Norris's erotics cast a wide net. 'Concupiscence or desire' has God as its primary object, but also finds God in all that we want or crave; 'our desire has many subordinate and secondary objects, which it tends to with more or less inclination according as the marks or footsteps of the universal good appears in them'.[32] The novel latitude of this eroticism lies in the ardency of mediation; objects track the deeper reality of a spirit whose pull on us is concupiscence unbound.

We are invited to imagine the world as one common object of our desire. Underlying this solicitation is a problem of increasing importance for the Enlightenment: what if not traditional hierarchy or revealed religion brings together the composite order of civil society? Norris's answer is that society is the name we give to the manifold bonds of concupiscence. 'The pulsation of the heart', he writes, 'is the great pulse of the body politic':

> 'Tis love that begets and keeps up the great circulation and mutual dependence of society, by this men are inclined to maintain mutual commerce and intercourse with one another, and to distribute their benefits and kindnesses to all the parts of the civil body, till at length they return again upon themselves in the circle and reciprocation of love.[33]

Since desire is the pull of the good, it may be no surprise that its cadence is fundamentally civil. The destiny of the erotic is to stitch together the aggregate of displaced individuals into a community whose fictive harmony has otherwise been dissolved. Norris presents this tailoring in two overlapping metaphors: circularity and penetration. The ostensibly antithetical pair blend into one positive image – 'circulation' *and* 'dependence', 'commerce' *and* 'intercourse', 'circle' *and* 'reciprocation' – with marked preference given to the first term. Penetration bends like a circle, even at the formal level in which Norris's sentence distends and then curves back into a sphere: love clasping to love. According to this round view of things, society is an amiable compound of desires, desire an ideal reciprocity of feeling and sexuality a sanguine form of re-enchantment. All the puzzles of modern living – the division of labour, the bonds of law, the exchange of commodities – may be explained by a concupiscence leached of opacity or tension.

In all of its zesty exuberance, *The Theory and Regulation of Love* may be taken to represent the extreme version of an argument that Locke moves steadily away from over the course of writing the *Essay*. In the first edition, he accepts the notion of the greater good but shies away from the related concept of desire, in so far as the latter carries with it the sundry mysteries of 'innate' dispositions that his plain-speaking empiricism seeks to vanquish. As he thinks about these matters, Locke slowly builds a new model of desire against the model he found in writers like More and Norris. The early version of the *Essay* agrees that we are moved by the idea of the greater good, but presents this as an act of logical calculation, not ecstatic feeling. More and Norris argued that desire led us to the good because it discovered the spiritual latency of objects. In what will later become a hallmark of empiricist method, the *Essay* consistently suggests that we have little access to this essential core of things. In the first edition, objects are simply matters of preference that test our rationality. But even this conception eventually seems too close to Norris's argument; as we shall see, rewriting the chapter leads to a notable recession of the object. The first edition had objects but no desire, the second desire but no objects. What is the upshot of this reversal? On the face of it, Locke appears to diminish the libidinal cast: ablegation and concupiscence give way to judgment; the coloured lights of the universal good fade to a monochromatic grey. Yet to understand the two-part change simply in these terms would be significantly misleading. Locke's difficulty with abiding models of desire does not so much reject the sexual as unfurl one set of erotics against the antecedent pressure of another. He fits desire to modern, secular uncertainty. Objects are no longer pre-given vehicles of the good; they are shaped by a wanting whose temper and timbre are difficult to predict. The targets of our longing are not set in advance but must constantly be invented.

During the years in which these erotics began to take shape, Locke conducted an extensive correspondence with the Irish scientist William Molyneux. The letters began when Locke stumbled upon Molyneux's book *Dioptrica Nova* (1692) and read that 'the incomparable Mr. Locke ... in his *Essay Concerning Human Understanding*, has rectified more received mistakes, and delivered more profound truths, established on experience and observation, for the direction of man's mind in the prosecution of knowledge ... than are to be met with in all the volumes of the ancients'.[34] Although they had not yet met, Locke's thankful response introduces an exchange of escalating intimacy; he writes on 16 July 1692 that he is pleased 'those who can be extreme and rigorous and exact in the search of truth, can be as civil and as complaisant in their dealing with those whom they take to be lovers of it', to which Molyneux responds on 27 August:

> I find by yours to me, that my ambition is not fallen short of its designe; but that you are pleased to incourage me by assuring me that I have made great advance of friendship towards you; give me leave to imbrace the favour with all joy imaginable. And that you may judge of my sincerity by my open heart, I will plainly confess to you, that I have not in my life read any book with more satisfaction, than your essay; Insomuch that a repeated perusal of it is still more pleasant to me.[35]

As the letters continue, Locke and Molyneux focus on problems that had vexed the chapter on power: ethics, will, objects and (eventually) desire. As the initial exchange would suggest, these are addressed in the register of convivial affection.[36] Alone among Locke's letters, the Molyneux correspondence radiates a sense of incipient and filial closeness: the 'complaisancy' of the one and 'incouragements' of the other; the shared quest for truth; the confessed joys of a satisfied heart. So much could have been said by Achilles to Patroclus. What gives these declarations their specificity are two interrelated facets of Enlightenment culture: in broad terms, the mediation of print and the division of knowledge. The plangent avowals of communion and like-mindedness occur between two writers whose only acquaintance is having read the other's published work. The pleasure Molyneux feels upon the receipt of Locke's letter leads him to recall the initial satisfaction he had in reading the *Essay* and to claim that rereading the book is perpetual delight. Desire, if we may call it that, is continually routed back to words on a printed page. Meanwhile, Locke only comes across the dedication because he and Molyneux share an interest in empirical philosophy and the natural sciences. He reaches out to the civility of a thinker who is as 'extreme and rigorous and exact' as he imagines himself to be. In this appeal lies an important variation in the wide course of the early-modern print market. The community brought together by publication is limited to the virtuosos of natural philosophy; Locke and Molyneux have, above all, a disciplinary familiarity.

Consider the reply of 20 September to Molyneux's solicitation, where Locke further warms the dialogue with what Maurice Cranston, in the standard biography, calls 'terms of unusual cordiality'.[37] The *billet-doux* is worth quoting at length:

> There being nothing that I think of so much value as the acquaintance and friendship of knowing and worthy men, you may easily guess how much I find my self obliged, I will not say by the offer of, but by the gift you have made me of yours. That which confirms me in the assurance of it is the little pretence I have to it. For, knowing myself, as I do, I cannot think so vainly of my self as to imagine that you should make such overtures and expressions of kindness to me for any other end, but merely as the pledges and exercise of it. I return you therefore my thanks, as for the greatest and most acceptable present you could have made me; and desire you to believe, that since I cannot hope that the returns which I make you of mine should be of any great use to you, I shall endeavour to make it up, as well as I can, with an high esteem, and perfect sincerity. You must therefore expect to have me live with you hereafter, with all the liberty and assurance of a settled friendship. For meeting with but a few men in the world whose acquaintance I find much reason to covet, I make more than ordinary haste into the familiarity of a rational enquirer after, and lover of truth, whenever I can light on any such. There are beauties of the mind, as well as of the body, that take and prevail at first flight; and wherever I have met with this, I have readily surrender'd my self, and have never yet been deceived in my expectation.[38]

What are we to make of these perfervid sentences? It is all too easy, I suppose, to reduce them to our modern categories of personal or sexual identity: on this account, the lifelong bachelor attempts to imagine a communion with his new friend, whom he had not yet met but who still prompts, within the relatively safe environs of personal correspondence, a fantasy of genial cohabitation set apart from the impediments of law and custom. As tempting as this reading may be, we would be closer to the amorous springs of the epistle if we consider it within the intimate context of expertise. On this reading, Locke's 'unusual cordiality' attempts to gild the pallid mural of Enlightenment with the hue it has apparently lost. Imaginative friendship and passionate collegiality compensate for the split of science from the subjective flux of social meaning. This wished-for end would then explain the excess of affect, unmatched as it is elsewhere in Locke's correspondence or in his published work. The chill of extremity and rigour leaves a proportionate warmth of affiliation. The result is a vertiginous swirl of feeling:

> your friendship must be genuine because I can return nothing but friendship of my own; so coupled, we will live together, for I will hastily join with one who shares my sober habits of mind, a mind which, after all, has its own ineffable and insuperable beauty. Each precipitous capture of the other leaves a breathless cession of the self: 'I hope you will see, by the freedom I have here taken with you, that I begin to reckon my self amongst your acquaintance. Use me so, I beseech you.'[39]

Remarkable as these declarations are, they take their cue and shape from the cultures of expertise. Witness this important interlarding: 'Wonder not therefore, if having been thus wrought on, I begin to converse with you with as much freedom as if we had begun our acquaintance when you were in Holland; and desire your advice and assistance about a second edition of my Essay, the former being now dispersed'.[40] The intimate salutation leads to a plea for help in emending his published work. But this is not to say that the letters are stripped of affect after they turn to the back-and-forth of revision. To be sure, the correspondence can hardly sustain the first epistle's purple passage. Still, the collaborative venture allows Locke to imagine relations of idealized transparency.[41] Shared vocation breeds like minds:

> I should be loath to differ from any thinking man, being fully persuaded that there are few things of pure speculation, wherein two thinking men who impartially seek truth can differ if they give themselves the leisure to examine their hypotheses and understand one another. I presuming you to be of this make, whereof so few are to be found (for 'tis not every one that thinks himself a lover or seeker of truth who sincerely does it) took the liberty to desire your objections, that I might correct my mistakes.[42]

Locke twice presents differing as a threat to transparent relations between thinking men. In this way, his letter may be said to typify an ideal often accorded to print culture writ large: the building of relations of radical similarity among readers who, as they peruse identical texts, are disembedded from the particulars of region, idiom and personality.[43] The speculative purity and impartial truthfulness that the two men share is made evident by their common response to what lies between them: a book, a set of problems. At the same time, the separation of empirical philosophy from other modes of analysis shapes a special closeness that is set apart from the larger amalgam of the print market. 'You are so desirous to hear the sense of others', Molyneux responds, 'you are so tender in differing from any man, that you have captivated me beyond resistance'. Shared habits of mind are removed from the multitude (alas, 'so few are to be found').

Within this irresistible and captivating sense of minority lies an important paradox. The same configuration that enables affective relations also thwarts them. In a subsequent letter, Locke returns to the image of Molyneux as, so to speak, a domestic partner – 'you have given me those marks of your kindness to me, that you will not think it strange that I count you amongst my friends, and, with those, desiring to live with the ease and freedom of a perfect confidence, I never accuse them to my self of neglect or coldness' – only to note with some sadness the expanse of geography that blocks their privacy. 'That request you press earnestly upon me', he responds to an appeal for manuscripts, 'makes me bemoan the distance you are from me, which deprives me of the assistance I might have from your opinion and judgment, before I ventur'd any thing into the public'.[44] Publication draws attention to distance in the very act of overcoming it. Conversely, intimacy takes form within public life by the act of shaping it, the 'speaking freely and candidly ones opinion upon the thoughts and compositions of another intended for the press'.[45] Each view makes recourse to print as the public condition in or against which intimacy is patterned: a colourless anonymity that proceeds 'after' personal relations; a necessary lineament of those relations.[46] Locke and Molyneux are brought together by the circuits of philosophical publication and debate, yet they enjoy the bond of a correspondence whose privacy is made all the more charged by its eventual disclosure.[47] Here is one further example. In this same letter, Locke promises to send Molyneux the draft pages of what will eventually become *Some Thoughts Concerning Education*, but cautions 'I know not yet whether I shall set my name to this discourse, and therefore shall desire you to conceal it. You see I make you my confessor, for you have made your self my friend'.[48] Confessor to penitent, friend to friend, colleague to colleague, so names the crosshatch of intimacy over the Enlightenment cultures of expertise.

We have been speaking, thus far, about desire in two ways: a conceptual absence in the first edition of the *Essay*, an affective presence in the letters. These may be brought together by considering the process in which desire is called out and named as such. Molyneux responded to Locke's request for help in preparing the second edition, as I mentioned earlier, by drawing attention to the 'finely spun' thread of Chapter 21. He was particularly concerned with that most curious aspect of Locke's early argument: 'you seem to make all sins to proceed from our understandings, or to be against conscience; and not at all from the depravity of our wills. Now it seems harsh to say, that a man shall be damn'd, because he understands no better than he does.'[49] This two-part reproach is concise: the authority given to judgment overlooks the agency of the will; failures of intellect should not damn our souls. On either side, Molyneux complains, the will is insufficiently developed as a concept. There must be something that runs below conscious deliberation and rational calculation that will allow us to understand human motivation and evaluate moral conduct. Molyneux here nervously lights on what is still only nascent in Locke's theory: the separation of ethics from what is not yet called desire. In the first edition of the *Essay*, blame lies with the great steering faculty of the understanding; the undercurrents of emotion and feeling are inculpable. For this reason, perhaps, Molyneux requests that Locke compose another book, 'the second member of your division of the sciences, the Ars Practica or Ethics', one that would presumably be concerned with managing the will.[50] He had been after Locke to write such a book since his first letter and would repeat his appeal frequently.[51] This time the plea is worked up into an entire programme for sociable ethics. Please compose for us a system, Molyneux asks, one that would bring morality down from the heights of the intellect into the give-and-take of the everyday: 'believe me Sir 'twill be one of the most useful and glorious undertakings I can implore you ... Be as large as tis possible on this subject, and by all means let it be in English'.[52] The practicality of the Ars Practica should lie in an expansion of the last section of Chapter 21, in which rational apperception of the future state guides daily choice-making. The problem with the present version of the argument is that it remains in the inhospitable form of a 'mathematical formula'.[53] Much more 'useful' would be a full discursive treatment of the subject in the vernacular, whereby moral instruction could assist social integration.

For whatever reason, Locke never wrote such a book. But he did respond, after a fashion, to the larger complaint. Ethics remain the property of the understanding. The infirmity of the will was to be compensated for by other means. 'I got into a new view of things', Locke writes to Molyneux during the summer of 1693, 'which if I mistake not, will satisfie you, and give a clearer account of humane freedom than hitherto I have done'.[54] He then lists twelve new sections, couched among which is the startling assertion that 'the greater good in view barely considered determines not the will, the joys of heaven are often neglected'.[55] Although Locke does not say as much, this scholium promises nothing less than a mirror inversion of his earlier position, a switch that would appear to widen rather than close the divide between desire and ethics. Writers like Norris had attempted to build a system in which individual goodness and social harmony were indelibly matched to desire. A committed empiricist, Molyneux would hardly have wanted so much from Locke; but he might not have expected the chapter to take the opposite direction and cleave the good from motivation *tout court.*[56] In place of the good, Locke avowed the importance of two novel terms, uneasiness and desire. According to the skeletal form presented by the correspondence, the argument was to run like this: when we desire something we are uneasy in its absence and consequently will its presence. *Desire* determines the will, but at the same time is subject to the rule of the understanding.[57] Freedom therefore lies in the ability to 'suspend the execution of our desires'.[58] Within this fateful joining of liberty and repression lie the germs of Locke's elaborated theory of the erotic. The emphasis on rationality that Molyneux had queried is reinforced by the 'suspension' of wants and cravings, while attraction to the good transforms into a morally-neutral appetite that Locke christens, for the first time, as desire.

Alongside the latter is the most enigmatic category of all. The cryptic charm of 'uneasiness' was not lost on Locke's readers. For many, the term was a fit response to the state of things at the beginning of the eighteenth century, one that captured the modern experience of risk and uncertainty.[59] But Molyneux might have been slightly puzzled to see the word raised to such prominence. As with desire, the dominion of uneasiness promises to be a significant addition to the chapter; in fact, the word does not appear at all in the first edition. But where desire's pedigree stretches back to the origins of philosophy itself (reworked as it may be by Locke) uneasiness brings no semantic tradition. In fact, Locke never defines the word in the letters and gives no clue of its derivation. He even left Molyneux unsure if it is desire's synonym or cause: 'That which in the train of our voluntary actions determines the will to any change of operation, is some present uneasiness, which is, or at least is always accompanyed with that of desire'.[60] Is uneasiness the same as desire or does it produce desire, and what does it mean to lack ease in the first place? These unanswered questions will remain into the second edition. Locke appears to introduce the equivocal word in order to strip the mystery from desire. One riddle steps in to replace another. The result is that desire is no longer 'doubtful' or 'remote' but set to become an integral faculty in the operations of the mind, presided over only by the sovereign act of judgment.

Or so Locke hints in the précis he sends to Molyneux, the only person with whom he shares his thinking on these matters prior to publication. The peculiar blurring of genres at this moment is consequential. Locke is not simply exchanging thoughts with his friend, nor is he presenting finished ideas in print; rather, he is furnishing, in epistolary form, what he plans for the revised edition of the published *Essay*. Desire is midway in its passage from experience to concept. This birth seems on first glance to deliver a concept that is at a considerable remove from the breathless passion of which Locke demonstrates himself quite capable. Viewed within the model of Enlightenment we have been tracing, however, this may not be such a surprise: Locke refuses to establish desire as a mode of re-enchantment and chooses instead to delimit its place within the division of knowledge. The concept presents neither a consoling retreat from a universe scoured of value nor a spring of social cohesion; it spells out, instead, a specific set of relations and type of longing. The severity of this blueprint matches the warmth of the letters; each is one side of a process that differentiates the erotic: an intimacy shaped by disciplines, an 'uneasiness' within the self.

The move from the letters back to the *Essay*, in any case, brings a significant change in altitude. Ardour gives way to precision, friendship to solitude. Yet the difference is not entirely stark. The language of the correspondence survives, in altered form, the shift in medium. This survival may be clarified by turning now to the 1694 *Essay*. In this version, 'Of Power' contains some twenty-six new sections and, as was promised to Molyneux, a new thesis. The opening discussion of the will and the concluding discussion of judgment and the future state each remain (although with several important modifications), while the middle section on the 'greater good' is replaced by a longer reflection on desire. The changes Locke introduces early on in the chapter are subtly indicative of the larger transformation to come. The 1690 version of section 5 defines the will as follows: 'we find in our selves a *power* to begin or forbear, continue or end, several thoughts of our minds, and motions of our bodies, barely by the choice or preference of our minds. This power the mind has to prefer the consideration of any *idea*, to the not considering; or to prefer the motion of any part of the body, to its rest is that, I think, we call the *will*.[61] The 1694 version is the same up until the final clause of the first sentence, where it reads, 'barely by a *thought* or preference of the mind ordering, or as it were commanding the doing or not doing such or such a particular action' (emphasis added).[62] The second sentence is also revised and expanded, and now reads: 'This power which the mind has, thus to order the consideration of any *idea*, or the forbearing to consider it; or to prefer the motion of any part of the body to its rest, and *vice versâ* in any particular instance is that we call the will'.[63] As Locke rewrites himself, the prose takes a dilatory form uncharacteristic of the first edition: each sentence wrangles into a multiple devolution of subordinate clauses. (Sentence-level pleonasm is recapitulated at a higher level, we soon discover, by the steady accretion of new sections to the chapter.) Once desire is in the wings, it would seem, there's no easy way to stop talking. Yet, not for the first time, content eddies against form. Locke grants little agency to things beyond our conscious reckoning. His writing may get quite ahead of itself, but what he has to say is that our mental operations are far more under control than he had first let on: we do not 'choose', we 'think'; we do not 'prefer', we 'order' or 'command'. Locke has a great deal of difficulty saying that it is very easy to direct one's will.

With this tension, we arrive at an entirely new discussion of desire and uneasiness in sections 29 through 47. These present the several themes Locke had sketched to Molyneux: the coupling of wanting and anxiety, freedom and repression and the final dominion of judgment. The new material begins by separating the will from desire. Locke represents this difference as an important philosophical distinction, one that draws attention to the rigor of his thinking and the specificity of his categories: 'I find the will often confounded with several of the affections, especially *desire*; and one put for the other, and that by men, who would not willingly be thought, not to have had very distinct notions of things, and not to have writ very clearly about them'.[64] In language besotted with compound negatives, Locke affirms clearly that doing is distinct from, and subject to, wanting. 'The will is perfectly distinguished from desire'; or, in other words, desire flows beneath and gives form to all actions.[65] But that is not to say that desire resides within what we would now call the unconscious; Locke is no precocious Freudian. On the contrary, the tremors of wanting lie on the surface of our daily *experience*. We are all too aware of what we fancy, especially when it is out of reach or in competition with other desiderata and so makes us uneasy.

The first appearance of desire and uneasiness is thus fairly simple. They are the feelings that exist before the will and summon the will to action. This initial simplicity sets the stage for Locke's most dramatic revision:

> To return then to the enquiry, *what is it that determines the will in regard to its actions?* And that upon second thoughts I am apt to imagine is not, as is generally supposed the greater good in view: But some (and for the most part the most pressing) uneasiness a man is at present under. This is that which successively determines the will, and sets us upon those actions, we perform. This, uneasiness we may call, as it is, *desire*.[66]

These are truly 'second thoughts'. Contrary to the stated opinion of the first edition, Locke draws the curtain on the greater good: we are not pulled toward it, we simply try to assuage the uneasiness caused by its absence. Locke is well aware of the fineness of this distinction and it takes several declarations for him to clarify the point. Here is an early one: 'Good and Evil, present and absent, 'tis true, work upon the mind: But that which immediately determines the will, from time to time, to every voluntary action, is the uneasiness of desire, fixed on some absent good'.[67] The second half of this formula gives back what the first half takes away: absent good does and does not determine the will. There are at least two ways of making sense of this apparent paradox. The first is that, unlike More and Norris, Locke distinguishes between moral and hedonic goodness. On this account, the subject is not motivated by an abstract sense of proper behaviour but does pursue what he or she declares to be good. The second is that Locke distinguishes between the object of goodness itself and the effect of that object's absence. We are not moved to act or forbear from acting by any given object; rather, we are made anxious by the absence of objects that we feel would be good if they were in our presence.

I am inclined to think that the importance of Locke's chapter lies in the conjuncture of these two arguments. The new version of the good that is attached to an absent object of uneasiness has an earthly cast. Locke nearly says as much in the third restatement of his thesis, which is more emphatic than ever about his process of self-revision. Where he had earlier written that the determination of the will by the greater good was 'the highest perfection of intellectual natures', he now writes:

> It seems so establish'd and settled a maxim by the general consent of all mankind, that good, the greater good, determines the will, that I do not at all wonder, that when I first publish'd my thoughts on this subject, I took it for granted; and I imagine, that by a great many I shall be thought more excusable, for having then done so, than that now I have ventur'd to recede from so received an opinion. But yet upon a stricter enquiry, I am forced to conclude, that good, the greater good, though apprehended and acknowledged to be so, does not determine the will, until our desire, raised proportionately to it, makes us uneasy in the want of it.[68]

Locke repeats himself. Moral goodness does not motivate the subject, only wanting some absent object that we declare to be good does. What is important about this repetition is not just that it brings together the hedonic and anxious dimensions to Locke's argument; it is also that the point is made in the idiom of progress. Locke's desire stages a break with the past, a split from the traditional way of conflating eros and ethics that had still dominated his thinking in the first edition. This intrepid division is bound to be unpopular, he claims, as the precise distinction that it proposes militates against received opinion. Yet, he continues, the lonely venture is worth taking since it opens the new continent of 'our desire' for future speculation. This gesture will be familiar to students of the Enlightenment: past ways of thinking are beholden to the mysteries; modern science has stripped the veil of superstition and provided fine distinctions for the future. On this basis, it is often said, were erected many of the categories by which we understand the modern world, from science to literature, the market to the public.[69] Where might Locke's revisionary terms stand in this list? It would surely be presumptuous to argue that we here witness the 'invention' of desire (with sufficient dexterity this could be placed at nearly any time or place). Yet it would not be too much, I think, to say that Locke's definition is an important moment within the ongoing division of knowledge: a turning inward toward the classification of feeling itself.

One might expect that as desire takes centre stage objects would have a proportionately greater role. What is desire, after all, if not a drive toward an object? Quite the opposite seems to be the case in Locke's emphasis on absence. The retirement of the greater good takes with it the objects in which the good was incubated. If desire is the experience of uneasiness and uneasiness is the anxiety of loss (in the empiricist lower-case, not psychoanalytic capitals), then the classification of desire necessarily entails a certain waning of the object. To see this more clearly, we should look again at the micro-level in which Locke revises himself. We observed earlier that the twenty-ninth section of the first edition postulates that 'pleasure and pain are produced in us, by the operation of certain objects' and 'therefore what has an aptness to produce pleasure in us, is that we labour for, and is that we call *good*'.[70] In the revised version of the section, 'the great motive that works on the mind' is not the apprehension of good objects; rather, 'the motive to change, is always some *uneasiness*'.[71] In the first account, the qualities of the object itself 'produce' the pleasure or pain that determines the will. In the second, the will is guided by a trepidation that there might be an object out there that could have such qualities. This anxiety, Locke is now able to argue in section 30, should be understood as desire: a wanting that precedes its target. The mind is free to fabricate whatever object it can imagine will bring it ease, a condition that is by definition always at some remove. In More, Norris and elsewhere, objects had solicited cravings that were naturally and ecstatically drawn to goodness. The circuit of desire and object was bound by an overarching sense of the ethical. Locke's response unfolds slowly: first he deliberately forswears the term desire and writes that the choice of the 'greater good' is rational, then he introduces desire in the very place of our moral 'perfection' and divides it from the object of longing.

The result is a benchmark in the Enlightenment's production and differentiation of categories. Desire is distinct from the will and so free from the antecedent penumbra of morality. It has become a centrepiece of philosophical expertise and experimental inquiry. How are we to understand the related loosening of the object? The answer lies partly in the wider strains of Locke's thinking. From the beginning chapters on innate ideas to the final pages on reason, the *Essay* remains suspicious of our ability to divine the 'real essence' of objects. We have little access to the inner structure of things whose 'nominal essence' we construct by reflecting on experience.[72] He strikes this resounding theme in the conclusion to both versions of the chapter: 'I shall not, contrary to the design of this essay, set my self to enquire philosophically into the peculiar constitution of bodies, and the configuration of parts, whereby they have the power to produce in us ideas of their sensible qualities'.[73] The sceptical perspective has a special bearing on Locke's revisions. His shift from assuming that objects solicit longings to postulating that we are uneasy about objects we fabricate adjusts the chapter to the *Essay*'s wider nominalism. The outcome is an object thrown into an unexpected instability. Now that 'the power of preferring' is no longer 'determined by the good', Locke is free to multiply and expand the variety of items that fall into the orbit of wanting:

> We are seldom at ease, and free enough from the solicitation of our natural or adopted desires, but a constant succession of *uneasiness* out of that stock, which natural wants, or acquired habits have heaped up, take the will in their turns; and no sooner is one action dispatch'd, which by such a determination of the will we are set upon, but another *uneasiness* is ready to set us on work.[74]

The subject does not confront an array of libidinal artifacts; rather, he or she finds a lack within him- or herself and then projects its imagined relief on the outside world. Objects are replaced by the process of their making. Once more, the result is of considerable moment. Locke's desire vacates the object, but it also initiates the process of what we would now call objectification. Cut loose from traditional relations, desire's unease is at once assuaged and prolonged by the ability to imagine that gratification can take concrete form in some absent thing.

The waning of the object and the construction of a subject founded on absence may seem overly familiar, even contemporary.[75] Speculation on this affinity should nevertheless abide placing Locke's vocabulary within the context in which it took on meaning. While Locke strives to retain the philosophical purity of his categories, his idea of uneasy inwardness was still a profoundly 'outward' development. Readers familiar with the *Second Treatise of Government* (1690) will recall the important argument that civil society precedes the state: individuals are lured to commerce without the threat of force and cede to the state the legitimacy to govern within set bounds. I draw attention to this turning point in the history of liberalism because it should guard against conceiving of Locke's subject in overly privatizing terms. For the Locke of the *Second Treatise*, the subject freely joins to the social order and also bears rights that are essentially private (including the right to property). This momentous fusion of our public and private selves provides the most recognizable version of the Enlightenment dialectics I have been adducing for the *Essay* and the letters.[76] The splitting off of the cultures of expertise from those of daily living replays in miniature the grand scission between state and civil society that forms the essential dynamic of Locke's political theory. As we have seen in the Molyneux correspondence, erotic relations form one way of imagining a mixture of public and private life within the delimited sphere of the philosophical community. In the *Essay*, this socio-sexual dynamic is disguised by the necessarily abstract register of the discourse – the establishment of 'desire' as a philosophical category inescapably occurs without reference to institutions and peoples – but it is not entirely obscured. 'Uneasiness' provides one bridge between the individual subject of desire and the social order in which that individual is placed. Not because society makes us anxious. Rather, anxiety makes society: 'uneasiness is the spur to action';[77] it is always 'ready to set us on work'.[78] Desire is the cause of labour and labour the foundation of society: 'When a man is perfectly content with the state he is in, which is when he is perfectly without any *uneasiness*, what industry, what action, what will is there left, but to continue in it?'[79]

Locke's question takes him to matters well outside the pristine language of the *Essay*, and so it is not surprising that the relation among desire, labor and society is largely unexplored. (It is taken up in the *Second Treatise* and later glossed at length by Mandeville.) The *Essay* appears to suggest this: our desires are uneasy because it is no longer simple to assign the place of their objects. Once fused by traditional religious and social forms, the origins and ends of wanting are set loose on an uncertain world. The result is a restlessness that founds modern society. We get a readier sense of this unease in the letters, where the exasperated pleasure of expertise is posed in informal terms. Yet the *Essay*'s concern to describe our longing for fabricated objects is not entirely removed from the relations spelt out in the correspondence. The development of empirical philosophy into an expert culture produced in Locke and Molyneux a sense of intimacy that was both bred and thwarted by that culture's differentiation from the wider currents of exchange. Enlightenment patterned an impassioned and idealized closeness braced against the solitude of the scientific vocation. The psychic model put forward by the second edition of the *Essay* has a similarly dual structure: a wanting subject serially imagines an end to anxiety.[80] In this sense, when Locke writes of the uneasiness we feel for absent objects he raises to a level of theoretical abstraction the relations that had animated his correspondence during the very years of the *Essay*'s major revision.

The homology between the philosophical intimacy evoked in the Molyneux correspondence and the melancholic object relations of the *Essay* may help to explain, finally, the sombre note struck in the last third of the revised edition. There Locke returns to the faculty of judgment that weighs the future consequences of our present behaviour. The newer version of this particular argument bears the imprint of the larger revision. Where he had earlier described how the understanding steps in to guide our choices, he now postulates that reason must contend with uneasiness. In an uncertain world, we are beset with the uneasiness of desire. How should we respond? Locke's initial answer takes the doleful form of repression, in which he finds the springs of all freedom:

> we have a power to suspend the prosecution of this or that desire, as every one daily may experiment in himself. This seems to me the source of all liberty; in this seems to me to consist that which is (as I think improperly) call'd *free will*. For during this suspension of any desire, before the will be determined to action, and the action (which follows that determination) done, we have opportunity to examine, view, and judge of the good or evil of what we are going to do.[81]

Freedom dwells in the mastery of one's desires, a wresting of composure from the realm of uneasiness. Or so it would seem. The negation enjoined on desire is not quite so one-sided. Locke does not let go of his argument that desire determines the will. Rather, the psychic model becomes reflexive. As we rationally perceive the consequences of our actions on the future state of our souls, we create a hitherto nonexistent uneasiness, a desire that (if judgment works correctly) will overtake all others. Locke returns to this notion at the end of his life, leaving one last revision of the chapter for the fifth and posthumous edition of 1706:

> a man may suspend the act of his choice from being determined for or against a thing proposed 'till he has examined, whether it be really of a nature in it self and consequences to make him happy, or no. For when he has once chosen it, and thereby it is become a part of his happiness, it raises desire, and that proportionably gives him uneasiness, which determines his will, and sets him at work.[82]

The final relation between judgment and desire obeys a now familiar circuit, although in reverse. Where earlier the will was summoned by desire, now desire is 'raised' by something outside itself. Reason inscribes desire on our consciousness. In this lapidary movement, we see a second and concluding recurrence of the division knowledge that Locke originally finds in the wider world.

The upshot is what we would now call a 'split subject', in which the recession of the object and the reign of judgment replay the prior differentiation of society. What does it mean to locate this process in Locke's philosophy? I will offer, by way of conclusion, three speculative answers to this question. The Enlightenment is often taken to be the venue for subjectivity of a most imperious sort: 'a proud culture of reflection', as Habermas put it, that builds empirical knowledge on the ruins of religious faith.[83] It has been the task of recent critical theory to disabuse the Enlightenment of these pretensions, and thus at least momentarily to will them into being.[84] Our review of Locke has revealed something distinct from this uniform oscillation between subjectivity and its annulment.

The differentiated character of the modern pours into the subject, whose newfound texture and depth assembles the precincts of an anxious, libidinal interior that will have a remarkable career in eighteenth-century literary history. In this sense, Locke's texts suggest that we might turn to empirical philosophy to see how the concept of desire was furnished for writers working in the representational genres with which literary critics are typically more comfortable. The establishment of desire, in the letters and over the course of the *Essay*, happened when that category disengaged from the ethical discourse in which it had previously been enmeshed. Locke is no hedonist, but he firmly divides desire from the process of moral choice-making that resides in the understanding. It seems to me that this is a fundamental differentiation of the Enlightenment from which it would be regressive to flinch. One need only glance at the present political context to see the dangers of recombining these separate domains. For Locke, desire was as distinct from the will as philosophy was from religion and civil society was from the state. In this compound division lay the shock and value of the modern age, the tremulous pleasures exhibited by the Molyneux letters. Locke's desire was, in this specific sense, 'modern', but that is not to say that it was like our own. This is a point worth emphasizing. Much of even the most interesting work on Enlightenment sexuality has endeavoured to make it seem familiar, as either the distant precursor or point of origin of sexual identity as we understand it today.[85] Our examination of the print relations and terms of debate that gave form to desire at the turn of the eighteenth century, I think, obliges a contrary reticence. The practices and meanings of desire ought to be made unusual to us and to our concerns, if only so we may grasp better how they were situated in the conflicts of their time. I would not want to be thought to be saying that our understanding of older forms of sexuality could ever be isolated from current issues and problems. But even the most utopian presentism should be rooted in the negativity of the past. For only by allowing that the past is different from the present can we imagine an uncharted future.

3 PHILOSOPHY AND POLITENESS, MORAL AUTONOMY AND MALLEABILITY IN SHAFTESBURY'S *CHARACTERISTICS*

Joseph Chaves

In 'Soliloquy, or Advice to an Author', the third essay in his *Characteristics of Men, Manners, Opinions, Times* (1711, 1714), Anthony Ashley Cooper, the third Earl of Shaftesbury, speculates on the 'two widely different roads' available to 'our ingenious and noble youths'. They may pursue 'pedantry or school learning, which lies amid the dregs and most corrupt part of ancient literature', or they may follow 'the fashionable illiterate world, which aims merely at the character of the fine gentleman and takes up with the foppery of modern languages and foreign wit'. Shaftesbury's concern here is not only education, but also the practice of philosophy and the conditions of the *Characteristics*' writing and reception. While it's far from obvious from this passage, academic philosophy and 'the fashionable ... world' represent the two pre-eminent norms of Shaftesbury's thought. Here and throughout the *Characteristics*, these 'two widely different roads' are contrary extremes, and – to a degree that has been underappreciated in critical commentary – Shaftesbury finds little firm ground between them: 'The sprightly arts and sciences are severed from philosophy, which consequently must grow dronish, insipid, pedantic, useless and directly opposite to the real knowledge and practice of the world and mankind'.[1]

Shaftesbury hoped to extricate philosophy from the cloistered confines of the school and the church, and to cure it of the dogmatism and pedantry he associated with those institutions. Having been 'immured ... in colleges', 'banished ... in distant cloisters and unpracticed cells', philosophy needed to be 'brought upon the public stage', to be relocated, as Lawrence Klein suggests, from 'solitary ... environments to worldly and sociable ones'.[2] In making philosophy sociable, Shaftesbury made it answer to the discursive imperatives of 'politeness', subjecting solitary modes of knowing to the dialogic play of sociable conversation. However, polite sociability serves Shaftesbury not so much as a substitute for customary philosophical contexts and practices as a corrective – which, in its turn, needs correcting. In 'good company' Shaftesbury complains, learning is dismissed as pedantry, and any discussion of morality is seen as tantamount to preaching.[3] 'The strain of modern politeness' is generally shallow, hyperbolic, insincere and obsequious – often indistinguishable from flattery or manipulation.[4] While Shaftesbury insists that the propensity for sociable fellowship, or 'associating inclination' is a natural appetite, the *Characteristics* also evinces an oft-remarked desire to distinguish sociable interaction from sense pleasures and physical gratification.[5] While politeness moderates philosophy, making it responsive to opinion exchange and active in the world, philosophy must be called upon to remedy the superficiality, indirection and sensuality of polite sociability. Moreover, in formal terms, the *Characteristics* alternates between programmatic unity and strategies of diversion, ellipsis and knowing self-contradiction. While the *Characteristics* aspires to the systematic coherence of the philosophical treatise, Shaftesbury's authorial persona vacillates between the position of the moral sage and that of the sociable companion. This, as well as his use of playfully mixed diction and a wide assortment of generic frames constantly undercut the book's consistency.

Central to these tensions is the manner in which Shaftesbury associates philosophy with moral autonomy and politeness with the malleability and permeability of character. Shaftesbury often sees the intersubjectivity of polite exchange as a threat to moral integrity. The 'real disadvantage of our modern conversations', for Shaftesbury, is 'that by such a scrupulous nicety they lose those masculine helps of learning and sound reason'.[6] His politeness is politeness strained of its 'effeminacy', which for Shaftesbury means excessive susceptibility both to sensations and to others.[7] Indeed, many critics have seen Shaftesbury as forcefully endorsing 'sociability' as an innate, ontological condition, and yet wholly suspect of sociability inasmuch as it entails practical dependence on others and places demands on the integrity of the self. John Barrell, influentially viewing the material independence of the landed gentleman as a pre-condition for impartial judgment, identifies Shaftesbury with the solitary, detached position of the aristocratic country freeholder.[8] Similarly, Ronald Paulson sees Shaftesbury's innovative vision of social order as replacing 'the king and his priests with an oligarchy of nobles', reading Shaftesbury in light of his supposed 'equation of virtue, disinterestedness, and civic-humanist landowning'.[9] While models of virtue based on the figure of the dispassionate sage tend to characterize the malleability of the self as anathema to moral integrity, however, conceiving of disinterest, opinion exchange, and moral self-maintenance in terms of sociable conversation allows Shaftesbury to discover ethical value in other-directedness and moral plasticity. As Klein suggests, Shaftesbury makes use of polite sociability 'not just as the basis for human moral capacity, but also as the criterion of moral communication'.[10] Recognizing the manner in which politeness serves as a corrective paradigm to philosophy can give us a better appreciation of Shaftesbury's openness to other-directedness, or to the manners in which selfhood is shaped and understood through interactions with others. But it can also give us a more acute sense of his attempt to negotiate between other-directedness and moral autonomy, between plasticity and integrity. Shaftesbury's concern over the dangers of the plasticity and permeability of character represents not so much a conservative response to their increasing relevance in a modern, commercial polity, but rather a new understanding of their ethical potential, and a consequent desire to separate out their ethical value from their potential dangers.

However, none of this is to wish away the tension between politeness and philosophy or that between moral autonomy and malleability. Indeed, resolving Shaftesbury's ambivalence between moral integrity and other-directedness through the rubric of 'polite philosophy' is to reduce what I want to suggest is a central animating tension in the *Characteristics*. To be sure, Shaftesbury is an enormously negative thinker; his social and aesthetic ideals are adumbrated not so much positively as in contradistinction to opposing values. Consequently, to a degree, we can say with Klein that Shaftesbury's ideal is a mean between contrary extremes: retirement and worldliness, seriousness and play, order and diversion, a stable, independent self and one that is highly mutable and responsive to others. Each side of this opposition, in its highest form, requires the other and serves as a corrective to the other. And yet this may be to overestimate Shaftesbury's capacity to remake politeness and philosophy in each other's image. Rather than seeing Shaftesbury as synthesizing two discrete conceptual vocabularies, embedded as they are in social institutions and cultural practices, we may view his desire to reconcile polite society with the school and the pulpit not as an accomplished fact but as a productive problem. In examining the 'odd agglomeration of arguments and artistic elements in *Characteristics*', for instance, Michael Prince suggests that the book is best understood 'as a scene of contestation where the period's most representative (if antagonistic) values are brought into proximity'.[11]

In Shaftesbury's famous formulation, 'To philosophize, in a just signification, is but to carry good breeding a step higher'.[12] To be sure, as Klein suggests, Shaftesbury 'elevat[es] and dignif[ies]' politeness 'by putting it to new and conspicuous use'. 'By the first decade of the eighteenth century', as Klein observes, '"politeness" had spilled beyond the limits of social behaviour and penetrated other areas of discourse', including learning, the arts, and philosophical debate.[13] While it's clear that this use of politeness renders philosophy conversable, there remains the question of the extent to which it transforms the practice of polite sociability itself. The answer depends, I would suggest, on how seriously we take Shaftesbury's instruction 'to carry good breeding *a step higher*'. To speak of '*moral grace*', or of '*decorum of an inward kind*' is to extend the relevance of politeness beyond scenes of sociable interaction, but it is also to filter from polite sociability some of its embodied, located and contingent nature (emphasis added).[14] If, for Shaftesbury, politeness tempers the monologism of the pedant and the moral dogmatist, he also calls on philosophy to correct the superficiality and material-ism of the fashionable world. In the *Characteristics*, sociable techniques such as raillery, the management of bearing, mutual deference, and even gallantry serve as conceptual paradigms for what Shaftesbury considers philosophical problems of the highest order, but only after undergoing a process of conceptual and for-mal elevation.

To 'elevate' politeness, as I am using the term, is thus to intensify or extend its significance, but it is also to tame it, to abstract face-to-face conversation from some of its particular and sensational aspects, which, for Shaftesbury, present a risk to moral autonomy. The 'private society', for example, serves Shaftesbury not only as a forum for the exchange of opinion, but also as a paradigm for civil soci-ety. The harmony of the abstract, impersonal connections that make up society at large is rendered comprehensible through the model of the forms of consensus obtained in the club. Similarly, Shaftesbury's practice of 'self-converse' is a mode of self-examination based on the practices of polite conversation. Like the anal-ogy of the private society for civil society, self-converse elevates polite sociability in a fashion that helps to mediate between the rival attractions, for Shaftesbury, of politeness and philosophy. Each of these forms of elevation both expands and filters politeness; each provides means of negotiating between the appeal of other-directedness and the desideratum of moral autonomy.

Philosophy and Politeness

In 'Sensus Communis', Shaftesbury opposes the advantage of a 'freedom in rail-lery' to ponderous, polemic forms of serious debate. The 'rational discourses' of scholars and churchmen are all too unidirectional and monologic; they 'have lost their credit and are in disgrace because of their formality'.[15] In contrast, the ludic intimacy of the club, or 'private society', normalizes expressions of discord that, outside the club, would appear as antagonistic or disrespectful. The club offers 'an allowance of unravelling or refuting any argument *without offence to the arguer*' (emphasis added), thus enabling what Steven Shapin has called 'dis-sension without disaster'.[16] The freedom of raillery allows conversants 'a liberty in decent language to question everything' through verbal play. By undermin-ing dogmatic assertions, raillery makes agreeable 'speculative conversations' that otherwise are 'rendered burdensome to mankind by the strictness of the laws prescribed to them and by the prevailing pedantry and bigotry of those who reign in them and assume to themselves to be dictators in these provinces'.[17]

Unlike unreflective appeals to common sense as an *a priori* mutual under-standing – such as the conversation-stopper, 'My opinion is just common sense'

– what Shaftesbury calls *sensus communis* is produced in conversation and produces further conversation. The techniques of sociable play shift the emphasis from the correctness of opinions and even from the goal of agreement to the peripatetic movement of polite conversation as an end in itself. For Shaftesbury, the defining moments of conversation arrive *before* the moment of agreement, in the process of moving, rather indirectly, towards it. If, in the dynamic movement of conversation, a 'great many fine schemes' are 'destroyed; many grave reasonings, overturned', sociable play makes conversation 'diverting' in both senses: good conversation is unmethodical, because its form follows the pursuit of mutual pleasure.[18]

For Shaftesbury, sociable exchange leads toward a brand of rationality that cannot be attained by the linear cogitations of the solitary philosopher: 'according to the notion I have of reason, neither the written treatises of the learned nor the set discourses of the eloquent are able of themselves to teach the use of it'.[19] Far from simply triumphing over contending opinions, play leads to a brand of consensus that cannot be imagined by conversants prior to the moment of sociable interaction, and that cannot be reached by mere assent. Grounding debate in mutual gratification, Shaftesbury finds in the club a domain in which sensation and affect complement (rather than compete with) reason. The impulse to rail, for example, derives not from a rational objection to the content of an argument, but rather as an affective response to its form – indeed, to the 'formality' that Shaftesbury associates with the 'set discourse'. The pursuit of mutual pleasure leads to an outcome that is more rational than those forms of reason exercised in the closet or pulpit. In describing the benefits of the 'diverting' pleasures of sociable play, Shaftesbury is 'persuaded, that had *Reason* herself been to judge of her own Interest, she would have thought she received more advantage in the main from that easy and familiar way, than from the usual stiff Adherence to a particular Opinion'.[20]

Shaftesbury's club, then, is not just an *alternative* discursive institution to the pulpit or the scholarly cell – although it is certainly that; it is also a mechanism for turning dogmatists and pedants into polite conversants. To be sure, Shaftesbury associates dogmatism and pedantry with the figures of the scholar and churchman, and with the corresponding institutions from which he seeks to distance the pursuit of philosophy. But in another, crucial sense, these are not identifiable, 'whole persons'. Dogmatism and pedantry are characteristics – even interior personae – of any person, which the processes of polite exchange serve to interrogate, socialize, subordinate, silence or extroject. Even beyond the value of sociable play for the flow of conversation and the shaping of consensus, the generous suspension of judgment in regard to the opinions of others is beneficial in itself. Raillery not only defends the flow of conversation from the monopolizing impulses of conversational 'dictators', but also promotes a salutary, even therapeutic form of self-suspicion in relation to one's own unreflective judgments.

Early on in 'Sensus Communis', for example, Shaftesbury takes up the experience of having raillery turned upon oneself. To participate fully in polite sociability, we must attain a disinterested relation not only to the outcome of the conversation, but also to our most engrained opinions:

> The question is ... whether it be not just and reasonable to make as free with our own opinions as with those of other people. For to be sparing in this case may be looked upon as a piece of selfishness. We may be charged perhaps with wilful ignorance and blind idolatry for having taken opinions upon trust and consecrated in ourselves certain idol-notions, which we will never suffer to be unveiled or seen in open light. They may perhaps be monsters, and not divinities or sacred truths, which are kept thus choicely in some dark corner of our minds. The spectres may impose on us, while we refuse to turn them every way and view their shapes and complexions in every light. For that which can be shown only in a certain light is questionable. Truth, it is supposed, may bear all lights, and one of those principal lights, or natural mediums, by which things are to be viewed, in order to a thorough recognition, is ridicule itself, or that manner of proof by which we discern whatever is liable to just raillery in any subject.[21]

The answer to the question that opens this paragraph is undoubtedly 'yes', but it is equally clear that this disinterested disposition towards 'our own opinions' is less an *a priori* requirement for polite sociability than an outcome of the process of sociability itself. Raillery promotes a degree of self-division that we tend to think of as one of the hallmarks of modern subjectivity, and as being realized in scenes of Romantic introspection. Here, however, the radical suspension of judgment (our own opinions '*may perhaps be* monsters') is brought about through the objections of others ('We may *be charged* perhaps with wilful ignorance', 'to be sparing in this case may *be looked upon* as a piece of selfishness'). Turned 'in every light', our own opinions appear as exterior to us. They may, indeed, bear the light of ridicule, or they may prove mere 'spectres' which 'impose on us'.[22] The dialogic force of raillery, then, is both centrifugal and centripetal, subtractive and expansive. The socializing movement into discursive play becomes at the same time a movement inward, a stripping away of the encrustation of customary self-understandings that now appear as mere prejudices: 'We polish one another and rub off our corners and rough sides by a sort of amicable collision'.[23] The winnowing away of unexamined, aprioristic mental dispositions is a method of 'becoming plural and enlarging [one's] capacity'.[24]

While politeness serves to render philosophy more dialogic, the merits of politeness are contested and relativized, in the *Characteristics*, by a set of contrary values that Shaftesbury associates with the practice of philosophy: systematic order, philosophical detachment and the integrity and durability of character.

Though the 'rallying humour' that Shaftesbury recommends in 'Sensus Communis' is a product of the fashionable world, he is extremely careful to distance the raillery he promotes from the mere 'buffoonery' he finds prevalent in Italy and, all too commonly, in contemporary England.[25] Shaftesbury's 'sober' raillery is also unlike that of the French court and town, which, Jean Starobinski suggests, reduced differences of opinion 'to the point where they are no longer productive of conflict but of play'.[26] For Shaftesbury, the usual 'gaiety' of 'men of pleasure' is inconsequential in both senses of the term: too confined to cheap puns and trifling subject matter, the disconnected sallies of 'airy' wits do not lead anywhere; they dispel tension without truly resolving discord.[27] Sociable play must be sufficiently serious to constitute real debate. As an institution for shaping conversation, Shaftesbury's 'private society' will navigate between the highly regulated, outcome-centered speech of the school and the trivial play of 'the gallant world'.[28]

Similarly, in friendship, 'sensation or mere bodily affection' must be distinguished from one's natural affection for the virtues that appear in the friend. 'The exalted part of love is only borrowed hence. That of pure friendship is its immediate self.'[29] Applying the non-instrumental imperative of politeness to the extreme, Shaftesbury counts even the accumulation of friends as another form of possessive attachment: it is better to 'adjust matters at home, rather than by making interest abroad and acquiring first one great friend, then another, to add still more and more to my estate or quality'. Similarly, Shaftesbury warns against one's 'imagination of something beautiful, great and becoming in things' degenerating into an attachment to mere things as such, now considered 'excellent in themselves'. Tellingly, Shaftesbury's examples consist of emblems of status and accouterments of polite refinement: 'such subjects as plate, jewels, apartments, coronets, patents of honour, titles or precedencies'.[30] Just as Shaftesbury protests against 'rat_ing] life by the number and exquisiteness of the pleasing sensations', the polite gentleman must eschew 'the care and culture of mere mechanic beauties' for 'that happier and higher symmetry and order of a mind'.[31] Guarding against 'placing worth or excellence in these outward subjects', we must rather 'place it where it is truest, in the affections or sentiments, in the governing part and inward character'. It is only in this manner that durability of character may be attained: 'the imagination or opinion remains steady and irreversible, and the love, desire and appetite is answered without apprehension of loss or disappointment'.[32]

Moreover, Shaftesbury's recovery of innate ideas seems to be at odds with the dialogism and other-directedness we have seen in his vision of sociable exchange. In particular, Shaftesbury posits a correspondence between the benevolent inclinations implanted in the individual and his theistic vision of providential order. The sensible and affective apprehension of harmony in the manifest world corresponds ideally and, at moments in the *Characteristics*, almost automatically to the rational dictates of providence. As Martin Price observes of Theocles's rhapsodic disquisition on the beauty of the providential order in 'The Moralists', 'Her plan is beyond his powers of understanding but not contrary to his reason'.[33] The highest feelings and interests of the individual and the rational ends of providence, as Howard Caygill suggests, '*must* be united, but how this is accomplished is unknowable'.[34] Moreover, the individual's predisposition towards the providential order amounts, at one remove, to the 'love of order and beauty in society'.[35] Consequently, as John Guillory has it, 'the order, proportion, or harmony of the social totality could be represented as analogous to the order, proportion, or harmony of a work of art, or any object of beauty'.[36] Shaftesbury's moral subject is like his ideal poet, a 'second Maker', who is able to 'imitate the Creator' in forming 'a whole, coherent and proportioned in itself, with due subjection and subordinacy of constituent parts', and yet who feels 'only by the effect while ignorant of the cause'.[37]

Moments like these, in the *Characteristics*, would seem to remove the process of judgment from the sociable context of consensus making to the scene of a solitary, disinterested individual, who experiences the dictates of providence with the immediacy of a perceptual faculty. Here *sensus communis* seems quite distant from the specific sense of commonality generated within a particular sociable grouping, and closer to an innate love of the common good – less the form of *phronesis* we have seen in the club, which is always 'directed towards the concrete situation' and capable of grasping 'the 'circumstances' in their infinite variety' (as Hans-Georg Gadamer says it is), than a 'purely theoretical faculty' (which, Gadamer claims, the term comes to mean for Goethe and Kant).[38] Indeed, commentators focusing on the transcendental principle of an accord between implanted inclinations and the ends of providence, to the neglect of the more sensible, affective and practical dimensions of *sensus communis*, have drawn a portrait of Shaftesbury as both philosophically incoherent and ideologically mystifying. As Caygill suggests, 'The capacity which mediates between the laws of providence and individual judgment, between individual interest and rational end, is itself irrational – a proportionable affection endowed with properties of rationality'.[39] A number of critics (including Paulson, Barrell and Caygill himself) make the easy conversion from philosophical-systematical inconsistency to ideological mystification, thus joining a long tradition that begins with Bernard Mandeville. The pursuit of particular desires, however enlightened or elevated, and the regard for the welfare of society as a whole, Mandeville argued, could be made to appear congruent only from the standpoint of aristocratic, land-owning privilege.[40] From this perspective, Shaftesbury's ideal subject appears to be self-contained and disengaged; others are, at best, a distraction.

This view, however, focuses on those values that Shaftesbury associates with philosophy to the detriment of those aspects of his writing that draw on polite sociability, and which strain against abstractive generalization and systematic order. Critics such as Caygill, Barrell and Paulson consider Shaftesbury's 'aestheticization of the social order' in light of his recurring analogies between the harmony of society and that of music, the plastic arts, or landscape.[41] However, it is in conceiving of the order of society on the model of polite conversation that Shaftesbury's caution and ambivalence towards transcendent abstraction surfaces most forcefully. In order to appreciate this, however, it will be necessary to consider how Shaftesbury's conceptual elevation of politeness problematizes both the 'inner sense' and the apprehension of the social order. The elevation of politeness mediates between the values Shaftesbury associates with clubbable conversation (contingency, diversion, other-directedness, sensation and affect) and those he associates with philosophy (consistency of character, detachment, the systematic coherence of the providential order and right reason).

Society and 'Society'

Shaftesbury's is not only a polemical version of politeness, an attempt to distinguish, among the myriad sociable practices and conceptual understandings of the term in contemporary Britain, the correct from the incorrect. In the *Characteristics*, the extension of the paradigm of polite converse into new domains is scarcely separable from its conceptual and formal elevation. To be sure, Shaftesbury seeks 'to recommend morals on the same foot with what in a lower sense is called manners and to advance philosophy, as harsh a subject as it may appear, on the very foundation of what is called agreeable and polite'.[42] But subjecting philosophical debate to the imperatives of polite sociability is also to make politeness philosophical; it raises politeness above its proper sphere of action, and distances it from the embodied and affective nature of sociable interaction. Shaftesbury's elevation of politeness, while making it relevant to new domains, also strains out those physical, interested, and sensational dimensions of face-to-face conversation that present a threat to the consistency and integrity of character. His desire to winnow politeness of its particular and embodied (and thus, for Shaftesbury, interested) nature stems from his desire to magnify its purview, in two opposing but complementary directions. As I will show, Shaftesbury draws on sociable conversation as a paradigm for performing self-examination. The practice of 'self-converse' regulates the interplay of disparate internal voices.

In the other direction, however, Shaftesbury abstracts and generalizes politeness. Shaftesbury looked to polite sociability not only as a means of regulating conversational exchange in the local, occasional arena of the club, but also as a model for harmonizing affections, opinions and interests beyond the club, in civil society at large. 'What would it be', Shaftesbury's Theocles proposes in 'The Moralists', 'if all life were in reality but one continued friendship ...?'.[43] For Shaftesbury, 'Society' would serve as a paradigm for 'society'.[44] The abstract, impersonal connections that make up civil society are rendered comprehensible on the model of the selective, face-to-face interactions of the 'private society'.[45] The movement, in Shaftesbury's aestheticization of the providential order, from sensible parts to rational wholes, is duplicated in the movement from immediate, practical forms of sociability to an enthusiastic apprehension of society as a congruent whole.

In 'The Moralists', for example, drawn by Palemon into the 'vein of philosophical enthusiasm', Philocles explains how, from the 'mysterious charms of the particular forms, you rise to what is more general and, with a larger heart and mind more comprehensive, you generously seek that which is highest in the kind'. Here, however, the progression is not only up the neoplatonic ladder from part to whole and from sense to reason, but also from personal and exclusivistic relationships to more general and intangible forms of sociability: 'Nor is the enjoyment of such a single beauty sufficient to satisfy such an aspiring soul. It seeks how to combine more beauties and by what coalition of these to form a beautiful society. It views communities, friendships, relations, duties and considers by what harmony of particular minds the general harmony is composed and commonweal established.' The harmony attained in sociable interaction, in turn, reveals and promotes the continuity between private affections and the affective investment in the public good. From the 'harmony of particular minds', the 'aspiring soul' naturally seeks to expand the circle, until eventually it comprehends the harmony of society as a whole: 'Nor satisfied even with public good in one community of men, it frames itself a nobler object and with enlarged affection seeks the good of mankind. It dwells with pleasure amid that reason and those orders on which this fair correspondence and goodly interest is established.' From 'the beauty of a part', it extends 'further its communicative bounty, seeks the good of all and affects the interest and prosperity of the whole'.[46] In this movement from part to whole, the particular-general relation we saw between the individual and the club is reproduced as a relation between the Society and society – between the 'private society' and civil society.

And yet, Shaftesbury evinces a fair bit of scepticism towards this ideal, generalized form of sociability, even while proposing it as a standard. Often, the easy alliance between sense and understanding, affect and reason that Shaftesbury finds in the intimate space of the club becomes strained as he considers more abstract forms of social cohesion: 'Universal good, or the interest of the world in general, is a kind of remote philosophical object. That greater community falls not easily under the eye. Nor is a national interest or that of a whole people or body politic so readily apprehended.' In 'less parties' of restrictive, face-to-face groupings, where 'men may be intimately conversant and acquainted with one another', they can 'better taste society and enjoy the common good of a more contracted public. They view the whole compass and extent of their community, and see and know particularly whom they serve and to what end they associate and conspire'. As we move outward, however, to ever more general forms of social cohesion, 'the social aim is disturbed for want of a certain scope. The close sympathy and conspiring virtue is apt to lose itself for want of direction in so wide a field.'[47] The sensational and affective modes of exchange that generate *sensus communis* in the club cannot easily span the distance of the nation or of civil society. In attempting to discern the harmony of interests beyond the sphere of personal acquaintance, durable relations and social parity, Shaftesbury's gentleman finds himself bereft of much of the apparatus that, in the club, renders the accord between private affections and the rational ends of the common good apparent. At this level of comprehensiveness, where 'perhaps the thousandth part of those whose interests are concerned are scarce so much as *known by sight*', the sensational dimension of *sensus communis* withers, and the 'combining principle' must be 'happily directed by right reason'. 'No *visible* band is formed, no strict alliance, but the conjunction is made with different persons, orders and ranks of men, *not sensibly, but in idea*, according to that general view or notion of a state or commonwealth' (emphasis added).[48]

Shaftesbury's frank confrontation of this problem complicates in advance the critique of Barrell, Paulson, and Caygill. In this passage, as Barrell suggests, Shaftesbury employs the metaphor of the 'comprehensive view'. He does so, however, not to preside in disengaged mastery over the social landscape, but rather to describe the coming apart, at this level of abstraction, of the club's synthesis of sensation, affect and reason. This passage does not represent the triumph of a rational capacity for apprehending the public good over particularity and contingency, but rather the unresolved conflict between two opposing ideals. In the club, as we have seen, disinterest is obtained not through aprioristic detachment, but through a process of generalization that takes place in sociable exchange; much of the value of the sort of *sensus communis* generated within the club inheres in its resistance to the abstractive rationalism of the 'general view', here consistently set in opposition to the activity of the senses. Shaftesbury insists on the continuity of the form of consensus attained through polite sociability and *sensus communis* in its broadest and most inclusive sense. And yet, he is at a loss to account for how this might happen without *sensus communis* being winnowed of its dialogic and sensible aspects.

The other, more serious problem with viewing Shaftesbury as wholly committed to an integral, disengaged subject who apprehends the social order from above inheres in the manner in which Shaftesbury problematizes the individual's apprehension of the providential order. As in other crisis moments in the

Characteristics, the burden of the theoretical tension between the abstractive rationalism of the 'general view' and the manner in which *sensus communis* is rooted in affect and particularity is not so much resolved conceptually as passed on to the process of individual judgment. In 'The Moralists', for instance, Theocles insists that 'No sooner are actions viewed ... than straight an inward eye distinguishes and sees the fair and shapely, the amiable and admirable, apart from the deformed, the foul, the odious or the despicable'. Access to this 'inner eye', however, must be tenuous and intermittent, since there remains, as Philocles points out, a 'perpetual variance among mankind, whose differences were chiefly founded on this disagreement in opinion'. Shaftesbury's ideal – which equates the affective motions of the individual and the rational interests of providence- sponsors a radical scepticism regarding the apparent plausibility of any given judgment. While '[a]ll own the standard, rule and measure', as Theocles concedes, 'in applying it to things, disorder arises, ignorance prevails, interest and passion breed disturbance'.[49]

Indeed, the standard of an accord between the individual's affect and the providential order provides a great deal of conceptual leverage for describing the (very likely) failure of the individual to maintain it. Potential errors in moral or aesthetic judgment are lent all the more force for dramatizing the individual's failure to accord not with some external standard of virtue or beauty, but rather with the very deepest resources of the self. Lack of consensus, in other words, signals not simply one party's inept apprehension of an aesthetic or moral object, but also internal 'disorder' and 'disturbance' – estrangement from oneself. Given that there is no ultimate verification of judgment and that, as we have seen, Shaftesbury elevates self-suspicion to the level of a moral duty, the *Characteristics* would seem to promote the very opposite of the account of placid, integral and durable selfhood that a spontaneous, automatic accord would deliver. (And indeed, this is borne out by many passages, which give us, instead, a highly corruptible 'moral sense' and the self's boundless aptitude for mutation.)[50] Whatever its attainability, the process by which 'the generous mind labours to discover that healing cause by which the interest of the whole is securely established, the beauty of things and the universal order happily sustained' not only subjects seemingly self-evident judgments to doubt, but also puts into question the seemingly evident nature of the self.[51]

Self-Converse

Shaftesbury calls the process he sets out for testing judgments and remedying the self's ineluctable permeability 'self-converse'.[52] Through the practice of self-converse, the relation to others prescribed by politeness may be experienced as a relation to oneself. Like the sociable version of 'becoming plural', self-converse ultimately promotes the integrity and durability of character. Among the terms Shaftesbury employs to refer to the 'improving art' of self-converse – including 'self-discourse', 'self-correspondence', and 'soliloquy' – 'self-correspondence' is especially suggestive: like the others, it presumes the dividedness or divisibility of the self, and suggests an activity, rather than an automatic or constant correlation between real and ideal selves.[53] But 'self-correspondence' also implies a process of realignment, through which self-division is recognized and remedied, serving the goal (as Shaftesbury has it in 'Advice to an Author') of 'our acquaintance, friendship, and good correspondence with ourselves'.[54]

The necessity for performing self-converse arises from the way that interests and desires become disaligned from the higher impulses of the moral sense, and yet masquerade as essential parts of the self: while everyone is 'convinced of the reality of a better self', the problem is that 'we are seldom taught to comprehend this self by placing it in a distinct view from its representative or counterfeit'.[55] Like dogmatic conversationalists, these counterfeit selves are found to be guilty of both *imposition* and *imposture* – a likeness Shaftesbury plays on throughout the *Characteristics* in representing both sociable converse and self-examination. In the context of polite exchange, to impose on one's interlocutor, by insisting on the transcendental truth of a given opinion or reserving judgment from the trial of sociable play, is almost always to commit imposture, and vice-versa. The dogmatist's gravity is proof, not so much of the error of his opinion, as its source in something other than the content of the opinion itself – the urge to convince, dominate or overwhelm. And the effect of the form of his enunciation is necessarily mystifying, whatever its truth in content: 'how specious soever may be the instruction and doctrine of formalists, their very manner itself is a sufficient blind or *remora* in the way of honesty and good sense'.[56] This holds equally well for self-converse as for sociable conversation: the tendency of appetites and narrow notions of self-interest to commit imposture is not just incidentally, but rather paradigmatically connected to their seeming essentialness and resistance to inspection: 'It is the grand artifice of villany and lewdness, as well as of superstition and bigotry, to put us upon terms of greater distance and formality with ourselves'.[57] And, just as raillery demystifies the serious pronouncements of dogmatists and pedants, self-converse exposes the dictates of counterfeit selves: the vicious or self-interested passion that 'make[s] me different with respect to myself and others ... must necessarily diminish as I discover more and more the imposture which belongs to it'.[58]

Self-converse, 'the narrowest of all conversations', is not just modelled on, but also dependent upon the continual practice of sociable exchange: 'nothing ... can so well revive this self-corresponding practice as the same search and study of the highest politeness in modern conversation'. As opposed to the common tendency of Britons to 'contract our views within the narrowest compass and despise all knowledge, learning or manners which are not of a home growth', the aspirant to self-converse 'must necessarily be at the pains of going farther abroad than the province we call home ... to gather views and receive light from every quarter'.[59] From 'practice abroad', we may 'learn the way of being free and familiar with [ourselves] at home'.[60]

Being free and familiar with oneself in this manner engenders a vertiginous degree of self-reflexivity. Deriving the technique of discovering inner impostures from the ancient genres of satire and dialogue, Shaftesbury proposes that we 'distinguish ourselves into two different parties', identified respectively with the figure of Socrates ('the commanding genius') and his interlocutor ('that rude, undisciplined and headstrong creature whom we ourselves in our natural capacity most exactly resembled').[61] The point is not that we could discern instantaneously the difference between higher and lower selves, for this is only the first step of the process. Indeed, the value of this separation does not inhere in anything the 'commanding genius' might have to say, for 'instead of giving himself those dictating and masterly airs of wisdom', he 'makes hardly any figure at all and is scarce discoverable'; he is an '*auditor* established within' (emphasis added).[62] The salutary effect of self-converse inheres in the peculiarly distanced manner in which it allows us to *hear*, as it were, our own thoughts, as the 'under-parts or second characters'.[63] To 'give ... voice and accent' to 'our thoughts', which 'have generally such an obscure implicit language', is to stand apart from them, to extroject them – at least temporarily – and to consider them as though they were the opinions of a sociable interlocutor or a persona taken on in a satiric vein: 'by a certain powerful figure of inward rhetoric, the mind apostrophizes its own fancies, raises them in their proper shapes and personages, and addresses them familiarly, without the least ceremony or respect'.[64] As in Persius's second *Satire*, where the prayer the speaker is revealed to utter secretly, while praying aloud for a sound mind, is the speedy death of a rich uncle, satires and dialogues 'hold us out a kind of *vocal* looking-glass, draw sound out of our breast, and instruct us to personate ourselves in the plainest manner'.[65] Just as, in the club, raillery demystifies those 'idol-notions, which we will never suffer to be unveiled or seen in open light', self-converse enables 'the suggestions of fancy' and 'the strong pleadings of appetite and desire' to be 'soundly reprimanded and brought under subjection', and thereby 'forced to quit their mysterious manner and discover themselves mere sophisters and impostors, who have not the least to do with the party of reason and good sense'.[66] Self-converse is a counter-personation, which, while, dividing the self in two, ultimately promotes self-identity by discovering inner impostures.

The discipline of self-converse closely resembles the procedure of Shaftesbury's *Askêmata*, or 'Exercises', which he employed as instruments of self-examination and moral self-reform. A 'textual version of an inner discussion', as Lawrence

Klein suggests, the notebooks represented the examination of opinions and beliefs as 'a discursive situation, a situation of speakers and listeners. In other words, Shaftesbury figured the inner world as a realm in which the conditions and capacities of discourse were applicable'.[67] Performing daily meditations on the model of Marcus Aurelius, Shaftesbury sought to record the quotidian fluctuations of the self, but also to marshal these various, partial selves into a coherent whole.

I have suggested that the need for self-converse, in the *Characteristics*, derives partly from the tensions generated in Shaftesbury's elevation of politeness through his analogy of 'Society' for 'society'. That analogy insists on the continuity of two disparate sets of values – contingency and stability, particularity and generality, sensation or affect and reason – and leaves the task of reconciling them to the process of the individual's inner deliberations. Like the analogy of 'Society' for 'society', however, the notion of self-converse itself constitutes a conceptual elevation of politeness, and in a similarly ambivalent sense. While self-converse provides a means of resisting the 'instruction and doctrine' of inner 'formalists', it also removes conversation from 'company', which, as Shaftesbury notes, is 'an extreme provocative to fancy and, like a hotbed in gardening, is apt to make our imaginations sprout too fast'.[68] Self-converse resituates conversation from scenes of other-directed sociability to one of 'close retirement and inward recess'.[69] In the process, polite conversation both loses and gains in its capacity for 'becoming plural' – that is, for absorbing otherness into the self. To be sure, asking one's various selves to be polite with one another is to take politeness almost absurdly seriously. Self-converse takes inward the polite imperative of mutual deference, which necessitates suspending opinionate predispositions in order to allow room for others' judgments. And it internalizes the practice of raillery, which results in radical forms of self-suspicion.

Questions remain, however, concerning the degree to which, in following out Shaftesbury's introjection of the norms of polite exchange, we can transfer the ethical imperatives of sociable conversation to the discipline of self-converse. For there seems to be a tension between the requirements of polite exchange and the demystifying function of self-converse. We might wonder how decidable, at any given moment, is the distinction between the 'commanding genius' and the lower versions of the self that impersonate him. Are we to imagine impersonation as an intermittent, quickly resolvable phenomenon, or does self-converse promote a continued scepticism concerning the plausibility of *any* given version of self? While it is clear that Shaftesbury intends the process of self-division in self-converse to be homeopathic – a form of counter-personation that reveals and eradicates impostures – it potentially sponsors an unremitting suspicion regarding the contents of the self, as well as a sustained openness to internal plurality, which Shaftesbury is eager to back away from.

Lawrence Klein observes that the form of self-conversation Shaftesbury pursues in the notebooks is '[n]ot a dialogue of equals', but rather 'like a Socratic dialogue, in which one voice was persuasively interrogatory and the other ... passively indicative'.[70] And, as we have seen, the *Characteristics* depicts self-converse as a relation of force, subjection and even violence.[71] Does Shaftesbury's vision of sociable conversation, which takes as its touchstone Juvenal's protest 'Am I always only to be a listener?', become, in its transition to a form of self-converse, a discursive situation in which 'speakers and listeners' can be distinctly separated?[72] At several points in the *Characteristics*, Shaftesbury addresses the discrepancy between the hierarchical, coercive nature of self-converse and the egalitarian, mutually deferential imperatives of sociable converse only to dismiss it: 'It appears ... like a kind of pedantry to be thus magisterial with ourselves, thus strict over our Imaginations, and with all the airs of a real pedagogue to be solicitously taken up in the sour care and tutorage of so many boyish fancys, unlucky appetites and desires, which are perpetually playing truant, and need correction'.[73] Given the manner in which Shaftesbury associates the 'magisterial voice and high strain of the pedagogue' with imposture, can he really endorse this manner of 'be[ing] thus magisterial with our-selves'?

The short answer to this question, based on Shaftesbury's account of self-converse, seems to be yes. By way of conclusion, however, I will briefly consider an aspect of the question that is much less decidable – the manner in which the *Characteristics* not only descants on self-converse as a practice, but also absorbs it as a technique of formal ordering. Self-converse elevates politeness not only conceptually, but also formally, and it serves Shaftesbury as a framework through which to stage the contest between philosophy and politeness as an internal debate. Like the *Askêmata*, the *Characteristics* is multi-voiced and self-contradictory, though less in terms of daily fluctuations of resolve and understanding than as a self-conscious strategy of placing contending voices, styles and perspectives in dialogue.

In the broadest terms, the *Characteristics* alternates generically between philosophic and belletristic form. By the latter, I mean that the *Characteristics* not only represents fictional scenes of sociability, but also embodies polite exchange in its very form. The exchange between reader and author is metaphorized throughout as coming 'into company' together, and the essays incorporate responses from real and imagined readers.[74] Drawing on belletristic genres such as the letter, familiar essay and dialogue, as Shaftesbury understands it, allows him to depart from the formal rigour and concision of the 'precise and formal treatise designed for public view'.[75] In 'Sensus Communis', for example, Shaftesbury tells the anonymous putative addressee that he will eschew the delineation of 'a formal scheme of the passions', because '[i]t would be out of the genius and compass of such a letter as this'.[76] Shaftesbury would like to have it both ways, however, and employs a variety of devices designed to unite the *Characteristics* into a coherent whole – a 'system', even.[77] He revised the previously published essays for the collection, commissioned engravings to serve as hinges among the various essays, and meticulously inserted a compendious series of footnotes, which cross-reference various topics within each of the essays. Not least of all, Shaftesbury assembled the various essays, which had circulated both in print and in manuscript, into a two-volume book. While critics have emphasized Shaftesbury's disdain for the mercenary world of print, it is important too to note the manner in which the printing of the *Characteristics* detaches it from the relatively particularized, personal scenes of manuscript circulation.[78]

Beyond its generic variety, the *Characteristics* brings into conversational frameworks a multiplicity of personae, all of which we are invited to associate with the author, but often it does so in a fashion that makes it quite difficult to assign a clear relation between leading character and some banished, now-former self. At moments, to be sure, the level of irony we are to attribute to a given voice seems clearly discernable. At other moments, however, the *Characteristics* seems to try on various personae – the intimate friend, the stolid philosopher, the miscellanarian, the witty interlocutor – as provisional selves, and to represent each of them less as the outcome of an inner struggle that has been resolved than in the very process of being tested through the textual analogues of sociable play and raillery. The *Characteristics* is rife with the kind of 'personation' Shaftesbury describes in outlining the practice of self-converse, alternating between the figures of the sage and the friend, the philosopher and the belletrist. Against the common interpretation of 'The Moralists' as Theocles's conversion of the sceptic Philocles to theism, for example, Michael Prince suggests that Shaftesbury 'will personify his inner antagonisms through the characters of Philocles, the radical sceptic, and Theocles, the rhapsodic defender of ancient order, hoping to reconcile these most representative divisions within a philosophical dialogue'.[79]

An even more explicit instance is the 'Miscellanies', five essays inserted at the book's end, where Shaftesbury proposes 'to descant cursorily upon some late pieces of a British author'.[80] The author is, of course, Shaftesbury himself in the previous five essays. From the perspective of Shaftesbury's 'airy paraphrast', the previous essays are too scholarly, linear and systematic: 'while I serve as critic or interpreter to this new writer, I may the better correct his phlegm and give him more of the fashionable air and manner of the world'.[81] Under the banner of the 'miscellaneous manner and capacity', happily, 'raillery and humour are permitted, and flights, sallies and excursions of every kind are found agreeable and requisite'.[82] Like the members of a club, the 'miscellanarian' is free to pursue 'the diverting manner in writing and discourse', and to range randomly from subject to subject, making 'what deviations or excursions I shall think fit, as I proceed in my random essays'.[83] Especially 'if the subject be of a solemn kind', it will be necessary 'to interrupt the long-spun thread of reasoning and bring into the mind, by many different glances and broken views, what cannot so easily be introduced by one steady bent or continued stretch of sight'.[84]

And yet even this principle of formal heterogeneity becomes inconsistent in the 'Miscellanies'. In general, embracing the 'familiar style', Shaftesbury decides to 'lay aside the gravity of strict argument and resume the way of chat ... which, through aversion to a contrary formal manner, is generally relished'.[85] However, in the very next paragraph, Shaftesbury raises the possibility that it 'may be objected to us by certain formalists of this sort that 'we can prove nothing duly without proving it in form'; 'condescend[ing] to their demand', he sets out to 'state our case formally and divide our subject into parts after the precise manner and according to just rule and method'.[86] A little later, Shaftesbury will interrupt himself, in a particularly playful moment, in order to offer a careful summary of philosophical precepts to 'the patient and grave reader', willing to 'retire into his closet as to some religious or devout exercise'.[87] Moreover, Shaftesbury's miscellanarian is himself ironized from the first paragraph, where he praises the genre (or anti-genre) of the miscellany for throwing off the yoke of 'the invidious distinctions of bastardy and legitimacy', so that 'wit, mere wit, is well received without examination of the kind of censure of the form'.[88]

Ultimately, if we associate Shaftesbury the philosopher with philosophical rigour and moral integrity, and Shaftesbury the belletrist with formal heterogeneity and moral plasticity, playing one off of the other as he does is bound to be a losing strategy for the philosopher (i.e., since this is in itself a type of formal heterogeneity). Reading the various, contradictory positions Shaftesbury takes in the *Characteristics* as forms of 'personation' allows us to understand the maxim 'humour was the only test of gravity, and gravity, of humour' not only as a prescription for philosophical debate, but also as a key to the *Characteristics'* composite form.[89] The self-reflexive title of 'Soliloquy, or Advice to an Author', along with its epigraph from Persius, 'No need to inquire outside yourself', may be taken as a guide not only to that essay, but also to the *Characteristics* as a whole.[90]

4 REID, WRITING AND THE MECHANICS OF COMMON SENSE

Alexander Dick

The eighteenth century was an 'age of machines'. This much we know. But recently literary critics and cultural historians have become concerned with just how controversial drawing instruments, hot air balloons, mechanical dolls and other products of virtuosi science were in the period.[1] Some thinkers used the analogy of machines and automata to prove that a well-governed, self-propelling society was not only desirable but possible. Others complained that the time and effort that went into exhibiting and selling mechanical trinkets and spectacular exhibitions proved that modern culture was economically corrupt and morally indiscriminate. Nevertheless, already by the first decades of the nineteenth century, machines had become part of the social and economic background. Even those whom we might expect to be against them found ways to accommodate machines *and* find a moral high ground from which to view them. A Tory naturalist, William Wordsworth could in 1833 look at a railway viaduct and declare:

> In spite of all that beauty may disown
> In your harsh features, Nature doth embrace
> Her lawful offspring in Man's art; and Time,
> Pleased with your triumphs o'er his brother Space,
> Accepts from your bold hands the proffered crown
> Of hope, and smiles on you with cheer sublime.[2]

The claim that the materialist revolution might be assuaged by the sublime is a stretch, but it proves the larger point.

How did this happen? The simple answer is that people just got used to new machines much like we have cell phones and iPods. A better answer has to do with how technologies appear in other technologies, a process that Jay David Bolter and Richard Grusin call 'remediation'. Normally, the word remediation means to remedy or clean up (as in an environmental spill), but as Bolter and Grusin use it, it also means to resituate one medium into another.[3] Googlebooks is a good example: printed books are photographed and then posted onto the web; the old linear medium *becomes* subject to the non-linear mechanisms of the computer interface; the limitations of print are thus remediated. The process works the other way as well. No one knew much about cyberspace until William Gibson wrote about it in his novel *Neuromancer*. Historians of science see something similar at work in the Enlightenment. Mechanism held a central place in eighteenth-century thought because the machines the philosophers used in their analogies were already part of the commercial and pedagogical landscape.[4] *Owning* a mechanical duck that sang 'Lillabulero' took the edge off its strangeness. Commodity fetishism excused the horrifying and exploitative means by which mass-produced commodities were made. Marketing mechanical utility helped to make mechanism itself self-evident.[5]

But the remediation of machines into books also allows us to query this process of ideological acclimatization. The straightforward satirical edge of a fictional episode parodying popular amazement and credulity over automata – as in the Cox's Museum scene in Burney's *Evelina* – becomes more complicated when the reader realizes that the object in his or her hand is itself a product of mechanical reproduction. Wordsworth's sonnet produces a like effect: the effort to subordinate the physical power of a steam locomotive to the sublime foregrounds the conventionality and, duplicated in hundreds of copies and poems just like it, the materiality of its myth of natural sublimity. Another example, the one I will focus on in this chapter, is the work of Thomas Reid, Professor of Philosophy first at Aberdeen (1749–63) and then at Glasgow (1764–80) and the founder of the so-called 'common sense' school. Reid had no truck with Hobbes, Leibniz and Hartley, who denied both subjective agency and Divine creativity; he thought the claim that all human action was mechanical was an absurd analogy.[6] Yet his published works and correspondence are full of references to machines. He idolized Newton and other 'inventors'. He championed the development of the portable perspective machine and the steam engine. He said that language was a 'huge and complicated machine'. Reid deflected the influence of mechanism by rendering it, as in Wordsworth's poem, both morally inferior and ideologically subordinate to natural and divine agency. But occurring in print, this effort also introduces an important complication to our sense of Reid as an anti-mechanist. By remediating mechanism into his *printed* books, Reid contributes to the formation of our modern, mediated world and shows us how that world was invented.

The Printing Press, the Puppet Show and the Perspective Machine

The first principle of Reid's philosophy of common sense is this: I must believe that the world exists as I perceive it because, if it did not exist then all the practical things that usually occur in it (including my powers of perception) could not occur, and since they do occur, the world must exist. Perhaps it is not surprising that Reid has had the dubious reputation of being the Scottish Enlightenment's most irascible and pragmatic philosopher – a reputation that dates back at least to Kant's complaint that Reid had merely begged Hume's question.[7] But recently philosophers have begun to see that Reid's epistemology is actually quite modern. Keith Lehrer, for instance, has suggested that Reid's philosophy anticipates the claims made by psychologists and linguists today that perception and representation are computational and systematic processes in which the mind and the world are intertwined rather than distinct. Rebecca Coperhaver labels Reid's realism 'mediated but direct', by which she means that our beliefs or concepts participate in the formation of the world that we perceive though that world also has a distinct existence from our concepts of it.[8] Illuminating though they are, these interpretations have nevertheless neglected the important rhetorical dimension of Reid's arguments. In the only account to date of Reid's style, Joseph Houston has suggested that the principal and quite distinctive elements of this style are 'analogy and ridicule, of quite common-o-garden kinds' used by Reid (often together) in 'technical philosophical' ways to undermine the pretension of scepticism and idealism.[9] I want to take this argument one step further by noting that these rhetorical devices involve placing a word or argument into a new context, in other words remediating it.

Here, for instance, is how Reid describes Hume's *Treatise* in the *Inquiry into the Human Mind* (1764):

> There is a certain character and style in nature's works, which is never attained in the most perfect imitation of them. This seems to be wanting in the systems of human nature I have mentioned, and particularly in the last. One may see a puppet make a variety of motions and gesticulations, which strike much at first view; but when it is accurately observed, and taken to pieces, our admiration ceases; we comprehend the whole art of the maker. How unlike is it to that which it represents! What a poor piece of work compared with the body of a man, whose structure the more we know, the more wonders we discover in it, and the more sensible we are of our ignorance! Is the mechanism of the mind so easily comprehended, when that of the body is so difficult? Yet by this system, three laws of association, joined to a few original feelings, explain the whole mechanism of sense, imagination, memory, belief, and of all the actions and passions of the mind. Is this the man that Nature made? I suspect it is not so easy to look behind the scenes in Nature's works. This is a puppet surely, contrived by too bold an apprentice of Nature, to mimic her work. It shews tolerable by candlelight, but brought into the clear day, and taken to pieces, it will appear to be a man made with mortar and trowel.[10]

The object of Reid's ridicule is Hume's theory of ideas; Reid's point is that the theory does not work because it is not put together very well. If a system reveals too much of its mechanics, then it cannot operate as a system. The purpose of philosophy is not to expose its own inner workings but to cultivate an idea of the mind that *works* and whose mechanism *cannot* be taken apart because it is an exact replica of real life. Hume's scepticism 'is a bold philosophy that rejects, without ceremony, principles which irresistibly govern the belief and the conduct of all mankind in the common concerns of life ... Such principles are older, and of more authority, than Philosophy; she rests upon them as her basis, not they upon her.' It therefore makes as much sense to trust the sceptic as it does to trust someone who claims to have shifted the earth off its axis: 'If [philosophy] could over turn [common sense principles] she must be buried in their ruins; but all the engines of philosophical subtlety are too weak for this purpose; and the attempt is no less ridiculous, than if a mechanic should contrive an *axis in peritochio* to remove the earth out of its place; or if a mathematician should pretend to demonstrate, that things equal to the same thing are not equal to one another'.[11] The sceptic is a charlatan.

Reid's caricature of Hume's system as a puppet show is a good example of how Reid uses ridicule, but it also registers a particular context for his critique. For much of the eighteenth century, people learned about the world at lectures, exhibitions and performances, including those put on by the members of the Royal Society.[12] By the middle of the century, commercial promoters were marketing the experiments as diverting spectacles and salacious curiosities. And as improvements in print technology made it easy and lucrative for philosophers to publish rather than display their results, 'visual education' became disreputable. But arguments *against* the commercialization of visual education did not entail a turn against visuality per se. Adherents of visual education simply attempted to overcome their reputation for amusement or demagoguery. George Turnbull, Professor of Moral Philosophy at Marischal College, Aberdeen during the 1720s and 30s and, as it happens, Reid's teacher argued that it was the responsibility of artists and scientists to provide 'moral "examples" or "Experiments in Philosophy"', and for the visual arts in particular to be the 'public ornaments' of virtue and truth. 'In the new moral climate of the mid-eighteenth century', Barbara Stafford notes, 'the follies and corruptions of humanity had to be painted veristically and not presented as a captivating spectacle'.[13]

Reid's criticism of Hume rests on the question of how best to produce this picture. What is interesting though is that the *terms* of these debates were concerned largely with the media in which philosophy itself was to appear. For many philosophers, Hume particularly, this medium was writing.[14] The first chapter of the *Treatise* begins: 'All the perceptions of the human mind resolve themselves into two distinct kinds, which I shall call IMPRESSIONS and IDEAS. The difference betwixt these consists in the degrees of force and liveliness, with which they strike upon the mind, and make their way into our thought or consciousness'. An analogy with the technology of printing – impression, force, strike – is not hard to discern. To avoid the sceptical crisis that ensues from this premise,

Hume postulates that we accept the customs already laid out for us in daily life even if reason itself tells us that such acceptance is irrational. And a readily available means of customization was, it turns out, print. In 'Of Essay Writing', which appeared only in the first 1742 edition of his *Essays*, Hume divides the world into two camps, 'the Learned' and the 'Conversible', the former of which he associated with 'being Shut up in Colleges and cells' and the latter with 'that Liberty and Facility of Thought and Expression, which can only be acquired by Conversation'.[15] Reading essays like Hume's and having sociable conversations are both parts of the same civilizing trend:

> 'Tis with great Pleasure, I observe, That Men of Letters in this Age, have lost, in a great Measure that Shyness and Bashfulness of Temper, which kept them at a Distance from Mankind; and, at the same Time, That Men of the World are proud of borrowing from Books their most agreeable Topics of Conversation. 'Tis to be hoped, that this League betwixt the learned and conversible Worlds, which is so happily begun, will be still farther improv'd to their mutual Advantage; and that to that End, I know nothing more advantageous than such *Essays* as these with which I endeavour to entertain the Public.[16]

Writing or 'impression' may be the root of Hume's sceptical crisis but it is by the general spread of writing that the crisis will be overcome.

Reid, of course, lambasts Hume's 'copy theory' of cognition. 'It is a fundamental principle of the ideal system, that every object of thought must be an impression, or an idea, that is, a faint copy of some preceding impression', he remarks in the *Inquiry*. But in the course of his critique of Hume, Reid also introduces a technological alternative:

> This is a principle so commonly received, that the author above mentioned [Hume] although his whole system is built upon it, never offers the least proof of it. It is upon this principle, as a fixed point, that he erects his metaphysical engines, to overturn heaven and earth, body and spirit. And indeed, in my apprehension, it is altogether sufficient for the purpose. For if impressions and ideas are the only objects of thought, then heaven and earth, and body and spirit, and every thing you please must signify only impressions and ideas or they must be words without meaning.[17]

The terms that Reid employs to describe the *Treatise* again recall the technologies of print: 'impression', 'faint copy' and 'engines'. But the idea that the principle of impression is a 'fixed point' also refers to mathematics. Fixed point theory assumes that no variable in a particular system will alter the functionality of the system as a whole.[18] The problem with Hume's solution is that it exists only on one plane, that it is two-dimensional. Reid's own position is informed by the more complicated geometry of three dimensions – one which includes depth – and which is based on the perspectivist notion of the 'vanishing' point, the point from which the world can be measured without assuming that its measurements will be fixed in one system.[19]

The vanishing point thesis derives from the art and mechanics of perspective drawing. Reid had a peculiar penchant for this technology. In December 1763, not long before the *Inquiry* was completed, Reid sent a portable perspective machine to his friend David Skene. The perspective machine was a device for reproducing three-dimensional objects exactly onto two-dimensional media. Looking through an eyepiece engrafted with horizon and perspective lines, the drawer could see an object as if it was already divided up into discrete sections. Moving a pencil attached by means of a jointed parallelogram to a metal pointer, the drawer could trace the object as if he were actually drawing around it. 'You will easily see by the construction of the parallelogram piece', Reid wrote enthusiastically 'that the pencil when fixed ... can easily be carried over the whole board; and that as you describe any figure whatsoever upon the paper applyed [*sic*] to the board, the upper end of the Index describes a figure to the imaginary perspective plain, exactly similar and equal'.[20] The particular machine that Reid sent to his friend is probably the portable perspective system invented by James Watt, who had been the mathematical instrument maker for the University of Glasgow (where Reid would soon assume the Chair of Moral Philosophy) in 1756.[21] Watt was working with a technology that was by that time already 300 years old: its portability was meant to simplify drafting techniques that were already in wide use.[22] The point of this technology was to make life easier for professional artists and, in turn, for the new technologies to achieve wider acceptability to the point that the technology itself would become a kind of second nature or, we might say, common sense.[23] Watt's machine seems to have been used quite widely among Reid's intellectual circle for, among other things, copying maps. 'I have seen the Machine used for taking off a smal [*sic*] Map from a large one', Reid comments. 'You will easily see that this is done by making the large Map the Object and the small one the perspective draught of that Object.'[24] What is important about perspective machines is how useful and trustworthy they are. They do not distort reality. They make it clearer.

I am suggesting, then, that the emphasis on sight in Reid's philosophy as the basis for common sense ('Of the faculties called *the five senses*, sight is without doubt the noblest')[25] correlates to his trust in observational technologies that he claims are more useful to knowledge than the scriptural ones which can deceive it. But Reid also insists that the act of perception and mechanics of seeing are distinct phenomenon. Reid must, in fact, make this distinction in order first to redeem the visual as a useful means of education. Just as the perspective machine is a device for making three-dimensional objects *and* is merely a tool for guiding the three-dimensional power of the artists' sight, so Reid's philosophy of perception demands that the mechanics of sight *and* the power of sight be elements of perception, though the latter in both cases is clearly more important. Indeed, many of Reid's later reflections on sight build on his derogations of claims that vision is a purely mechanical process. 'A man cannot see the Satellites of Jupiter but by a telescope. Does he conclude from this, that it is the telescope that sees those stars? By no means; such a conclusion would be absurd. It is no less absurd to conclude that it is the eye that sees, or the ear that hears. The eye is a natural organ of sight, by which we see; but the natural organ sees as little as the artificial'.[26] The analogy is a telling one: materialism presumes that the body is a machine, but is it the case that we trust machines more than we trust our own eyes? Reid concedes that the 'eye is a machine most admirably conceived for refracting the rays of light, and forming a distinct picture of objects upon the retina'; but this is by no means the same as saying that the eye actually *sees*: 'it sees neither the object nor the picture'. The eye cannot see for us; it is only a device that helps us to see. The perspective machine is much the same.

In fact, Reid takes this distinction even further. Perception is an intentional act of consciousness, not a mechanical or animal process. This distinction applies to all forms of sensation as well as perception. 'If one should tell of a telescope so exactly made as to have the power of feeling', Reid quips, 'of a whispering gallery that had the power of hearing; of a cabinet so nicely framed as to have the power of memory; or of a machine so delicate as to feel pain when it is touched; such absurdities are ... shocking to common sense'. 'It is the same absurdity', he concludes 'to think that the impressions of external objects upon the machine of our bodies can be the real efficient cause of thought and perception'.[27] Reid attacks Leibniz's view that 'the mind was originally formed like a watch wound up; and that all its thoughts, purposes, passions, and actions, are effected by the gradual evolution of the original spring of the machine'.[28] Leibniz's philosophy had as much merit for Reid as Hartley's, Hume's and Priestley's or any other philosophy that presumed that matter had or could have agency: 'To account for the regularity of our first thoughts, from motions of animal spirits, vibrations of nerves, attractions of ideas, or from any other unthinking cause, whether mechanical or contingent, seems equally irrational'.[29] In the *Essays on the Active Powers of Man*, Reid makes a more determinate effort to distinguish common sense from mechanical philosophy. 'Our power to move our own body is', he admits, 'in its nature subject to mechanical nature'.[30] Accordingly 'principles of action which require no attention, no determination, no will ... we shall call mechanical'. But these mechanical actions are fundamentally distinct from both the social and solitary actions of communicating and thinking that Reid deems worthy of theorization.

The distinction between the mechanical means of sight and the intentional power of perception is, of course, crucial to Reid's theory of mind. And yet, the distinction is also highly rhetorical, as the preceding examples show. The question is, if power is distinct from mechanics, where does power come from? Reid is notoriously reticent about this; he usually ignores the question and when he does address it, he tends to defend it through a kind of negative natural theology. Since God made human consciousness then it is in the divine that the ultimately source of human agency must be found. But since we cannot question the will of the divine, there is no point in trying to understand or contemplate it. On the surface, then, divine will represents the end point of Reid's philosophy.[31] But I want to suggest that there is another limit point to Reid's arguments about perception, one that, given what I have already noted about his critique of Hume's puppet show, actually steers Reid's philosophy of common sense far into the realm of equivocation, that is, into the realm of writing.

Reading, Writing and Inventing

Lying behind Reid's critique of Hume is a debate about what kind of technology could represent nature best: writing or perspective drawing. But what is interesting about Reid's metaphorical references to machines is that they also concede Hume's point: it is the circulation of writing – in the form of letters, or pamphlets, or philosophical treatises – that ends up grounding our understanding or belief that a three-dimensional world exists. Only by being remediated into print, as reports, illustrations or metaphors within philosophical debates would the utility of perspective drawing become widely known. Reid's own analogical rhetoric, which champions the new forms of visual observation over their rival writing, gains popularity and acceptability by being discussed and taught in publication. Reid's rhetorical uses of analogy and illustration enable him to accommodate mechanism in the philosophy of common sense without risking contradiction.

In the *Inquiry*, observations on the operations of a machine and the examination of natural phenomenon are treated as like instances of perception.

> The more obvious conclusions drawn from our perceptions, by reason, make what we call common understanding; by which men conduct themselves in the common affairs of life ... The more remote conclusions which are drawn from our perceptions, by reason, make what we commonly call *science* in the various parts of nature, whether in agriculture, medicine, mechanics or in any part of natural philosophy.[32]

The understanding of the farmer 'dwells so near to perception, that it is difficult to trace the line which divides one from the other. In like manner, the science of nature dwells so near to common understanding, that we cannot discern where the latter ends and the former begins.'[33] The farmer 'traces the prints of his horses feet in the soft ground, and by them discovers which road the thief has taken'; likewise the natural philosopher perceive[s] that bodies lighter than water swim in water, and that those which are heavier sink. Hence I conclude, that if a body remains wherever it is put under water, whether at the top or bottom, it is precisely of the same weight with water ... Thus every man, by common understanding, has a rule by which he judges of the specific gravity of bodies which swim in water; and a step or two more, leads him into the science of hydrostatics.[34]

The use of terms such as 'print' and 'rule' here suggest that what underlies Reid's idea of perception is not seeing but *reading.*

A similar argument is made in the *Essays on Intellectual Powers.* In the essay 'Of Reasoning in general, and of Demonstration' Reid makes clear that a professional mechanic has knowledge and powers well beyond that of an ordinary person:

When men of equal natural parts apply their reasoning power to any subject, the man who has reasoned much on the same, or on similar subjects, has a like advantage over him who has not, as the mechanic who has store of tools for his work, has of him who has his tools to make, or even to invent.[35]

Yet the comparison here again implies that thinking and observing are parallel phenomenon. Custom, we might say, breeds familiarity, which in turn breeds expert knowledge. That this knowledge is based on custom and familiarity plays into the next essay, 'On Beauty', where the mechanic exemplifies aesthetic judgment:

Suppose ... that an expert mechanic views a well constructed machine. He sees all its parts to be made of the fittest materials, and of the most proper form; nothing superfluous, nothing deficient; every part adapted to its use, and the whole fitted in the most perfect manner to the end for which it is intended. He pronounces it to be a beautiful machine. He views it with the same agreeable emotion as the child viewed the pebble; but he can give a reason for his judgment, and point out the particular perfections of the object on which it is grounded.[36]

What is stressed here is the unity of the machine as an object of perception. That the mechanic can understand its distinct functions and intricacies demonstrates that his knowledge is acquired rather than immediate, which is what distinguishes it from the more instinctive response of the child.[37] 'In a train of reasoning', Reid states, 'the evidence of every step, where nothing is left to be supplied by the reader or hearer, must be immediately discernable to every man of ripe understanding who has a distinct comprehension of the premises and conclusions, and who compares them together'. Yet, he goes on, this 'natural ability' toward reasoning 'may be much improved by habit'. The more we know, the better we see.

Of course, Reid does not say here – as Hume did not – that when he says 'habit' or 'custom' he actually means writing. To clarify how important the technologies of print were to Reid's ideas about knowledge and custom, I turn to his remarks on inventing.

> The highest talent in reasoning is the invention of proofs; by which, truths remote from the premises are brought to light. In all works of understanding, invention has the highest praise; it requires an extensive view of what relates to the subject, and a quickness in discerning those affinities and relations which may be subservient to the purpose ... In this chiefly, as I apprehend, and in clear and distinct conceptions, consists that superiority of understanding which we call *genius*.[38]

Although there is in Reid's use of the term 'invention' something of the sense of creation or fabrication (that was already being used in the eighteenth century), Reid is using the word in an archaic sense to mean observation. There is then a direct correspondence between the invention of genius and the power of perception.

The exemplary 'inventive genius' for Reid was Isaac Newton. Much of Reid's early career was devoted to defending Newtonian mathematics from those whom he thought were using and abusing it. In the 'Essay on Quantity', delivered to the Royal Society in 1748, Reid openly attacked Francis Hutcheson's claim in his *Inquiry into the Origin of Our Ideas of Beauty and Virtue* that ethics could be modelled on Newtonian science. Reid argued that such a premise was a ludicrous analogy. There are, Reid argues, proper quantities and improper quantities. Proper quantities are those that can be measured in their own right. A line is a quantity because it can be doubled in length and thus observed to be twice as long as before. An improper quantity is a quantity that has none of the 'extention, duration, number, and proportion' of proper quantities.[39] Improper quantities include moral virtues, which can be judged 'more or less' but cannot be measured because, to put it simply, they have no natural form. Yet when Reid defends Newton's hypotheses for the existence of forces in nature that cannot be seen, he concedes that improper quantities can be useful. 'I conceive', Reid writes, 'that the applying of Measures to things that properly have not Quantity, is only a Fiction or Artifice of the Mind, for enabling us to conceive more easily, and more distinctly to express and demonstrate, the Properties and Relations of those things that have real Quantity'. Measures might be invented to quantify improper quantities, as long as these measures are useful to the progress of scientific inquiry. The contradiction here is tempered by the commonsensical function to which it is to be applied. Where fictions provide a useful means of measuring things which are otherwise impossible to measure, they provide a useful service. Though Newtonian concepts like 'force' or 'fluxion' are fictional, and therefore improper, they are nevertheless useful. They save time, a positive judgment that Reid further ascribes in the essay to scientific books:

> The Propositions contained in the two first Books of *Newton's Principia* might per-
> haps be expressed and demonstrated, without those various Measures of Motion,
> and of centripetal and Impressed Forces which he uses; But this would occasion such
> intricate and perplexed Circumlocutions, and such a tedious Length of Demonstra-
> tions as would fright any sober Person from attempting to read them.[40]

The larger point that needs to be made here is that for Reid scholarly transmission is as useful as empirical observation. What legitimates the actions of the
inventor over that of the philosophical charlatan (or mechanist) is the utility of
their observation in transmitted form. In an oration he delivered to his students
at King's College, Aberdeen in 1753, for example, Reid clearly suggests that
advances in science that had taken place over the preceding two hundred years
were a direct result of the invention of the magnifying glass and the telescope:

> The discovery of the magnifying glass rendered the subject matter of natural phi-
> losophy greater, since it revealed many objects that were not seen by the naked eye
> because of distance or small size. By the use of the telescope, the movement of the
> heavenly bodies was observed by Galileo, Helvetius, the Cassinis, father and son,
> Huygens and Flamsteed, with trustworthiness, labour, and watchfulness very great,
> strong, and worthy, of kings, and they have opened a way for the establishment of
> true physical astronomy. This subject the most sagacious Kepler has grasped to some
> extent, and the leader of geometry and physics, Isaac Newton, has led it to that sum-
> mit which all gaze at.[41]

What is impressive about this statement (from the point of view of the history
of science) is its assumption that scientific advances would not have been possible without the invention of the telescope. Nevertheless, the further assumption
is that the truths established through these epoch-making acts of perception
would not have been known had it not been for their dissemination in print.
This genealogy ends, importantly, with Newton. The 'supreme genius of Newton', Reid declares,

> fitted for revealing the laws governing the greatest bodies, has explained reflections
> of the rays of light, refractions, and color, having detected them by experiments with
> equal care and acuteness ... whatever progress in natural philosophy the followers of
> this mighty man have made, which to be sure is very small ... it is almost all owed
> to the questions and conjectures proposed by Newton with a modesty singular and
> worthy of a philosopher.

The natural philosophers who have followed Newton, Reid goes on, can do
nothing but ratify his laws:

> this physical astronomy of Newton has been reluctantly accepted by foreign phi-
> losophers and not sufficiently understood. At last, it has been illustrated by the
> *Minimorum Romanorum Commentarium* and confirmed by the recent observations
> of the most glorious Edmund Halley in particular, of Bradley and those of the French

Academy sent to Lapland and Peru, to such an extent that the most stubborn opponents have been compelled to submit.

Reid's basic argument here is that Newton got astronomy right but it contains
a more fundamental claim as well. Like the observations made through the
telescope, Newton's laws circulate from philosopher to philosopher: they are
recorded and *remembered*. Newton's contributions to science would not have
been possible without the circulation of ideas, from 'glorious' English scientists, whose understanding is much more pronounced that the more 'reluctant
foreign' rivals.[42] Writing of some kind is necessary to the establishment of an
episteme, especially one that transcends regional or even national and linguistic
boundaries.

'A Huge and Complicated Machine'

I have been arguing that Reid models his epistemology of common sense on
the visual technologies of the telescope and the perspective machine and, to a
lesser extent, a reformed visual education. We believe in the world as it exists
because we see that it exists. The best kind of philosophical reasoning, then, is
one that is built on the supremacy of sight rather than just on impressions or
the circulation of ideas. But Reid also makes clear that the equivalence between
mental power (common sense, genius) and sight assumes that writing and reading are fundamental to the establishment of the mature powers of cognition and
understanding that he associates with common sense. In the final section of this
chapter I will examine the way this equivocation plays out in Reid's theory of
signs.

Throughout the *Inquiry* and in *the Active Powers* Reid distinguishes 'natural'
and 'artificial' signs. 'By language', he says,

> I understand all those signs which mankind use in order to communicate to oth-
> ers their thoughts and intentions, their purposes and desires. And such signs may be
> conceived to be of two kinds: First, such as have no meaning but what is affixed to
> them by compact or agreement among those who use them; these are artificial signs:
> Secondly, such as previous to all compact or agreement, have a meaning which every
> man understands by the principles of his nature.

He then divides what he calls language into these two generic classes. 'Language,
so far as it consists of artificial signs, may be called *artificial*; so far as it consists of
natural signs, I call it *natural*'. Reid goes on to conjecture that without a natural
language there could be no artificial one, because people would have to be able
to communicate in order to determine 'by compact' what artificial signs mean.
'Had language in general been a human invention', Reid conjectures 'as much as
writing or printing, we should find whole nations as mute as the brutes'.[43] There

is, then, an ur-language, a natural or universal language of which the artificial is merely a derivation or supplement.[44]

There are, however, complications in this scheme. First, believing in what signs tell us does not entail that the relation between a sign and an object belongs to the object itself: 'There is', Reid says 'no necessity of a resemblance between the sign and the thing signified: and indeed no sensation can resemble any external object'. But, he continues,

> there are two things necessary to our knowing things by means of signs. First, that a real connection between a sign and thing signified be established, either by the course of nature, or by the will and appointment of men. When they are connected by the course of nature, it is a natural sign; when by human appointment, it is an artificial sign. Thus smoke is a natural sign of fire; certain features are natural signs of anger; but our words, whether expressed by articulate sounds or by writing, are artificial signs of our thoughts and purposes.

In order to establish that a natural sign is not an artificial sign we already have to know that a relationship between sign and thing exists. At times these connections are instinctive, but Reid could not say, in keeping with his own theories of perception, that our understanding of natural signs is a matter strictly of instinct.

Second, it is not easy to tell the difference between artificial and natural signs. Artificial language is made by 'appointment'. It presumes its own fabrication and thus its timeliness. The difficulty with an artificial sign is that it 'very much resembles, and hath all the force of a natural one'. Artificial signs come with the risk of lifting us out of a social and even psychological equilibrium that Reid associates with the physical closeness of common sense. Artificial 'stimuli' create appetites for more stimulation which then makes us confuse our natural beliefs with artificially-stimulated ones. Usually, Reid says, these artificial stimulants produce a 'depression' which we then only correct by repeated application of the stimulus. Thus, he notes, 'It is in this manner that men acquire an appetite for snuff, tobacco, strong liquors, laudanum, and the like'.[45] Artificial signs, like language and writing, are contagious and harmful.

Third, the seemingly categorical distinction between natural and artificial signs does not hold when Reid comes to list forms of communication under each category. Under the heading 'artificial signs' Reid includes the 'articulate sounds' that human beings use when they speak to each other rather than simply gesture or emote. Under the heading 'natural' Reid includes the fine arts but also aesthetic taste. Music, drama and the visual arts are real 'natural' signs in contrast with the artificiality of language and writing:

> It were easy to show, that the fine arts of the musician, the painter, the actor and the orator, so far as they are expressive; although the knowledge of them requires in us

> a delicate taste, a nice judgment, and much study and practice; yet they are nothing
> else but the language of nature, which we brought into the world with us, but have
> unlearned by disuse and so find the greatest difficulty in recovering it.

The reason why this is surprising is because it presumes that certain skills, ones
that take years to learn, are accounted for by instincts equivalent to facial gestures and emotions.

> Abolish the use of articulate sounds and writing among mankind for a century, and
> every man would be a painter, an actor, and an orator ... as men are led by nature and
> necessity to converse together, they will use every mean in their power to make them-
> selves understood; and where they cannot do this by artificial signs, they will do it as
> far as possible by natural ones: and he that understands perfectly the use of natural
> signs, must be the best judge in all the expressive arts.[46]

Fourth, the criteria for trusting in natural as opposed to artificial signs are also
not clear. In the *Intellectual Powers*, Reid distinguishes between what he calls
'combinations' and 'compositions'. Writing was invented, Reid states, in order to
'embalm' the system of classes and species with which God had endowed nature
and that we perceive instinctively. It is, therefore, an artificial sign. The use of
writing (composition) is to imitate the systems of nature (combination). Reid
says further that writing is perfect when it is wholly transparent, when it behaves
like a natural sign: 'of the works of human understanding our conception may
be perfect and complete. They are nothing but what the author conceived, and
what he can express by language, so as to convey his conception perfectly to
men like himself.' We know what a written work *means* because we speak the
same language, because we are part of the same linguistic community. He then
remarks that compositions are 'more the objects of judgment and taste, than of
bare conception or simple apprehension.'[47]

But when he compares the system of nature to composition Reid makes it
clear that although natural combinations 'are works of creative power' and 'have
a real existence' (they are natural signs, in other words) 'our best conceptions of
them are partial and imperfect'. We believe that natural objects exist, but we do
not necessarily explain *why* we trust them. True to his empiricism, Reid says that
our experience of the world begins with the sensation of objects and qualities.
But sensation does not produce or impress ideas in the mind. Instead sensation
'suggests' objects and concepts to us that we accordingly perceive or believe. The
choice of the word 'suggests' is odd, and Reid is unusually wary of employing
it: 'I know not one more proper, to express a power of the mind, which seems
entirely to have escaped the notice of philosophers, and to which we owe many
of our simple notions which are neither impressions nor ideas, as well as many
original principles of beliefs'. But then Reid's own formation of his account of
suggestion becomes decidedly visual:

> I shall endeavour to illustrate, by an example, what I understand by this word. We all know, that a certain kind of sounds suggests immediately to the mind, a coach passing in the street; and not only produces the imagination but the belief, that a coach is passing. Yet there is here no comparing of ideas, no perception of agreements or disagreements, to produce this belief; nor is there the least similitude between the sound we hear, and the coach we imagine and believe to be passing.[48]

How, Reid asks, can cognitive functions be the same as 'the suggestion' of a sound? In one sense the idea is absurd, and indeed, his own example 'is not natural and original; it is the result of experience and habit'. Nevertheless, he carries on with the analogy: 'I think it appears from what hath been said, that there are natural suggestions'.[49] These suggestions include the fact that something present to me exists or that something I remember existed. What is interesting about the word 'suggests' is that it implies intentionality. It is *as if* the world were speaking to us. Sensations, then, naturally signify objects, but only in so far as they *speak to* the power of perceiving. What I want to underline here again is the extent to which this commitment to the naturalness of orality hinges on Reid's own use of the language of vision which, as I argued above, also presumes the primacy of reading. The suggestions of sensation have escaped the 'notice' of philosophers. He will 'endeavour to illustrate' his meaning of suggestion. The metaphor of the coach exemplifies a phenomenon of hearing, but that phenomenon can only serve as an illustration here because Reid's readers are encouraged to *see* the whole scene of the listener in the street and the coach passing.

Several commentators have noted similar contradictions in Reid's theory of 'social acts' outlined in the fifth essay of the *Active Powers*, 'on contracts'. There Reid subtly and some have said contradictorily argues (again contra Hume) that whereas some signs are the result of 'solitary reflection' others only have legitimacy in as much as they occur in social situations which then, by common sense, become the criteria for their own efficacy. The promise is for Reid the basic form of this social act. But the sticking point remains one of trust: how do we know that a contract is valid? Reid's solution to this problem is to suggest that intention is not the only part of the promise that makes it valid, but also that 'a promise, being a social transaction between two parties, without being expressed can have no existence'.[50] In other words, we must know by virtue of the fact that we promise that promises are valid otherwise we would not make them in the first place.

In a way, then, our relationship to social acts is like that of the farmer or the mechanic who can 'read' the signs that make up their relationship to the world. But this analogy entails that Reid thinks of language – social acts – as akin to that of a machine. In fact, this is precisely what he thought. In a letter he wrote to James Gregory in 1787 (not long before completing the *Active Powers*), Reid said that 'the art of communicating by articulate sounds is certainly, of all human arts, the most ingenious, and that which has required most of thought, of abstraction, and nice metaphysical discrimination', but he thinks of it basically

> as a huge and complicated machine, which was very imperfect at first, but gradually received improvements from the judgment and invention of all who used it in the course of many ages ... It is a machine which every man must use, and which he finds of such utility and importance that, if he has any genius, he has sufficient inducement to employ it in making language more subservient to his purpose.[51]

Reid's analogy here has all the hallmarks of the problematic relation to technology that I have already outlined: a tension between observation and fabrication, between utility and judgement, even between writing and sight. It suffices to say that the mere fact that Reid calls language a 'machine' points precisely to the technological core of his epistemology.

Yet, this technological foundation was by no means a settled idea. In a later passage, Reid makes a further analogy between language, the steam engine and a tree. Combining artificiality, nature, time and 'invention', the story summarizes the role technology plays in common sense philosophy:

> The steam engine was invented not much more than a century ago; but it has received so many and so great improvements in that short period, that, if the inventor were to arise from the dead, and view it in its improved state, he would hardly be able to discern his own share of the invention. Language is like a tree, which, from a small seed, grows imperceptibly, till the fowls of the air lodge in its branches, and the beasts of the earth rest under its shadow. The seed of language is the natural sign of our thoughts, which nature has taught all men to use, and all men to understand. But its growth is the effect of the united energy of all who do or ever did use it. One man pushes out a branch, another a leaf, one smooths a rough part, another lops off an excrescence. Grammarians have, without doubt, contributed much to its regularity and beauty, and philosophers, by increasing our knowledge, have added many a fair branch to it, but it would have been a tree without the aid of either.[52]

Natural signs, Reid says, are the 'seeds' of language: in the *Inquiry* Reid had made it clear that these seeds are not grammatical or articulate but gestural and artistic and even, we might say, technological. The final clause of this passage makes the final gesture that aims to confirm the triumph of nature over technology: 'it would have been a tree without the aid' of anyone anyway. In so undermining both the historical and exemplary force of his own mechanical analogy, Reid invents a general concept, language, that has no history or material foundation but that exists universally and in all social situations.

But as I have been arguing throughout it is vital that we keep in mind not only how rhetorical this description of language is but also how much it depends on its material context in a written document, in this case a letter but also evident in Reid's inquiries and essays. The equivocation that Reid mounts here (and tries to hide) is an apt way of understanding the place of writing and other technologies in Scottish Enlightenment thought: always there, often a useful analogy, but often in the same breath denied relevance. It is equally important that rather than reducing this to a purely philosophical conundrum compatible with Derrida's grammatology for instance, we understand that it belongs to a particular moment in the history of Scottish philosophy and to the development of a technologically-mediated and remediated modernity. If Reid is important to the history of technology, it is because he transformed technology from a problem to be sceptically addressed into a convenience that could be epistemologically ignored. But this transformation is also crucial to the history of philosophy. Reid's insights and his equivocations both demonstrate the powerful place that it must hold if we are to fully understand both the historical and material conditions for human knowledge.

5 PREPOSTEROUS HUME

Mark Blackwell

Ye haue another manner of disordered speach, when ye misplace your words or clauses and set that before which should be behind & *è conuerso*, we call it in English prouerbe, the cart before the horse, the Greeks call it *Histeron proteron,* we name it the Preposterous, and if it be not too much vsed is tollerable inough, and many times scarse perceiueable, vnlesse the sence be thereby made very abused. (George Puttenham, *The Arte of English Poesie* (1569))[1]

'You can scarce,' said he, 'combine two ideas together upon it, brother Toby, without an hypallage' – What's that? cried my Uncle Toby. The cart before the horse, replied my father – (Laurence Sterne, *The Life and Opinions of Tristram Shandy, Gent.* (1760–5))[2]

A quarter century ago, John Richetti published the most sustained literary analysis to date of Locke, Berkeley and Hume's major works, arguing that 'Philosophical writing in this period is self-conscious about the difficult relationship between thought and the expository necessity whereby thought acquires style and becomes persuasive by extralogical or rhetorical means'.[3] He distinguished Hume as 'a rather more interesting writer than Berkeley or Locke', one who 'always conceived of his philosophy in literary terms and saw his problems as essentially rhetorical'.[4] Thus, Richetti rendered Hume exemplary of a set of eighteenth-century thinkers whose work must be approached as philosophical *writing* rather than as philosophy *tout court*. Characterizing Hume's writing as 'a distinct rhetorical enactment and a crucial supplement to his thought', Richetti paid particular attention to the ways in which his 'tightly controlled style', with its 'terse understatement, irony, mock concession, and ... austerity of ornament', often served as a counterweight to the enormity of his claims and the 'extreme implications of his findings', especially in the *Treatise of Human Nature* (1739–40).[5]

Like Richetti, I am interested in the 'larger, cumulative effects' of Hume's prose and in its 'operation and sequence', particularly in the ways that complicated manipulations of serial order generate its curious accretive power.[6] However, I differ from Richetti in my understanding of how those effects are produced and how they typically perform their work, largely because I do not see in Hume an absolute 'refusal of overseeing and organizing analogies or of master metaphors'.[7] My main contention is that the preposterous functions as the governing rhetorical device of Hume's *Treatise*. Rather than merely enacting or supplementing his thought, as Richetti suggests of Hume's writing, the preposterous acts as a master figure that conditions his philosophy. Thus, putting the cart before the horse serves not as a means to a philosophical end in the *Treatise* but rather forms part of the very fabric of its philosophical system. Perhaps the most compelling example of this thoroughgoing preposterousness lies in the nonlinear relationship between Book I, in which Hume fails to articulate a satisfactory theory of personal identity, and Books II and III. Even as Hume leaves behind the epistemology of the self and shifts to the passions and morals in the later books, he all the while recurs to the problem left unresolved in Book I, constructing personal identity from the outside in and from the end of the *Treatise* back to the beginning.

This is no mere rhetorical maneuver on Hume's part. In 'Of Eloquence' (1742), an essay roughly contemporary with the *Treatise*, Hume no sooner distinguishes 'rhetorical tricks' from 'good sense' than he confounds that distinction:

> [The ancient orators] hurried away with such a torrent of the sublime and pathetic, that they left their hearers no leisure to perceive the artifice, by which they were deceived. Nay, to consider the matter aright, they were not deceived by any artifice. The orator, by the force of his own genius and eloquence, first inflamed himself with anger, indignation, pity, sorrow; and then communicated those impetuous movements to his audience.[8]

Hume has in mind orators such as Demosthenes and Cicero, whose use of the pathetic and sublime rendered their style superior to the 'Attic eloquence ... calm, elegant, and subtile, which instructed the reason more than affected the passions'. Yet the *Treatise* teaches us to be wary of too-easy distinctions between orderly reason and the disordering passions, and 'Of Eloquence' treats 'the sublime and passionate' style of ancient eloquence not as different in kind from 'the argumentative and rational' approach of the moderns, but as superior in degree of persuasive force.[9] With Hume, as perhaps with no other eighteenth-century philosophical writer, it makes sense to think of a rhetorical figure not as the dress of philosophy, but as its skeleton, as a structuring principle that gives distinctive shape to a body of thought.[10] Hume's *Treatise*, I propose, is preposterous.[11]

Anachronic Composition

Even a cursory survey of, say, Puttenham's *Arte of English Poesie*, Johnson's *Dictionary*, the *OED* and *The New Princeton Encyclopedia of Poetry and Poetics* quickly demonstrates that figures such as hypallage, hyperbaton, anastrophe and hysteron proteron can be difficult to distinguish. The epigraphs to this essay, in which Puttenham uses the proverb 'the cart before the horse' to exemplify hysteron proteron while Sterne's Walter Shandy associates it with hypallage, illustrate the problem, though it is likely that Walter's Lockean joke about the rhetorical consequences of Toby's inability to associate ideas properly is accompanied by a joke at Walter's expense which derives from his own problems of association: his confusion of different forms of syntactic disorder and his misapplication of rhetorical terms. Samuel Johnson includes only anastrophe and hypallage in his 1755 *Dictionary*, and his definitions are also unfortunate. Hypallage he calls 'A figure by which words change their cases with each other', and his emphasis on cases, by narrowing the word's application to changes in the endings of Greek and Latin words, obscures the ways in which exchanges of syntactic relation that involve shifts in word order create a like effect in English.[12] He defines anastrophe as 'A figure whereby words which should have been precedent, are postponed', and glosses its Greek original as 'a preposterous placing', thereby rendering it the equivalent of Puttenham's hysteron proteron and Walter Shandy's hypallage. Puttenham identifies a number of 'figures Auricular working by disorder', using hyperbaton (Englished as the 'trespasser') as the general term for such figures before specifying parenthesis (the inserter) and hysteron proteron (the preposterous) as the only two that count as 'bewties of language'.[13] Hypallage (the changeling) Puttenham identifies as the only figure 'working by exchange' that English shares with Greek and Latin; the others depend upon certain 'Grammaticall accidents, or verball affects' that derive from 'their diuers cases, moodes, tenses, genders, with variable terminations'.[14] *The Princeton Encyclopedia* distinguishes hypallage, hysteron proteron, and anastrophe and classes them under hyperbaton, which, as in Puttenham, serves as 'the genus for several figures of syntactic dislocation, i.e. alteration of the normal (that is, prose) word order'.[15]

Hysteron proteron is the term that best captures Hume's practice in the *Treatise*. The *Princeton Encyclopedia* describes it as a 'figure in which the natural order of time events occur in is reversed'.[16] Puttenham called it a 'manner of disordered speach, when ye misplace your words or clauses and set that before which should be behind & *è conuerso*', choosing as his English equivalent the preposterous, which Johnson defined as 'Having that first which ought to be last'. Nathan Bailey pithily glossed hysteron proteron as 'a preposterous Way of Speaking, putting that first which should be last'.[17] The definitions of Bailey, Johnson and the *Princeton Encyclopedia* do not clearly distinguish local inversions, those at the level of syntax, from reversals at the level of narrative, for which anachrony, the achrono-logical presentation of events, might seem the preferred term.[18] For my purposes, the preposterous shall designate all reversals of expected sequence, all instances of 'a "before" (*prae*) "coming after" (*posterus*)'.[19]

As Joel Altman notes, Puttenham grouped the preposterous among the figures possessing a 'vividness or luminosity usually associated with figures of amplification that offer circumstantial evidence to the eyes of the mind'.[20] Such a device might furnish Hume with one way of inspiring his readers' belief by providing him with a means of bringing his ideas alive, of investing them with sufficient vivacity – 'vividness or luminosity' – to raise them to the level of impressions. Belief, after all, 'is nothing but *a more vivid and intense conception of any idea*' for Hume.[21] Indeed, Longinus associated such 'transposing of Words or Thoughts out of their natural and grammatical Order' with the forceful oratory of Demosthenes, one of Hume's favorites:

> *Thucydides* is still more of a perfect Master in that surprising Dexterity of transposing and inverting the Order of those things which seem naturally united and inseparable. *Demosthenes* indeed attempts not this so often as *Thucydides*, yet he is more discreetly liberal of this kind of Figure than any other writer. He seems to invert the very Order of his Discourse ... so that by means of his long Transpositions he drags his Readers along, and conducts them thro' all the intricate Mazes of his Discourse ... At length after a long ramble, he very pertinently but unexpectedly returns to his Subject, and raises the Surprize and Admiration of all by these daring but happy Transpositions.[22]

Longinus is alive to the ways in which transpositions and inversions generate for readers and listeners alike an experience of surprise that has sublime suasive power – the power to compel belief. Nonetheless, Hume's own 'discreetly liberal' manipulation of sequence serves less as a means of communicating 'impetuous movements to his audience' and more as a distinctive structural feature of his thought – one operating at several discursive levels simultaneously, and one dependent in part on the materiality of the book as distinct from that of, say, the unfolding lecture or strictly linear proof.[23]

For an example of the preposterous functioning at the broadest level, that of the multivolume narrative, one need only consider Hume's *History of England, from the Invasion of Julius Caesar to the Revolution in 1688*. Richard Hurd, an early critic, complained about Hume's decision to compose the volumes about the Stuarts first and those treating England's origins last: 'For having undertaken to conjure up the spirit of absolute power, he judged it necessary to the charm, to reverse the order of things, and to evoke this frightful spectre by writing (as witches use to say their prayers) *backwards*'.[24] Norman Kemp Smith made a like claim over sixty years ago, arguing that the *Treatise*, like the *History*, was writ-ten out of sequence. Smith adduced evidence intended to demonstrate that the originary insight which opened for Hume 'a new scene of thought' was derived from Francis Hutcheson's moral sense philosophy, specifically from the notion that judgments are based not upon reason or evidence, but upon feeling. Smith drew from his hypothesis that Hume 'entered into his philosophy through the gateway of morals' two important conclusions concerning the composition of the *Treatise*.[25] First, he maintained that Hume's theory of ideas and impressions, laid out in Sections i to vi of Book I, was 'predetermined' by the argument about belief which comes later in Book I. Second, he argued that 'Books II and III of the *Treatise* are in date of first composition prior to the working out of the doctrines dealt with in Book I'.[26] A good part of Smith's internal evidence for the latter claim came from a careful attention to Hume's contradictory treatment of the self, a treatment as unrelentingly searching and rigorous in Book I and the Appendix as it is unexamined in Book II.[27]

The merits of Smith's argument about the composition of the *Treatise* concern me less than does his intuition that the work's philosophy does not develop straightforwardly from beginning to end, that the apparent sequentiality of Hume's movement from understanding (Book I), to passions (Book II), to morals (Book III) – and thus from isolated intellect to affective life, sociability and their political consequences – conceals a less linear, more retrograde relationship among the *Treatise*'s parts. This, I take it, is what Gilles Deleuze has in mind when he contends that 'Hume is a moralist and a sociologist, before being a psychologist' – that Hume treats the mind as a product of the social and material life of the self.[28] Thus, even if Smith's specific claims about the writing of the *Treatise* cannot be verified, his sense that Hume's thought folds back upon itself communicates something important about the way that the *Treatise* performs its philosophical work.

Some local examples of its recursive, nonlinear organization come in the Appendix. In a worried addendum to Book I, Part iii, Section xiv, 'Of the idea of necessary connexion', Hume amends his analysis of the efficacy of causes before abruptly shifting to a review of the inconsistencies in his discussion of personal identity, which comes in Book I, Part iv, Section vi:

> I had entertain'd some hopes, that however deficient our theory of the intellectual world might be, it wou'd be free from those contradictions, and absurdities, which seem to attend every explication, that human reason can give of the material world. But upon a more strict review of the section concerning personal identity, I find myself involved in such a labyrinth, that, I must confess, I neither know how to correct my former opinions, nor how to render them consistent.[29]

The strange placement of this reconsideration of personal identity is typical of Hume, who throughout the *Treatise* establishes ordered sequences and priorities provisionally, only to complicate or supersede them. The passage's position also reveals the complex relation between Hume's analysis of causation and belief, which undergirds his epistemology, and his treatment of personal identity. Since causation is a principle necessary to the elaboration of a theory of selfhood, its discussion comes before that of personal identity in the *Treatise*. But this unidirectional model of necessity becomes increasingly difficult to sustain as Hume's investigation continues. The passage cited here registers such stress in its anticipation of the section on personal identity and in its juxtaposed discussions of selfhood and cause.

Why should Hume's crisis of faith in his analysis of personal identity come in a footnote to a section that precedes that account of selfhood by tens of pages? Originally, the Appendix was included at the end of Volume III, 'Of Morals', which appeared over a year after the first two books had been published. In this sense, there is nothing temporally out-of-order about Hume's reflections on personal identity being appended to a section that precedes his thoroughgoing treatment of that subject near the end of Volume I. The few contemporary readers who had purchased and read Books I and II shortly after publication might consider the Appendix published with Book III as part of Hume's continuing conversation with the earlier work. Those who had purchased the new volume independently, without having entered 'into all the abstract reasonings contain'd' in the first books – a buying strategy Hume had encouraged in the Advertisement to Volume III after the poor reception of the first volumes – could simply ignore the Appendix. Nonetheless, the placement of this note is curious for modern readers of the standard edition of Selby-Bigge and Nidditch. An asterisk in the section entitled 'Of the Idea of Necessary Connexion' refers us to a long passage in the Appendix that should be inserted, as it were, at the spot marked. This passage begins by continuing Hume's discussion of the power of causes, but then proceeds, after a section break, to a careful reconsideration of Hume's analysis of personal identity, which the conscientious and straightforward first-time reader has still not encountered. Hume's addendum refers proleptically to an argument that we have yet to see.

Nor is this the only preposterous peculiarity of Hume's Appendix. As P. H. Nidditch notes, 'An odd feature of it is that amendments to Parts iii and iv precede those to Parts i and ii'.[30] Parts iii and iv, 'Of Knowledge and Probability' and 'Of the Skeptical and Other Systems of Philosophy', rest upon foundations laid in Parts i and ii, 'Of Ideas, Their Origin, Composition, Connexion, Abstraction, Etc.' and 'Of the Ideas of Space and Time'. Yet by the time Hume was composing the Appendix, problems with the later sections seemed sufficiently grave to merit a reevaluation of priorities. What had once seemed the proper order, a linear movement from small building blocks to more elaborately constructed theories, has been altered to address the most forceful objections first.

The *Treatise*'s resistance to orderly, sequential reading may also signal that Hume has a more sophisticated understanding of the printed book – and of the reading practices peculiar to it – than has heretofore been recognized.[31] The curious relationship between text and addendum, like the Advertisement to Volume III and other manipulations of sequence discussed below, perhaps provides evidence of Hume's complicated conception of the variety of ways in which readers interact with texts in different reading environments. N. Katherine Hayles has coined the term 'technotext' to describe works self-conscious about the manner in which their physical form 'affects what the words (and other semiotic components) mean'.[32] It may make sense to think of Hume's *Treatise* as an early experiment in technotext or hypertext, exploring and manipulating the tension between its linear, hierarchical presentation and the multiple reading paths and alternative networks – associative, recursive – that 'constitute subversive texts-behind-the-text'.[33] However unwitting, Hume was an experimentalist with print media, like the Wittgenstein described by Jay Bolter, who wanted 'to produce a conventional treatise' but whose inability to 'cast his philosophy in linear-hierarchical form' resulted in the hypertextual organization of the *Philosophical Investigations*.[34]

First Things First: Ideas and Impressions, Effects and Causes

The first example of the preposterous – and perhaps also the smallest in scale – comes early in the first book of *Treatise*. Hume begins Book I by defining terms, clarifying their relations with one another and establishing tidy sequences. He distinguishes impressions from ideas, associates the former with sensations and the latter with perceptions and demonstrates that 'impressions are the causes of our ideas, not our ideas of our impressions'.[35] Having hammered home his incontrovertible first principle, that 'our simple impressions are prior to their correspondent ideas'. Hume posits that 'method seems to require we should examine our impressions, before we consider our ideas'. That 'seems' surely gives the careful reader pause, and indeed, Hume quickly complicates this system of basic priorities by identifying a whole class of impressions (those of reflection) that derive from our ideas: 'impressions of reflexion are only antecedent to their corresponding ideas; but posterior to those [ideas] of sensation, and deriv'd from them'.[36] The consequence is an unanticipated transposition in Hume's order of presentation, with what seemed secondary being discussed first: 'as the impressions of reflexion, *viz* passions, desires, and emotions, which principally deserve our attention, arise mostly from ideas, 'twill be necessary to reverse that method, which at first sight seems most natural; and in order to explain the nature and principles of the human mind, give a particular account of ideas, before we proceed to impressions'.[37] Noteworthy is the explicitness with which Hume frames this volte-face, establishing a linear, chronological and apparently logical sequence only to reverse field. His devotion of an entire section, entitled '*Divi-*

sion of the subject', to a justification of his inverted order of presentation suggests that the question of sequence has a significance in excess of this single instance, and that readers are being instructed in a habit of thought that will continue to be important in the *Treatise*.

Indeed, the very next section, treating memory and imagination, distinguishes the two on the basis of the vivacity of the ideas they present to the mind and the 'order and position' in which those ideas are presented. Ideas of memory enjoy greater liveliness but are restricted to 'the original form, in which its objects were presented', while the imagination preserves a liberty 'to transpose and change its ideas'.[38] For Hume, the faculties have literary analogies; poems and romances are genres of the imagination, while history is construed as the form most closely approximating memory. Still, Hume acknowledges that 'An historian may, perhaps, for the more convenient carrying on of his narration, relate an event before another, to which it was in fact posterior; but then he takes notice of this disorder, if he be exact: and by that means replaces the idea in its due position'.[39] The historian, in other words, has the preposterous at his disposal, a capacity to effect 'a dislocation between the natural order of things and its representation'.[40] Yet the form of preposterousness Hume himself displayed in deciding to treat ideas before impressions did not consist in reversing 'the natural order of things'; rather, it involved redefining that natural order by demonstrating that linear sequentiality may be a figment of the imagination, a simplified misrepresentation of a more complex and recursive disposition of things.

That recursiveness is most apparent in Hume's lengthy discussion of causation. Once again, he proposes 'To begin regularly' by tracing the origin of our idea of causation:

> 'Tis impossible to reason justly, without understanding perfectly the idea concerning which we reason; and 'tis impossible perfectly to understand any idea, without tracing it up to its origin, and examining that primary impression, from which it arises. The examination of the impression bestows a clearness on the idea; and the examination of the idea bestows a like clearness on all our reasoning.[41]

Hume's earlier manipulation of our expectations about whether ideas or impressions need be examined first should prepare us for complications to the neat linearity of Hume's suggested method of analysing causation. Hume offers a series of regular steps, using anaphoric repetition (''Tis impossible to reason ... without understanding ... and 'tis impossible ... to understand, without tracing'; 'The examination ... bestows a clearness ... and the examination ... bestows a like clearness') to establish a pattern that demonstrates the orderliness of his method while also habituating readers to systematic, sequential thinking. However, just as it proved inappropriate to treat impressions before ideas at the very beginning of the *Treatise*, so it proves impossible for Hume to identify any 'primary impression' of causation in his 'direct survey' of the question. Unable to 'begin regularly', Hume must abandon straightforward priorities, regular procedures and first principles. In their stead, he proposes a haphazard search in the hope both that he will stumble upon something worth finding and that this discovery will retroactively – or preposterously – impose order on an investigation whose course has been irregular: 'We must, therefore, proceed like those, who being in search of any thing that lies conceal'd from them, and not finding it in the place they expected, beat about all the neighbouring fields, without any certain view or design, in hopes their good fortune will at last guide them to what they search for'.[42] Here is an instance of what Hume later calls 'philosophy in this careless manner', whose primary injunction is that one indulge one's 'disposition' and 'follow [one's] inclinations'.[43]

Hume's deliberate indirection later achieves a happy result when he happens upon the concept of constant conjunction: 'Thus in advancing we have insensibly discover'd a new relation betwixt cause and effect, when we least expected it, and were entirely employ'd upon another subject'.[44] There is an anachrony in play here, a manipulation of sequence that returns us to the very question about causation abandoned ten pages earlier. A logical ellipsis – the setting aside of the question of necessary connection – is recuperated ex post facto as consistent with chronological and logical continuity. Following one's disposition now seems less like careless, unsystematic inquiry and more like a crafty strategy of rhetorical disposition. As Longinus says of Demosthenes, Hume's 'Order seems always disordered, and Disorder carries with it a surprising Regularity'.[45]

Nonetheless, the question of causation remains unsettled, for Hume still cannot explain how contiguity, succession and constant conjunction give rise to causal inference: 'From the mere repetition of any past impression, even to infinity, there never will arise any new original idea, such as that of necessary connexion'. His analeptic return to the problem of causal relations thus instigates a proleptic anticipation of a theory of causation he has yet to elaborate: 'Perhaps 'twill appear in the end, that the necessary connexion depends on the inference, instead of the inference's depending on the necessary connexion'.[46] Hume's forecast of his conclusion is preposterous in two senses: it places early in the *Treatise* a hypothesis that may appear only 'in the end', and it suggests the possibility of a reversal in the causality of causation. The structure of Hume's argument about causation is topsy-turvy, as conclusions appear before the inferences that lead to them. Yet the substance of that argument is likewise disorderly, as Hume intimates that the causal inference we had expected to be the effect of necessary connection may in fact be its cause. Inelegantly put, causal inference may turn out to be the cause of what we thought to be the cause of causal inference. The cart may belong before the horse.

Roughly eighty pages later, Hume indeed reaches the conclusion that 'necessity is something, that exists in the mind, not in objects', and immediately anticipates the objection that this conclusion is preposterous: 'Thought may well depend on causes for its operation, but not causes on thought. This is to reverse the order of nature, and make that secondary, which is really primary.'[47] Moreover, Hume recognizes that his method, like his account of causation, carries the whiff of hysteron proteron:

> 'Tis now time to collect all the different parts of this reasoning, and by joining them together form an exact definition of the relation of cause and effect, which makes the subject of the present enquiry. This order wou'd not have been excusable, of first examining our inference from the relation before we had explain'd the relation itself, had it been possible to proceed in a different method. But as the nature of the relation depends so much on that of the inference, we have been oblig'd to advance in this seemingly preposterous manner, and make use of terms before we were exactly able to define them, or fix their meaning. We shall now correct this fault by giving a precise definition of cause and effect.[48]

Hume apologizes for going about things backwards. Proleptically, he has deployed terms before glossing them and justifying their use, while analeptically, he has reached conclusions upon which his premises depend.[49] The very syntax of the second sentence of this passage captures his jugglings of sequence through the jarring interpolation of a lengthy prepositional phrase via a figure (parenthesis, or the inserter) that Puttenham considers a close relation of the preposterous: 'This order wou'd not have been excusable, *of first examining our inference from the relation before we had explain'd the relation itself*, had it been possible to proceed in a different method' (emphasis added).[50]

Hume has gathered his inferences by relying on the terms, the concepts, indeed, the very process – causation – which the inferences are supposed to explain, and his procedure is itself an example of what it purports to describe. His careless inferential method is thus implicated in the relation of cause and effect which it discovers; hence his insistence that 'the nature of the relation depends so much on that of the inference'. Yet Hume contends that he has been '*oblig'd* to advance in this seemingly preposterous manner', that he cannot but begin by using terms before he exactly understands them – by assuming, for example, that impressions alone give rise to ideas before he has come to grips with causation (emphasis added).[51] In other words, his misguided early assumptions about straightforward reasoning are necessary mistakes, integral to the retrospective elaboration of a preposterous method.

To understand that method, one must comprehend the distinction between inferences and relations of cause and effect in the *Treatise*: 'We infer a cause immediately from its effect; and this inference is not only a true species of reasoning, but the strongest of all others, and more convincing than when we interpose

another idea to connect the two extremes'.[52] As Hume uses the term here, inference proceeds immediately, habitually, unreflectively upon the appearance of an
idea, 'without any choice or hesitation'.[53] Its very strength lies in our ignorance of
its dynamics, in the fact that, as Hume puts it, we perceive no 'sensible interval' as
we pass straightforwardly from one idea to another.[54] The idea of causation, on
the other hand, involves mediation, the interpolation of a relation between two
objects or two ideas. As Hume shows, the idea of causation arises from reflection, from observation of our tendency to call up an idea upon the appearance
of another with which it is customarily conjoined. We necessarily infer before
we know how, why or even *that* we do so. Then, our awareness of our tendency
to infer generates an idea of causation retrospectively, or preposterously, even
as it saps the strength of our belief in that inference. The rhetorical power of
inference, and of reason, depends upon our ignorance of its mechanism, or what
Hume calls 'inadvertence'.[55]

Hume faces this very problem with regard to the force of his own arguments.
Having explained the mechanics of causation, he realizes that his very success,
measured by our willingness to grant the necessity of his inferences,

> may seduce us unwarily into the conclusion, and make us imagine it contains nothing
> extraordinary, nor worthy of our curiosity. But tho' such an inadvertence may facili-
> tate the reception of this reasoning, 'twill make it be the more easily forgot, for which
> reason I think it proper to give warning, that I have just now examin'd one of the most
> sublime questions in philosophy, *viz. that concerning the power and efficacy of causes;*
> where all the sciences seem so much interested. Such a warning will naturally rouze up
> the attention of the reader, and make him desire a more full account of my doctrine,
> as well as of the arguments, on which it is founded.[56]

Readers may thoughtlessly, carelessly grant Hume his conclusions, but such
intellectual complaisance does not pay due acknowledgement to the sublimity
of Hume's achievement. Hume must 'give warning' in order to break the spell of
inadvertent inference and point us back to what he has just accomplished, a bit
like the peasant in *The Prelude* who reminds Wordsworth and his companion
that they have already crossed the Alps.

Hume's warning not only rouses his readers, but also makes them disinclined
to believe what they had been content to take for granted moments before; 'Loth
to believe', like Wordsworth at Simplon Pass, we readers question Hume 'again,
and yet again'.[57] Our late-born resistance to his suasion – once roused, we 'desire
a more full account of [his] doctrine, as well as of the arguments, on which it
is founded' – is a preposterous projection of the difficulty we think we should
have encountered in believing him in the first place, in passing from premise
to premise. It is a retrospective effort to remember the radical contingency of
reason which has been forgotten in the service of our habituation to belief, to
rediscover a time of fear and wonder when one idea did not necessarily lead to

another and one step was not sure to carry us safely forward to solid ground. Our minds must lead us forward easily, unconsciously and habitually in order that our smooth trajectory of thought convince us, but that smoothness also paints over the cracks and dampens the jarring thuds which would otherwise permit us to mark shifts, changes or progress.[58] The idea of causation springs from an impression which makes no impression and which can only be narrated analeptically, after the fact.[59]

Hysteron Proteron: Causing Personal Identity

However backwards it may seem, Hume finds a solution to the problem of cause and effect not in any necessary connection between objects themselves, but in the tendency of an observer to anticipate their relation and project this expectation upon the objects. Causation thus presupposes a perceiving self who can unite distinct experiences of contiguity and succession into an idea of necessary connection. A comprehensive theory of personal identity, then, an account of a mind with the imaginative power to melt a series of resembling instances into a single idea, is the linchpin of Hume's epistemology.

Hume's problem in his attempt to construct this theory is that he cannot make sense of the idea of self. Since, as he reminds us in the section 'Of Personal Identity', 'It must be some one impression, that gives rise to every real idea', there must be some impression or perception of self to subtend our mental idea of personal identity. But as Hume recognizes, 'self or person is not any one impression, but that to which our several impressions and ideas are suppos'd to have a reference'.[60] Hume cannot find this reference point, this impression of unitary identity to which all our other impressions are subordinate: 'When I turn my reflexion on myself, I never can perceive this self without some one or more perceptions; nor can I ever perceive any thing but the perceptions. 'Tis the composition of these, therefore, which forms the self'. As Hume puts it elsewhere, human beings 'are nothing but a bundle or collection of different perceptions, which succeed each other with an inconceivable rapidity, and are in a perpetual flux and movement'.[61]

Hume's task in the section on personal identity – to discover in what consists the identity of our flux of impressions, what is the 'principle of connexion' that composes our particular perceptions – is, of course, a version of the problem of causation previously confronted earlier in Book I. Hume has already shown in that discussion that 'no connexions among distinct existences are ever discoverable by human understanding. We only feel a connexion or a determination of the thought, to pass from one object to another.'[62] In other words, Hume finds the origin of the idea of causation in the mind, which spreads upon the distinct objects it observes its own determination to move from one to another. This explanation may suffice where causation is concerned, but the notion that the mind somehow constitutes itself by projecting coherence upon the various perceptions that compose it is, he recognizes, less satisfying. Hume describes the problem of personal identity as an inability to reconcile contradictory beliefs: 'In short, there are two principles which I cannot render consistent; nor is it in my power to renounce either of them, viz. *that all our distinct perceptions are distinct existences,* and *that the mind never perceives any real connexion among distinct existences'.*[63] Hume's treatment of necessary connection seems always already to presume the existence of necessary connection in the form of a coherent, self-constituting self.

The apparent circularity of Hume's reasoning here is not peculiar to personal identity. Our belief in causation, like the trust we repose in general rules, is a fiction of our imaginations, but it undergirds the operations of reason which permit us to correct other illusions of the imagination: 'The following of general rules is a very unphilosophical species of probability; and yet 'tis only by following them that we can correct this, and all other unphilosophical probabilities'. Perhaps 'preposterous' is a better term than 'circular' for Hume's analysis of the paradox of general rules, 'a new and signal contradiction in our reason' whereby 'all philosophy [is] ready to be subverted by a principle of human nature, and again sav'd by a new direction of the very same principle'.[64] First-order particularities (impressions) enable the elaboration of a second-order generality (rules) which somehow becomes constitutive of the realm of the particular in a way that compromises simple distinctions between primary and secondary: "Tis thus the understanding corrects the appearances of the senses, and makes us imagine, that an object at twenty foot distance seems even to the eye as large as one of the same dimensions at ten'.[65]

Though Hume establishes a system of priorities and distinctions, with original impressions (of sensation) and secondary impressions (of reflection), impressions and ideas, general rules (judgment) and exceptions (lively imagination), the question of personal identity brings Hume to the limit of this epistemological system, to a point of blockage where the difference between subject and object, outside and inside, mind and world threatens to disappear. The confusing sequential questions raised by the relationship of mutual dependency between the self and causation recalls other preposterous aspects of the *Treatise* discussed thus far:

> I had entertain'd some hopes, that however deficient our theory of the intellectual world might be, it wou'd be free from those contradictions, and absurdities, which seem to attend every explication, that human reason can give of the material world. But upon a more strict review of the section concerning personal identity, I find myself involved in such a labyrinth, that, I must confess, I neither know how to correct my former opinions, nor how to render them consistent.[66]

Unsatisfied by contradictory theories of the material realm, Hume begins the *Treatise* with an attention to the intellectual world – not to objects 'out there', but to ideas and impressions 'in here'. The very structure of the *Treatise*, moving from the understanding to the passions and then to morals, suggests that for Hume, a proper philosophy must trace a straight-line path from the inside out. But that path becomes increasingly labyrinthine as Hume discovers that external and internal are mutually constitutive, and that distinctions between them – and, for that matter, between intellectual and material worlds – cannot be easily maintained. Hume's growing realization of the tautological relationship between causation and subjectivity helps account for the abrupt appearance of his thoughts on personal identity in a note appended to his discussion of the efficacy of causes, for Hume needs a theory of personal identity to explain causation and a theory of necessary connection to account for identical selfhood.[67]

Hume's section 'Of Personal Identity' is followed directly by the justly famous conclusion of Book I, which stages a philosophical crisis that functions as a transition to and a set-up for Books II and III.[68] Annette Baier devotes the first chapter of *A Progress of Sentiments: Reflections on Hume's Treatise* to this critical section, arguing that 'it brings the line of thought in Book One to its preordained conclusion, and moves us on to the themes of Book Two'.[69] Indeed, Baier sees Book I's conclusion as 'a microcosm of the work as a whole', for, by dramatizing a dialectical tension between the solitary, self-absorbed philosopher and the carefree, gregarious backgammon player, it bridges the gap between 'Book One's *reductio ad absurdum* of Cartesian intellect and the rest of the *Treatise*'s development of its more passionate and sociable successor'.[70]

Philosophical speculation is clearly associated by Hume with a radical self-consciousness and a pathological self-scrutiny that paradoxically threaten to unravel the singular self. 'Where am I, or what?' Hume asks in the deepest throes of the crisis that ends Book I. His malaise can only be remedied by 'carelessness and in-attention', by 'indolent belief', by some 'lively impression of [the] senses', which enables him to 'obliterate all these chimeras' and, in a sense, forget himself: 'I dine, I play a game of back-gammon, I converse, and am merry with my friends'. Engaging in social activities ensures both that Hume resumes habitual patterns of behavior and that others reinforce such patterns by expecting him 'to live, and talk, and act' like everyone else 'in the common affairs of human life'.[71] Nonetheless, Hume finally becomes 'tir'd with amusement and company' and, having 'indulg'd a *reverie* in my chamber, or in a solitary walk by a river-side, I feel my mind all collected within itself, and am naturally inclin'd to carry my view into all those subjects, about which I have met with so many disputes in the course of my reading and conversation'. The mind fragmented by doubt having been re-collected with help from without, Hume can again indulge an ambitious urge to acquire 'a name by my inventions and discoveries'.[72] The collapse of self engendered by radical scepticism can only be cured through an engagement with the world which interrupts introversion yet also steels one for the return to philosophical introspection.

Thus Book I points forward to the books of passions and morals which follow it, demonstrating that, as Baier contends, there is 'progression of thought within the work as a whole' and, as Richetti observes, 'The *Treatise* is a progression of related and progressively involving subjects'.[73] Yet progression may be a misleadingly straightforward term, for the dialectic of self and world at the end of Book I proleptically anticipates Hume's accounts of passions and morals, and a proper account of selfhood depends upon a retrogressive application of the work of Books II and III to the unsatisfactory account of personal identity in Book I. If, in Fred Wilson's words, 'The sort of personal identity one can have is dependent upon the social structure ... and the stability of that identity depends upon the stability of that social structure', and if Hume's acknowledgement of this fact is manifest in the conclusion to Book I, then Hume's positioning of the section 'Of personal identity' shortly before the transition to Books II and III is preposterous.[74]

Pride Goeth before the Self

Book II, 'Of the Passions', picks up with the questions of identity left open at the end of the first book. However, the problem of the basis of identity seems to disappear as Hume deploys the self as an established concept with roots in the world, as the common object of the passions of pride and humility: 'According as our idea of ourself is more or less advantageous, we feel either of those opposite affections, and are elated by pride, or dejected with humility'.[75] Remarkably, pride even has the ability to produce the idea of self that Hume found so hard to account for in Book I: 'nature has given to the organs of the human mind, a certain disposition fitted to produce a peculiar impression or emotion, which we call pride: To this emotion she has assign'd a certain idea, viz. that of self, which it never fails to produce'.[76] Though the self is pride's object, it cannot be pride's cause: 'We must ... make a distinction betwixt the cause and the object of these passions; betwixt that idea, which excites them, and that to which they direct their view, when excited'.[77] The cause consists of a quality – something that operates on the passions to produce pleasure or pain – and a subject – something related to the self in which the quality inheres.

Questions of sequence become confusing yet again. Hume seems to be delineating a preposterous system of self-production that resembles his treatment of the paradox of general rules. Pride may help produce the idea of self, but that idea of self must antecede pride, since the relation to an idea of self is among the necessary components of pride's cause. This conundrum resembles that involving personal identity and causation discussed above, where each seems necessary to the constitution of the other. The trajectory is not a forward-plodding movement from (small) first principles to (big) accounts of complicated phenomena assembled from these basic units, but a tortuous course – what Hume calls a double relation – which confounds simple narrative linearity.

Most interesting, then, is Hume's contention that 'pride requires the assistance of some foreign object'.[78] Hume suggests that the production of an idea of self depends upon one's relation with objects external to the self, or, to push the logic a bit further, that ownership, with the relations to possessions and other possessors that it entails, is inextricably, doubly related to personal identity. This may simply be a different model of the confusing dynamics of internality and externality involved in the production of personal identity. The unification of disparate perceptions into a self only occurs when a more 'internal' mental agency can fuse these objectified memory traces into a coherent, forceful package. But what to do with the gap between the fusing imagination and the newly produced idea of self? And can distinctions between outside and inside be assumed, a priori, before a coherent idea of self has been constructed? Do our bodies or our ideas belong to us in some essential and fundamental way, or are they claimed, made ours by a deeper mental force in the same way that we arrogate property or possessions to ourselves?

Hume refutes our commonsensical suppositions that 'our own body evidently belongs to us' and that, 'as several impressions appear exterior to the body, we suppose them also exterior to ourselves'.[79] He notes 1) that we do not perceive our body, but merely impute a corporeal reality to impressions 'which enter by the sense'; 2) that what is and is not external to the body is unclear; and 3) that 'Even our sight informs us not of distance or outness (so to speak) immediately and without a certain reasoning and experience'.[80] Hume's last example suggests that general rules, or customs, regulate the mapping of the contours of our physical being and thus guide our elaboration of an idea of personal identity, which means that our sense of self must constantly be measured against new impressions and variations in these general rules. Our idea of what is and is not our body is intimately connected with our experience of the objects around us, or our impressions of those objects. Perhaps this explains the connection between Hume's emphasis on the role of foreign objects in the feeling of pride and the considerations of property that begin in Book II, Part ii and continue in Book III. Just as causation presumes a self and self-identity assumes causation, and just as studious solitude inspires social interaction and social pleasures nudge one back to solitary pursuits, Hume's unsatisfactory theory of personal identity in Book I leads him to examine the self's position in a world of feelings and possessions, and his account of such passions as pride in Book II and of such social artifices as property and justice in Book III relies upon the coherent and distinct selves who experience emotions and make adjudicable claims.[81] The preposterousness that characterizes specific arguments in the *Treatise* also governs the broader structural dynamics of the work as a whole.

Hume furnishes examples of foreign objects in his discussion of pride, presumably in order of increasing foreignness: 'excellency in the character, in bodily accomplishments, in cloaths, equipage or fortune'.[82] His 'Abstract' of the *Treatise* provides a more complete list, following a similar trajectory from the inside out: 'Pride or self-esteem may arise from the qualities of the mind; wit, good-sense, learning, courage, integrity: from those of the body; beauty, strength, agility, good mein, address in dancing, riding, fencing: from external advantages; country, family, children, relations, riches, houses, gardens, horses, dogs, cloaths'.[83] The slippage from 'personal' qualities to possessions is consistent with Hume's position at the opening of Section viii, 'Of Beauty and Deformity', where he admits that it is possible to consider the body as just another category of 'external advantages'.[84] It is also consistent with Hume's emphasis on quantitative distinctions as the sole markers of the boundary between inside and outside; only their greater force and vivacity distinguish impressions from ideas, and this distinction is in fact subverted not only in such diseases of the mind as madness and enthusiasm, but in processes central to the proper exercise of our mental capacities, like belief and judgment. Hume's lists suggest that there are only relative distinctions between body parts, personal qualities and possessions, that all may be properties of the self. Read this way, the *Treatise* seems to anticipate recent work that, as N. Katherine Hayles puts it, 'seeks to redefine the human as part of a distributed cognitive system rather than as an autonomous unit' and as a 'creature whose distinctive characteristic is continually and aggressively to enroll objects in its extended cognitive system'.[85]

Nonetheless, Hume expresses concern in Section ix, 'Of external advantages and disadvantages', about the infiltration of the self by foreign objects that are too foreign: 'But tho' pride and humility have the qualities of our mind and body, that is self, for their natural and more immediate causes, we find by experience, that there are many other objects, which produce these affections, and that the primary one is, in some measure, obscur'd and lost by the multiplicity of foreign and extrinsic'.[86] As causes of pride, foreign and extrinsic objects clearly help constitute a fictive self. They allow the self to organize a system of proximities and distances, a set of rules of identity that enable it to delineate its bounds. (Hume's Section vi, 'Limitations of this system', offers a surveyor's guide to these rules.) But the passage above reveals Hume's ambivalent feelings about a means of self-constitution that must rely upon something external. For him, it would seem, something 'primary' may be lost in these fuzzy exchanges at the self's limina.[87]

Pride works by transferring a pleasant sensation from the object with which it is associated (the cause) to the self (the object). Through pride, pleasure is co-opted by the self in an exchange that recalls both Locke on the appropriation of property and Longinus on the dynamics of the sublime: 'we come to believe we have created what we have only heard'.[88] The self-consolidation and self-aggrandizement that attend this move seem advantageous, particularly when the 'natural and more immediate causes' of pride are involved, that is, 'the qualities of our mind and body'. But as 'the relation which is esteem'd the closest, and which of all others produces most commonly the passion of pride, is that of property', the advantages accruing to the self from the operation of this passion most often depend upon externalities, upon 'unnatural' or 'secondary' causes.[89]

The dangers of this dependency can perhaps be elucidated by means of an analogy with Hume's miser: 'a miser receives delight from his money; that is, from the power it affords him of procuring all the pleasures and conveniences of life, tho' he knows he has enjoy'd his riches for forty years without ever employing them'.[90] Because it can be easily exchanged for any number of things, money provides one with the means of procuring pleasure, but it can also become an end in itself. As riches are to pleasant conveniences, so property is to the self. The problem, as Hume states it, is that the 'anticipation of pleasure is, in itself, a very considerable pleasure', that possessions may come to constitute, may even displace the more primary qualities of that self which they are supposed to help consolidate.[91] Hysteron proteron.

Preposterous Property

Hume seems to be of two minds about his treatment of morals at the opening of Book III. The Advertisement that prefaces this book, while reminding the reading public that it is 'a third volume of the *Treatise of Human Nature*', takes pains to describe it as 'in some measure independent of the other two' and to encourage the view that it may be read as a stand-alone treatise of morals. Yet the opening paragraph of Book III characterizes the final volume as part of 'a long chain of reasoning' that 'will acquire new force as it advances', asserting that 'our reasonings concerning *morals* will corroborate whatever has been said concerning the *understanding* and the *passions*'. Indeed, by musing upon the 'inconvenience which attends all abstract reasoning' and by alluding to leaving the closet so as to 'engage in the common affairs of life', Hume returns us to the close of Book I just as Book III begins.[92] It is not clear whether 'Of Morals' conveys us altogether beyond Books I and II or carries us back to the questions raised there, whether it functions independent of earlier volumes or only makes sense in conjunction with them.

There is evidence for both views. Hume's claim early in the third volume that 'The rules of morality ... are not conclusions of our reason', which anticipates the moral sense theory he elaborates immediately thereafter, is consistent with his treatment of belief in Book I, which subordinates reason to feeling: 'all probable reasoning is nothing but a species of sensation'.[93] Later in Book III, when Hume notes that 'Vice and virtue ... may be compar'd to sounds, colours, heat and cold, which, according to modern philosophy, are not qualities in objects, but perceptions in the mind', an echo of his argument about causation as a mental projection rather than a property of objects may be discerned.[94] There is even a complex structural and temporal analogy between his argument about causation, which he portrays as a kind of back-formation from habit-driven, unconscious inferences that inspired belief, and his account of justice, wherein self-interest leads to the imposition of artificial rules whose observance produces the natural pleasure we dignify with the term morality.[95] And there is the deliberate play with the primacy of the natural evident in Hume's claim that the rules of justice are human artifices that may properly be called '*Laws of Nature*' nonetheless.[96] One feels in Book III, then, some reverberations of Books I and II, including resonant examples of Hume's self-conscious manipulation of commonplace expectations about order of presentation and logical priority.

Yet arch reversals of field and sly rhetorical maneuvers, evident especially in Book I, are less frequent in the more earnest-seeming third book. If Smith is right about the order of the *Treatise*'s initial composition, then this difference may signal an evolution in style, or reveal tactical shifts intended to address the burgeoning complexity of Hume's thinking about impressions and ideas; personal identity, pride and property; reason, the passions and morals; and so on. If not, as Richetti suggests, the tonal difference may proceed from both the 'diminished ambition' of Books II and III and from Hume's 'growing sense of the near incompatibility between stylish clarity and abstract difficulty'.[97] Book III is a departure from Book I, either because it is a renunciation of the sorts of difficulty embraced by Hume the metaphysician, or because it is the residue of a Hume who has yet to recognize and accept the preposterousness of his project.

Hume's use of the word 'preposterous' in Book III's discussion of the relationship between property and justice differs markedly from its deployment in Book I, in which he apologizes, with a wink, for proceeding in a 'seemingly preposterous manner'. Hume is comfortable with sequential inversions and calculated manipulations of order in Book I; his ostensible apologies for preposterousness always seem more like shrewd – and proud – vindications of his complicated patterns of reversal. Yet there is no irony in his use of the term to debunk others' accounts of the origins of property:

> Those ... who make use of the word *property*, or *right*, or *obligation*, before they have explain'd the origin of justice, or even make use of it in that explication, are guilty of a very gross fallacy, and can never reason upon any solid foundation. A man's property is some object related to him. This relation is not natural, but moral, and founded on justice. 'Tis very preposterous ... to imagine, that we can have any idea of property, without fully comprehending the nature of justice, and shewing its origin in the artifice and contrivance of men.[98]

The preposterous procedure upon which Hume relied in his analysis of belief – 'mak[ing] use of terms before we were exactly able to define them, or fix their meaning', and 'examining our inference from the relation [of cause and effect] before we had explain'd the relation itself' – becomes a 'very gross fallacy' in this passage, an irrecuperable philosophical error.

Yet Hume's account of the origin of property is not quite as straightforward as this eschewal of the preposterous might lead one to expect. Men quickly 'become sensible of the infinite advantages that result from' society, Hume contends, and

> when they have observ'd, that the principal disturbance in society arises from those goods, which we call external, and from their looseness and easy transition from one person to another; they must seek for a remedy, by putting these goods, as far as possible, on the same footing with the fix'd and constant advantages of the mind and body. This can be done after no other manner, than by a convention enter'd into by all the members of the society to bestow stability on the possession of those external goods, and leave everyone in peaceable enjoyment of what he may acquire by his fortune and industry.[99]

Hume's insistence on the progressive, sequential movement from immediate possession to the stability of socially-ratified property ownership cuts against the grain of the circular, serpentine patterns he traces in Books I and II, and his certainty about the distinction between loose, transferable external goods and 'the fix'd and constant advantages of mind and body' likewise flies in the face of the earlier volumes' more nuanced account of both the fungible border between body and world and the mutually constitutive relationship between property and self. Nonetheless, Hume's contention that the improvement of goods is 'the chief advantage of society', while their instability is 'the chief impediment', strangely renders the stability of goods both a cause and a consequence of social stability.[100] Perhaps, as Hume suggests, it is preposterous to think that property may exist before socially ratified rules of justice have been established, yet only the stability of possession that property brings – and the broad agreement that such stability is in everyone's best interest – makes social life possible in the first place.

Moreover, property, it turns out, merely sanctions a preexisting form of possession, immediate possession, so natural and so customary that there is no question about the redistribution of goods when property conventions are first established:

> 'Tis evident, then, that their first difficulty ... after the general convention for the establishment of society, and for the constancy of possession, is, how to separate their possessions, and assign to each his particular portion, which he must for the future inalterably enjoy ... it must immediately occur, as the most natural expedient, that every one continue to enjoy what he is at present master of, and that property or constant possession be conjoin'd to the immediate possession. Such is the effect of custom, that it not only reconciles us to any thing we have long enjoy'd, but even gives us an affection for it, and makes us prefer it to other objects, which may be more valuable, but are less known to us. What has long lain under our eye, and has often been employ'd to our advantage, *that* we are always the most unwilling to part with; but can easily live without possessions, which we never have enjoy'd, and are not accustom'd to.[101]

It is hard to reconcile this passage, which emphasizes our imagined forebears' contentment with what they already possess, with Hume's profound concern about the dangers of avidity, which he describes as 'insatiable, perpetual, universal, and directly destructive of society'.[102] If all are content to keep what they already have, why the need for justice and property law in the first place? Hume's narrative of social development implies a progress of avidity, as boundless greed gives way to a form of rationalized acquisitiveness that sees in constant possession its most likely path to satisfaction. Yet Hume's myth of the social origins of property depends on a distinction between immediate possession and constant possession that slowly unravels as his description of humans' customary attachment to objects long enjoyed begins to sound like a form of property avant la lettre.

Indeed, the distinction becomes especially unstable when, having maintained the social importance of the stabilizing effects brought by constant possession, and having asserted possessors' contentment with the establishment of property rights in their present possessions, Hume begins to enumerate the 'very considerable inconveniences' that attend 'stability of possession', inconveniences that proceed from the fact that, thanks to the chance distribution of goods at the first establishment of society, 'persons and possessions must often be very ill adjusted'.[103] These inconveniences can only be mitigated by putting in place a system of property transference so as to create a new form of the circulation and 'looseness' that constant possession was designed to eliminate. The social worlds that exist before justice and after justice, pre-property and post-property, seem preposterously interlaced.

This essay has attempted to identify in Hume's *Treatise of Human Nature* a habit of mind, a tic, one most easily described using the rhetorical terms hysteron proteron or the preposterous, and to trace this figure of thought at various discursive levels throughout his most sustained piece of philosophical writing. Further, it has tried to demonstrate that recognizing Hume's penchant for the preposterous does not simply disclose a characteristic means of embellishment or emphasis in the *Treatise*, but also helps us understand the overarching architecture of its argument, and the important relationship between that argument and its material embodiment.

6 AESTHETIC SENSIBILITY AND THE CONTOURS OF SYMPATHY THROUGH HUME'S INSERTIONS TO THE *TREATISE*

Adam Budd

Shortly after Samuel Richardson published the second installment of his tragedy *Clarissa* (1747–8), one reader warned that its heroine's death would hit her 'like a mortifying stroke'. Another insisted that 'the desire of having your piece end happily (as 'tis called) will ever be the test of a wrong head, and a vain mind'.[1] Both readers sought to use their aesthetic reactions to display their moral sentiments, believing that the practice of reading led to important social consequences. For the first reader, sentimental fiction aroused her moral abilities; for the second, such claims to sensitivity only suggested one's inability to recognize true right and wrong.

It has become something of a classroom cliché to depict eighteenth-century readers voicing moral reactions to sentimental novels, and a scholarly truism that the source of the connection between moral feelings and literary response was celebrated (if not defined) by David Hume's theory of sympathy in *A Treatise of Human Nature* (1739–40). This would seem to be straightforward both in terms of the *Treatise*'s theoretical positions and of the psychology it depicts – for when Hume presented the now-famous 'philosophical melancholy and delirium' that was brought on by his relentless scepticism, it was non-cognitive 'lively impressions of my senses' that restored him to 'a relaxed frame of mind'.[2] Earlier in the same book, Hume had defined the provision of such lively impressions as the unique ability of eloquent authors who are thus like our close friends – that is, like those with whom we sympathize.[3] So it would seem that Hume had epistemological and even therapeutic reasons for celebrating the moral value of powerful fiction. Yet this chapter will argue that Hume's aesthetic theory from the early 1740s provides a fresh interpretive context for making sense of contemporary aesthetic claims to moral practice. This argument will clarify not only why Hume's theory of fiction serves as a weak source of belief at the level of his own philosophy, but also why it is important to recognize Hume as a theorist of the kind of self-conscious reading that ultimately makes reading a process of adjustment and response rather than of credulous reaction. In the process, I hope to direct attention to passages in the text of Hume's *Treatise* that have been marginalized by editors, largely overlooked by textual scholars, and therefore have been prone to neglect by literary historians.

One reason why readers have found in Hume a moral proponent of sentimental reading is that Hume adopted numerous literary styles and generic forms to popularize his moral theory, 'that propensity we have to sympathize with others, and to receive by communication their inclinations and sentiments'.[4] Moreover, he did so throughout the 1740s, which was precisely the time when sentimental novels first gained a measure of critical respectability. Hume also argued for a link between virtuous feelings and human nature which, together, helped to spawn a moral vocabulary that was itself featured in the works of sentimental novelists.[5] Catherine Gallagher's understanding of Hume is representative of current interpretations of sentimental reading: '[Humean] sympathy is that process by which the emotions [of others] come to be experienced as our own ... fiction, then, stimulates sympathy'.[6] Gallagher's confidence in 'the link between fiction and sympathy that usually goes without saying' assumes a merger of moral and aesthetic notions that helps to explain Paul Goring's observation: 'there grew up around sentimental novels a culture in which bodily responses were widely lauded as signs of moral status'.[7] This view of Hume's notion of sympathy would recognize ethical value in Richardson's attempt to stir the passions of his readers, and it would justify reactions to the heroine's suffering as a demonstration of their moral sense.

More recently, John Richetti has pointed to the philanthropic projects that were proudly proclaimed but quickly abandoned by sentimental readers during this period, leading him to observe that 'by cultivating private sympathy and self-indulgent emotional responses to misery and injustice, fiction [offered] a controlling evasion or consoling moral gesture that [stood] in place of analytical understanding or systematic criticism'.[8] By indicating that sentimental reading was actually a quasi-public performance that must be understood in its social context – one which featured actual and imagined suffering – Richetti has brought us closer to the moral and aesthetic concerns that Hume had in mind. Hume may be the most prominent philosopher to emerge from literary studies of 'the culture of sensibility', but Hume's less familiar texts of this period reveal his view that aesthetic experience invites causal associations that always refer to the real social world of human relations rather than to the 'weak' impressions brought on by 'the fictions of poetry'. This aesthetic theory carries important practical meaning and historical insight since it teaches, unsentimentally and yet at the emergence of the sentimental novel, that our responses to aesthetic experience are in fact empty of moral value. While Hume did not go so far as to confront readers by asking them to consider the moral terms with which they voiced their aesthetic feelings, his plan for a revised *Treatise* in 1740 and the publication of two essays (in 1742 and 1748 respectively) sought to encourage such critical thinking about aesthetic experience. Before I examine Hume's thought concerning fictional writing and dramatic performance in his moral and epistemological theory, I will outline what might well be the editorial origins of current misinterpretations.

Textual History of the Early Aesthetic Theory

From the nineteenth until the twenty-first century, L. A. Selby-Bigge's reprint of the first edition of the *Treatise* largely defined the Hume canon; it left Hume's earliest published views on aesthetics in an Appendix following Book III, rather than integrated into the prominent main text of Book I, as Hume had intended. Conceptually, this overlooked material clarifies important elements of his moral theory of that period. Textually, given the apparent scarcity of literary discussion in the otherwise elaborate *Treatise*, readers interested in Hume's aesthetic theory have focused, nearly exclusively, on his much later essay 'Of the Standard of Taste'.[9] Mary Mothersill has articulated the consensus view: this essay represents Hume's 'final and *indeed his only attempt* to deal with questions in critical theory ... [such that] we may take it as definitive of Hume's position'.[10] But Hume's earliest published views on aesthetics are important specifically because they were articulated during a formative and self-consciously important period in his career – when he sought entry into the worldly discourse of *belles lettres* by engaging with topics of contemporary moral and literary interest.[11] Peter Jones is right to suggest that '"Of the Standard of Taste" is Hume's most interesting essay on aesthetics' but this essay simply cannot stand in for Hume's normally overlooked principles on the relation of sympathy to aesthetic experience – principles which Hume articulated in brief but still specific ways, through each of his earliest works.[12] Paradoxically, Hume's concern for his reputation during this period (despite his famous claims to the contrary in *My Own Life*) has led even his closest readers to misinterpret his contemporary attacks on 'the fictions of poetry' as a social critique rather than a philosophical argument.[13]

Hume's early theory of aesthetic perception is integral to his 'Science of Man', and not only because his *Treatise* sought to integrate aesthetics into a unified project: 'in these four sciences of Logic, Morals, Criticism, and Politics, is comprehended almost every thing, which can in any way import us ... [and] can tend either to the improvement or ornament of the human mind'.[14] At the core of Hume's earliest aesthetic writings is an attempt to discern 'that act of the mind, which renders realities more present to us than fictions, causes them to weigh more in the thought, and gives them superior influence on the passions and imagination'.[15] This approach may have helped to transform the strictly qualitative notion of *criticism* as 'a standard of judging well' (in Samuel John-son's definition) toward the more philosophically complex project formulated by Alexander Gottlieb Baumgarten in his *Aesthetica* of 1750: 'an epistemology of less-than-rational-knowing' – from which time *criticism* addressed wider moral concerns that were more pressing than earlier worries about defining good taste.[16]

Hume never published the book-length critical theory that he envisioned on the opening page of his *Treatise*, for he did not receive 'the good fortune to meet with [the] success' that would enable him 'to proceed to the examination of Morals, Politics, and Criticism; which will compleat this *Treatise of Human Nature*'. However, Hume included nine textual insertions with the manuscript of the *Treatise*'s second installment (and third book), *Of Morals* (1740). Seven of these insertions represent Hume's plan to integrate his aesthetic theory into the *Treatise*; the other two clarify related arguments. They constitute the Appendix whose inclusion was announced prominently on the title-page of the second installment, which claimed to 'illustrate' and 'explain' *Of the Understanding* (1739).[17] This newly-illustrated theory of aesthetic sensibility comprises an integral element of Hume's epistemological and only consequently of his moral philosophy (of which the theory of sympathy constitutes a part), because it is in *Of the Understanding* and in the *Philosophical Essays* (1748) that Hume placed his comments on literature and on literary perception – these were also the texts that Hume expected his readers to encounter first.[18] Hume was so convinced of the importance of these insertions that, several days before he submitted his manuscript, and despite his worries about poor sales, he remarked, 'I wait with some Impatience for a second Edition principally on Account of Alterations I intend to make in my Performance'.[19] But no new edition of the *Treatise* would appear until 1817 – forty years after Hume's death.[20] The next edition, edited by T. H. Green and T. H. Grose (1874, second edition 1886), integrated Hume's insertions into the main text as Hume intended. So when L. A. Selby-Bigge 'reprinted' Hume's insertions to Book I as an Appendix following Book III in his Clarendon edition of 1888, he was turning back to Thomas Longman's 1740 copytext.[21] Long-standing reliance on Selby-Bigge's edition, the only edition of the *Treatise* to remain in print throughout the twentieth century, and the one which Peter Nidditch has described as having provided 'a significant and helpful factor in the *fortuna* of Hume's book and reputation in the twentieth century' has meant, paradoxically, that Hume's early aesthetic principles have remained in the textual margins until the publication of the David Fate Norton and Mary J. Norton's excellent critical text of 2000.[22]

Even textual scholars have neglected Hume's insertions. Since the discovery in 1975 of Hume's manuscript notes for a revision of the *Treatise*'s second book, critics have tried to envision Hume's plan for a full revision of the three-book text.[23] By disregarding those insertions that Hume had published, readers may have overlooked the only surviving evidence of Hume revising and qualifying the first installment of his longest and most detailed philosophical work.[24] This is only the formal reason why even an authority as eminent as Ernest Mossner has stated that Hume's aesthetic theory exists only 'in pregnant hints and fruitful ideas [which] are scattered throughout his works'.[25] Peter Kivy claims that 'Hume's *Treatise* contains no extended treatment of aesthetics at all, either before, after, or in any other relation to his moral theory'.[26] Indeed, one must consult the neglected insertions to discern Hume's position on the relation between aesthetic experience and the moral value of sympathy.

A further reason for overlooking Hume's aesthetic theory during the 1740s follows his own decision, some twenty years later, to excise the extensive discussion of literary genres from 'Of the Connexion of Ideas', which first appeared in the *Philosophical Essays*. In the 1764 edition of his *Essays and Treatises on Several Subjects*, Hume began to cut those remarks as part of an editorial process that, in the final posthumous edition of 1777, survives as the two-page 'Section III' of *An Enquiry Concerning Human Understanding*.[27] Yet 'Of the Connexion of Ideas' had provided the most detailed discussion of literature in all of Hume's published works, and its inclusion in Hume's first popularization of his epistemology emphasizes the centrality of literary practice to his early theories of perception and belief. Even T. E. Jessop's otherwise indispensable *Bibliography of David Hume and of Scottish Philosophy* neglects to mention that Hume excised roughly 340 words of his 'loose hints' on 'compositions of genius' for the 1764 and some 2,800 words for the 1777 editions.[28] Hume may have made these deletions to highlight his more recent and more substantial essays 'On Tragedy' and 'On the Standard of Taste', which would appear alongside his earlier essays in all editions of *Essays and Treatises* from 1758. In any event, Selby-Bigge's 1902 edition of *An Enquiry Concerning Human Understanding* (Hume's title for the *Philosophical Essays* after 1758) follows Hume's final excisions, thereby displaying Hume's only apparent silence on aesthetic issues and their moral significance during this period in his career.

Once I point to the primacy of social and devaluation of aesthetic experience in Hume's moral theory, I will revisit the literary material that he dropped from his *Philosophical Essays*. Together with the material Hume inserted into the *Treatise* and his early essay 'On the Delicacy of Taste and Passion', his aesthetic concerns of the first decade of his career as a published author focused on our instinctive tendency to draw social connections from our aesthetic experiences. Tracing Hume's early critical principles through his 'anatomy of the mind', we can better appreciate his self-conscious theory of reading.

'Fictions of Poetry' and the Force of Belief

Hume designed his insertions to clarify the arguments he made in the first book that deal with belief, 'that act of mind which renders realities more present to us than fictions, causes them to weigh more in the thought, and gives them a superior influence on the passions'.[29] Setting out to show that 'the effect of belief is to raise up a simple idea to an equality with our impressions', Hume points out that this requires a psychological process distinct from those caused by 'chimeras of the brain', in which 'a present impression and a customary transition are now no longer necessary to enliven our ideas'.[30] This means that the process of converting ideas into beliefs must be governed by those two elements that Hume emphasizes throughout his *Treatise*: 'When we pass from the impression of one [thing] to the idea or belief of another, we are not determined by reason, but by custom or a principle of association'.[31] Hume indicates that our acquiescence to custom is instinctive; it 'operates before we have time for reflection'.[32] Our adherence to belief is likewise involuntary and immediate: 'belief is a judgement of causes and effects by a secret operation, and without being thought of'.[33] This version of the theory of belief seems, at first, to invite affinities with the emotional enticements raised by the novel: for instance, John Sitter has observed that Hume's intense reflections on his own emotions provide 'the philosophical equivalent of what Richardson would call "writing to the moment"' – that the *Treatise* invites a 'private relationship' with the reader that in turn leads us to invest emotionally in Hume's 'melodrama of momentary intensities'.[34] Hume's 'self-revelatory appeals to the writer's [that is, his own] sentiments' leads us to share what Hume calls 'that forlorn solitude, in which I am plac'd in my philosophy'.[35]

However, the parallel with sentimental reading, indeed with any moralistic modeling of emotion, must be troubled by the fact that Hume's insertions specify that when we experience aesthetic impressions, 'how great soever the pitch may be, to which [their] vivacity arises, 'tis evident, that in poetry it never has the same *feeling* with that which arises in the mind, when we reason, even upon the lowest species of probability'.[36] Richardson understood that his readers should be conscious of what he saw as the essentially qualitative difference between depicted and actual impressions, which is why Richardson described his readers' 'historical faith' as a literary rather than moral phenomenon: 'the *Air* of Genuiness [would] be kept up ... to avoid hurting that kind of Historical Faith which Fiction is generally read with'.[37] For Hume, in order for an idea to inspire belief, the idea must bear a particular kind of quantitative and not simply representational weight: 'belief must please the imagination by means of the force and vivacity which attends it'.[38] This force will be experienced only as a sensation and not as an idea: ''tis *felt*, rather than conceived', and this force refers directly to intimate experience: it 'approaches the impression, from which it is deriv'd'.[39]

In a summary of his *Treatise* printed that same year, Hume repeated his now customary caveat, for those who attended to his insertions, lest readers judge the moral value of their response to the voice of a literary protagonist in a way similar to responding to a real person: 'Poetry, with all its art, can never cause a passion, like one in real life: It fails in the original conception of its objects, which never *feel* in the same manner as those which command our belief'.[40] If this sounds like common sense now, it seemed to Hume as philosophically compelling then – compelling enough to be inserted into his text and iterated in his self-published *Abstract*.

The emotive power that will enable belief derives from our instinct to reflect on the nature of our impressions, a reflection which precedes even the compulsion to believe: 'We observe, that the vigour of conception, which fictions receive from poetry and eloquence, is a circumstance merely accidental, of which every idea is susceptible; and that such fictions are associated with nothing that is real'.[41] To be sure, Hume does imply that aesthetic perception can enable a certain kind of imaginative transport, but he attaches specific value both to the emotional quality of that experience and to our conscious observance of its ultimate 'inferiority' as an impression: 'This observation makes us only lend ourselves, so to speak, to the fiction: But causes the idea to feel very different from the external establish'd perswasions founded on memory and custom. They are somewhat of the same kind: but the one is much inferior to the other, both in its causes and effects'.[42] Despite a novelist's effort to portray his characters as real people, and the epistolary protagonist's notoriously urgent 'drama of potential interruption', Hume underlines our consciousness of the fact that fiction does not exist in the social realm of real engagement with real people:[43] custom and memory derive solely from uniquely social relationships, those relationships which touch on 'the passions, [which] always turns our view to ourselves, and make us think of our own qualities and circumstances'.[44] Simply put, perceptions which arise from poetry (or from any other literary genre or aesthetic experience) must fail to inspire strong impressions, due to 'the want of resemblance, or contiguity, [which] render its force inferior'.[45] Hume specifies in the *Treatise* that associations based on resemblance and contiguity to the self – that is, those associations which turn on their uniquely social nature – are required to generate those impressions that can bear the force of communicable passions. They also provide the elements through which 'the understanding corrects the appearances of the senses'.[46]

Hume's published insertions to the first book *Of the Understanding* clarify those ambiguities in the subsequent two books that together have led to suggestions that aesthetic experience can animate sympathy. In fact, the insertions specify Hume's argument that aesthetic impressions are ultimately weak: 'A passion, which is disagreeable in real life, may afford the highest entertainment in a tragedy, or epic poem ... it lies not with that weight upon us: It *feels* less firm and solid: And has no other than the agreeable effect of exciting the spirits, and rouzing the attention' (emphasis added).[47] Hume is elaborating an earlier insertion, in which he proposed that it is our capacity to discern 'the manner of conception, and in their *feeling* to the mind' which 'distinguishes the ideas of the judgment from the fictions of the imagination ... and renders them the governing principles of all our actions' (emphasis added).[48] This matter is of particular importance for critics of the eighteenth-century novel, since the presumption of 'its faith in language to affect the behaviour of readers' is among the genre's most salient features, as current and contemporary critics have long argued.[49]

Hume allows that there are times when the imagery of poetry nearly raises passions, by attempting to replicate the force of our impressions: sometimes, 'it approaches so near, in its influence, as may convince us, that they are deriv'd from the same origin'.[50] Indeed, poets depend on associations based on resemblance to bring us closer to real experience: 'poets make use of this artifice of borrowing the names of their persons, and the chief events of their poems, from history, in order to procure a more easy reception for the whole, and cause it to make a deeper impression on the fancy and affections'.[51] Yet, ultimately, 'the vivacity they bestow on the ideas is not deriv'd from the particular objects of these ideas, but from the present temper and disposition of the person'.[52] Hume intended to clarify this point by indicating in the accompanying insertion that 'we shall afterwards have occasion to remark both the resemblances and differences betwixt a poetical enthusiasm, and a serious conviction'.[53] No such remarks appear in these three books, but as I pointed out earlier, Hume had already indicated his confidence in our ability to discern what is only a 'feigned association', when he stated 'the imagination reposes itself indolently on the idea, and the passion, being soften'd by the want of belief in the subject, has no more than the agreeable effect of enlivening the mind, and fixing the attention'.[54]

In contrast, when Hume deals with those associations that refer to relations with people, he finds that our faculty of belief is much more conducive to yielding its powers of assent. Like literary representations, the ideas that will incite sympathy are at first understood only by their visual appearance: 'When any affection is infus'd with sympathy, it is at first known only by its effects, and by those external signs in the countenance and conversation, which convey an idea of it'.[55] The crucial element of those associations that govern our appreciation of such external signs is causation: 'when I see the *effects* of passion in the voice and gesture of any person, my mind immediately passes from these effects to their *causes*, and forms such a lively idea of the passion, as is presently converted into the passion itself'.[56] This is why perception and association – rather than mere contagion – is central to Hume's theory: 'no passion of another discovers itself immediately to the mind. We are only sensible of its causes or effects. From *these* we infer the passion: And consequently *these* give rise to our sympathy'.[57]

Hume also shows that 'resemblance and contiguity are relations not to be neglected; especially when by an inference from cause and effect, and by the observation of external signs, we are inform'd of the real existence of the object, which is resembling or contiguous'.[58] Those external indications of passion relate to not just anyone, but to those people who most resemble ourselves: 'we find that where, beside the general resemblance of our natures, there is any peculiar similarity in our manners, or character, or country, or language, it facilitates the sympathy'.[59] Hume emphasizes this point: 'The stronger the relation is betwixt ourselves and any object, the more easily does the imagination make the transition, and convey to the related idea the vivacity of conception, with which we always form the idea of our own person'.[60] By suggesting that the basis of sympathetic feelings resides in our sense of ourselves, and yet by indicating the importance of feeling in establishing that basis, Hume combines his sensory theory of belief with his previous discussion of personal identity. As Hume repeats numerous times throughout the second book of the *Treatise*, 'as we are at all times intimately conscious of ourselves, our sentiments, and passions, their ideas must strike upon us with greater vivacity than the ideas of the sentiments and passions of others'.[61] More pointedly: 'the idea of ourselves is always intimately present to us, and conveys a sensible degree of vivacity to the idea of any other object, to which we are related'.[62]

Hume argued that in order for the passions to be raised, and for sympathy to operate, our perceptions must strike us with so much force that they approach the vivacity of those impressions which define our very identity. For Hume, that genesis of sympathy can be achieved only through the threefold principle of association: the psychological relations of objects through their resemblance, contiguity, and causation – 'the mind ... conceives [a given idea] with an additional force and vigour, by the united operation of that principle, and of the present impression'.[63] This cannot be achieved through aesthetic experience, because while fictional imagery can gain affective force through its associations, our primary impression of it is always defined by the fact that we are experiencing fiction – the experience is essentially second-hand. In fact, Hume teaches that we ought to be aware of the effect our associations have on our sense of primary impressions, since it is by those effects that we come to understand the nature of our perceptions: such awareness will help us to resolve those moments when 'we feign the continu'd existence of the perceptions of our senses ... and confound identity with relation'.[64] Although each of these three relations is crucial for the construction of personal identity, Hume indicates that causation is the strongest of them, since 'as the power, by which one object produces another, is never discoverable merely from their ideas, 'tis evident *cause and effect* are relations, of which we receive information from experience, and not from any abstract reasoning or reflection'.[65]

In his longest insertion, Hume stresses that aesthetic representations cannot excite the passions and thus sympathy, since 'the ideas [that a poetical description] presents are different to the *feeling* from those, which arise from the memory and judgement', and it is those two latter elements that create the requisite subject for all passions: 'passion always turns our view to ourselves, and makes us think of our own qualities and circumstances'.[66] Moreover it is the human ability to communicate passion, which for Hume comprises sympathy, that governs our sense of morality: 'Justice is certainly approv'd of for no other reason, than because it has a tendency to the public good: and the public good is indifferent to us, except so far as sympathy interests us in it'.[67] Since Hume will assert that only uniquely social impressions can evoke those associations which will excite the passions – that is, those which relate to memory and judgement – literature cannot substitute for interaction with real people. Hume remarks that 'the rules of art are founded on the qualities of human nature', and just as perception and sympathy form the basis of all knowledge and all social relations, so his theory of aesthetic sensibility provides a lucid reflection of human morality and sociability.[68]

Commentators have frequently suggested that 'Hume sees sympathy as a kind of emotional infection' that affects us from without, during an aesthetic experience, operating independently of those internal mechanisms of belief which inform our judgments of experience.[69] Instead, as Hume strove to point out in a 1740 popularization of his theory, 'it is by means of thoughts only that any thing operates upon our passions ... [the three principles of association] really are *to us* the cement of the universe'.[70] And those associations, which animate all thoughts, require certain beliefs: this means that, for Hume, our consciousness of our beliefs instinctively degrades aesthetic representations, disabling them from arousing the passions or from stimulating sympathy. Moreover, the faculty of belief eliminates those ideas which do not affect the passions, and so Hume effectively argues in his insertions to the *Treatise* that responses to literature do not imply moral sensibility.

Despite his concerns about the *Treatise*'s poor reception, Hume wrote in 1740 that 'if any thing can entitle the author to so glorious a name as that of an *inventor*, 'tis his use of the principle of the association of ideas, which enters into most of his philosophy'.[71] Hume's 'use' of association is indeed effective, both for clarifying his 'anatomy of the mind' and for explaining his insistence that 'the vigour of conception, which fictions receive from poetry and eloquence, is a circumstance merely accidental' – that is, a circumstance that that natural principle of association will correct.[72] While the theory of association explains the role of the imagination in the creation of perceptions, Hume had subordinated those creative abilities in the foundational opening pages of the *Treatise*: 'The ideas of the memory are much more lively and strong than those of the imagination ... when we remember any past event, the idea of it flows in upon the mind in a more forcible manner'.[73] Given the critical role of memory in the formation of personal identity, the imagination operates at that time only by assembling (and not creating) those experiences which touch on intimate past experience.[74] When Hume uses the association of ideas to explain sympathy, he shows that, like the memory, the communication of passions can only take place when we have previous experience of those passions we recognize in others.

The first definition of sympathy to appear in the *Treatise* again allows for literature to be an instrument of sympathetic communication: 'No quality of human nature is more remarkable, both in itself and in its consequences, than that propensity we have to sympathize with others, and to receive by communication their inclinations and sentiments, however different from, or even contrary to our own'.[75] Adela Pinch is correct when she observes that, for Hume, 'people's ability to feel other people's feelings is the sign of humanity's essentially social nature'.[76] Hume indeed proposed that 'we can form no wish that has not a reference to society', and that 'the minds of men are mirrors to one another, not only because they reflect each other's emotions, but also because those rays of passions, sentiments, and may often be reverberated'.[77] But in fact, by indicating that aesthetic experience cannot incite passions –"tis too weak to take any hold of the mind, or be attended with emotion' – it is precisely this *social* element of human nature that Hume underscores, at the affective and moral expense of literary experience.[78]

Hume observes that 'sympathy depends on the relation of objects to ourselves', and since 'the passions, both direct and indirect, are founded on pain and pleasure', our perception of those objects must carry enough force 'so that the ideas of the affections of others are converted into the very impressions they represent, that the passions arise in conformity to the images we form of them'.[79] Since belief arises through the association of ideas in the memory, and since those associations which are based on causation are strongest, our immediate causal sense of our own identity determines the intensity of our feelings. Since poetry does not reveal causation of anything but the imagination's creativity, which is inferior to memory, Hume *required* a peremptory dismissal of fiction for his subsequent definition of sympathy. Those particular kinds of powerful sensations that Hume requires for the sympathetic communication of passions derive solely through actual social relationships, and not through aesthetic representations.

Sensibility in Hume's Own Writing

Within five years, Joseph Warton would declare 'Invention and Imagination to be the chief faculties of a Poet', in one of a number of definitions that refer to a kind of aesthetic experience that Hume's theory of association could not allow and whose moral theory would not validate.[80] Richard Wendorf has argued persuasively that 'this new poetic of the 1740s ... involves an emotional response to a picturesque or literary rather than a social environment'; and later in the century, Warton would characterize the poetry of this particular period by suggesting that 'the use, the force, and the excellence of language, certainly consists in raising *clear*, *complete*, and *circumstantial* images, and in turning *readers* into *spectators*'.[81] Just as Warton sought to produce poetry that would arouse the passions and provide vicarious imaginative experiences, Richardson's sentimental readers went further. When Richardson's *Pamela* appeared, only one week after *Of Morals* and the insertions were printed, Richardson proclaimed that his novel 'shall engage the Passions of every sensible Reader', so that his 'particular Examples ... will be followed' – as if an aesthetic experience could guarantee moral compliance.[82]

Writing in his insertions of 1740, his *Essays Moral and Political* of 1742, and his *Philosophical Essays* of 1748, Hume argued that human nature will not allow mere depictions of emotion to animate the passions, nor their fictional figures to elicit moral behaviour through sympathy aroused through fictional imagery. So what was Hume's design when he provided his own instance of emotional modelling in the conclusion to the first book of the *Treatise*?

> The *intense* view of these manifold contradictions and imperfections in human reason has so wrought upon me, and heated my brain, that I am ready to reject all belief and reasoning, and can look upon no opinion even as more probable or likely than another. Where am I, or what? From what causes to I derive my existence, and to what condition shall I return? Whose favour shall I court, and whose anger must I dread? What beings surround me?[83]

Hume's anonymous reviewer in the *History of the Works of the Learned* responded sarcastically, adopting the language of maudlin sentiment: 'What Heart now would not almost bleed? What Breast can forbear to sympathize with this brave Adventurer?'[84] But by depicting his own state of mind, Hume was not trying to evoke sympathy in his reader; rather, his emotional modelling was designed to depict the organic basis of his theory of human nature: 'Most fortunately it happens, that since reason is incapable of dispelling these clouds, nature herself suffices to that purpose, and cures me of this philosophical melancholy and delirium, either by relaxing this bent of mind, or by some avocation, and lively impression of my senses, which obliterate all chimeras'.[85] Even if Hume had not provided this pointed demystification of emotional depiction, the philosophy which immediately preceded it was designed to define the perceptual mechanisms by which we resist sympathetic investment in aesthetic experience. Literary modelling of emotion, for Hume, provides a colourful instance of a mind in action, useful for the critical emphasis on causality that it naturally invites: the depiction of exhaustion leads us to inquire critically and not emotionally into its cause.

The psychology that Hume depicts in *Essays Moral and Political*, and particularly in 'Of the Delicacy of Taste and Passion', draws closely on passages from *On the Passions* (1740), which themselves refer closely to the insertions that Hume submitted for publication around the same time. Consistent with Hume's stylistic effort to avoid the 'abstract reasoning' that had alienated readers of his neglected *Treatise*, the essays feature 'a desultory method' that nevertheless provides philosophical learning – as Hume would show in his gradual revisions over successive editions.[86] The first observation of Hume's essay, which was evidently calculated both to flatter and instruct his readers' own notions of aesthetic and emotional sensibility, is that 'delicacy of taste has the same effect as delicacy of passion: It enlarges the sphere of both our happiness and misery, and makes us sensible to pains as well as pleasures, which escape the rest of mankind.'[87] Hume then proposes that 'nothing is so proper to cure us of this delicacy of passion, as the cultivating of that higher and refined taste, which enables us to judge of the characters of men, of compositions of genius, and of the productions of the nobler arts'.[88] This therapeutic ability to make aesthetic judgments rests on our inherent and instinctive tendency never to lose sight of our emotional state of mind. In the essay, Hume simply makes this assumption, for his recommendation that his readers simply 'study the beauties ... of poetry, eloquence, music, or painting', does not clarify the mechanism by which such aesthetic experiences will 'render the mind incapable of the rougher and more boisterous emotions'.[89]

In *Of the Passions*, Hume had emphasized the natural fact that 'the idea, or rather impression of ourselves is always present with us': we are always present of what we feel and of what we are capable of feeling.[90] This immediate and continual emotional self-consciousness provides important aesthetic and moral functions, for it enables us to temper our experiences as readers by cultivating our judgment while it allows us to cultivate our sympathetic relationships by seeking out others who reflect that view of ourselves. Hume closes his essay on delicacy of taste and passion by pointing out, in a further gesture to the *Treatise*, that 'delicacy of taste is favourable to love and friendship', since those who possess a refined taste will seek out each other's company.[91] Therefore aesthetic sensibility carries a social function in both the *Treatise* and in this early critical essay, but it does so only for the relationships that readers cultivate amongst other readers apart from their imaginative experience. For Hume, when aesthetic experiences are powerful, they refer us to our social sense of ourselves, and this is based on the primacy of causation among the association of ideas.

Similarly, in 'Of the Association of Ideas', Hume uses his theory of association to validate familiar classical principles. He argues that historians, epic poets, and dramatists can be confident of a specific response because all readers create mental associations on the same primary basis of causation. Just as historians emphasize 'the knowledge of causes' since it is 'the most instructive' and '[the] relation or connexion [that is] the strongest of all the others', poets and dramatists also focus their readers on events that provide the logical basis for the action which follows.[92] Indeed, for Hume, the very enjoyment that we derive from aesthetic experience is a product of the artist exercising our natural associations: 'on no occasion, can our thoughts be allowed to run at adventures, if we would produce a work, which will give any lasting entertainment to mankind'.[93] Poets also must work hard to maintain their readers' attention, since this entails distracting us from our instinctive emotional and social self-consciousness.

Interestingly, while Richardson worried about the ease by which his readers could mistake his heroine for a real person, and Warton celebrated the power of his poems to captivate his readers' imaginations, Hume focused on the considerable difficulty that poets and dramatists must encounter when they try to maintain an 'enlived imagination and enflamed passion'. They do this by combining a certain etiquette with a particular technique – by not to allowing 'a breach in the connexion of ideas ... by exciting a new concern [or] new scene of action', so that the poet 'preserves the affections still in the same channel and direction'.[94] Hume's conclusion, 'that a certain unity is requisite in all productions' based on 'the relations of cause of and effect', phrases Aristotle in his own psychological terms. For Hume, human nature provides both the inherent bounds that contain our aesthetic experience, and the key to our realizing moral abilities – through the true social relationships that associations based on causality define.[95]

7 DAVID HUME AND JANE AUSTEN ON PRIDE: ETHICS IN THE ENLIGHTENMENT

Eva M. Dadlez

David Hume and Jane Austen would, on the face of it, appear to have little in common, unless we take into account the sojourn of each in eighteenth-century Britain. In fact, their lives barely coincided, for Hume left this world a scant eight months after Austen had entered it. He was an empiricist philosopher, probably an atheist. She was a novelist and a clergyman's daughter. Attempts at comparison appear unpromising on those grounds alone. Hume was, after all, sometimes regarded as The Great Infidel, the title of a recent biography. Austen was a believer, further buttressed in respectability by clerical and religious relations who burned her more revealing letters and represented her, repeatedly and in print, as a kindly old maid, humble and placid, contented with her domestic duties, having taken up writing as a kind of genteel alternative to darning socks. The whitewash job did not begin to fade until the latter half of the twentieth century. This conventional image of Jane Austen is one that would appear entirely incompatible with infidels both great and small, and it is the falsity of that purposely promulgated version of Austen that prompts the contrast to which I have initially called attention. It has been argued more effectively, by those less inclined to relegate Austen to saccharine respectability, that the works of Jane Austen are best understood as deriving from the sceptical traditions of the Enlightenment. Austen's constant predilection as a writer for 'stick[ing] to the observable', in the words of Peter Knox-Shaw, suggests an affinity for the empirical method.[1] Indeed, Knox-Shaw goes further and proposes that if Hume's *Treatise of Human Nature* 'is less a scientific study of mankind than a philosophy of science with an attached discourse on humanity that is consistent in principle with it, the same sort of consistency could be claimed for other discourses, including fictional ones'.[2] The claims made in this paper are more specific, aligning the moral perspective and moral reasoning presented in Austen's work with those of David Hume.

Because it focuses principally on human character and human interaction, Austen's work has been the subject of ethical analyses by philosophers and literary critics alike. We cannot be certain whether Austen read or reflected on philosophy, particularly ethics, although many possibilities have been suggested. Austen scholars have detected the influence of Aristotle, of Shaftesbury, of Adam Smith, of Kant, even of Hobbes. Austen herself denied any familiarity with philosophy, though some suspect the denial was disingenuous. What is possible, however, and possible without indulging in excessive speculation, is to consider the question of which philosopher's ethical theories and systems are brought most to life in the course of Austen's fictional narratives. It will be maintained here that Austen's work brings to life the ethics put forward in David Hume's *Treatise of Human Nature*.

How can it be maintained that fiction takes up an ethical stance? Hume believed, as did Austen, that fiction engages us on a moral level and elicits moral reactions. This is borne out by Hume's claim in 'Of the Standard of Taste' that, in our interaction with fiction, we resist 'bear[ing] an affection to characters, which we plainly discover to be blameable' or feeling 'sentiments of approbation or blame ... different from those to which the mind ... has been familiarized'.[3] The imaginative resistance is not due to a simple imposition of one's own standards on the fiction, but rather to the capacity of fiction to make us complicit in its ethical perspective. If we cannot imagine what we cannot conceive, then our capacity to imagine that some act is right commits us to the possibility of the rightness of that kind of act in a context a good deal wider than that of the fiction's world. But whether or not we choose to accept it, it remains clear that Hume sees fiction as a purveyor of moral perspectives.[4] Indeed, Jane Austen agrees, calling a novel a 'work in which ... the most thorough knowledge of human nature, the happiest delineation of its varieties' is to be observed.[5] Jane Austen's descriptions of moral character, of moral reasoning, of the ways in which people judge and evaluate others can be aligned on different levels with claims made in Hume's *Treatise*. But the contention here is not simply that Austen provides us with soft *illustrations* of Hume's ethical dilemmas, though it will be necessary to establish a range of such similarities at the outset. I would like to argue that Austen's novels are *demonstrations* of precisely the kind of moral reasoning that Hume advocates; that is, the novels are thought experiments in a hard philosophical sense.

Consider the simplest kinds of thought experiments in ethics and how these work. Thought experiments are intended to test the effectiveness or applicability of moral principles (often by providing counterexamples) in a way that depends almost entirely on our immediate reactions to particular cases. Utilitarians present us with examples in which a rigid adherence to moral rule, the rule of promise-keeping say, prevents the saving of a life. Deontologists, on the other hand, muster an arsenal of cases in which insignificant increases in utility are obtainable only at the cost of human life, attempting to show that utilitarians would be required by their ethical system to take lives. Such examples cannot assume the truth of the presenter's ethical stance without begging the question;

they clearly do not assume the truth of the principle they are intended to criticize. The point of such thought experiments *must* be to confront the audience
with a case to which they *react* as wrong, in order to demonstrate the inadequacy
of the principle under consideration. Since this reaction should properly depend
neither on the principle under review nor on that preferred by the presenter
of the example, it seems clear that what is essential to the entire process is the
emotional reaction of the auditor. That is, thought experiments, and the manner in which ethicists deploy them, suggest in themselves that emotion can play
a serious role in ethics, something that Hume maintains from the outset when
he claims that the source of morality is to be found in sentiment, and that our
emotional reactions of approbation and disapprobation provide the key to identifying virtue and vice.

Some may maintain that if Austen were conducting thought experiments,
she would have joined Hume as a *teller* of moral principles, and assume with Roy
Sorensen that literary works cannot be regarded as thought experiments because
their authors did not create them with this purpose in mind.[6] But philosophers
like Noel Carroll, Eileen John, Martha Nussbaum and others have suggested
that fiction can cause us to examine what concepts mean and can lead readers
to apply them to characters and events on the basis of their actual conceptual
commitments, ascribing to fiction the kind of clarificatory function typically
associated with thought experiments. The same mechanism is thought to govern
our reactions to fiction and to the world, leading these philosophers to stress,
just as Hume has done, the connection between ethical salience and emotional
response. Fiction is not a work of philosophy, but it can have philosophical value
nonetheless. In this sense, then, it can be held by even the most conservative to
do some of the work of a thought experiment.

Add to the preceding the consideration that fictions are intended to elicit
emotion from their audience. Imaginative immersion in fiction requires emotional involvement which, as we have seen, and especially for Hume, brings with
it moral engagement. So the claim here is that Austen's fiction, both in the nar-
rowness of its focus on a small group of closely related individuals and in its
purposeful investigation of the effects of traits of character, provides us with a
working out of Humean hypotheses and with the opportunity to participate in,
actually to undertake, what is a distinctively Humean method of moral evalua-
tion in the course of our imaginative engagement with her works. It is impossible
to do justice to the sheer range of parallels in a single paper, of course. Instead of
generalizing, I will attempt to focus on both Hume's and Austen's treatment of a
single disposition: pride. We will begin by establishing strong parallels between
Hume and Austen, and end with an example of Austen's fiction as a clarifier and
elucidator of Humean concepts. Pride is especially interesting for those engaged
in the study of ethics, because it has been characterized both as a virtue and as a

vice. Indeed, the contention that there can be both proper and improper pride is characteristic of both Hume and Austen.

Hume and Austen often use the words 'pride' and 'vanity' interchangeably. Roughly, both terms are used to signify a habitual pleasure taken in some action, trait or object exhibited by, possessed by, or associated with oneself. When the terms appear to differ in meaning, 'vanity' is more likely to signify a vice than is 'pride' and is sometimes, though not invariably, characterized as a concern to elicit admiration from all and sundry. However, the purpose of this paper is to see which dispositions fit within the compass of these terms as they are actually used in Hume and Austen, not to draw distinctions which neither of them feels inclined to make. No speculations as to the meaning of these terms beyond those canvassed by Hume and Austen will be offered.

It should first be noted that neither Austen nor Hume condemns pride (or vanity) categorically as a vice. Both acknowledge a sense in which there can be a proper pleasure in one's achievements, abilities, and condition – what Hume sometimes calls self-respect. There is also, for both, a sense in which pride may be inappropriate, as when, feeling contempt for someone, we are 'elevated with the view of one below us' or when we estimate our talents or capacities unrealistically.[7] Hume considers both pride and humility in terms of 'the vice or virtue that lies in their excesses or just proportion', sounding positively Aristotelian as he does so. 'An excessive pride or over-weening conceit of ourselves is always esteem'd vicious, and is universally hated; as modesty, or a just sense of our weakness, is esteem'd virtuous, and procures the good will of every-one.'[8]

Still, Hume reminds us that the same 'qualities and circumstances, which are the causes of pride and self-esteem, are also the causes of vanity or the desire of reputation'.[9] That is, proper pride and improper pride have the same causes. Pride, it should be remembered, is for Hume an indirect passion. The object of this passion is always the self. Its cause is an idea or thought concerning a quality that is esteemed valuable and inheres in some subject associated with the self. That is, the causes of sentiments like pride involve those qualities which are thought to be instantiated in something affiliated with the object of the emotion. The cause of the passion, an idea, is also the cause of a sensation of pain or pleasure.[10] This sensation is intimately connected to the quality (pleasure, in the case of pride) which the thought ascribes to a subject (which must be something related to or associated with the object of the emotion: the self). Consider pride in the ownership of a beautiful house. Hume indicates that 'the quality [beauty is used here as an example of an agreeable quality] which operates on the passion [pride], produces separately an impression resembling it [pleasure]; the subject [a house] to which the quality adheres [i.e., beautiful house], is related to self [i.e., *my* beautiful house], the object of the passion: No wonder the whole cause, consisting of a quality and a subject, does so unavoidably give rise to the passion.'[11]

However, this does not mean that we can only feel pride on our own account. 'The virtue or vice of a son or brother not only excites love or hatred, but by a new transition, from similar causes, gives rise to pride or humility. Nothing causes greater vanity than any shining quality in our relations; as nothing mortifies us more than their vice or infamy.'[12] This certainly holds true in Austen. Few are likely to be more mortified than Elizabeth Bennett at the conduct of her flighty sister Lydia or than Edmond Bertram at the illicit affair engaged in by his sister Maria. Each young woman is taken to have disgraced her family. Grim prognostications are issued about the outer darkness into which the reputations of all family members will be cast by their behaviour. In the same way that the vices of one's relatives enforce a kind of global family embarrassment, one's vanity expands to encompass the accomplishments of one's relations. Mrs Norris is in perpetual raptures over the perfections of the very niece whose misconduct will later embarrass her nearest and dearest: 'Maria was indeed the pride and delight of them all – perfectly faultless – an angel'.[13] Equally affectionate but much more honest, is Mrs Norris's neighbour Mrs Grant, who 'having never been able to glory in beauty of her own ... thoroughly enjoyed the power of being proud of her sister's'.[14] Indeed, the affiliation between the self and the object of the emotion may be more tenuous still. Consider the kind of sympathetic pride an entire village might experience in tandem with a beloved inhabitant: Mr Weston 'saw his son every year in London and was proud of him; and his fond report of him as a very fine young man had made Highbury feel a sort of pride in him too'.[15]

As will become evident, the causes of pride are various indeed, according to Hume, who remarks on the 'vast variety of subjects, on which they may be plac'd. Every valuable quality of the mind, whether of the imagination, judgment, memory or disposition; wit, good-sense, learning, courage, justice, integrity; all these are the cause of pride; and their opposites of humility'. Jane Austen's novels confirm this. Emma Woodhouse and Elizabeth Bennet pride themselves on their perceptiveness, Mary Bennet on her learning, and Mr Collins on his humility, though some are less justified than others in doing so. 'Nor are these passions confin'd to the mind', Hume continues, 'but extend their view to the body likewise. A man may be proud of his beauty, strength, agility, good mein, address in dancing, riding, and of his dexterity in any manual business or manufacture.' Again we find examples in Austen: Sir Walter Elliot of *Persuasion* is more than a little vain of his appearance, John Thorpe of *Northanger Abbey* brags about his riding, Emma Woodhouse is pleased to be as good a dancer as Jane Fairfax. 'But this is not all', Hume indicates. 'The passions looking farther, comprehend whatever objects are in the least ally'd or related to us. Our country, family, children, relations, riches, houses, gardens, horses, dogs, cloaths; any of these may become a cause either of pride or of humility.'[16] Since there are many examples in Austen's work of cases such as these and given that vanity is one of her chief sources of amusement, I will focus on those examples that evidence the most striking similarities in ethical insight between Hume and Austen.

As has been indicated, Hume does not regard pride as inevitably vicious. On the whole, he maintains, vanity is not so bad. For one thing, it is sometimes the only reward for and the only spur to virtuous behaviour.[17] Surely we will not begrudge someone a little cheerful moral smugness when there is not much else to prompt an act of kindness, an act which might have remained undone without the inducement of self-satisfaction. 'Vanity is ... closely allied to virtue ... to love the fame of laudable actions approaches ... near the love of laudable actions for their own sake'.[18] Further, there are purely practical considerations to keep in mind: "twoud be more advantageous to over-rate our merit than to form ideas of it, below its just standard', for fortune is hardly likely to favour the self-effacing or the diffident instead of the bold.[19] Moreover, Hume believes that 'A genuine ... self-esteem, if well conceal'd and well-founded, is essential to the character of a man of honour'.[20] It is necessary to know our rank in the world, to understand what is due to us and what deference we owe to others, and that makes it necessary 'to feel the sentiment ... of pride in conformity to' that understanding.[21] This last pronouncement is especially in line with the sentiments of Jane Austen when she considers proper, as opposed to improper, pride.

Many kinds of pride might be proper and desirable if we take some of Austen's characters as examples. First, there is a pride that constitutes a resistance to being humbled before others, which prevents one from advertising one's weaknesses, errors and vulnerabilities. As Hume repeatedly points out, humility is painful and disagreeable, just as pride is agreeable. Clearly then, there is reason to avoid exposing one's mistakes and embarrassing susceptibilities, if only to prevent additional unpleasant sensations that could occur as the result of sympathy with the potentially negative reactions of others, as Hume might suggest. For instance, Elinor Dashwood urges upon her sister Marianne a 'reasonable and laudable pride'. That is, she urges Marianne to attempt to restrain her display of wretchedness at Willoughby's desertion and to exercise a modicum of self-control.[22] Interestingly, and very much in line with Hume's remark about pride in its just proportion, this particular sort of pride is not inevitably virtuous, since it can prove excessive.

Both Maria Bertram of *Mansfield Park* and Captain Wentworth of *Persuasion* are rejected by the respective objects of their affection, and subsequently suffer from a pride fuelled by resentment, a pride that leads them to conceal or to deny their feelings about being spurned. The prolonged absence of Henry Crawford rightly convinces Maria that he was never serious in his advances. She therefore decides to marry a man whom she does not in the least care for to be 'safe from the possibility of giving Crawford the triumph of governing her actions, and destroying her prospects'. She 'retire[s] in proud resolve', refusing to allow her father to extricate her from the unfortunate engagement.[23] 'Henry Crawford had destroyed her happiness, but he should not know that he had done it; he should not destroy her credit, her appearance, her prosperity too. He should not have to think of her as pining in the retirement of Mansfield for *him*, rejecting Sotherton and London, independence and splendour for *his* sake.'[24] The results of Maria's pride are, as we know, disastrous.

Captain Wentworth, on the other hand, manages to conquer his pride and resentment, though only after several years have passed. At first 'the attempts of angry pride' lead him to court a woman with whom he will not be happy.[25] Fearing he has attached her, he begins to 'deplore the pride, the folly, the madness of resentment, which had kept him from trying to regain' his first love.[26] 'Six years of separation might have been spared' had Wentworth not been 'proud, too proud to ask again'.[27] He and Anne are happily united at last, but only because his pride has finally given way to an inclination to be happy.

Proper pride, however, usually involves more than a defence against externally imposed humility or self-exposure. Hume indicates that 'a genuine and hearty pride, or self-esteem, if well conceal'd and well founded, is essential to the character of a man of honour'.[28] The antecedent of the conditional suggests that we are not permitted to lord it over those we consider inferior, and that pride is not considered appropriate when it is based on a mistaken apprehension of our merits, talents, or actions. However, 'there is no quality of the mind', Hume continues, 'which is more indispensibly requisite to procure the esteem and approbation of mankind', when it *is* well founded. For instance,

> there are certain deferences and mutual submissions, which custom requires of the different ranks of men towards each other; and whoever exceeds in this particular, if thro' interest, is accus'd of meanness; if thro' ignorance, of simplicity. 'Tis necessary, therefore, to know our rank and station in the world, whether it be fix'd by our birth, fortune, employments, talents or reputation. 'Tis necessary to feel the sentiment and passion of pride in conformity to it, and to regulate our actions accordingly.[29]

This is not a defence of snobbery on account of class or wealth against which, as we will see eventually, Hume inveighs. It is more a question of being able to negotiate one's way within one's social milieu without arousing either enmity or contempt, of knowing how much one can expect from one's fellows and how much they can expect from oneself, and of knowing how much is too much or not enough.

In this context, we can consider Elizabeth Bennet's ultimate happy certainty of Darcy's having 'no improper pride',[30] or the 'bright proud eye' of Captain Wentworth, which speaks of taste, discrimination, and a strong sense of what is his due.[31] There is Emma's mild indictment of Frank Churchill, who has nothing of the pride or reserve of the wealthy snobs by whom he was raised: 'Of pride, indeed, there was, perhaps, scarcely enough; his indifference to a confusion of rank, bordered too much on inelegance of mind'.[32] And there is Emma's much more justifiable surprise at the ability of Jane Fairfax to tolerate the company of superficial and unpleasant intellectual inferiors: 'This was astonishing! – She could not have believed it possible that the taste or the pride of Miss Fairfax could endure such society and friendship as the Vicarage had to offer.'[33] To venture a further example, we may consider how seriously Emma Woodhouse takes her social responsibilities. She dreads meeting the repellent Elton, whose advances she has recently repulsed, yet nonetheless pays a conventional call on his new wife. This is presented more or less as a requirement of rank and of the kind of pride that Hume describes. 'Emma had feelings, less of curiosity than of pride or propriety, to make her resolve on not being the last to pay her respects.'[34]

Of course, proper pride can simply involve not allowing oneself to be contemptible. Anne Elliot of *Persuasion* sets her own proper pride at odds with her family's sycophantic attentions to distant relatives of higher rank: 'She had hoped for better things from their high ideas of their own situation in life, and was reduced to form a wish which she had never foreseen – a wish that they had more pride'.[35] 'I suppose ... I have more pride than any of you', she tells her cousin, 'but I confess it does vex me, that we should be so solicitous to have the relationship acknowledged, which we may be sure is a matter of perfect indifference to them ... I am certainly proud, too proud to enjoy a welcome which depends entirely upon place'.[36]

Improper pride, on the other hand, is something of which both Hume and Austen sometimes offer acerbic critiques. As in the case of proper pride, there are several kinds of pride or vanity which might be termed improper or vicious. First, there is the kind of pride which Hume would not consider 'well founded', a pride that is based on an unwarranted overestimation of one's merits. We see just such an overestimation in the conceit exhibited by Mr Collins and Lady Catherine de Bourgh of *Pride and Prejudice*. Collins sets his merits so high that he is incapable of understanding why a young woman would reject his proposal of marriage. Moreover, he exhibits a kind of false piety, an unrealistic conception of his duties as clergyman. He appears to believe that being a clergyman confers upon him the right to dictate proper conduct to others in areas of life having nothing whatsoever to do with religion, and certainly has an inflated notion as regards his own importance in being a member of the clergy: 'I consider the clerical office as equal in point of dignity with the highest rank in the kingdom'.[37] Elizabeth Bennet finds this maddening and is ashamed to be related to him. Hume's writings contain more than one reflection on the hypocritical character of the clergy, and sometimes dwell in particular on their 'great facility in entering into the views of ... princes' and despots.[38] This is like Mr Collins's instantaneous, sycophantic adoption of any view put forward by his patron, Lady Catherine, whose condescension he is wont to extol at every opportunity. Lady Catherine is a petty tyrant whose own estimation of her merits is grossly inflated. She is even vain of skills that she is certain she *would* have possessed had she bothered to try and acquire them: 'There are few people in England, I suppose, who have more true enjoyment of music than myself, or a better natural taste. If I had ever learnt, I should have been a great proficient'.[39]

The next species of pride to come under review will be the sort of pride that elevates the self at another's expense, and that involves either unwarranted contempt toward someone else or unwarranted assumptions about one's own superiority. The bare fact that one's pride is accompanied by contempt is not enough to make it improper pride, of course. As Hume points out, in considering the qualities of another, we may regard them as they are in themselves, compare them to our own traits, or both. 'The good qualities of others, from the first point of view, produce love; from the second, humility; and from the third, respect; which is a mixture of these two passions. Their bad qualities, after the same manner, cause either hatred, or pride, or contempt, according to the light in which we survey them.'[40] So there is an admixture of pride in contempt (or humility in respect), which arises from 'a tacit comparison of the person contemn'd or respected with ourselves ... These passions, therefore, arise from our observing the proportion; that is, from a comparison.'[41]

So contempt, as well as pride, is not inevitably vicious. Feelings of contempt can be quite appropriate, as when Captain Wentworth takes the true measure of Anne's relations, and she cannot but notice and sympathize with his disdain: 'Anne caught his eye, saw his cheeks glow, and his mouth form itself into a momentary expression of contempt'.[42] Mrs Dashwood's contempt for the money-grubbing Fanny is equally understandable: 'The contempt which she had, very early in their acquaintance, felt for her daughter-in-law, was very much increased by the farther knowledge of her character, which half a year's residence in her family afforded'.[43]

It also appears to follow (both from Hume's observations and from Austen's depictions) that the proud and contemptuous will be held to have erred in so far as they have been mistaken about the badness of the other person's qualities or the preferability of their own, or in so far as they have illegitimately generalized from the superiority or inferiority of a single quality over the entire character. There are clear examples in Austen of wholly inappropriate contempt and pride. Consider Emma's inability to resist mocking poor Miss Bates for her interminable chatter. Knightly rebukes Emma for her contemptuous treatment of someone worthy of respect:

It was badly done, indeed! You, whom she had known from an infant, whom she
had seen grow up from a period when her notice was an honour, to have you now,
in thoughtless spirits, and the pride of the moment, laugh at her, humble her – and
before her niece, too – and before others, many of whom (certainly some,) would be
entirely guided by your treatment of her.[44]

One of Jane Austen's most believable depictions of personal shame and guilt
(more convincing by far than Willoughby's declarations of regret in *Sense and
Sensibility*, but then it is not clear how convincing those are meant to be) is
her description of Emma's distress at her own conduct: 'She was most forcibly
struck. The truth of this representation there was no denying. She felt it at her
heart. How could she have been so brutal, so cruel to Miss Bates! How could she
have exposed herself to such ill opinion in any one she valued! And how suffer
... [Knightly] to leave her without saying one word of gratitude, of concurrence,
of common kindness!'.[45]

Part of what makes this so believable, of course, is Emma's concern about
what others think of her. Hume speaks of the influence of sympathy

on pride and humility, when these passions arise from praise and blame, from reputation and infamy. We may observe, that no person is ever prais'd by another for any
quality, which wou'd not, if real, produce, of itself, a pride in the person possest of
it ... 'Tis certain, then, that if a person consider'd himself in the same light, in which
he appears to his admirer, he wou'd first receive a separate pleasure, and afterwards a
pride or self-satisfaction ... Now nothing is more natural than for us to embrace the
opinions of others in this particular; both from sympathy, which renders all their
sentiments intimately present to us; and from reasoning, which makes us regard their
judgment, as a kind of argument for what they affirm.[46]

For such reasons are infamous flirts like Austen's Henry Crawford driven to
elicit admiration at all costs, even to their own eventual detriment. They simply
cannot resist being found irresistible. But the same kind of process is involved in
the case of less pleasant reactions like shame. When Emma considers herself in
the same light in which she appears to someone who *disapproves* of her conduct,
she suffers an additional pain, followed by shame and self-contempt. She enters
into Knightly's disapprobation and into his judgment. There is the added irony
of Emma having committed the same error for which she held Miss Bates in
contempt: self-indulgently saying more than she should have done and producing thereby an effect she did not intend to create. That Emma was motivated by
contempt makes this more contemptible rather than less. Her distress is very
convincing.

Hume points out that excessive conceit on an individual's part causes
uneasiness in everyone else, especially as that conceit presents observers with a
disagreeable comparison in which they come out the losers. After all, ''tis our
own pride, which makes us so much displeas'd with the pride of other people;

and that vanity becomes insupportable to us merely because we are vain'.[47] When we look for a demonstration of this in Austen, there is no dearth of examples. For instance, Darcy 'was looked at with great admiration for about half the evening, till his manners gave a disgust which turned the tide of his popularity; for he was discovered to be proud, to be above his company, and above being pleased; and not all his large estate in Derbyshire could then save him from having a most forbidding, disagreeable countenance, and being unworthy to be compared with his friend'.[48] It is Elizabeth's injured pride, ably assisted by Wickham's lies, that leads to her initial unflattering and inaccurate assessment of Darcy's character. Indeed, Elizabeth's pride is injured by the pride of Darcy, who at first considers her to be beneath his notice. When various false allegations concerning Darcy are exposed for what they are, Elizabeth realizes that she has laboured under a misapprehension. She blames her vanity, and overconfidence in her own abilities, for that mistaken assessment:

> I, who have valued myself on my abilities! who have ... gratified my vanity, in useless or blameable distrust. – How humiliating is this discovery! – Yet, how just a humiliation! – Had I been in love, I could not have been more wretchedly blind. But vanity, not love, has been my folly. – Pleased with the preference of one, and offended by the neglect of the other, on the very beginning of our acquaintance, I have courted prepossession and ignorance, and driven reason away, where either were concerned. Till this moment, I never knew myself.[49]

Unjustified contempt for others is also often tied to the kind of pride that is accompanied by insolence or arrogance. Characters exhibiting these traits emerge repeatedly in Austen. *Emma*'s Mr Weston says of Mrs Churchill that 'her pride is arrogance and insolence', a description that also applies to Lady Catherine de Bourgh of *Pride and Prejudice*.[50] Frank Churchill speaks of the Eltons' 'insolence of imaginary superiority' when he considers the air of familiarity they adopt with Jane Fairfax.[51] Catherine Morland reflects on the fact that there is no 'apology that could atone for the abruptness, the rudeness, nay, the insolence of' General Tilney's behavior in summarily dismissing her from Northanger.[52] Mrs Ferrars's 'cold insolence' toward Elinor distresses Marianne, who knows that it is prompted by a resistance toward a match between Elinor and Edward Ferrars.[53] Emma Woodhouse reflects in regret on her own overestimation of her abilities and on what she terms arrogance: 'With insufferable vanity had she believed herself in the secret of every body's feelings; with unpardonable arrogance proposed to arrange every body's destiny'.[54]

It should be remembered that, according to both Hume and Austen, one may take pride in one's possessions as well as one's personal merits and accomplishments (real or imagined). External objects acquire a relation to ourselves, Hume indicates, and the 'same object causes a greater or smaller degree of pride, not only in proportion to the encrease or decrease of its qualities, but also to the distance or nearness of the relation'.[55] We can, in fact, be vain of any object that bears a relation to us. And if the ownership of anything that gives pleasure by its utility, its beauty or its novelty can produce pride, then the *power* or means to acquire those things – namely wealth – should give rise to pride as well.[56] Hume also reflects on pride in wealth and rank, and the kind of economic and class snobbery that go with them: 'As we are proud of riches in ourselves', says Hume,

> so to satisfy our vanity we desire that every one, who has any connexion with us, shou'd likewise be possest of them, and are asham'd of any one that is mean or poor among our friends and relations. For this reason we remove the poor as far from us as possible; and as we cannot prevent poverty in some distant collaterals, and our fore-fathers are taken to be our nearest relations; upon this account every one affects to be of a good family, and to be descended from a long succession of rich and honourable ancestors.[57]

Consider, against this backdrop, Sir Walter Elliot's outrage at Anne's choosing to spend the evening with her old schoolfellow Mrs Smith instead of joining the family in their attentions to Lady Dalrymple:

> and who is Miss Anne Elliot to be visiting in Westgate Buildings? – A Mrs. Smith. A widow Mrs. Smith. And who was her husband? One of the five thousand Mr. Smiths whose names are to be met with everywhere. And what is her attraction? That she is old and sickly. – Upon my word, Miss Anne Elliot, you have the most extraordinary taste! Everything that revolts other people, low company, paltry rooms ... disgusting associations are inviting to you ... A poor widow, barely able to live, between thirty and forty – a mere Mrs. Smith, an everyday Mrs. Smith, of all people and all names in the world, to be the chosen friend of Miss Anne Elliot, and to be preferred by her to her own family connections among the nobility of England and Ireland![58]

A less subtle example of precisely the species of vanity that Hume describes is to be found in the boasting of *Northanger Abbey*'s repellent John Thorpe. Flattered by General Tilney's request for information about Catherine Morland and her family, and laboring under the conviction that Catherine will accept his proposals and his sister those of Catherine's brother, Thorpe's

> vanity induced him to represent the family as yet more wealthy than his vanity and avarice had made him believe them. With whomsoever he was, or was likely to be connected, his own consequence always required that theirs should be great, and as his intimacy with any acquaintance grew, so regularly grew their fortune. The expectations of his friend Morland, therefore, from the first overrated, had ever since his introduction to Isabella been gradually increasing; and by merely adding twice as much for the grandeur of the moment, by doubling what he chose to think the amount of Mr Morland's preferment, trebling his private fortune, bestowing a rich aunt, and sinking half the children, he was able to represent the whole family to the general in a most respectable light. For Catherine, however, the peculiar object of the

general's curiosity, and his own speculations, he had yet something more in reserve, and the ten or fifteen thousand pounds which her father could give her would be a pretty addition to Mr Allen's estate.[59]

The severance of Thorpe's connection with the Morlands has exactly the reverse effect on their fortunes. Once Thorpe has been roundly rejected, he informs the General that the family is necessitous, 'numerous too almost beyond example; by no means respected in their own neighborhood ... aiming at a style of life which their fortune could not warrant; seeking to better themselves by wealthy connections; a forward, bragging, scheming race'.[60]

What will constitute wealth or plenty for a given person is determined by comparison, according to Hume.

> What is an immense fortune for a private gentleman is beggary for a prince. A peasant wou'd think himself happy in what cannot afford necessaries for a gentleman. When a man has either been acustom'd to a more splendid way of living, or thinks himself intitled to it by his birth and quality, every thing below is disagreeable and even shameful.[61]

None illustrate this better than the disinclinations of Sir Walter Elliot and his daughter Elizabeth to restrain their expenditures, even though they have been living beyond their means for years:

> The Kellynch property was good, but not equal to Sir Walter's apprehension of the state required in its possessor', and they search in vain for any prospect 'of lessening their expenses without compromising their dignity, or relinquishing their comforts in a way not to be borne ... There was only a small part of his estate that Sir Walter could dispose of; but had every acre been alienable, it would have made no difference. He had condescended to mortgage as far as he had the power, but he would never condescend to sell. No; he would never disgrace his name so far.[62]

To curtail lavish living entails a loss of dignity and pride, something that failing to pay one's debts apparently does not. Hume points out that

> Every thing belonging to a vain man is the best that is any where to be found. His houses, equipage, furniture, cloaths, horses, hounds, excel all others in his conceit; and 'tis easy to observe, that from the least advantage in any of these, he draws a new subject of pride and vanity. His wine, if you'll believe him, has a finer flavour than any other; his cookery is more exquisite; his table more orderly; his servants more expert; the air, in which he lives, more healthful; the soil he cultivates more fertile; his fruits ripen earlier and to greater perfection.[63]

Compare to this the professions of Anne Elliot's father and sister as they welcome her to their lodgings in Bath: 'Their house was undoubtedly the best in Camden Place; their drawing-rooms had many decided advantages over all the others which they had either seen or heard of; and the superiority was not less in the style of fitting up, or the taste of the furniture'.[64]

One final example involves a connection that might be found between pride and indolence. Indolence itself might become an object of pride, for instance. Someone could have been a contender, his friends might claim on his behalf, were it not for his dislike of business or his lack of personal ambition. 'And this a man sometimes may make even a subject of vanity; tho' with the air of confessing a fault: Because he may think, that his incapacity for business implies much more noble qualities; such as a philosophical spirit, a fine taste, a delicate wit, or a relish for pleasure and society'.[65] A similar reversal occurs in *Pride and Prejudice*. Bingley is a sloppy, impatient correspondent: 'he leaves out half his words and blots the rest'. He assumes an attitude of humility and, very much with the air of confessing a fault, agrees that his letters seldom convey any ideas at all to his correspondents. He explains, however, that this failure is due to the fact that his ideas flow so rapidly. Darcy takes issue with this:

> Nothing is more deceitful ... than the appearance of humility. It is often only ... an indirect boast ... you are really proud of your defects in writing, because you consider them as proceeding from a rapidity of thought and carelessness of execution, which if not estimable, you think at least highly interesting. The power of doing any thing with quickness is always much prized by the possessor, and often without any attention to the imperfection of the performance.[66]

A flaw which ought to inspire humility is, by means of an air of humility, neatly converted into a subject of vanity. The preceding examples demonstrate, like thought experiments, Hume's stipulation that the contrary passions of pride and humility have the same object, the self, and that 'according as our idea of ourself is more or less advantageous, we feel either of those opposite affections, and are elated by pride or dejected with humility'.[67] When an apparent incapacity (to write coherently, or to bring oneself to attend to business) is presumed a symptom of 'valuable qualities of the mind', humility is transformed into pride. Interestingly, the mental qualities in question are the kinds of intellectual traits that resist a concrete demonstration which would require effort of their possessor, whereas the flaws that are conveniently taken to signal their existence require just such an effort for their rectification.

The examples presented by Austen demonstrate Hume's analysis of the indirect passions; they may thus be thought to provide the kind of conceptual clarification typically associated with thought experiments. First, a quality, which is given a positive or negative valence, inheres in a subject associated with the self, for the self is always the object of pride or humility. Qualities such as 'a philosophical spirit' or 'fine taste' or 'rapidity of thought' have a positive valence. When associated with the self, they give rise to pride, just as they can give rise to love when associated with another, when that other person is the object of emotion. The test cases show us how a shift from a negative to a positive valence in the quality associated with the self (a shift away from the negatively valenced qualities of sloppiness and laziness to positively valenced intellectual qualities) necessitates a shift in the passion that is felt, a shift from humility to pride. Strictly speaking, it is not that individuals can be proud of what they perceive as flaws, but rather that they mine the flaws for evidence of estimable traits (with what commitment to accuracy, we should not inquire too closely), without the idea of which pride would not be possible.

8 HUME, RELIGION, LITERARY FORM: *DIALOGUES CONCERNING NATURAL RELIGION*

John Richetti

Completed in 1751 and read in manuscript in the early 1750s by friends, Hume's *Dialogues Concerning Natural Religion* was not published until three years after his death, in 1779.[1] Hume's friends had advised him not to publish during his lifetime, and he clearly saw the wisdom of not confirming the suspicions of a public that regarded him as a dangerous infidel, even if the opinions in the *Dialogues* could readily be found in his earlier works. Nonetheless, as J. C. A. Gaskin notes, Hume revised the manuscript in 1761 and again in 1776, making two fair copies of the revised work and telling Adam Smith in a letter that he intended to publish the *Dialogues* if he lived a few years longer.[2] Although he did not mention it in the short autobiographical piece he wrote just before his death, 'My Own Life', Hume clearly thought of the *Dialogues* as among his best works.[3] Indeed, he wrote to Adam Smith 'that nothing can be more cautiously and more artfully written'.[4]

During the composition of the first version of the *Dialogues* in March 1751 Hume outlined to his friend Gilbert Elliot his approach to the crucial generic problem inherent to the philosophical dialogue. Hume's aim was to avoid the 'vulgar Error ... of putting nothing but Nonsense into the Mouth of the Adversary'.[5] Oddly, having claimed that he has made Cleanthes (the more or less anthropomorphic theist) the 'Hero' of the dialogues, he appealed to Elliot for material to strengthen 'that Side of the Argument'. He also admitted that his propensity for the anti-theist position, 'to the other Side, crept in upon me against my Will' and recalled his recent burning of a manuscript he wrote in his teens in which he attempted to 'confirm the common Opinion' about religion but found that doubts kept stealing in upon him in a 'perpetual Struggle of a restless Imagination against Inclination, perhaps against Reason'.[6] Had he and Elliot been neighbours, says Hume, they might have enacted the dialogue, with Elliot as Cleanthes and Hume playing Philo (the sceptic), a part he 'coud have supported naturally enough'.[7]

Three related issues come into play in this letter that help to contextualize the *Dialogues* as part of Hume's approach to the vexed question of natural (as opposed to revealed) religion. He is concerned, first of all, to take 'dialogue' seriously as a staging of competitive positions rather than using it as a means or mere assertion or polemic. As Norman Kemp Smith put it, Hume worked to maintain genuine dramatic balance by giving Demea and especially Cleanthes a larger share of the argument than one might have supposed, thus keeping up the reader's respect for Cleanthes, whose views are never completely rejected: 'a chief danger against which he had to guard was lest his argument should become so one-sided that the dramatic interest of the *Dialogues* would be destroyed'.[8] Such literary finesse reflects Hume's guiding stylistic programme in his career as a mature writer in which he sought to persuade and delight as much as to convince (a key distinction that I hope in what follows to emphasize), to function as an orator and moral essayist as well as a philosopher.[9] Secondly, that drive to generic propriety is for Hume a means of taming or at least refining his own radical religious scepticism by objectifying it within the dramatic structure of a purified philosophical dialogue. Thirdly, in his invitation to Elliot not only to play the role of Cleanthes but to participate in making the intellectual conception of that character more coherent, Hume places his philosophical project within a social and collegial relationship in which Elliot will as Cleanthes help to make 'formal & regular' the moderate theistic anthropomorphic argument to which the mind has a natural 'Propensity'. Such friendship has for Hume the highest moral value, and philosophical discussion like the *Dialogues* is the perfect opportunity for expressing it. As Hume tells Elliot, for the 'Antients ... If a Man made Profession of Philosophy, whatever his Sect was, they always expected to find more Regularity in his Life and Manners, than in those of the ignorant & illiterate'.[10] W. B. Carnochan has gone so far as to propose that the *Dialogues* are essentially a dramatization of the 'overriding Ciceronian virtue of friendship' (in philosophical inquiry) between Philo and Cleanthes, and he reads the work as a comic dramatization of their alliance against the dogmatic fideist Demea. The *Dialogues*, says Carnochan, are a dramatic enactment of 'the social order of friendship that merges with the discursive commentary on natural religion'.[11] That is I think exactly right, although if one follows the dramatic plot of the *Dialogues* to the bitter end, some serious qualifications of that 'friendship' are in order.

Reacting to Carnochan's (and a 'host of recent commentators') highlighting of the neglected 'rhetorical, dramatic, or literary qualities of the *Dialogues*', Michael B. Prince has argued strongly that Hume's prime purpose was to attack rational theism and by extension Christianity, and that the *Dialogues* have a clear philosophical and polemical point. Noting Shaftesbury's and Berkeley's use of the dialogue to defend religion wherein an initial conflict of opinions were made to yield a consensus among the participants, Prince's thesis is that in Hume the *'failure* to achieve consensus dramatized the deeper structural fallacies of natural religion'.[12] Hume was out to expose 'the vacuity of the dominant argument for the writing of dialogue within a religious context', and his explication of the *Dialogues* seeks to show that they reveal the irrelevance of rational inquiry to religion.[13] Prince makes a convincing case, and he avoids the approach of philosophical and historical commentators who treat the ideas in the *Dialogues* apart from their dramatic and literary articulation. Carnochan and other literary commentators on the *Dialogues* also point to rhetorical instabilities and ironic flourishes that create dramatic tension in the work and take readers beyond the mid-eighteenth-century debate about natural religion.[14] Literary approaches show that the *Dialogues* is not so much a (deliberately) failed philosophical dialogue as Prince would have it but a return of the genre to its proper dimensions as Hume understood them. To put this another way, Hume dramatizes not only how theistical arguments, both *a priori* and *a posteriori*, wilt in the face of (Humean) rational examination, but also how in the dramatic give and take of the *Dialogues* such beliefs reveal their (entertaining) plausibility when defended by an articulate and intelligent proponent like Cleanthes.

Hume makes his accusation against modern philosophical dialogues as vulgar polemic not only in the letter to Gilbert Elliot but at the opening of the *Dialogues*. Pamphilus declares in the introductory letter to Hermippus the rather combative opinion, ignoring (or disparaging) Shaftestbury's, Berkeley's and Mandeville's efforts in the genre, that modern philosophical dialogues have not succeeded: 'though the ancient philosophers conveyed most of their instruction in the form of dialogue, this method of composition has been little practised in later ages, and has seldom succeeded in the hands of those who have attempted it'.[15] In seeking to avoid the author/reader relationship natural to systematic philosophy, 'to give a freer air to his performance', the writer of philosophical dialogue, says Pamphilus, blunders into an even worse relationship: *'pedagogue* and *pupil*'.[16] And even if he avoids this didactic heaviness and implicitly coercive relationship, there is still a loss in the lively articulations of dialogue represented 'in the natural spirit of good company' with the 'proper balance among the speakers', since achieving these graces involves sacrificing 'order, brevity, and precision'.[17] Why then write philosophical dialogues at all? Because, says Pamphilus, 'There are some subjects ... to which dialogue-writing is peculiarly adapted, and where it is still preferable to the direct and simple method of composition'.[18] Accordingly, Pamphilus outlines two kinds of topics and gives distinct reasons why the dialogue form is desirable and indeed superior to 'the direct and simple method'. 'Obvious' topics that are not disputable but happen to be 'so *important*' that they cannot be too often treated are one kind, and, contrariwise, so too is any topic that is 'so *obscure* and *uncertain*, that human reason can reach no fixed determination with regard to it; if it should be treated at all, seems to lead us naturally into the style of dialogue and conversation'.[19] In the case of 'NATU-RAL RELIGION', he continues, both of these circumstances apply.

Pamphilus's rhetoric in these pages is remarkable in its slippery good humour and latent irony, and these smooth and silky tones anticipate in their distinct ways the approaches that Cleanthes and Philo take in the dialogue proper.

> What truth so obvious, so certain, as the being of a God, which the most ignorant ages have acknowledged, for which the most refined geniuses have ambitiously striven to produce new proofs and arguments? What truth so important as this, which is the ground of all our hopes, the surest foundation of morality, the firmest support of society, and the only principle which ought never to be a moment absent from our thoughts and meditations?[20]

At the same time that Pamphilus articulates these pious truisms (which as rhetorical questions can easily come under the sign of irony once the reader enters the *Dialogues* proper), he follows with the paradox that discussing the obvious truths of natural religion leads, logically, to the darkest obscurity. God exists, of course, but just what is the deity like? he asks in the same calm voice, carrying on in the same truistic spirit – precisely what a theist is not really prepared to grant – that the very process of articulating the obvious and morally and socially beneficial existence of the deity raises or highlights the vexed question of his nature: 'in treating of this obvious and important truth, what obscure questions occur concerning the nature of that Divine Being, his attributes, his decrees, his plan of providence? These have been always subjected to the disputations of men; concerning these human reason has not reached any certain determination.'[21] Philosophical dialogue that rehearses the 'obvious' natural proofs of God's existence, thereby promoting social and moral good, is the cause, it seems, of a crucial, indeed a radical, awareness of doubt about his nature and being, so that the assumption with which the *Dialogues* ostensibly begin that he exists is in fact undermined in the course of things.

Given this perplexity that philosophical dialogue about natural religion is bound to provoke, the question remains, why then enter into such discussions? Pamphilus's answer evokes the inevitability of philosophical inquiry for certain individuals: 'these are topics so interesting, that we cannot restrain our restless inquiry with regard to them; though nothing but doubt, uncertainty, and contradiction, have as yet been the result of our most accurate researches.'[22] That implicit satisfaction in disrupting the calm belief in a deity with these dark uncertainties anticipates the paradoxical intellectual pleasures of the dialogues to follow. Philosophy is characterized as an intellectual compulsion to grapple with the unknown, yet the word 'interesting' suggests a social pleasure and solidarity in thinking and discussing that tends to cancel the horror of 'doubt, uncertainty, and contradiction'. As the *OED* notes, 'interesting' in the mid-eighteenth century hovered between its now obsolete meaning of that which 'concerns, touches, affects, or is of importance', and the still current meaning, 'having the qualities which rouse curiosity, engage attention, or appeal to the emotions'. For Hume (and for Philo), questions surrounding natural religion have the latter emphasis (in their perennial inevitability they induce fascination and pleasurable speculation), while for Demea and to a lesser extent for Cleanthes it is the former set of meanings or personal implications (the existence of God is for them more than an 'interesting' issue and is rather a personal and urgent matter) that impels them in the *Dialogues*.

But there are moments in the *Dialogues* when Cleanthes seems to share in the philosophical pleasure of theistic speculation, when, despite his disagreements with him and his anti-theistic arguments, what he calls Philo's 'suppositions' strike him 'with no horror', which is an intimate putdown of what Philo expects to be shocking. He enjoys and even admires Philo's 'rambling way' and declares that his arguments give him 'pleasure', since they show 'that by the utmost indulgence of your imagination, you never get rid of the hypothesis of design in the universe, but are obliged at every turn to have recourse to it'.[23] Cleanthes from time to time shows that he appreciates the special qualities of Philo's intellectual pugnacity. For example, in Part IX after Demea tries to insist on a return to the *a priori* proof for God's existence, Cleanthes beats Philo to the punch, testifying to his delight in his opponent's alertness and eagerness for the fight: 'I shall not leave it to PHILO, said CLEANTHES, though I know that the starting objections is his chief delight, to point out the weakness of this metaphysical reasoning'.[24] For Philo the pleasures of the debate are less qualified, since he is attracted to the 'interesting' arguments surrounding the existence of the deity by virtue of his character as a thoughtful philosopher who also enjoys the play of ideas. His eagerness for debate is a recurring note; in the very last part he is still enjoying himself, indeed defining himself precisely as someone who takes pleasure in establishing truth and driving out superstition, even it means violating certain intellectual decorums: 'in proportion to my veneration for true religion, is my abhorrence of vulgar superstitions; and I indulge a peculiar pleasure, I confess, in pushing such principles, sometimes into absurdity, sometimes into impiety'.[25] And as the *Dialogues* proceed the attraction seems to be complemented by his engagement with the social and moral implications of theism, his emotional opposition to belief in a creator deity who has (if he exists) made a very bad job of things. In the very end, Philo too acquires a personal even urgent 'interest' in the issues; one of the startling qualities of Hume's dramatic development of this character is this transition from cool detachment to intense, even passionate involvement in the moral importance of the question of the existence of God. Such involvement is a sign of Hume's dramatic distance from Philo, who becomes far more intense and committed than Hume was in life.

Demea opens Part I of the *Dialogues* by observing that in educating his children he has avoided or postponed exposing them to 'the science of natural theology' and instead has striven to 'season their minds with early piety' and by his own example to 'imprint deeply on their tender minds an habitual reverence for all the principles of religion'.[26] He adds that in their education he has stressed 'the eternal disputations of men; the obscurity of all philosophy; and the strange, ridiculous conclusions, which some of the greatest geniuses have derived from the principles of mere human reason'.[27] Philo applauds these sentiments and launches into an eloquent extension of Demea's suspicion of human reason:

> Let Demea's principles be improved and cultivated: Let us become thoroughly sensible of the weakness, blindness, and narrow limits of human reason: Let us duly consider its uncertainty and endless contrarieties, even in subjects of common life and practice: Let the errors and deceits of our very senses be set before us; the insuperable difficulties which attend first principles in all systems; the contradictions which adhere to the very ideas of matter, cause and effect, extension, space, time, motion; and in a word, quantity of all kinds, the object of the only science that can fairly pretend to any certainty or evidence. When these topics are displayed in their full light, as they are by some philosophers and almost all divines; who can retain such confidence in this frail faculty of reason as to pay any regard to its determinations in points so sublime, so abstruse, so remote from common life and experience?[28]

Pamphilus notes at the end of Philo's disparagement of reason 'a smile in the countenances both of DEMEA and CLEANTHES' but where Demea's looks indicate 'unreserved satisfaction in the doctrines delivered', Cleanthes displays in his features 'an air of finesse; as if he perceived some raillery or artificial malice in the reasonings of PHILO'.[29] As Carnochan puts it, Philo and Cleanthes are clearly 'in league' and in Philo's opening speech 'the plot has been opened up for anyone with eyes to see'. Carnochan adds that every word in this speech is 'double-edged', and he's right.[30] But despite its archness, Philo's scepticism is authentically Humean, and Philo will argue often enough in the *Dialogues* using just these terms with unqualified urgency. In addition to the plot against Demea, the larger joke is that in the discussions that follow such scepticism will be employed not to buttress Demea's fideism but to exploit it in order to further Philo's demolition of the theistic positions that Cleanthes occupies.

This opening part establishes precisely the playful sparring of the two well-matched debaters. Shrewdly, Cleanthes sees Philo's endorsement of scepticism as tactical and offers a joke about the distance between theory and practice: 'Whether your scepticism be as absolute and sincere as you pretend, we shall learn by and by, when the company breaks up: We shall then see, whether you go out at the door or the window; and whether you really doubt if your body has gravity, or can be injured by its fall; according to popular opinion, derived from our fallacious senses, and more fallacious experience'.[31] In his philosophical distrust of total scepticism, Cleanthes is echoing Hume's own position as expressed in his *Enquiries*.[32] So, too, in Cleanthes's joke that follows about Pyrrhonian sceptics and Stoic philosophers, 'both of them seem founded on this erroneous maxim, That what a man can perform sometimes, and in some dispositions, he can perform always, and in every disposition', he is introducing that delicious Humean (and British Augustan) theme that philosophical 'enthusiasm' or absolutism subsides eventually and often enough collapses comically under the pressure of common life: 'But how shall he support this enthusiasm itself? The bent of his mind relaxes, and cannot be recalled at pleasure; avocations lead him astray; misfortunes attack him unawares; and the philosopher sinks by degrees into the plebeian.'[33] Such Humean tendencies have led some commentators over the years to identify Cleanthes with Hume. But these intellectual resemblances are part of the attempt to make the *Dialogues* a fair fight. Here in the opening section Cleanthes's attack on scepticism provokes Philo's agreement in general terms: 'To whatever length any one may push his speculative principles of scepticism, he must act, I own, and live, and converse, like other men; and for this conduct he is not obliged to give any other reason, than the absolute necessity he lies under of so doing'.[34] But this is followed by a spirited defence of the sceptical turn of mind as wholly appropriate to 'theological reasonings', where we are 'like foreigners in a strange country, to whom every thing must seem suspicious'.[35] Cleanthes, in response, gives as good as he gets, sharply observing that we accept Newton's analysis of light and Copernicus's and Galileo's astronomical discoveries and do we say that 'these subjects were too magnificent and remote to be explained by the narrow and fallacious reason of mankind?'[36] And Cleanthes shows in this opening part that he is capable not simply of strong reasoning but of playing to the reader, as it were, shifting the discourse to self-expressiveness and competitive dialogue:

> Our senses, you say, are fallacious; our understanding erroneous; our ideas, even of the most familiar objects, extension, duration, motion, full of absurdities and contradictions. You defy me to solve the difficulties, or reconcile the repugnancies which you discover in them. I have not capacity for so great an undertaking: I have not leisure for it: I perceive it to be superfluous. Your own conduct, in every circumstance, refutes your principles, and shows the firmest reliance on all the received maxims of science, morals, prudence, and behaviour.[37]

So Part I of the *Dialogues* initiates the special balance in them between rational disputation and self-expressive or even self-dramatizing discourse in which Philo and Cleanthes understand each other perfectly and precisely and speak not just to each other and to Demea and Pamphilus but to that larger audience of read-

ers. At the opening of Part II, Demea, the naive and impatient theist, the butt
in Carnochan's reading of the joke concocted by Philo and Cleanthes, declares
that in fact the nature of God is 'from the infirmities of human understanding ... incomprehensible and unknown to us'.[38] Demea has been scandalized by
Cleanthes's moderate rationalism, in response to Philo's historical survey of the
decline of superstition and the rise of sceptical reason, so that as Cleanthes avers
'If we distrust human reason, we have now no other principle to lead us into
religion'.[39] In what follows closely in Part II, Cleanthes reacts calmly to Philo's
sceptical questioning of the argument from Design (*a posteriori*), provoking even
greater alarm and recriminations from Demea: 'Good God! cried Demea, interrupting him, where are we? Zealous defenders of religion allow, that the proofs
of a Deity fall short of perfect evidence! And you, Philo, on whose assistance I
depended in proving the adorable mysteriousness of the Divine Nature, do you
assent to all these extravagant opinions of Cleanthes?'[40] Demea takes no pleasure, in short, in the playful essence of philosophical dialogue as conducted here
by the other two participants, and Pamphilus's characterization of the discussion
as 'interesting' (in the second sense of arousing curiosity) is lost on him.

In an important sense elided by purely philosophical commentators, Philo
and Cleanthes are entertaining one another with their arguments in the early
parts of the *Dialogues*, which are serious but also playful, to some extent tactical rather than fixed or final, part of what seems a friendly agon. Pamphilus
notes at one point near the end of Part II that Philo's 'vehement manner' is
located as it seems to him 'somewhat between jest and earnest'.[41] Absolute truth
or certainty is implicitly suspended through tone, although Demea's dogmatic
impatience points us to the tentative and exploratory quality of the main lines of
the dialogues. One recurring sentiment, in fact, is that these exchanges are not
'disputation in the schools', the absurd and egomaniacal wranglings of clerical
Medieval philosophers, but civilized and secular discussions like those in Cicero's philosophical dialogues.[42] Moreover, Pamphilus's awareness of the complex
quality of Philo's manner of presentation shows that Hume aspires to turn the
dialogue toward dramatic utterance, to alert the reader to these tonal and situ-
ational qualities of the discourse. Of course, Demea's blustering is part of that
performativity, and as Carnochan has shown a crucial part of the comic plot of
the *Dialogues*.

I want to propose, however, a plot that slides from this easygoing comedy
to a darker and more consequential development in the final parts that is more
comprehensive than Carnochan's and that may be said to drive the *Dialogues*, to
provide the rhetorical impetus and persuasive force that make them more than
simply a series of arguments for or against natural religion. In the to and fro of the
Dialogues, Philo may be said to look for a way not actually to convince Cleanthes
and to make him change his mind (that's not really possible as Hume sets things

up; Cleanthes is too smart, too confident in his own position) and perhaps not even to convince but to please his other audience, the reader, and thereby for the moment at least to persuade the reader (not just the silent and neutral auditor, Pamphilus) by what are essentially rhetorical means of the absurdity and inconsistency of rational or natural religion. To do that Hume arranges opportunities to dramatize not just arguments as such but Philo's mode of thinking in framing or arriving at those arguments. Between Philo and Cleanthes, let us say, the issue is almost at first a matter of form: how each presents the issues rather than what is being argued. Cleanthes himself regularly admires Philo's impressive rhetorical skill, concedes that he is 'puzzled' and to that extent temporarily persuaded but of course not convinced by his 'fertility of invention'.[43] He admits all this at the very end of Part VII:

> I must confess, PHILO, replied CLEANTHES, that of all men living, the task which you have undertaken, of raising doubts and objections, suits you best, and seems, in a manner, natural and unavoidable to you. So great is your fertility of invention, that I am not ashamed to acknowledge myself unable, on a sudden, to solve regularly such out-of-the-way difficulties as you incessantly start upon me: though I clearly see, in general, their fallacy and error. And I question not, but you are yourself, at present, in the same case, and have not the solution so ready as the objection: while you must be sensible, that common sense and reason are entirely against you; and that such whimsies as you have delivered, may puzzle, but never can convince us.[44]

Cleanthes's praise is to some extent ironic, a concession but also a complaint. Philo is skilled, he says, at raising doubts, and his arguments are specious and clever rather than convincing. Cleanthes's accusation that Philo's objections to theism are 'whimsies' marks them as essentially for him rhetorical rather than substantive. But earlier we have seen Cleanthes himself succumb to rhetoric, making propositions designed to dramatize and persuade rather than to induce conviction. For one example that resembles his refusal in Part I to succumb to scepticism, consider his complaint to Philo in Part IV that his method of reasoning is extreme, demanding knowledge of final causes that is simply not available. The end of his response is oratorical rather than argumentative, a fairly desperate challenge and rational withdrawal, a declaration of personal certainty, of hope against hope with no firm basis in the argument.

> You alone, or almost alone, disturb this general harmony. You start abstruse doubts, cavils, and objections: You ask me, what is the cause of this cause? I know not; I care not; that concerns not me. I have found a Deity; and here I stop my inquiry. Let those go further, who are wiser or more enterprising.[45]

What philosopher, asks Cleanthes, 'could possibly submit to so rigid a rule?'.[46]

The implicit joke is of course that David Hume is just that kind of philosopher. Philo's rigorous examination, before Cleanthes's outburst, paraphrases and

in the process literalizes what he calls Cleanthes's anthropomorphism: 'there is
no ground to suppose a plan of the world to be formed in the divine mind, consisting of distinct ideas, differently arranged, in the same manner as an architect
forms in his head the plan of a house which he intends to execute'.[47] Philo is
practicing a rigorous literalism that insists upon what he calls 'experience', which
teaches: that 'a mental world, or universe of ideas, requires a cause as much, as
does a material world, or universe of objects; and, if similar in its arrangement,
must require a similar cause'.[48] And then again, in other words, he issues the same
challenge to Cleanthes, what is the cause of that cause you call God?:

> How, therefore, shall we satisfy ourselves concerning the cause of that Being whom
> you suppose the Author of nature, or, according to your system of anthropomor-
> phism, the ideal world, into which you trace the material? Have we not the same
> reason to trace that ideal world into another ideal world, or new intelligent principle?
> But if we stop, and go no further; why go so far? why not stop at the material world?
> How can we satisfy ourselves without going on *in infinitum*? And, after all, what sat-
> isfaction is there in that infinite progression?[49]

Philo concludes this stage of the argument in Part IV with the charge that the
theistical claim that the order and proportion visible in the world are proof of a
divine rationality that created them is no more than circular reasoning or playing
with words, like saying that bread nourishes because it has a 'nutritive faculty'.
With mounting irony that looks back to philosophers' invocation of such '*faculties* or *occult qualities*', which was 'nothing but the disguise of ignorance', Philo
equates such mumbo jumbo with the anthropomorphites' leap from apparent
design to deity:

> It is only to say, that such is the nature of material objects, and that they are all origi-
> nally possessed of a faculty of order and proportion. These are only more learned
> and elaborate ways of confessing our ignorance; nor has the one hypothesis any real
> advantage above the other, except in its greater conformity to vulgar prejudices.[50]

Philo's literalism is grounded in his insistence on empirical rigour. When in Part
V he brings up the expanded order of the natural world, a 'new universe in miniature', that modern science has revealed, for example, by the microscope, he draws
the inference that 'the universal cause of All to be vastly different from mankind,
or from any object of human experience and observation'.[51] As Philo begins to
enumerate other discoveries in 'anatomy, chemistry, botany', Cleanthes interrupts,
with marked complacency that sits somewhat at variance with Philo's increasing intensity, that these scientific advances in our knowledge 'only discover new
instances of art and contrivance. It is still the image of mind reflected on us from
innumerable objects'.[52] Philo pounces on that assertion, and Cleanthes is equally
quick with his response: 'Add, a mind like the human, said PHILO. I know of
no other, replied CLEANTHES. And the liker the better, insisted PHILO. To

be sure, said CLEANTHES'.[53] Occasional stichomythic moments like this, it is worth noting, are what help to make the *Dialogues* effectively dramatic and debate-like, as each of the two main disputants acquire personalities and display emotion amid all their cerebration. There is a hint of bad temper and impatience, suddenly, in this bitten-off and curt exchange. Philo takes off, however, with a series of uninterrupted implications ('with an air of alacrity and triumph') that he says follow from Cleanthes's admission, which is within the range of empirical reality. Who, after all, knows any mind but a human one? That granted, then Cleanthes's position, Philo argues with great vigour and a hint of impatience, involves the logical impossibility of finding an infinite cause in a finite effect: 'as the cause ought only to be proportioned to the effect, and the effect, so far as it falls under our cognisance, is not infinite; what pretensions have we, upon your suppositions, to ascribe that attribute to the Divine Being?'[54]

Philo's extrapolations here at the end of Part V from what he takes to be Cleanthes's steadfast adherence to the design argument are deliberately outrageous, one *reductio ad absurdum* after another. If we judge by analogy, as Philo says we have no other way of proceeding in Cleanthes's frame of arguing, then a deity who made the universe may resemble, say, the maker of a ship, 'so complicated, useful, and beautiful a machine', whom if we question we may find 'a stupid mechanic, who imitated others, and copied an art' that has been perfected 'through a long succession of ages'.[55] Worth noting here, by the way, is the class bias built into these dialogues: the elegant leisure (in Cleanthes's library) and cultural privilege the participants possess are made at times explicit. For example, in Part V, Philo wonders about the implicit metaphor Cleanthes invokes of God as a 'perfect author' of the universe, and he asks how we are to read his works since we lack knowledge of the literary system and values by which such an author can be said to operate. In this position, he argues with great wit but unsettling social hauteur that we are in the position of an untrained reader: 'you must acknowledge, that it is impossible for us to tell, from our limited views, whether this system contains any great faults, or deserves any considerable praise, if compared to other possible, and even real systems. Could a peasant, if the Aeneid were read to him, pronounce that poem to be absolutely faultless, or even assign to it its proper rank among the productions of human wit, he, who had never seen any other production?'[56] There are no peasants or stupid mechanics in Cleanthes's library, although the 'vulgar' are invoked on occasion, and indeed one may say that the untutored perceptions of the vulgar are in the final analysis central to the empiricist analysis Philo pursues.

Maliciously, and indeed one can imagine for Demea blasphemously, Philo proposes at this same point in Part V as a thought experiment that there may have been any number of false starts in creation: 'Many worlds might have been botched and bungled, throughout an eternity, ere this system was struck out;

much labour lost, many fruitless trials made; and a slow, but continued improvement carried on during infinite ages in the art of world-making'.[57] Or even, as he continues and as he milks this gambit for all it is worth, there may have been several deities involved, just as it takes many men to build a ship or a house or a city. Or at the end of this mounting series of subversive although tongue-in-cheek speculations, Philo asks Cleanthes why he takes half measures, why not become a perfect anthropomorphite?

> Why not assert the deity or deities to be corporeal, and to have eyes, a nose, mouth, ears, &c.? EPICURUS maintained, that no man had ever seen reason but in a human figure; therefore the gods must have a human figure. And this argument, which is deservedly so much ridiculed by CICERO, becomes, according to you, solid and philosophical.[58]

As the *Dialogues* progress Philo becomes more and more rhetorically inventive and intellectually aggressive in this vein, but he argues as Part VIII begins in response to Cleanthes's complaint that what his opponent labels his 'fertility' is not something he has planned but is, rather, owing to 'the nature of the subject', which lies beyond the 'narrow compass of human reason':

> But in such questions as the present, a hundred contradictory views may preserve a kind of imperfect analogy; and invention has here full scope to exert itself. Without any great effort of thought, I believe that I could, in an instant, propose other systems of cosmogony, which would have some faint appearance of truth, though it is a thousand, a million to one, if either yours or any one of mine be the true system.[59]

So the various reductions to absurdity, the flights of fancy that Philo offers along with his philosophical arguments, he claims are merely the result of his opponent's theistic stance. He has been provoked by Cleanthes's arguments.

This is more than a bit disingenuous, and it seems to me that the gradually darkening plot of the *Dialogues* that I am in search of can be located exactly in this issue, in Philo's fertility and inventive extensions that add up to a rudely aggressive philosophic parody of his opponent's assumptions about the deity. As Norman Kemp Smith notes, Cleanthes is never definitively refuted, and his positions are always ably if not, for me and other Humean sympathizers, convincingly presented. Philo makes his points very strongly, but he is at times kept from being definitive by what Kemp Smith calls Hume's trick of making Philo speak 'on the necessary occasions somewhat irresponsibly, and so making it appropriate that Cleanthes should excuse himself from replying'.[60] To a significant extent, this imaginative verve represents a partial turning away from the properly dramatic or dialogical qualities of the *Dialogues* to a more monological effect. Philo moves from speaking to his interlocutors and engaging with their arguments to addressing an implied audience of readers. That is to say, Philo's mode of discourse inclines in the last few parts of the book to triumphalist satire and complacent moral essay rather than to philosophic argumentation per se, and I think it is safe to assume given what we know about Hume's aspirations in his mature work after *A Treatise of Human Nature* to reach a wide audience that the *Dialogues* is aimed at a broadly educated and thoughtful but not philosophically-defined readership. From philosopher, Philo edges into the postures of the man of letters. Looking back, in fact, to the opening of the *Dialogues* (and this may be the main generic problem in the philosophical dialogue), we can trace a tension in some large sense between arguing and responding to (and thereby respecting) your opponent and speaking in full oratorical or literary mode, self-expressively, aiming your discourse beyond or above your interlocutor (and we've seen that dual approach occasionally in both Philo and Cleanthes from the beginning of the *Dialogues*).

As it happens, of the three disputants Demea for all of his simple-mindedness is the one who at the opening of Part IX moves the discussion to a new stage as he wonders if given the 'many difficulties' that attend the argument for the existence of God *a posteriori* whether we should not 'better adhere to that simple and sublime argument *a priori*, which, by offering to us infallible demonstration, cuts off at once all doubt and difficulty?'.[61] Confused and frustrated by the drift of the discussion so far, Demea proposes a return to pure logic and more technical philosophical assertion. On its own terms, his protest is stated in purely ontological terms (what Cleanthes hastens to label derisively 'metaphysical reasoning'):

> Whatever exists must have a cause or reason of its existence; it being absolutely impossible for any thing to produce itself, or be the cause of its own existence. In mounting up, therefore, from effects to causes, we must either go on in tracing an infinite succession, without any ultimate cause at all; or must at last have recourse to some ultimate cause, that is necessarily existent.[62]

Cleanthes's quick response is very much in the Humean spirit, and indeed as Gaskin's note points out, the idea that 'nothing that is distinctly conceivable implies a contradiction' and whatever we can conceive as existing we can as easily conceive as non-existent echoes Hume's *Enquiry Concerning Human Understanding* in several places.[63] Cleanthes even goes so far in his rebuttal as to suggest the materialist dangers of the *a priori* argument: the 'necessarily existent Being' may just be the 'material universe' and just as we can imagine the non-existence of the material world 'the same argument extends equally to the Deity, so far as we have any conception of him; and that the mind can at least imagine him to be non-existent, or his attributes to be altered'.[64] Cleanthes's response is tightly and elegantly argued but of course necessarily abstract in the spirit of Demea's invocation of the argument *a priori*, so much so that Philo concludes Part IX by observing (the kiss of death for empirical philosophers) that such an argument has 'seldom been found very convincing, except to people of a metaphysical head, who have accustomed themselves to abstract reasoning'.[65] Even people disposed to theism, he adds, 'feel always some deficiency in such arguments, though they are not perhaps able to explain distinctly where it lies; a certain proof that men ever did, and ever will derive their religion from other sources than from this species of reasoning'.[66]

This concluding observation of Part IX sets the stage for the final three parts, which mark, I would argue, a transition from physico-theology and ontology to moral philosophy, from rigorous argumentation about whether the deity can be found in the order of the universe to meditations on the problem of evil that approach in Philo's hands a repudiation of any deity that could fashion such a misbegotten world. The result is almost a sort of negative theodicy as Philo moves from rigorous discussion to fairly repetitive reiteration of certain moral themes. This alteration in theme is also a transformation in style and a modification of the genre, from argumentative, fairly polite and pleasurable exchanges to moral assertion and satiric exposition that have a distinctly rough edge. One might almost read these last three parts of the *Dialogues* as articulating Hume's ultimate irony as the philosophical dialogue yields not to consensus but to reinforced and increasingly hardened and antagonistic affirmations of the disputants' original positions. Once again, it is Demea who for all his naiveté and inconsistency sets what turns out to be the tone of this part by his impulsive assertion. Provoked by the dismissal of his *a priori* reasoning in Part IX, he embraces the opposite and contradictory position. Or, rather, he undermines the whole principle of rational dialogue by invoking pure feeling. Sounding like the frightened primitives Hume evokes in *The Natural History of Religion*, he begins Part X by declaring that religion is man's response to human unhappiness and fear, stemming 'from a consciousness of his imbecility and misery, rather than from any reasoning, [man] is led to seek protection from that Being, on whom he and all nature is dependent'.[67]

Philo says as much at the beginning of Part X:

> I am indeed persuaded, said PHILO, that the best, and indeed the only method of bringing every one to a due sense of religion, is by just representations of the misery and wickedness of men. And for that purpose a talent of eloquence and strong imagery is more requisite than that of reasoning and argument. For is it necessary to prove what every one feels within himself? It is only necessary to make us feel it, if possible, more intimately and sensibly.[68]

This strikes me as not quite genuine, since in what follows Philo will represent not simply the misery and wickedness of men but offer a startling indictment of a natural order that depicts it in relentlessly pessimistic terms. One cannot help being struck by the change in emphasis from 'reasoning and argument' to 'eloquence and strong imagery', which comes across as almost a form of violence rather than philosophic interrogation and investigation. In the opening pages of Part X Philo and Demea trade eloquence and imagery with great energy and mounting intensity, surrendering the special contemplative perspective of philosophy for the agreement of the 'learned' and the 'vulgar', for who can doubt as Demea says 'of what all men declare from their own immediate feeling and experience'.[69] In these complementary exchanges between Philo and Demea, they vie with one another in the force of their dark pessimism, and Demea seems the warmer and more extreme:

> The whole earth, believe me, PHILO, is cursed and polluted. A perpetual war is kindled amongst all living creatures. Necessity, hunger, want, stimulate the strong and courageous: Fear, anxiety, terror, agitate the weak and infirm. The first entrance into life gives anguish to the new-born infant and to its wretched parent: Weakness, impotence, distress, attend each stage of that life: and it is at last finished in agony and horror.[70]

But Philo offers after this outburst from Demea a crucial qualification whereby it is not natural (dis)order that is the scandal but rather man's conjuring up of '*imaginary* enemies, the daemons of his fancy, who haunt him with superstitious terrors, and blast every enjoyment of life'.[71] Demea rushes to agree with Philo and in fact outdoes him in evoking human misery as a self-inflicted condition. He concludes in so sweeping a fashion that invades even the privileged sanctuary of the world of the *Dialogues* and suggests in its closing statement something like suicide as an option:

> Labour and poverty, so abhorred by every one, are the certain lot of the far greater number; and those few privileged persons, who enjoy ease and opulence, never reach contentment or true felicity. All the goods of life united would not make a very happy man; but all the ills united would make a wretch indeed; and any one of them almost (and who can be free from every one?) nay often the absence of one good (and who can possess all?) is sufficient to render life ineligible.[72]

These pages constitute a remarkable satiric panorama, a rhetorically powerful diatribe that is all the more significant for coming near the end of what had been a fairly decorous philosophical dialogue. This violent rhetoric may be said to infect this elegant scene with the virus of tragic everyday existence. As it turns out, however, these melodramatic reflections with their seeming abandonment of thoughtful discussion are a trap, and Demea is once again the unwitting tool of the clever Philo. Listening to this long exchange, Cleanthes's only contribution is a mild demurral: 'I can observe something like what you mention in some others, replied CLEANTHES: but I confess I feel little or nothing of it in myself, and hope that it is not so common as you represent it'.[73] But then Philo pounces, asking Cleanthes if after all these unchallenged 'reflections, and infinitely more which might be suggested', he can still persevere in his anthropormorphism.[74] The natural and the strictly human order, Philo says, reveals only an instinct for self-preservation, and the deity held responsible for this order is simply from this perspective an inscrutable monster. In perhaps his smoothest and most subversive moment, Philo admits that Cleanthes is right, that there is 'a purpose and intention to nature', but then he asks 'But what, I beseech you, is the object of that curious artifice and machinery, which she has displayed in all animals?'[75]

Cleanthes is at first amused by Philo's plot, still admiring the form of his discourse, his 'noble spirit of opposition and controversy':

> And have you at last, said CLEANTHES smiling, betrayed your intentions, PHILO? Your long agreement with DEMEA did indeed a little surprise me; but I find you were all the while erecting a concealed battery against me. And I must confess, that you have now fallen upon a subject worthy of your noble spirit of opposition and controversy. If you can make out the present point, and prove mankind to be unhappy or corrupted, there is an end at once of all religion. For to what purpose establish the natural attributes of the Deity, while the moral are still doubtful and uncertain?[76]

But when Demea, ever the blunt instrument, responds in self-satisfied and conventionally religious terms that these 'phenomena' that Cleanthes sees as destructive of the argument from design will be 'rectified in other regions, and in some future period of existence. And the eyes of men, being then opened to larger views of things, see the whole connection of general laws; and trace with adoration, the benevolence and rectitude of the Deity, through all the mazes and intricacies of his providence', Cleanthes rises for the first time in the *Dialogues* into an agitation close to anger: 'No! replied CLEANTHES, No! These arbitrary suppositions can never be admitted, contrary to matter of fact, visible and uncontroverted. Whence can any cause be known but from its known effects? Whence can any hypothesis be proved but from the apparent phenomena?'[77] Finally, in this most consequential and least leisurely of all the *Dialogues*, Philo responds and accuses Cleanthes of insisting against common experience that 'human happiness in this life, exceeds its misery' so that he is 'unawares introducing a total scepticism in to the most essential articles of natural and revealed theology'.[78] Philo presses here upon the ineradicable problem of evil, and his final speech in Part X concludes with a dramatic flourish: 'Here, CLEANTHES, I find myself at ease in my argument. Here I triumph', he declares.[79] But then in a winning nod to the athletic challenges of matching Cleanthes ('I needed all my sceptical and metaphysical subtility to elude your grasp') and to the seductive and apparent 'beauty and fitness of final causes', he rises reluctantly to a triumphant and unforgiving conclusion:

But there is no view of human life, or of the condition of mankind, from which, without the greatest violence, we can infer the moral attributes, or learn that infinite benevolence, conjoined with infinite power and infinite wisdom, which we must discover by the eyes of faith alone. It is your turn now to tug the labouring oar, and to support your philosophical subtleties against the dictates of plain reason and experience.[80]

This last sentence, Philo's challenge, is the culmination of what has become something of a shouting match. We are witnesses to a transformation in these pages of what had been a communal inquiry meant to give intellectual pleasure and to serve friendship into a bitter opposition that Philo polemically defines as between his 'reason and experience' and Cleanthes's 'philosophical subtleties'. Philo is playing to the crowd, those readers beyond the text and the scene, outside the boundaries of what had been a sedate dialogue, labelling Cleanthes as a proponent of what is clearly now bankrupt logic chopping and entrenched positioning in the face of the core values of empirical honesty. Part XI, therefore, is the most rancorous and unpleasant of the dialogues, as Cleanthes notes at the very beginning of Part XII, after Demea has left at the very end of Part XI. He observes, tactfully or perhaps just ruefully, that the decorum of the philosophical dialogue has been unbalanced by Demea's presence and by Philo's unscrupulous exploitation of Demea's impressionability:

> I should rather wish to reason with either of you apart on a subject so sublime and interesting. Your spirit of controversy, joined to your abhorrence of vulgar superstition, carries you strange lengths, when engaged in an argument; and there is nothing so sacred and venerable, even in your own eyes, which you spare on that occasion.[81]

But at the beginning of Part XI Cleanthes did attempt to answer Philo's challenge by retreating, perhaps too far. If we abandon all human analogy, he says, in imagining the deity, as Demea has proposed, then 'we abandon all religion'.[82] He offers as a surprising compromise, what he labels 'this new theory', that we suppose the

> Author of nature to be finitely perfect, though far exceeding mankind, a satisfactory account may then be given of natural and moral evil, and every untoward phenomenon be explained and adjusted. A less evil may then be chosen, in order to avoid a greater; inconveniences be submitted to, in order to reach a desirable end; and in a word, benevolence, regulated by wisdom, and limited by necessity, may produce just such a world as the present.[83]

In response to this sweetly reasonable statement, Philo delivers a mini treatise that stretches in the Oxford paperback edition of the *Dialogues* for a full uninterrupted nine pages, making good on Cleanthes's somewhat hostile characterization of him as one who is 'so prompt at starting views and reflections, and analogies'.[84] Philo's treatise is actually quite imaginative, beginning with a thought experiment, proposing a sort of Man from Mars visitor to earth, 'a very limited intelligence, whom we shall suppose utterly unacquainted with the universe'.[85] If we were to ask this being what a world would be like that had been created by 'a very good, wise, and powerful Being', Philo asserts that this being's idea of the world would be very different from what we experience.[86] Continue the experiment, says Philo, and bring this being to our earth with the continued assurance of the power and wisdom of the creator. Our stranger would be disappointed by what he found, 'but would never retract his former belief, if founded on any very solid argument; since such a limited intelligence must be sensible of his own blindness and ignorance, and must allow, that there may be many solutions of those phenomena, which will for ever escape his comprehension'.[87] And, finally, bring this visitor to earth leaving him 'to gather such a belief [in a wise and benevolent creator] from the appearances of things ... He may be fully convinced of the narrow limits of his understanding; but this will not help him in forming an inference concerning the goodness of superior powers, since he must form that inference from what he knows, not from what he is ignorant of'.[88]

The world as we experience it is such, Philo argues, that its phenomena 'can never afford us an inference concerning his ['such a Deity] existence'.[89] In one of the most stylish sentences in this stylish work, Philo sums things up with a flourish: 'We know so little beyond common life, or even of common life, that, with regard to the economy of a universe, there is no conjecture, however wild, which may not be just; nor any one, however plausible, which may not be erroneous', a sentence whose perfect paradoxical symmetries have a Johnsonian fullness and weight.[90] The rest of his speech reprises in systematic and amazingly confident (a believer would say presumptuous) terms the evocations of earthly imperfection and human misery that Philo and Demea combined to produce in Part X. Philo outlines '*four* circumstances, on which depend all ... that molest sensible creatures', adding that these circumstances, these sources of evil and mortal misery, are probably all 'necessary and unavoidable'.[91] These four circumstances add up to a high-spirited indictment of the botched and decidedly unsatisfactory creation, a theodicy in reverse: 1. why is pain and not simply a diminution of pleasure involved for all creatures 'in the great work of self-preservation'? Philo asks; it should be possible 'to carry on the business of life without any pain';[92] 2. the 'conducting of the world by general laws', he continues, is unnecessary for a perfect being, who might 'easily, by particular volitions, turn all these accidents to the good of mankind, and render the whole world happy, without discovering himself in any operation', and he insouciantly provides a few examples derived from the topoi of satire:[93]

A fleet, whose purposes were salutary to society, might always meet with a fair wind. Good princes enjoy sound health and long life. Persons born to power and authority, be framed with good tempers and virtuous dispositions ... Some small touches given to CALIGULA's brain in his infancy, might have converted him into a TRAJAN. One wave, a little higher than the rest, by burying CAESAR and his fortune in the bottom of the ocean, might have restored liberty to a considerable part of mankind;[94]

3. 'the great frugality with which all powers and faculties are distributed to every particular being', which is an index of an unimaginative creator who provides no more than is barely necessary for each creature to survive, and Philo adds for humans this frugality is especially debilitating because of the idleness, from which 'almost all the moral as well as natural evils of human life arise';[95] 4. the most damning inadequacy of all is 'the inaccurate workmanship of all the springs and principles of the great machine of nature', in which 'There is nothing so advantageous in the universe, but what frequently becomes pernicious, by its excess or defect; nor has Nature guarded, with the requisite accuracy, against all disorder or confusion'.[96] This last circumstance offers the greatest challenge to the design argument, and its sweeping negation will, in fact, be retracted by Philo in Part XII.

Like the tailor in the joke Clove tells in Samuel Beckett's *Endgame* who responds to his outraged client when he complains about the time it has taken to make his trousers, since God made the world in six days: 'But my dear Sir, my dear Sir, look—at the world— (Pause.) and look— (loving gesture, proudly) — at my TROUSERS!' Philo is not entirely serious in this satiric exposition of how a better world would have been fashioned by any deity worth the name. He is, however, not only serious but eloquent and forceful when he comes to the peroration of his speech and boasts at first that his claim that 'these circumstances are not necessary, and that they might easily have been altered in the contrivance of the universe'.[97] But then he retreats as he notes that these claims seem 'too presumptuous for creatures so blind and ignorant'.[98] What Philo offers, overall, is worth quoting at some length, since it marks I think the fullest cancellation of the dialogue format by that 'talent of eloquence and strong imagery' that Philo in Part X observed was 'the only method of bringing every one to a due sense of religion'.[99] The enormous irony at this point is that eloquence and strong imagery are now being employed to disabuse us of theism as literature trumps philosophy:[100]

> Let us allow, that, if the goodness of the Deity (I mean a goodness like the human) could be established on any tolerable reasons *a priori*, these phenomena, however untoward, would not be sufficient to subvert that principle; but might easily, in some unknown manner, be reconcilable to it. But let us still assert, that as this goodness is not antecedently established, but must be inferred from the phenomena, there can

be no grounds for such an inference, while there are so many ills in the universe, and while these ills might so easily have been remedied, as far as human understanding can be allowed to judge on such a subject. I am Sceptic enough to allow, that the bad appearances, notwithstanding all my reasonings, may be compatible with such attributes as you suppose; but surely they can never prove these attributes. Such a conclusion cannot result from Scepticism, but must arise from the phenomena, and from our confidence in the reasonings which we deduce from these phenomena.

Look round this universe. What an immense profusion of beings, animated and organised, sensible and active! You admire this prodigious variety and fecundity. But inspect a little more narrowly these living existences, the only beings worth regarding. How hostile and destructive to each other! How insufficient all of them for their own happiness! How contemptible or odious to the spectator! The whole presents nothing but the idea of a blind Nature, impregnated by a great vivifying principle, and pouring forth from her lap, without discernment or parental care, her maimed and abortive children![101]

This almost frightening paragraph, along with some others in the speech, was among Hume's last revisions, written on the last sheet of Part XI and marked for insertion. In making these revisions, Hume was confirming what I have been tracing as the demolition (or radical disruption) of the genre of the philosophical dialogue. In this long disquisition, in what Pamphilus at the end of Part XI calls 'his spirit of opposition, and his censure of established opinions', Philo shifts defiantly to the rhetorical and assertive and away from the argumentative and tentative mode proper to philosophical dialogue.[102] As Cleanthes remarks to the appalled Demea, Philo has 'been amusing himself at both our expense', which is an economical way of saying that dialogue has been superseded by satire and moral essay and that Philo has effectively silenced his interlocutors as debate and discussion are forced to yield to imaginative monologue.

This generic shift explains why Philo makes some at first glance startling concessions to Cleanthes ('with whom I live in unreserved intimacy', he remarks, as if at this point he thinks some kind of affirmation of a compromised relationship is necessary), at the beginning of Part XII.[103] He declares that 'notwithstanding the freedom of my conversation, and my love of singular arguments, no one has a deeper sense of religion impressed on his mind, or pays more profound adoration to the divine Being, as he discovers himself to reason, in the inexplicable contrivance and artifice of nature'.[104] With what looks at first like a newly-found conventional piety and conciliatory spirit, Philo seems to be saying that we must not take his extraordinary performance in Part XI too seriously, that he has simply been carried away by his own pleasure in paradoxical argumentation and in the sound of his own voice. In what follows, he seems to admit Cleanthes's argument from design, asserting

that the works of Nature bear a great analogy to the productions of art, is evident; and according to all the rules of good reasoning, we ought to infer ... that their causes have a proportional analogy. But as there are also considerable differences, we have reason to suppose a proportional difference in the causes; and in particular, ought to attribute a much higher degree of power and energy to the supreme cause, than any we have ever observed in mankind. Here then the existence of a DEITY is plainly ascertained by reason.[105]

But as we read on, what looks like Philo's astonishing turnabout is considerably less than it appears, and in fact his qualification and apparent conciliatory retreat is his last and most subversive gesture. Belief in a deity, he quickly adds, is nothing but 'a mere verbal controversy', and in another late addition to the manuscript Hume has him say in the next paragraph that 'All men of sound reason are disgusted with verbal disputes, which abound so much in philosophical and theological inquiries'.[106] As Gaskin points out in a nice phrase, Philo is conceding just about nothing, since the argument from the world to some sort of deity enables a 'virtually contentless affirmation'.[107] Moreover, as the exceptionally strong word 'disgust' signifies, truly rational individuals, says Philo, are appalled by the philosophic futility of such disputes. A bit later on, Philo briefly stages just such a dispute, imagining himself in debate with an imaginary theist and atheist in order to dramatize this time that the difference between them is 'merely verbal, or perhaps, if possible, still more incurably ambiguous'.[108] Both of them, he argues, would have to admit what he has just conceded, that for the theist there is 'a great and immeasurable, because incomprehensible difference between the human and the divine mind', and the atheist is compelled to admit as probable that there is 'some remote inconceivable analogy to the other operations of nature, and, among the rest, to the economy of human mind and thought'.[109] Having withdrawn from the actual dialogue in the library and declared a kind of truce in renewing his friendship with Cleanthes, Philo stages an imaginary exchange among more useful because more polarized opponents: 'Will you quarrel, Gentlemen, about the degrees, and enter into a controversy, which admits not of any precise meaning, nor consequently of any determination?'.[110]

So Part XII marks a complete and ironic circle, a return to Pamphilus's observations at the outset. Philo concedes that there is in some sense a deity, but the nature of that being is shrouded in such mystery that he is a ghostly, radically attenuated figure, not a presence in the lives of rational human beings in any sense of the word. Although in the last few pages Philo repairs his friendship with Cleanthes, his debate partner is essentially defeated, reduced to warning his friend to take care that his 'zeal against false religion' not 'undermine your veneration for the true'.[111] Carnochan calls this a 'reconciliation' of the two friends, as indeed it is, but Cleanthes is a diminished thing at the end.[112] The only defence he can now find to invoke is that religion is consoling: 'Forfeit not this principle, the chief, the only great comfort in life; and our principal support amidst all the attacks of adverse fortune'.[113] Philo dismantles even this poor defence, pointing out that when in need of consolation from religion men will imagine 'unknown Beings, suitably to the present gloom and melancholy of their temper', producing 'the tremendous images [that] predominate in all religions'.[114] Cleanthes is silent, dramatically perhaps abashed, for the rest of Part XII, unable to respond we are left to gather as Philo demolishes 'popular religion' of the sort that consoles and also terrifies ordinary people as it projects a deity with 'one of the lowest of human passions, a restless appetite for applause', or a 'capricious Demon who exercises his power without reason and without humanity'.[115]

To conclude by returning to the terms with which I began this essay, Philo cannot be said to have *convinced* Cleanthes, although he often enough delights him with his argumentative and rhetorical powers. A converted Cleanthes would have violated what Hume thought of as the proper form of the philosophical dialogue and turned it into a purely literary event, a palpable fiction no different from the set-ups in Christian philosophical dialogues like Berkeley's. But in his final reconciliation with his friend after the bruising contests of Parts X and XI, Philo is expressing his satisfaction through small concessions and gestures and implicitly declaring himself the winner of the contest, partly by his condescending to admit an extremely reduced version of the theistic position. He has been the most persuasive and delightful of the three disputants, displaying a verbal fertility and rhetorical intensity that have carried the day. Hume has obviously allowed Philo to dominate the latter parts of the discussion, and he has in his revamped guise as moral essayist/man of letters simply overwhelmed his opponents by adding rhetorical force to his arguments. He has also exploited the innocent Demea, in league as Carnochan says with Cleanthes, who is thereby co-opted, drawn into the determining arc of the plot. So *Dialogues Concerning Natural Religion* is true to the genre as Hume envisioned it, preserving the philosophic openness and dramatic structure that he claimed to be seeking by endowing Cleanthes with integrity, intelligence, modesty and real honesty about the difficulties of theistic belief. But it is also a variation on the genre in its granting Philo a knock-out victory by any means necessary and moving the *Dialogues* into a triumphant monologue for the anti-theist champion.

9 THE EPISTEMOLOGY OF GENRE

Jonathan Sadow

Mais je n'avais pas dessein de faire durer la conversation de Cidalise et de Pharsamon, et cependant elle est plus que raisonnablement longue. Auteurs, ne jurez jamais de rien, ne promettez rien; ce que l'on promet aux lecteurs est souvent la chose que l'on tient le moins: tel nous annonce du beau, qui ne nous fournira que du laid. Pour vous, monsieur le critique, qui direz peut-être qu'on se serait bien passé de cette conversation, en ami je vous conseille de quitter le livre; car si vous vous amusiez à critiquer tout ce qu'il y aurait à reprendre, votre critique deviendrait aussi ample que le livre même, et dès lors mériterait une critique aussi.

(I did not intend to prolong this conversation between Pharsamon and Cidalise, and yet it is already unreasonably long. Authors: swear to nothing, promise nothing. What one promises to readers is often the thing one honours the least; he who says that beauty will follow provides us with nothing but ugliness. For you, Mr. Critic, who will perhaps suggest that we could have done without this conversation; as a friend, I advise you to leave the book; for if it would amuse you to criticize everything that might be redone, your critique would become as large as the book, and at that point would deserve a critique as well.) (Marivaux, *Pharsamon* (1713))[1]

Crucial questions surrounding the nature of genre have often been left out of the project of understanding eighteenth-century fiction. Classification itself has often been the goal of historians of the novel, a project that largely ignores many compelling critiques of such an activity. More importantly, what is often obscured in criticism is the degree to which 'genre' itself, as an object of philosophical reasoning, is an important object of understanding for many eighteenth-century novelists. Not only did many writers of eighteenth-century fiction see theoretical questions of genre as being directly connected to issues of linguistic figuration, they often saw them as them being inextricably linked or, rather, as the same problem. I suggest that questions of genre were in fact inextricable from the activity of writing, and that the anxiety about genre produced by this form of reflection was an active force in the institution of eighteenth-century fiction, bridging both its theory and practice.

This chapter is therefore concerned with an approach to genre that apprehends literary objects alongside the epistemological questions they raise. Its approach is not 'new' – it is, in fact, central to eighteenth-century writers' understanding of their own projects – but it differs from the conception of genre presented by many literary historians who are concerned with the nature or emergence of a transhistorical literary mode such as the novel. 'Genre', rather, represents neither metaphysical objects nor collections of features, but a form of ongoing cultural discourse and production inextricable from questions surrounding the classification and understanding of knowledge and language.

That eighteenth-century writers often understood genre in just this way is perhaps most easily demonstrated by the ongoing analogy between fictional practice and an essentially Lockean anxiety surrounding figuration and the mixed mode. Locke's *An Essay Concerning Human Understanding* generated a number of genre questions and of course provided one of the most important templates for the overall classification of enlightenment knowledge. However, the mixed mode – which the *Essay* both theorizes and models – creates a particularly productive form of anxiety that has a number of consequences for eighteenth-century fiction. This anxiety becomes an actual conundrum for fictional representation while at the same time being a trope for that conundrum:

> *The Mind* often *exercises an active Power in making these* several *Combinations*. For it being once furnished with simple *Ideas*, it can put them together in several Compositions, and so make variety of complex *Ideas*, without examining whether they exist so together in Nature ... as if they had the Original, and constant Existence, more in the Thoughts of Men, than in the reality of things.[2]

The Cervantick trope of the active and disordered mind mistaking the figural for the real becomes, in Locke, tentatively associated with classification. The mixed mode is, of course, a necessary concept for Locke, since it is the method by which the mind can understand abstract categories. It is also a source of philosophical trouble, a fraught concept even in the chapter that it is introduced. Even more dubious for Locke is associative thought, which is similarly disconnected from nature and attached to 'madness', despite being a universal condition. As readers of Sterne well know, the disability surrounding cognitive figuration was often understood much more literally than Locke had intended. However, this implicit detachment from reality becomes a question for eighteenth-century literary genre long before *Tristram Shandy* (1759–67).

Locke and 'The Epistemology of Metaphor'

It is necessary to address the question of tropes per se, since to a great degree Locke's metaphors resonated with eighteenth-century fiction as much as his logic. This was Paul de Man's line of inquiry in 'The Epistemology of Metaphor'. De Man portrays the transformation of Lockean tropic anxiety – the fear that the metaphorical nature of language will disrupt understanding – into what he describes as a proto-gothic narrative in philosophical texts. However, he largely ignores the complement – the way eighteenth-century fiction begins to tell its own tale of Lockean figuration and combination. It is true that philosophy tells a tale of figurative distress, but its interactions with eighteenth-century fictional narrative create a situation that is more complex than de Man proposed, and one that I would like to examine further.

De Man analyses the problem of figural language in Locke, Condillac and Kant, and reminds us that the proliferation of figuration in language is a central difficulty for eighteenth-century philosophy. Suggesting that 'when Locke then develops his own theory of words and language, what he constructs turns out to be in fact a theory of tropes', he proposes that the anxiety of metaphoric proliferation forms a link between eighteenth-century philosophy and twentieth-century literature.[3] There are a number of hints in the essay about the general effect of this problem on 'literary' texts, and de Man suggests that literature and philosophy are joined as disciplines by their generic murkiness. That is, it is precisely the problem of figuration that places literature and philosophy within the same discursive field. At the same time, they are condemned to be fundamentally inarticulate:

> Our argument suggests that the relationship and the distinction between literature and philosophy cannot be made in terms of a distinction between aesthetic and epistemological categories. All philosophy is condemned, to the extent that it is dependent on figuration, to be literary and, as the depository of this very problem, all literature is to some extent philosophical. The apparent symmetry of these statements is not as reassuring as it sounds since what seems to bring literature and philosophy together is, as in Condillac's argument about mind and object, a shared lack of identity or specificity.[4]

De Man, curiously enough, provides examples from philosophy while (aside from an oblique reference to the gothic novel) largely ignores the 'depository of the problem', literature. And yet, readers of Sterne will find de Man's subject – the fear of metaphoric proliferation in eighteenth-century philosophy in general, and Locke in particular – very, very familiar, and not as radical as he suggests. In a sense, this 'counterintuitive' reading of Locke and Condillac provides an apt description of the explicit epistemology of Sterne and Diderot. The figurative power of language itself becomes a figure for narrative and identity and, importantly, the instability of genres. The central crisis that metaphor causes for language – as far as Locke is concerned – is the mixed mode, the philosophical equivalent of catachresis.[5] This abuse of language is a problem for Locke because of its tendency to be non-referential: 'He that thinks the name *centaur* stands for some real being, imposes on himself and mistakes words for things'.[6] De Man points out that Locke's examples are, inevitably, physical 'mixed modes' as well: centaurs, monsters, changelings, fetuses that are half-man, half-beast.

De Man, strangely, does not make what would seem to be an obvious point in an essay alluding to the relationship between 'literary modernity' and the anxieties of eighteenth-century philosophy: that a narrative exploring the non-referentiality of metaphoric language and its consequent proliferation of abstractions, is liable to be a 'mixed-mode' itself. However, de Man hints at this point when he talks about literature and philosophy's shared 'lack of specificity', and very generally about the consequences of his argument for writing a history of either discipline. This is not true for purely philosophical reasons: once the anxiety regarding the referentiality of language spills over into fictional narrative, the issues regarding a narrative's own self-referentiality inevitably move to centre stage. Its own fuzziness becomes apparent, self-conscious, the elephant in the room. That is why *Pharsamon*'s narrator claims that he is writing about nothing, and why Diderot claims that he is not writing a romance, but the truth. Far from being a chimera, this kind of claim spins out a narrative of figurative difficulty.

De Man's mischievous suggestion that philosophy and literature's primary homology is a lack of specificity deserves further attention. His central interest at the time was in linking Lockean philosophy to literary modernity, claiming that Locke's theory of language was 'really' a theory of tropes. Therefore, suggests de Man, if we read ahistorically – that is, against 'received' history – we may discover that the insights of enlightenment philosophy and poststructuralism are essentially the same: metaphoric proliferation creates an inescapable instability in the foundation of knowledge. This, too, deserves further scrutiny, despite the dubious nature of the claim. As he pointed out, it is a 'literary' model of epistemological anxiety that helped to produce a theory of tropes in eighteenth-century philosophy. However, the exploration of rhetorical 'mixed modes' in eighteenth-century narrative has a profound effect on those narratives' relationship to genre. De Man points out that 'Like the blind man who cannot understand the idea of light, the child who cannot tell the figural from the proper keeps recurring throughout eighteenth-century epistemology as barely disguised figures of our universal predicament'.[7] Once this question – a question even more integral to Cervantes, Marivaux, Fielding, Sterne and Diderot than it is to Locke and Condillac – takes centre stage as a narrative subject, the consequences for genre are enormous. The form that this takes is generally genre parody, since it is through the attention to 'mixed modes' that the satire of figuration takes place.

In one sense, de Man's argument now seems banal, a cliché of deconstructive or postmodern criticism. His 'ahistorical' reading may contain some inaccuracies, as well. Even though de Man makes a show out of reading against received notions about Enlightenment thought, he does not claim that Locke's and Condillac's theories of tropes are a marginal aspect of Enlightenment thought or that they subvert empirical philosophy. In truth, difficulties presented by metaphoric language are not, in fact, a submerged, unconscious anxiety but a widely-recognized philosophical problem. Since this is indeed the case, it is even more curious that de Man does not connect this to the 'literary' history of Condillac's contemporaries. Although de Man is ostensibly interested in the literary qualities of philosophy, he ignores the fact that eighteenth-century fiction often saw itself as a philosophical collaborator.

The 'mixed mode' in Locke presents a problem that extends well beyond the question of tropes. Anxiety about mixed modes does not simply stem from the proliferation of metaphor; the difficulty is that the mixed mode sometimes falsely passes for ideas rooted in the senses. For Locke, there needs to be a way to retain morality and the law while excluding gnomes and sprites. It is important, as well, to distinguish the difficulties presented by the mixed mode with the tropic issues created by associative thought. While association is necessarily tied to illogic, trepidation about the mixed mode is largely concerned with the fictionality of concepts produced by an active operation of the mind. At the same time, the mind's ability to produce a mixed mode – as suggested in Book III, Chapter 5 of the *Essay* – is the active function by which the mind categorizes understanding through language. Locke makes this clear in the next chapter:

> *The common names of Substances*, as well as other general Terms, *stands for Sorts*; which is nothing else but the being made signs of such complex *Ideas*, wherein several particular Substances do, or might agree, by virtue of which, they are capable to be comprehended in one common Conception ... which, by the way, may shew us how much the Sorts, or if you please, *Genera* and *Species* of Things ... depend on such Collections of *Ideas*, as Men have made; and not on the real Nature of Things.[8]

Since Locke wields his theory of language primarily as a critique of rationalist metaphysics, one might suggest that it is somewhat more concerned with typology than with metaphor. It is in any case clear that anxiety over the mixed mode is embodied by concerns with both metaphor and classification in eighteenth-century conceptions of genre. This anxiety was self-consciously extended to genre travesty: the satirical mix of genres that formed a template for many novels. It was a recognition on the part of eighteenth-century writers that the didactic anxiety regarding language and the same didacticism regarding genre were explicitly connected.

One might be tempted to view the simultaneous parody of metaphor and genre in these works as a philosophical sidebar, but one would be wrong to do so. Exploration of generic epistemology is a direct consequence of linking the satire of didacticism to both philosophical and literary forms. Genre ceases to represent the form of the text and becomes a figure which produces an incoherent narrative; this in turn is often the object of satire. I will demonstrate the explicit operation of this process in three key texts – Marivaux's *Pharsamon*, Fielding's *Tom Jones* and Sterne's *Tristram Shandy* – but I suggest from the outset that the anxiety over mixed modes is at work in many other less 'self-conscious' eighteenth-century works as well.

Writing about Nothing

Marivaux's *Pharsamon* should provide us with a good object lesson. Aside from being a useful exposé of some early eighteenth-century genre critique, it is a work that is usually excluded from the history of the novel per se. At the same time, it exerts some usually-ignored weight upon this history, having patently influenced Fielding.[9] The allusion to Marivaux in the text of *Tom Jones* almost undoubtedly includes a knowledge of this work, and its similarity to Diderot's *Jacques le fataliste* seems unquestionable, as well. It is, at the same time, specifically a satire of the romance, titled after – but very different from – *Don Quixote*, and deals with epistemological questions in a very different fashion from Cervantes.

That the narrator claims continually to be writing about 'nothing' is of course what we would now describe as a self-conscious gesture. However, this nothingness is directly linked to the play of generic categories, and it is precisely the combination of modes that creates a lack of referentiality. On the one hand, the Quixotic mind of the hero thematizes the problems of figuration. Since the inability to distinguish the figural from the proper is, of course, represented best by the Cervantick tradition in the *roman*, *Pharsamon*, like *Don Quixote*, uses this motif relentlessly. At the same time, it is a parody of a more recent work, La Calprenède's *Faramond*, as well as the romance tradition generally speaking.

However, rather than providing a springboard to a series of humorous adventures, *Pharsamon*'s narrative dwells endlessly on the rules of romance. The aimless uneventfulness of the plot, however, resembles the later non-adventures in the generic woods of *Jacques le fataliste*. In fact, the word *roman* is repeated so often in the text that the whole exposition becomes quite tiresome, which may help to explain the work's relative obscurity. The narrator's claims are in some sense true; virtually nothing happens in the novel other than discussion, and what results is an exposition of the artificiality of genre, as well as the lack of connection to reality presented by a fictional narrative. As we shall see, the novel specifically links the issues raised by the Lockean mixed mode to the combination of literary genres.

Marivaux wrote *Pharsamon* between 1712 and 1713 almost simultaneously with an equally ignored work, *Les Aventures de *** ou les Effets surprenants de la sympathie*. Although the text is the kind of hackneyed *roman* that Marivaux lampoons in *Pharsamon*, the prefatory 'Avis au Lecteur' is worth our attention. In it, the narrator critiques the *nouvelle* while upholding the values of the *roman*:

> Je trouve à mon gré qu'on a retranché des romans tout ce qui pouvait les rendre utiles, et souvent même intéressants. Ceux qu'on compose à présent ne sont que de simples aventures racontées avec une hâte qui amuse le lecteur à la vérité, mais qui ne l'attendrit, ni ne le touche; il est simplement curieux, et rien de plus.[10]

> (I have found that romances have been stripped of everything which could make them useful, and often times even entertaining. Those which are being composed at present are no more than simple adventures related with a haste which truly amuses the reader with the truth, but which does not move him or touch him.)[11] The reader is simply curious, nothing more.

Marivaux writes a *roman* full of clichés, explicitly championing the genre, at the same time that he is writing a romance travesty in which the features of the romance are exhaustively exhumed and satirized. Additionally, the narrator of the 'Avis au Lecteur' suggests that the noble emotions of women are a better guide for the artist than the rules of critics: 'C'est au goût et à sentiment secret, indépendant des lois stériles de l'art, que l'auteur a tâché de conformer le langage et les actions de ses personnages'.[12] ('It is to taste and to secret sentiment, independent of art's sterile laws, that the author has worked to make the language and the actions of his characters conform.') The sterile laws, allegedly a quality of modern writers, are in *Pharsamon* attributed to the outmoded genre of the *roman*. Though this dissonance, or disingenuousness, does little to provide a coherent theory of genre or romance, it suggests an intense engagement with genre as law. In fact it is with the *laws* of romance that the narrator of *Pharsamon* sheepishly claims to comply:

> Que d'évanouissements, dira quelqu'un! Un seul aurait suffi: il est vrai, le premier était naturel, et le second n'était que par forme : c'était un de ces évanouissements de commande, qui semblait nécessaire à Cidalise pour revêtir son aventure de toutes les formalités requises; elle aimait mieux pécher par le trop que par le trop peu.[13]

> ('So much fainting, someone will say! Once would have been enough. It is true, the first was natural, the second only for form. It was one of those spontaneous swoonings that seemed necessary to Cidalise to flesh out her adventure with all of the formal requirements; she would rather sin too much than too little.')

Pharsamon is replete with comments of this nature. However, despite the tone of this commentary, the *roman* does not follow the rules of romance satire, let alone the rules of romance. After a brief, initial comic adventure in the manner of Cervantes, we find this passage:

Voici, dira quelque critique, une aventure qui sent le grand : vous vous éloignez du goût de votre sujet ; c'est du comique qu'il nous faut, et ceci n'en promet point. Dans le fond il a raison : j'ai mal fait de m'embarquer dans cette aventure. Le plaisant pourra peut-être y faire naufrage. Je dis peut-être, car je tâcherai de le sauver. Cependant il serait plus prudent de ne point l'exposer. Il me prend presque envie d'effacer ce que je viens d'écrire : qu'en dites-vous, lecteur? Allons, c'est bien pensé; mais c'est de la peine de plus, et je la crains : continuons. Ne semble-t-il pas après tout à monsieur le critique, que parce qu'il a ri quelque part, on soit obligé de lui fournir toujours de quoi rire? Qu'il s'en passe s'il lui plaît; un peu de bigarrure me divertit. Suivez-moi, mon cher lecteur, à vous dire le vrai, je ne sais pas bien où je vais; mais c'est le plaisir du voyage. Nous voici dans une solitude; restons-y puisque nous y sommes, nous en sortirons comme nous pourrons avec nos personnages.[14]

(Here, some critic will say, is a great adventure: You are deviating from the treatment decorum demands of your subject. What we need is comedy, and this doesn't promise any. He is mainly right; it was a bad idea to start this adventure. Amusement will possibly be shipwrecked there; I say possibly since I will endeavor to save it. However, it would be more prudent not to let it show at all. I almost think I should erase what I have just written. What do you say, reader? Go ahead, it's a good idea; but wait, I fear this would be more trouble. Let us continue. After all, does not the esteemed critic think that, just because he laughed at some point, he should be made to laugh by everything? Let him skip over it if he pleases; a patchwork pleases me. Follow me, my dear reader, to tell you the truth, I don't know where I'm going, but I'm enjoying the trip. We are here alone; let us remain there since we are here. We will get out of it, along with our characters, as best we can.)

These discussions with the reader and critic continue throughout, and we are in fact provided with the promised variety in the form of three inset genre exercises. The first self-conscious narrative is of a *solitaire* whose sad tale is foreshadowed by her own youthful performance in tragic drama. The narrator's defence of the second, Colin's 'realistic' childhood tale, suggests the overall artifice of storytelling while disputing the idea that high genre requires elevated subjects. The third inset story is an adventure narrative, complete with pirates and savages. These three tales are the only real 'stories' in the book, since the bulk of *Pharsamon* consists of wandering and chatting. Each exercise serves to both highlight and dispute genre commonplaces, and the discussion of high and low modes uses the same metaphors that Fielding will use in *Tom Jones*. Genre per se is, as Ralph Cohen would put it, placed under the strict control of didactic narrative, and the mixture of genre in *Pharsamon* is often addressed self-consciously: 'tout le burlesque de son caractère cède alors à un ressouvenir confus de ce qui'il a lu dans les romans'.[15] ('All of the burlesque part of his character yields to a confused remembrance of what he had read in romances.') This mixture is contiguous with the satire of figuration; there is, obviously, the protagonist who believes he is a knight living in a romance. But this error gets spun out into a generality about mistaking the figurative for the real. 'Vous êtes livré vivant, et précisément ce qu'il me faut', Pharsamon tells Cidalise.[16] ('You are delivered alive, precisely what I need.') Later on, he kisses her picture. But mistaken or jokey comparisons are the general concern of the entire work:

> Voilà comment elles sont faites toutes, continua le paysan, quand elles ont perdu quelque chose, elles sont plus sémillantes qu'un chien dans un tournebroche : dame, c'est sans comparaison; car je sais bien que Mlle Babet n'est pas une chienne; mais ôtez cela, c'est tout de même.[17]

> (See, They're all like women, continued the peasant, when they've lost something, they are livelier than a dog on a spit. Lady, it's no comparison, and I know Miss Babet is not a bitch; But other than that, it's all the same.)

Pharsamon is filled with jokes of this kind. But mistaken identity in genre and the errors in figuration are essentially the same narrative device in the text. Later on, Cliton (or Colin) engages in a confused discussion with Fatime in which burlesque metaphors and romantic metaphors are clumsily intermixed. The topic of the discussion turns to the value of comparisons and to the question of whether the adoption of a romantic title may cause one to become the thing that is named. Cliton eventually blows it by suggesting that words are important, and tells Fatime that she would not like it if he called her a monkey. The substitutions of metaphor, of genre, and of class are essentially all part of the same gag:

> ... et effectivement toutes ces choses burlesques le chagrinaient véritablement; ces aventures ne marchaient pas d'un pas égal ... que lui manquait-il d'avantage pour que rien ne démentît la noblesse de sa conduite: cependant il fallait se battre contre des cuisiniers ... il ne se souvenait point d'avoir rien lu dans la vie de ses maîtres, qui composât un si monstrueux mélange ... et qu'il ne devait point être surpris que des hommes moins accoutumés qu'autrefois au respect qu'on leur devait, donnassent par leur étonnement en le voyant, occasion à tout ce qui se mêlait de comique à ses plus nobles aventures
>
> En vérité, dira mon critique, Pharsamon est bien posté pour faire de si grandes réflexions; sans doute, un homme de son espèce réfléchit sur tout et partout; au reste ces réflexions que je lui fais faire, étaient bien plus promptes dans sa tête qu'elles ne le paraissent, lorsqu'il les faut mettre sur le papier : car, en un instant, Pharsamon réfléchit, raisonna, et jugea tout ce que je n'ai pu dire moi, qu'en beaucoup de mots.[18]

> (... and indeed all of these burlesque things caused true chagrin; these adventures did not proceed as at a steady pace ... What more did he need for the nobility of his conduct to be unquestionable? And yet he was forced to fight with cooks ... he could not remember reading anything in the lives of his masters that made up such a monstrous mixture ... and he should not be at all surprised that men less accustomed than before to the respect they deserved, should provide, through their astonishment in seeing him, the opportunity for all of the comedy that mixed with his most noble adventures.
>
> In truth, my critic will say, Pharsamon is well situated to make such deep reflections; there is no doubt that a man of his species reflects on all and everything; besides,

the reflections I have him make happened much faster in his head than it seems when it comes time to put them on paper; in a moment, Pharsamon reflected, reasoned, and judged all those things that I could not say myself, except in many words.)

The narrator cannot specifically describe Pharsamon's reflections precisely because language *is* figurative. The *monstrueux mélange* clearly refers to the entire text as well as the frustration of the moment. It is interesting to note, also, that the narrative diverges into a discussion of writing and cognition, with a particular emphasis on the difficulty of representing thoughts and things with words. It is not the only moment in *Pharsamon* where this occurs, and there are frequent references to the madness in Pharsamon's brain: 'Vous nous changiez nos noms à tous tant que nous sommes: est-ce rêverie de maladie, ou bien pure folie?'[19] ('You've changed all of our names; is this a fever dream, or pure madness?') However, the mixing of modes in the brains of the characters and the mixed modes of the narrative itself are frequently compared. The confusion of names and of generic modes is frequently associated with madness. This association will, of course, be familiar to readers of Sterne; however, *Pharsamon* places this discourse more firmly in the realm of genre, with continuous and explicit reference to the *roman*. It is notable that *Pharsamon* uses the same rhetoric as Locke when discussing the problem of 'mistaking words for things': monstrousness. De Man, writing of the development of the theory of metaphor from Locke to Condillac, suggests:

> From the recognition of language as trope, one is led to the telling of a tale ... The temporal deployment of an initial complication, of a structural knot, indicates the close, though not necessarily complementary, relationship between trope and narrative, between knot and plot. If the referent of a narrative is indeed the tropological structure of its discourse, then the narrative will be an attempt to account for this fact.[20]

This phenomenon occurs throughout *Pharsamon*. The narrator often claims that he is writing about nothing, a move that prefigures the more specifically 'philosophical' *Jacques le fataliste*. However, the narrative accounting leads directly to a critical consciousness of the generic mixed mode. Between the two Marivaux texts, a somewhat paradoxical discourse emerges. On the one hand, critical rules are decried by each. On the other, the *roman*, and perhaps genres and modes in general, both are and are not associated with those rules. In any case, *Pharsamon*'s self-referential account of the anxious trope of the 'active Power' of mental combination creates a story of mixed generic modes. *Pharsamon* consistently and explicitly veers between them, mediating its fuzzy paths between the burlesque and the romance with ambivalent narrative uncertainty. The haziness that Pharsamon feels when thinking about romance is part of the exposition, since the traditional genre can only exert its full ideological force when the specifics of its historical production are obscured. The boundary-mark of generic identification, the Derridean *clause de genre*, becomes fetishized to the extent that it becomes the text's structural and thematic principle.[21] The Lockean conundrum – the inability to tell the real from the figural – is played out universally through these texts as a kind of loss, echoing Locke's qualms about the inadequacy of substitution. Simply put, the metaphor is not simply the mistake of the figural for the real, but the nostalgic figure of the past 'mistaken' for the literal present.

The Mixed Mode

Tom Jones adopts this particular, highly self-conscious and ambivalent brand of 'Lockean' discourse, pointing to a link between Marivaux and Fielding that rises above the level of surface influence and historical curiosity. In particular, Book IV, Chapter 1 contains a striking parable of genre ossification. In the chapter, both 'news' and 'romance' are parodied as discursive practices. The narrator compares two kinds of historians: one the dull chronicler, another the one who chronicles revolutions. He likens the first to coach service which runs whether or not there are passengers. The other relevant analogy here is that of the newspaper; it has the same number of words whether or not it has anything to say, or anything contained in it at all but endless humdrum nothingness. Fielding's narrator compares himself to the second, the chronicler of revolutions.

This active travesty of genre inflexibility brings different genres to bear upon each other, particularly the interaction of high and low genres, critical theory and practice (Fielding distinguishes beginning and advanced critics). In the parable of the King and the Stagehands, the narrator compares his introductory chapters to the pomp of the arrival of the hero in tragedy and epic poetry.

But he then shifts the discussion to the *masters* of those poets, the theatre-owners. He expostulates about a time when, for a performance of a play, the actor playing the king has bribed the stagehands to show up late and be lackadaisical so that he can continue eating his mutton (importantly, eating and the stage, two variety-laden and 'low'-genre experiences, are the most sustained metaphors). The audience is then forced to wait through the music and the scene-shifters. The scene-shifting is important, since this is what is most directly being compared to the introductory chapters of *Tom Jones*. But lest we take the analogy too seriously, Fielding then speculates about how politicians and other pompous types look more upscale in a procession when surrounded by paid-off flower girls. This scene is a satirical convention in its own right, but that convention becomes a self-conscious narrative of genre play in *Tom Jones*. This analogy highlights the degree to which many eighteenth-century works of interest tend to be plays of genre, and of different kinds.

Fielding, however, travesties even this analogy, submerging the importance of any individual metaphor. All of the critical analysis then becomes a chain of mixed-metaphors not only for writing, but also for genres. Much of what historians of the novel generally claim to be 'essential' qualities of the novel – news, empiricism, probability, history, etc. – is brought into satirical play in *Tom Jones* in a conscious display of genre juggling. Moreover, many of the formal aspects of genre, even the idea of formal aspects of genre, are often lampooned in terms of reader-reception. The spectacle of scene-shifters is the most important factor in contemporary response to those critics who sanctimoniously impose rule upon genres; really, they should be more like clerks. As the narrator makes clear in Book IX, Chapter 1, the objection to the term 'romance' is not so much that it is romance, but that romance is associated with ignorance of other disciplines. The writer who undertakes a new province of prose ought to have knowledge of other disciplines and other areas of knowledge; it is 'generification' itself that the narrator objects to. The rhetoric employed by Fielding in the chapter bears a remarkable resemblance to Marivaux's: 'As truth distinguishes our Writings, from those idle Romance which are filled with Monsters, the Productions, not of Nature, but of distempered Brains; and which have been therefore recommended by an eminent Critic to the sole Use of the Pastry-cook'.[22] The comparison of the romance to monstrosity is not limited to Fielding or Marivaux. Shaftesbury had referred to novels and romances as 'Things the most *unnatural* and *monstrous*,' and it is in any case an extremely common eighteenth-century metaphor. However, Fielding follows this description with an *explicit* reference to Lockean catachresis; 'Thus the Hero is always introduced with a Flourish of Drums and Trumpets, in order to rouse a martial Spirit in the Audience, and to accommodate their Ears to Bombast and Fustian, which Mr. *Lock's* blind Man would not have grossly erred in likening to the Sound of a Trumpet'.[23] This is a kind of double joke, inasmuch as the narrator is misusing a figure which signifies the misuse of language. This metaphor reappears several times in *Tom Jones*, however, and often as part of the discussion of high and low modes.[24] More important is the degree to which both Fielding and Marivaux adopt a similar attitude to genre, a self-conscious mixing of high and low that is closely associated with complications in eighteenth-century philosophy, and which specifically singles out the romance as a hackneyed genre. Cohen, among others, has convincingly demonstrated that many critics and writers saw literary forms as being interrelated, and had no difficulty mixing them, especially for didactic purposes:

> Truth statements were a necessary part of didactic poems and could be found in panegyric, elegy, most prose forms. Readers, therefore, were addressed, challenged, guided and goaded to discover the proper distinctions, not because earlier theories had not made them, but because mixtures had become so prevalent.[25]

Cohen makes a case for the relatively distinct identity of certain forms, and it is undoubtedly true that many eighteenth-century writers saw them as such. However, he also points out (perhaps without meaning to) the theoretical weaknesses behind those distinctions in eighteenth-century criticism:

> Interrelations among forms were reinforced by the form-mode distinction since modes of satire, for example, could appear in most other forms. The specification of parts of any form was minimally defined, and it was precisely because this specification of parts was left open that the critics relied upon 'propriety' and 'decorum' as comparative (historical) guides[26]
>
> The stipulation of 'rules' was primarily cautionary and relative, urging writers not to take certain freedoms. But the interrelation of forms made such guides questionable, especially since the forms were part of a hierarchy not fully understood.[27]

Cohen goes on to suggest that 'No literary work in the period can be understood without recognizing that it is a combination of parts or forms'.[28] By and large, this is something better understood by eighteenth-century writers than many twentieth-century critics, and Fielding's analysis of genre was a response to the surrounding literary terrain. Fielding connects both of Locke's anxious motifs in the same paragraph: the distempered brain's monstrous associations and the inability to distinguish between species. The invocation of Locke's blind man in the middle of a complex genre parable is, of course, no accident. It is worth remembering that story of the blind man in Book II of the *Essay* involves, literally, the inability to distinguish different forms (sphere and cube). Fielding's attack on critical enforcers of genre is directly related to this distinction, since the species is purely an abstract invention rather than a natural distinction. One might object, of course, that mixed modes in Locke are the necessary result of the mind's distinguishing ability, but – as de Man points out – it is this unresolved paradox that spins the tale. The mind must be at a remove from nature in order to apprehend and categorize it. In *Tom Jones*, again, the story of genre combination and distinction is embedded into a narrative of mental figuration and detachment from reality.

'A Shared Lack of Specificity'

Sterne is, of course, the most elaborate literary inheritor of Lockean philosophical anxiety, and perhaps needs little further explication on this score. It is nevertheless worth remarking that Sterne adopts Lockean philosophy as a 'literary' genre, a self-conscious move in which philosophy and historiography – two genres perhaps already linked for Sterne by Humean theory – are subsumed under the same trope. Sterne's famous characterization of Locke's *Essay* as a 'history-book ... of what passes in a man's own mind' locates historical narration squarely within subjectivity.[29] Philosophy is, in a sense, a form of historiography, a notoriously unreliable genre: 'The literary histories of past ages ... what terrible battles, 'yclept logomachies, have they occasioned'.[30]

Sterne self-consciously addresses questions raised by Humean historical rhetoric. Hume, in a rather un-Humean fashion, regarded the mechanism of history as operating through a 'Secret Spring'. In Sterne, this metaphor echoes Hume but carries different connotations: 'Figuratively speaking, dear *Toby*, it may, for aught I know, said my father; but the spring I am speaking of, is that great and elastic power within us of counterbalancing evil, which like a secret spring in a well-ordered machine, though it can't prevent the shock – at least it imposes upon our sense of it'.[31] The secret spring in this case is not the natural order of history, but a much less substantial spring: a sensibility that tentatively and occasionally suggests order over chaos. This does not, however, mean that Sterne has given up on historical representation; it simply means that he has not accepted Hume's model for it. Toby is emblematic of the difficulties of the historian, insomuch as his eloquence depends upon his empirical experience and particularity, rather than upon the study of causal chains. Yet, it is precisely this complexity that makes his accounts more confusing than those of the traditional historian:

> I must remind the reader, in case he has read the history of King *William*'s wars ... my uncle *Toby* was an eye-witness at *Namur*, – the army of the besiegers being cut off, by the confluence of the *Maes* and *Sambre*, from seeing much of each other's operations, – my uncle *Toby* was generally more eloquent and particular in his account of it; and the many perplexities he was in, arose out of the almost insurmountable difficulties he found in telling his story intelligibly, and giving such clear ideas of the differences and distinctions between the scarp and counterscarp, – the glacis and covered way, – the half-moon and ravelin, – as to make his company fully comprehend where and what he was about.
>
> Writers themselves are too apt to confound these terms; – so that you will the less wonder, if in his endeavors to explain them, and in opposition to many misconceptions, that my uncle *Toby* did oft times puzzle his visitors, and sometimes himself too.[32]

Although Toby – 'no chronologer' – is bewildered upon this point, he later makes the importance of historical accuracy clear:[33]

> As for *Chronology*, I own, *Trim*, continued my uncle *Toby* ... that of all others, it seems a science which the soldier might best spare, was it not for the lights which that science must one day give him, in determining the invention of powder ... the world cannot be too exact in ascertaining the precise time of its discovery, or too inquisitive in knowing what great man was the discoverer, and what occasions gave birth to it.[34]

Passages such as this one, along with the exceptionally extensive documentation regarding the consistency of Sterne's own chronology, should make us aware that we are in the realm of historiographic, rather than historical, subjectivity.[35]

Sterne believes that narration of history is subjective, but never suggests that this is true of history itself. The secret spring of historiography, like the secret spring of morality, is essentially a substitution:

> SOMETHING therefore was wanting, as a *succedaneum*, especially in one or two of the more violent paroxysms of the siege, to keep up something like a continual firing in the imagination, – and this *something*, the corporal, whose principal strength lay in invention, supplied by an entire new system of battering of his own, – without which, this had been objected to by military critics, to the end of the world, as one of the great *desiderata* of my uncle *Toby's* apparatus.[36]

Toby's actual experiences with the specificity of history prevent him from creating a compelling historical narrative. The historian's conundrum locates itself in the inability of a narrative to follow the actual contour of history. Historiography is not a representation of history, but rather a substitute. As R. G. Collingwood points out, Hume's work as a historian tended to contradict his scepticism of Lockean causality; his historiographic practice never conformed to his historiographic theory.[37] In this sense, Sterne parries Hume with Hume, since Hume's *Treatise*'s contribution to philosophy is partially a critique of Lockean causality. Hume had pointed out in his *Enquiry Concerning Human Understanding* that 'all our reasonings concerning matter of fact are founded on a species of Analogy, which leads us to expect from any cause the same events, which we have observed to result from similar causes'.[38] If history did possess any secret springs, they would certainly not be directly accessible to the historian. Again, this is Toby's problem; historical narrative is a trope, not an explanation. As de Man suggests, the inability to tell the figural from the proper becomes the most vexing metaphor, a trope that leads to the narrative of Hume's *Treatise*, on the one hand, with its demotion of causality to non-metaphysical scientific naturalism, and Sterne, who essentially leaves the problem unsolved. As Christina Lupton claims, Sterne's approach leaves the problem within a comforting space by the conversion of language into a primary, material object – the novel itself.[39] Hence, its scepticism is 'a cock and a bull', unserious and confined to the secondary realm of literary device.

But it is the materiality of secondary impressions that – for Hume and Sterne alike – destroys the notion of Lockean, metaphysical notions of causality. Not only are they analogies, they are fundamentally unable to articulate 'primary' impressions, since they do not follow the contours of the objects they describe, but possess their own 'grammatical' logic. This is in opposition to Hume's own later description of the role of the historian; on a literal level, it's opposed to *Tristram Shandy*'s own presentation of history, with its disordered narrative but orderly chronology. Although there is no easy resolution to Sterne's overall relationship to Hume's philosophy and historiography, it is at least safe to say that

Sterne's central metaphor of Lockean causality is mediated through Hume and questions of historical representation. Sterne's oft-quoted comment about the *Essay* is not a throwaway line; it is an allusion to the Humean problem of the secondary nature of causality, and its paradoxical twin, the primary nature of secondary impressions. At the same time, Lupton is correct that Sterne never tries to impose a solution onto the problem of historical representation, or causality in general.[40] The secret spring is *not*, in fact, causality, but a process of figuration by which philosophical inquiry is converted into a narrative genre marked by the inability to properly represent.

This is, of course, yet another instance where self-reference is the result of the combination of abstractions. Sterne represents a true epistemology of genre, one in which representational modes, both literary and philosophical, are subject to the same succadaneous story. One might suggest that this form of scepticism is the essential engine for a narrative work which indeed subsumes a variety of genre travesties under a didactic voice, the primary theme of which is the inability to narrate. Certainly Diderot – whose *Jacques le fataliste* expands a fragment of *Tristram Shandy* by recasting the question of narrative ambivalence in terms of romance parody once again – perceived it that way. In many ways, Sterne's formulation is much as de Man describes. What binds philosophy to literary and historical narration is, in fact, a shared lack of specificity. As in Marivaux, figuration leads to a tale of repetition and loss. Needless to say, *Tristram Shandy* also resembles *Pharsamon* in its endless self-questioning and genre variety. It is, of course, a more 'sophisticated' exposition, but one can also see Sterne as the latest development in what is by now an old story, a story where the anxiety surrounding mixed modes in eighteenth-century philosophy is self-consciously extended to genre travesty – a recognition on the part of eighteenth-century writers that the didactic anxiety regarding language and the same didacticism regarding genre were explicitly connected.

An examination of Sterne's treatment of historiography may lead us towards a revision of de Man's thesis. It is true, in a sense, that the novel acts as a sort of 'depository' of philosophical anxiety, since that anxiety is able to play itself out as an unresolved narrative of self-reference and substitution, whereas a philosophical text must attempt to resolve problems of reference and categorization. However, the evidence suggests something closer to continuous engagement than a homology, since the legacy is a theory of genre that both apprehended and produced forms of eighteenth-century fiction. In this sense, genre was *essentially* epistemological, and even formulations such as a 'new species of writing' recognised the relationship between the creation of a type and a mixed mode. To write a novel was not to conform to a literary mode, but to engage in a self-reflective practice of combination. Genre was a story, again, of being led from theory to practice, and trope to tale.

10 THE PRIMITIVE IN ADAM SMITH'S HISTORY

Maureen Harkin

The life of a savage, when we take a distant view of it, seems to be a life either of profound indolence, or of great and astonishing adventures; and both these qualities serve to render the description of it agreeable to the imagination. The passion of all young people for pastoral poetry, which describes the amusements of the indolent life of a shepherd; and for books of chivalry and romance, which describe the most dangerous and extravagant adventures, is the effect of this natural taste for these two seemingly inconsistent objects. In the descriptions of the manners of savages, we expect to meet with both these: and no author ever proposed to treat of this subject who did not excite the public curiosity. (Adam Smith, Letter to the *Edinburgh Review*, March 1756)[1]

1

On the night of 11 July 1790, a few days before his death, Adam Smith ordered his two literary executors, Joseph Black and James Hutton, to burn all of his manuscripts, with the exception of a handful of essays.[2] Smith thus ensured that, barring these short pieces, no incomplete work would be posthumously added to the two monuments of his career, *The Theory of Moral Sentiments* (1759) and *The Wealth of Nations* (1776). It is generally assumed that the manuscripts destroyed that night were versions, or portions, of two major works, long projected by Smith, one a treatise on the 'History of Law and Government', and the other a study of 'the different branches of Literature'. These are the 'two ... great works' Smith described as 'upon the anvil' in his letter of 1 November 1785 to the Duc de la Rochefoucauld.[3] Detailed student notes from Smith's lecture courses on jurisprudence and on literature and rhetoric later surfaced, collected as the *Lectures on Rhetoric and Belles Lettres* and the *Lectures on Jurisprudence*, and give us some access to Smith's thought on these topics. However, the loss of these two long-planned works on literature and legal-political history is enormous. This failure to complete the projects and the destruction of his papers mean that Smith's corpus can be seen as shaped, to an extraordinary degree, by the major absences of these long-meditated works, as well as by the accomplishments of the *Theory of Moral Sentiments* and *The Wealth of Nations.* These absences in Smith's oeuvre necessarily influence our understanding of the work available to us from his hand and generate a number of pressing questions. Why, for example, did Smith find it so difficult to bring his thinking on literature and history to fruition in a major work – a *Theory of Literature* or a *History of Civil Society* that would be a companion work to his two other great treatises on ethics and economic systems?

Looking at his early career, one would indeed have far sooner expected major works on literature and history from Smith than on political economy. His education at Oxford had consisted in large part of classical and recent European literature; he began his career as a man of letters, giving three series of public lectures on rhetoric in Edinburgh from 1748–51; and by all accounts Smith made the study of rhetoric and literature an important part of his classes throughout his career at the University of Glasgow (1751–63) after he was appointed Professor of Logic in 1751, and then Professor of Moral Philosophy in 1752.[4] Smith was deeply involved in thinking about questions of historiography from early on in his career. His thinking about the history of forms of government had occupied him from at least 1759 on: the study of law and government he mentions to la Rochefoucauld had in fact been promised to the public in the closing lines of *The Theory of Moral Sentiments*, and he lectured on jurisprudence at the University of Glasgow throughout the 1750s and early 1760s.[5] From 1754 to 1762 he also had the great example of his friend David Hume's six-volume *History of England*, which appeared in instalments, to progressively greater public acclaim. Why then, given the quality of his surviving contributions to the theory of history in the Lectures, did Smith fail to complete the projected treatise on the history of laws and political institutions?

Critical commentary on Smith has of course frequently lamented these absent works, but with few exceptions has tended to treat them as unfortunate gaps in the record rather than as significant silences.[6] However, our own historical moment, with its legacy of poststructuralist (and more distantly, psychoanalytic) interpretation, makes it more obvious, even inescapable, that we should not treat these works as simply missing. Instead these gaps in Smith's oeuvre can be understood as significant, even crucial to Smith's published writings and project. Such discontinuities should be attended to as symptoms of larger meanings and contradictions. Certainly the explanation Smith himself provided in his letter to la Rochefoucauld for not completing his projected two 'great works' does not put the matter to rest. He cites age and fatigue as reasons for leaving off work, but also manifests a certain palpable disinclination to finish what he has so evidently long laboured over:

> The materials of both [the treatises on History and on Rhetoric and Literature] are in a great measure collected, and some Part of both is put into a tollerable good order.

But the indolence of old age, tho' I struggle violently against it, I feel coming fast upon me, and whether I shall ever be able to finish either is extremely uncertain.[7]

Without denying the losses and difficulties Smith faced in the mid- and late 1780s – the death of his mother and his own various health problems, for example – this statement seems to express at least as much a will to drop the two projects as any incapacity, especially if we note the two projects' unusually long gestation and the fact that this letter is written almost five years before his death – years of considerable intellectual and professional activity for Smith.[8]

The gap in Smith's corpus, I would suggest, should be read not as a symptom of simple fatigue or incapacity, but rather as the sign of a struggle with problems or contradictions in his own grand narratives of literature and history. In the case of writing history, which I will focus on here, recent work by Karen O'Brien and J. G. A. Pocock has shed new light on the complexity of the situation facing Smith's generation of historians (in Britain, Hume, Smith, William Robertson, Adam Ferguson and, of course, Gibbon), and the particular difficulties posed by the conflicting claims and objectives of Enlightenment historiography. To write history in the second half of the eighteenth century was to negotiate a complex relationship to the past and to prestigious ancient models of history-writing, to comment quite directly on the current political situation by the invocation of the example (positive or negative) of the past and to work with an unusually heightened sense of the forms and genres of historiography.[9] Pocock describes a situation in which there was considerable tension between the classical inheritance of Enlightenment historians, in which a history was typically that of a narrative 'which related exemplary deeds, to be imitated or avoided, of ruling individuals', and the newer, self-appointed task of Smith and the rest of his cohort, of constructing an overarching narrative of the 'progress of the human spirit' from ancient times to the present.[10] At the same time, Pocock notes eighteenth-century authors' constant 'need to vindicate the superiority of modern commercial civilisation in the face of incessant neo-republican challenges to its virtues'.[11]

Pocock's account of the complex interactions between narratives of exemplary actions, philosophizing generalization, and antiquarian scholarship in the field of Enlightenment historiography stresses the competing demands of these various subgenres on authors and the difficulty of getting the blend right. In this densely textured account of the field of eighteenth century historiography and of Smith's particular sensitivity to its conflicts, Pocock makes some of the conceptual problems of writing history at this time very clear.[12] He also suggests, in passing, one or two possible causes for Smith's inability to finish his own historical account: the conflict between an understanding of history as macro-narrative of the processes of social change and the older, classical sense of 'exemplary and instructive narrative', for example; and Smith's fear of a certain repetitiousness in recounting narratives of development. Pocock does not, however, explore the question at any length, concluding that, 'on the whole, [Smith] left 'history' where ... he had placed it, in the role of a heuristic device needed to organize information to be treated by other disciplines, ranging from moral philosophy to political economy'.[13]

Pocock's discussion helps clarify Smith's relation to the larger field of eighteenth-century historiography and the problems of defining the nature of historical narrative at this point, but we are still left with the question of why Smith in particular, unlike his contemporaries Hume, Robertson, Ferguson and the rest, did not work through in print his difficulties with the field. His absence from the rolls strongly suggests that, in addition to being as concerned as his contemporaries with the same general refashioning of forms of historical writing that was taking place at this time, Smith was also wrestling with something unique to his own understanding of the historical past and how to write it. That problem, I want to suggest here, is that of settling on a consistent model of the relation of past to present, of committing to a notion of historical unfolding as either a form of progress, an ascent to modernity, or a decline. The following account explores this difficulty in Smith, as a means of finding at least a partial explanation for his failure to bring his historical researches to completion.

The assertion that Smith's understanding of the relation of the past to his own historical moment shows shifts and contradictions may seem surprising; Smith's various surviving writings on historical development – the *Lectures on Jurisprudence*, and the passages on history and society from *The Theory of Moral Sentiments*, and the *Wealth of Nations* – have generally been read as an account of progress from barbarism to civilized modernity, which places commercial society at the summit of historical development.[14] This is indeed a dominant part of his narrative of the relation of past to present – but as an attentive reading demonstrates, it is by no means the only account he gives. Smith's writings on history, especially the passages on primitive societies of North America in the *Theory of Moral Sentiments*, include both accounts of progress to modern European capitalism *and* a strong counter-narrative questioning the benefits, if not the inevitability, of such an unfolding. In reading some of these passages on 'the North American Savages' and their relationship to his models of historical development, we are able to see some of the difficulties and contradictions Smith struggled with in his thinking about history, specifically the challenge posed by the savage to a progress model of history. This reading of Smith on the primitive, therefore, should help elucidate some of the reasons why he could not resolve, or reunify these contradictions in the great treatise on history of forms of government he had so long projected.

2

Perhaps the best-known contribution of mid-eighteenth-century Scottish intellectuals to writing and thinking about history is their conceptualization of a particular notion of progress. In 1741, for example, Hume describes the intellectual benefit and aesthetic appeal of historical study as deriving from the tableaux depicting the rise of civilization that such study supplies. What could be more agreeable, Hume asks in his essay 'Of the Study of History', 'than to be transported into the remotest ages of the world, and to observe human society in its infancy, making the first faint essays towards the arts and sciences: To see the policy of government, and the civility of conversation refining by degrees, and every thing which is ornamental to human life advancing towards its perfection'?[15] The general sensation of being at the apex of historical development which Hume evidences is made systematic in the writings of the Scottish Historical School of the 1750s to 1770s.[16] This group, which included William Robertson, Adam Ferguson, John Millar, Henry Home, Lord Kames and Smith, developed and shared a series of theories about social development, key among them being a notion of history as progress through four successive socio-economic stages, each based on a specific mode of subsistence that determined government, property relations and other institutions.[17] According to the stadial thesis, human society had progressed – or, in the case of non-European societies was still uncertainly progressing – from a miserable subsistence hunting and gathering in the age of barbarism (stage one), through the progressive accretions of property and the accompanying establishment and refinement of government in pastoralism (stage two) and agriculture (stage three), to emerge into an 'age of commerce' characterized by the division of labour, the spread of manufacture and trade and general prosperity.

Pocock has pointed out that this sequence of historical stages is first presented by Smith in the *Lectures on Jurisprudence* as a provisional, conjectural ordering, 'a heuristic device' employed to illustrate the links between modes of subsistence and particular forms of law rather than to describe an actual account of historical development.[18] Smith invites the reader (or auditor of the original lectures) to imagine a group of ten or twelve on an otherwise uninhabited island and to trace the progressively more complex methods the group would employ to support themselves and regulate their society: 'the first method they would fall upon for their sustenance ... would be the chase. This is the age of hunters. In process of time, as their numbers multiplied, they would find the chase too precarious for their support ... Hence would arise the age of shepherds.'[19] And so on. It is certainly true that the odd mix of conditional and declarative statements at this point in the *Lectures*, and the indefinite, isolated location of this group of castaways makes it difficult to link this history to a generalizable model. At the same moment that Smith introduces the four stages model of history, then, he could be described as wavering a little about its applicability. Nonetheless, by the end of his account, the original image of the desert island has entirely faded away, and Smith sums up in decisive language, asserting that he has given 'a generall account of the history of government in Europe', and expressing a sense of being the beneficiary and end-point of this historical sequence: '... Thus at last the age of commerce arises ... such a society has done all in its power towards its ease and convenience'.[20]

This sense of the authors' historical good fortune indeed tends to permeate accounts of the four-stages theory, with its tale of progress upward from precariousness to 'ease and convenience'.[21] And ease and plenty is not all there is to it. According to the stadial thesis, human society had progressed through stages that marked increases not only in material abundance, but also in delicacy of feeling and social and intellectual freedoms. The suggestion that life in a commercial society revealed some kind of latent human possibility or promise is manifest in the historical writings of Millar, Kames, Smith and their predecessor Hume. Such a conception marked the modern inheritors of this historical march as not only more fortunate, but also somehow more expansive, richer in sympathy and imaginative range than their predecessors. This is the burden, for example, of James Millar's comments on the intersection between the conditions of material life and the human type they make possible in his *The Origin of the Distinction of Ranks* (1771): 'as men ... find less difficulty in the attainment of bare necessities, their prospects are gradually enlarged, their appetites and desires are more and more awakened and called forth ... There is a natural progress from ... rude to civilised manners'.[22] Or, as Hume puts it in his essay, 'Of Refinement in the Arts', 'The ages of refinement are both the happiest and the most virtuous'.[23]

This model of history gives the 'age of commerce' historical necessity and a certain finality, buttressing Smith's claims in the *Wealth of Nations* that modern commercial society is the best arrangement for harnessing individual effort to general social benefit. Different social or economic systems are essentially defined by the writers of the Scottish Historical School as stages to be superseded by the inevitable triumph of modern commercial society, rather than challenges or plausible alternatives to current arrangements.[24]

Along with his colleagues, Smith offers current European social and economic arrangements as the acme of progress, as his assessment of the civic benefits of commerce – 'order and good government ... liberty and security of individuals' – in the *Wealth of Nations*, for example, attests.[25] Yet a very different current also runs through much of Smith's writing on history, one that constitutes a challenge to the idea of history as progress, and which has the effect of negating this tone of self-satisfaction in the progress model. One could point to the repining for the lost practices of a less rationalized and specialized economy in his account of the prodigious hospitality and intense local loyalties of the feudal estate in the *Wealth of Nations*; and to the attacks on the effects of commerce on character in both the *Lectures on Jurisprudence* and the *Wealth of Nations*.[26] These passages acknowledge distinct and major losses, as well as gains, in the move to a commercial society. The elements of a critique of his age and of capitalism surfacing in the *Wealth of Nations*'s analysis of economic systems are, unsurprisingly, even more evident in Smith's writings on moral and cultural phenomena, and it is for this reason that the earlier *Theory of Moral Sentiments* is of such importance in tracing Smith's ideas on the culture of capitalism. There is a major shift in focus, discipline and tone between the two works, with the *Theory*'s concern with developing an ethics of social interaction replaced by the later work's analysis of economic systems, a difference once described as 'the Adam Smith problem'.[27] Without revisiting this older debate about how to reconcile the supposedly conflicting worldviews of Smith's two major works, we can certainly acknowledge the very marked differences in the atmosphere, as well as the mode of analysis, of the two books: while the *Wealth of Nations* does register some strong criticisms of commercial society, the earlier *Theory* articulates a much sharper sense of nostalgia, of the personal and social losses incurred by developing capitalism, and along with this sense of loss it offers a more questioning version of the course of historical development. Hence the evidence the *Theory* supplies of Smith's thinking about history will be of particular interest here.

Smith's sense of some of the limits and losses of his own historical moment can be seen most vividly in his critical discussion of the figure of 'the primitive', specifically that of the North American Indian, who returns repeatedly in the *Theory of Moral Sentiments*.[28] The voluminous literature of European encounters with other native peoples preceding Smith had constructed a general native type, characteristically though not invariably seen as validating the dominance of European culture.[29] Hume's argument in 'Of National Characters', for example, provides an obvious instance of the ways in which European intellectual discourse put these encounter and voyage narratives to use as proof of the superiority of European culture ('I am apt to suspect the negroes to be naturally inferior to the whites. There scarcely ever was a civilized nation of that complexion, nor even any individual eminent either in action or speculation ...').[30] Smith's texts share elements of this dismissive characterization, what Ronald Meek calls the tradition of the 'ignoble savage'.[31] But in general Smith is far less persuaded than Hume and his own contemporaries that an age of commerce and modernization represents an advance.

The sense of history as progress is both asserted and questioned in Smith's writings, and a large part of the challenge to the notion of modern Europe as representing a pinnacle of cultural development resides in the North American 'savage'. For Smith, this figure offers both an image of backwardness and paucity familiar from accounts like Hume's, but also a compelling alternative to modern forms of subjectivity.[32] Descriptions of Native American culture and customs – especially the accounts of astonishing bravery, endurance, nobility and cruelty in works published by the Jesuit missionaries, Joseph-François Lafitau (1724) and Pierre François-Xavier de Charlevoix (1744) – had strongly impressed Smith, who repeatedly alludes to them in passages on the social and ethical values of primitive societies in the *Theory of Moral Sentiments*.[33] However, while Smith was evidently fascinated by these accounts, they also posed something of a methodological problem for him. For it was clear from the works of Lafitau, Charlevoix and the other European descriptions of Native American societies that Smith included in the *Theory* that the four-stages theory did not accurately explain the workings of these cultures, which mixed elements from supposedly separate phases of historical development, cultivating crops while keeping no flocks, for example.[34]

In describing this variation on a supposedly universal law of development and the difficulty it posed to the stadial schema of the Scottish Historical School, Pocock lays out the three possible solutions to the problem that these societies represent for Smith and his fellow historians. The historian or philosopher 'might say that the progress of society had not occurred in the continents of the New World; he might find some new theory in which it progressed through a different series of stages; or he might join Rousseau in regarding the paradigm of progress ... as itself open to criticism'.[35] Pocock stresses that the first solution is the one generally adopted by Smith, Hume, Robertson and Ferguson, but I would suggest that the third, Rousseauvian response, here offered as a merely hypothetical position not really seriously considered by the Scottish group, in fact actually comes quite close to describing the sympathetic and often admiring accounts Smith gives of Native Americans.[36] The example of the North American in Smith's work comes to stand for a vision of history dominated less by themes of ascent and accumulation and more by those of difference and loss. An examination of the figure of the 'savage' or 'barbarian' (terms Smith uses interchangeably), contrasting with the modern subject Smith characterizes as essentially linked to others by sympathy, is thus central to understanding the conflicting impulses in Smith's thinking about history, and ultimately to finding our way back to the problem of what prevents Smith from writing it.

What we find when we are looking at the relationship between the modern and the savage or primitive is an intense unresolved ambivalence about the value of the latter, making it possible to read Smith both as believer in history as progress towards commercial civilization *and* as Rousseauvian elegist of a lost social harmony. This mix of attraction and condemnation for the primitive is on display most clearly in two areas of the *Theory of Moral Sentiments*: the accounts of sympathy and its absence among savage peoples, and the related discussions of these groups' supposed silence and non-communicativeness. These passages therefore deserve some extended scrutiny.[37]

To take sympathy first: Smith's account of sympathy in the *Theory* stresses the element of spectacle involved: *seeing* suffering, joy, danger and so forth helps generate fellow-feeling:

> When we *see* a stroke aimed and just ready to fall upon the leg or arm of another person, we naturally shrink and draw back our own leg or our own arm; and when it does fall, we feel it in some measure ... The mob, when they are *gazing* at a dancer on the slack rope, naturally writhe and twist their own bodies, as they see him do ... Persons of delicate fibres and a weak constitution of body complain, that in *looking* on the sores and ulcers which are exposed by beggars in the streets, they are apt to feel an itching or uneasy sensation in the correspondent part of their own bodies.[38] [emphasis added]

This notion of sympathy as an experience of the visible is a consistent thread in Smith. The orientation toward the *spectacle* of feeling, indeed the constitutive theatricality which has been observed in Hume's and Smith's accounts of the workings of sympathy produces a notion of the social that is in many ways inseparable from the scopic.[39] Smith's sense of the dependence of modern social relations in general, and sympathy in particular, on the regime of the visible is, moreover, not just a distinctive element in his account but also a source of anxiety. The *Theory* makes use of the realm of the visible as both an indispensable and fundamentally deluding condition of social bonding. For example, Smith's comments on the illusory gratifications of wealth include the remark that these exist rather in the spectators' observation than in the actual possessor's experience: 'In this, as in all other cases, we constantly pay more attention to the sentiments of the *spectator*, than to those of the person principally concerned, and consider rather how his situation will appear to other people, than how it will appear to himself' (emphasis added).[40]

Along with this anxiety about social spectacle, Smith demonstrates concern about the overall effects of sympathy, a concern which also emerges most clearly in his account of the savage's (contrasting) indifference to the suffering of others. The portrait of the savage as immune to sympathy is presented in some detail in Part V of the *Theory*, where Smith discusses the influence of various local customs and cultures on morality. Here Smith asserts a fundamental opposition between civilized and barbarous nations, with North American Indians as his primary exemplar: 'Among civilized nations, the virtues which are founded upon humanity, are more cultivated than those which are founded upon self-denial and the command of the passions. Among rude and barbarous nations it is quite otherwise, the virtues of self-denial are more cultivated than those of humanity.'[41] The savages' lack of 'humanity', or sympathy, is initially presented as the result of a paucity of resources, a move which presents their value-system as essentially a response to a lack:

> Every savage undergoes a sort of Spartan discipline, and by the necessity of his situation is inured to every sort of hardship. He is in continual danger: he is often exposed to the greatest extremities of hunger, and frequently dies of pure want. His circumstances not only habituate him to every sort of distress, but teach him to give way to none of the passions which that distress is apt to excite. He can expect from his country men no sympathy or indulgence for such weakness. Before we can feel much for others, we must in some measure be at ease ourselves. If our own misery pinches us very severely, we have no leisure to attend to that of our neighbour: and all savages are too much occupied with their wants and necessities, to give much attention to another person. A savage, therefore, whatever the nature of his distress, expects no sympathy from those about him ...[42]

Sympathy, feeling for others, then, depends on the kind of material surplus that is only possible in the latter stages of historical development, an argument also made by Millar and Hume, and which Smith repeats in the *Lectures on Rhetoric and Belles Lettres*.[43] The *Theory*'s characterization of the benefits and achievements of modern commercial life, and of sympathy as a mode of social cohesion deriving from a certain wealth and ease, would seem then to gain by the contrast with the figure of the insensible savage, supporting a logic of cultural progress from barbarism to modern Britain.

But as Smith's account develops, this apparently secure placing of the savage in the pre-history of modern society begins to founder. The absence of sympathy shifts from being simply the product of lack, to the far more positive value, for Smith, of self-denial – 'a heroic and unconquerable firmness' as he later terms it, 'which the custom and education of his country demand of every savage'.[44] This characterization marks a slide in Smith's argument. Now it is polite society which evinces loss and a kind of poverty, and the savage begins to appear as the bearer of the kind of self-regulating rationality that is a dominant value not only in Smith's ethics, but in the Enlightenment conception of the subject. Hence 'insensibility' or self-denial by itself does not securely demonstrate the contrastive virtues of sympathy, nor locate the savage as a stage of human development since surpassed by European history.

In fact, this picture of the savage indifferent to his own fate strongly resembles that of the ancient Stoic, given an admiring portrait in the *Theory*. The characterization of the Stoic, with his 'contempt of life and death' and a wholehearted 'submission to the order of Providence' is discussed at some length in the *Theory*, and evokes strong parallels with the North American savages.[45] The prestige and prominence Smith accords the Stoics in his moral system is increased in the sixth and final edition of the *Theory* in 1790, where he expands the treatment of Stoic philosophy in his concluding survey of different ethical systems and gives them this commendation: 'The spirit and manhood of their doctrines make a wonderful contrast with the desponding, whining and plaintive tone of some modern systems'.[46] Smith overtly links the Stoics to the American Indians, both of whom are ready to face the calamities of life with equanimity, and notes that both share a contempt for 'life and death ... and, at the same time, the most entire submission to the order of providence'.[47] The alignment of the modern primitive with the figure of the ancient Stoic suggests continuities and values very foreign to the 'four stages of progress' model of history.

This shifting valuation of 'primitive morality' continues in Smith's discussion of the second distinguishing characteristic of primitive peoples, their supposed circumspection, or tendency to conceal their feelings, rather than to reveal them to observers in a scene of exchange of sympathies. In a typical comment Smith notes of the native subject, 'his passions, how furious and violent so ever, are never permitted to disturb the serenity of his countenance, or the composure of his conduct and behaviour'.[48] The theatricality which we observed above in Smith's accounts of the workings of sympathy meets its opposite in the account of the determinedly *anti-theatrical* social space of the savage. Where Smith had famously opened, and exemplified, his discussion of the workings of sympathy with the spectacle of a man on the rack, observed by a sympathetic spectator attempting to imaginatively recreate the victim's experience of suffering, his discussion of the self-command of primitive peoples replaces this scenario with one in which both physical pain and the spectatorial gaze have lost most of their significance:

The savages in North America ... [possess a] self-command almost beyond the conception of Europeans ... When a savage is made prisoner of war and receives, as is usual, the sentence of death [by torture] from his conquerors, he hears it without expressing any emotion, and afterwards submits to the most dreadful torments without discovering any other passion but contempt of his enemies. While he is hung by the shoulders over a slow fire, he derides his tormentors, and tells them with how much more ingenuity he himself had tormented such of their countrymen as had fallen into his hands. After he has been scorched and burnt, and lacerated in all the most tender parts of his body for several hours together, he is often allowed, to prolong his misery, a short respite, and is taken down from the stake: he employs this interval in talking upon all indifferent subjects, inquires after the news of the country, and seems indifferent about nothing but his own situation. The spectators express the same insensibility; the sight of so horrible an object seems to make no impression upon them; they scarce look at the prisoner, except when they lend a hand to torment him. At other times they smoke tobacco, and amuse themselves with any common object, as if no such matter was going on. Every savage is said to prepare himself from his earliest youth for this dreadful end. He composes for this purpose, what they call the song of death, a song which he is to sing when he has fallen into the hands of his enemies, and is expiring under the tortures which they

inflict upon him. It consists of insults upon his tormentors, and expresses the highest contempt of death and pain ... The same contempt of death and torture prevails
among all other savage nations ...[49]

The contrast this scene makes with the spectacle of suffering that compels the
gaze and sympathy of the spectator could hardly be sharper. The familiar aspects
of this death scene – the savage's incredible tolerance for and silence about pain,
his invincible inwardness and the tradition of the death song – call up some of
the by-now stock images of European accounts of American and other indig-
enous peoples, from at least Behn's *Oroonoko* on.

Smith initially identifies this inwardness as simply a form of 'falsehood and
dissimulation' common to all savage nations.[50] But in a reversal similar to the one
we saw on the status of sympathy, he also suggests the suffering savage's total self-
command and spectators' indifference is honourable, even admirable. A certain
tone of respect permeates Smith's descriptions of the harsh details of these practices. Moreover the portrait of the savage's supreme self-control, self-denial and
inwardness, corresponds in several striking details with Smith's characterization
of the so-called 'impartial spectator'. The impartial spectator, or 'ideal man within
the breast' that Smith establishes as the supreme arbiter of moral conduct, is in
effect a limiting principle introduced into the *Theory* as a means of directing and
establishing limits to the potentially excessive workings of emotion and sympathy. He represents what the proper level of emotional response to a given event
should be, establishing a standard to which participants in the scene of sympathy
properly aspire and by which, most importantly, they regulate and restrain their
own expression of feeling: 'We must ... in all cases, view ourselves not so much
in that light in which we may naturally appear to ourselves, as according to that
in which we naturally appear to others ... If [an individual] would act so as that
the impartial spectator may enter into the principles of his conduct ... he must
... upon all ...occasions ... bring [his emotion] down to something which other
men can go along with'.[51] The vision of discipline and self-denial offered by the
figure of the impartial spectator clearly offers something of a parallel to the self-
control of the savage.

These musings on the meaning of the savage again raise the question about
how the age of commerce has surpassed or improved on a supposedly primitive form of social organization. Due to Smith's extremely ambivalent account of
modernity in the *Theory*, the primitive shifts meaning from exotic variation, or
earlier and outmoded stage of development, to an alternative which is implied
to be more desirable than the regime of sympathy that otherwise dominates in
Smith's text. In making these comparisons and evaluations, Smith manifests a
strong resistance to the idea of history as a series of advances to the present, and

an intense nostalgia for the losses of past forms of social organization which seriously challenges the overt claims of the *Theory* about the benefits of commercialism.

This strain, while at its strongest in his early writings like the *Theory*, is found throughout Smith's corpus. His list of 'the disadvantages of a commercial spirit' in the *Lectures on Jurisprudence* specifies: under its influence 'the minds of men are contracted and rendered incapable of elevation, education is despised or at least neglected, and heroic spirit is almost utterly extinguished'.[52] As late as the *Wealth of Nations*, Smith's description of the effect of commerce and manufacture on personality and social relations is often unsparingly hostile. Smith's well-known assessment of the negative effects of specialization on workers, for example – that after years spent in repetitive tasks a worker 'becomes as stupid and ignorant as it is possible for a human creature to become' – is underlined by the contrast he makes between this state and the range of skills and mastery demanded of hunters, pastoralists, and even farmers: 'in such societies the varied occupations of every man oblige every man to exert his capacity'.[53] The representation of the savage, throughout Smith's corpus and especially in the *Theory of Moral Sentiments*, provides a challenge to the assumed dominance of a commercial society and the regime of sympathy. Smith's fascination with the primitive illuminates the profound concerns the first great theorist of the age of commerce held about the problems and limitations of the modern subject, and about the idea of progress itself.

3

In Smith's version of history, then, the primitive and the modern compete for dominance, and the celebration of progress clashes with an intensely felt sense of decline and nostalgia. These sentiments, despite his better-known assessments of the benefits of the age of commerce elsewhere, not infrequently align Smith more closely with Rousseau than with Hume.[54] However, this real, if partial, affinity is usually either denied or explained away.[55] But both Rousseau and Hume are influences on Smith's historical thinking, even if they cohabit very uneasily.

Smith's historical thinking here might be understood as anticipating the kind of revisionist Enlightenment historicism Johann Gottfried von Herder outlines in his *Reflections on the Philosophy of the History of Mankind* (1784–91). Without completely abandoning the idea of progress, Herder proposes in the *Reflections* a vision of multiple individual and social types that seems to find a permanent place for social arrangements that are seen as strictly transient in a progress model of history. Herder argues that the kind of human variety and difference of values that Smith mourns as lost in his historical narrative can and will continue to co-exist, and, in fact, even to flourish: this variation of types has something of an evolutionary imperative backing it. Describing the nature of human sociability, Herder elaborates a principle of diversification that completely undermines the notion of any particular society's supremacy:

> The practical understanding of man was intended, to blossom and bear fruit in all its varieties: and hence such a diversified Earth was ordained for so diversified a species ... As man is the most artfully complicated of all creatures, so great a variety of character occurs in no other ... Man, from his very nature, will clash but little in his pursuits with man; his dispositions, sensations, and propensities, being so infinitely diversified, and as it were individualized. What is a matter of indifference to one man, to another is an object of desire: and then each has a world of enjoyment in himself, each a creation of his own. Nature has bestowed on this diverging species an ample space ... over which the most different climates and modes of life have room to spread.[56]

Instead of making the familiar assumption that certain cultures and climes were more civilized than others, Herder argues that the variety of human societies cannot be ranked or reduced to stages in some unitary narrative, in effect giving up the earlier Enlightenment ideal of establishing a 'universal norm' for human development.[57]

This kind of acknowledgement of the limits of totalizing narratives is precisely what is anticipated in Smith's own conflicting attitudes to social formations and ideas of progress. Anticipated, but never quite concluded, as Smith remains uneasily suspended between triumphalism and melancholy in comparing his own historical and social situation to others. It is, one must suspect, precisely this unresolved conflict that prevents Smith, for all the depth and complexity of his meditations on history, from completing the long systematic treatment he had undertaken; and presumably, that is responsible for precipitating the deathbed bonfire of his papers. Why could Smith not resolve the conflict he spent so much time rehearsing and revisiting? And, if he could not write a resolution, why could he not be content to leave the evidence of this dualism for his readers to ponder?

Without claiming to provide final answers to all the questions raised by Smith's ceremonial act of destruction, one can point to two models of historical discourse, two conflicting notions of professional identity, that play out in this scene of sacrifice. The first model is that of the philosopher or system-builder. It is notable that, despite his own interest in literary narrative and the example of Hume, who famously moved from experimental moral philosophy to the essay form (with all its more literary, unscientific associations) in the 1740s, Smith resisted writing in any form other than the treatise. Smith produced very few essays, and the ones he did produce were evidently designed in almost every case to form part of a projected large study which remained unfinished: the systematic or scientific survey always remained his preferred genre.[58] In response, for example, to Henry Mackenzie's invitation to contribute to his periodical *The*

Mirror (1779–80), Smith ultimately declined, explaining that 'My Manner of Writing ... will not do for a Work of that Sort; it runs too much into Deduction and inference'.[59] In his preference for a particular form, the philosophical treatise, Smith highlights his commitment to the systematic ideal of philosophy and his evident conviction of its fundamental difference from the fragmentary, impressionistic, or unsystematic essay.

The four-stage model of history, in its reduction of all social forms to four basic types, has a certain austere appeal for a writer so invested in the prestige of philosophical system-making, and this appeal should not be underestimated. The stadial model's undeniable economy of explanation is an ideal to which Smith himself acknowledges all philosophical or systematic thinkers are particularly susceptible. In his accounts of various *deformations professionelles* (a topic which Smith, in quest of disciplinary self-definition, visits with some frequency in his writings), he identifies as the philosopher's particular weakness his love of elegant explanations. Smith describes a desire for simplicity and closure in explanation in the *Theory of Moral Sentiments* as a 'propensity ... natural to all men, but which philosophers in particular are apt to cultivate with a peculiar fondness, as the great means of displaying their ingenuity, the propensity to account for all appearances from as few principles as possible'.[60]

Countering this impulse in Smith to see history driving forward to a uniform modernity are, as we have seen, the appeal of the varied primitive social forms and practices he describes, the example of Rousseau and, perhaps most importantly, an emphasis on history writing as a literary genre, rather than a branch of philosophical or scientific enquiry. Smith's detailed characterization of the goals of history writing in the *Lectures on Rhetoric and Belles Lettres* repeatedly stresses the status of history as a more or less literary narrative, one governed by strict rules of veracity to be sure, but also concerned with matters of style, the psychology of principal agents, and above all, how best to affect and instruct the reader through shaping an effective story.[61] From his comments on the literary appeal of the savage's (supposed) life of adventurousness combined with pleasurable idleness in the early letter to the *Edinburgh Review*, quoted above, to the descriptions of narrative and sympathy in the *Theory* and the *Lectures on Rhetoric and Belles Lettres*, Smith consistently stresses the form historical narratives should take if they are to be successful in engaging their readers. In the *Lectures* Smith gives, for example, a detailed account of techniques for involving the reader's sympathies in the events narrated by the historian, concluding that the most powerfully affecting narratives are those describing misfortune: 'It is with the misfortunes of others that we most commonly as well as most deeply sympathise. – A Historian who related a battle and the effects attending, if he was no way interested would naturally dwell more on the misery and lamentations of the vanquished than on the triumph and exultations of the Victors.'[62]

This sentimentalist theory of history, as Smith here expounds it, could have been inferred from his own practice, with his habit of memorably recreating the pleasures and accomplishments of cultures now lost or irremediably transformed, and his suggestions of something vital lacking in modern European culture.[63] Few theorists of history before Walter Benjamin have had quite so keen an appreciation for those who are, in Benjamin's terms, 'lying prostrate ... in the triumphal procession' of history, and for the unique value of what has been lost in this march.[64] Here we can say that Smith's commitment to a history understood as conforming to an efficient if not quite benevolent model of systematic advance collides, not only with the fact of loss, but also with his conviction as a student of literature and theorist of sympathy that narratives of decline make the best stories. This conflict between literary and philosophical/scientific discourses and forms of knowledge is played out throughout Smith's corpus and opens up the question of the relation between Smith's literary researches and the rest of his work – the question that inevitably leads us on to Smith's other missing treatise, that on literature. But for now, at least, we can say that Smith's inability to write his projected history derives from a thoroughgoing questioning about which social values to espouse and, at a deeper level, from an anxiety about how to write history and about what he as an author is producing when he writes it: a systematic philosophical analysis, with all the claims to authority that entails, or an unscientific literary narrative that commands the reader's deepest sympathies.

11 CAN JULIE BE TRUSTED? ROUSSEAU AND THE CRISIS OF CONSTANCY IN EIGHTEENTH-CENTURY PHILOSOPHY

Nancy Yousef

The cleft between being and appearance in interpersonal and social relations has long been regarded as the unifying and driving problem in Rousseau's work.[1] In the context of eighteenth-century moral psychology, Rousseau's preoccupation with 'seeing through' others imports empiricist concerns with the limitations of the senses into the realm of relations between persons and thereby imagines ethical aspirations as consistent with and contingent upon epistemological possibilities. Rousseau's ideal of transparency, whether expressed as nostalgia for a lost period of human or personal history, or as utopian yearning for inescapably public forms of life, or as indulgent surrender to imaginative visions of harmonious beautiful souls, can be understood as displacing an ideal of sympathy that many of Rousseau's philosophical precursors and contemporaries assumed to be a natural, irresistible feeling for others.

Earlier in the eighteenth century, questions about the moral implications of natural sympathy arise among proponents of sentimentalism even as epistemological questions about access to the thoughts and feelings of others are foreclosed. Shaftesbury, for example, assumes an uncomplicated continuity between natural affections and benevolence or good will towards others. Hume, by contrast, offers a more complex view of sympathy: it is the source of the 'sentiments' upon which 'all morality depends', but does not, in itself, motivate virtuous action and at times conflicts with the broader humanitarianism of justice.[2] Kant would later separate the question of feeling from duty towards the other, arguing that sympathy is an amoral sentiment, contingent, inconsistent and unrelated to recognition of the other as an intrinsically valuable being, worthy of respect and esteem.[3] And yet the recognition Kant's ethics demands might itself best be understood as an abstract distillation of sympathy in its most basic sense – as involving appreciation of the other as like oneself, as an equal.[4] What Rousseau appears to take from the contradictions and complexities of eighteenth-century moral sentimentalism is an insistence on the ethical orientation towards others entailed by sympathy which is proto-Kantian in its austerity and absoluteness (where to feel for the other obliges me to respect and respond to the other as a fellow human being) and an unrepressed anxiety about the epistemic basis of sympathetic recognition (how can I know the other to be human, like me, and therefore worthy of respect and esteem?).

Implicit in Rousseau's ameliorative approach to the challenge of intersubjectivity is an interpretation of the underlying individualism of empiricist psychology – the very idea that apparently similar creatures might experience radically different sensations and ideas (of sweetness, say, or justice) – as itself a philosophical symptom of a social world that has engendered divisive particularity. Although for Rousseau perceptual constraints always literally and metaphorically obstruct our access to one another, limiting us to the body of the other (which conceals his mind and heart), the face (which masks thought and feeling), the spoken word (which might contradict the secretly held belief or idea), the achievement of conditions in which we can be sure that we see and hear and the other as he really is does not entail a transcendence of those empirical bounds (a more insightful gaze, more acute hearing, telepathy). Rather Rousseauvian transparency seems to entail something stranger and more radical than penetrating access to the other. What is imagined is an emptying out of the interior. Rousseau in effect, approaches the problem of knowing others from the inside out. Instead of imagining a special capacity for feeling or judging or perceiving the thoughts and feelings 'hidden' inside another mind or heart, he imagines what individuals would have to be like in order to be readily perceived and recognized as sympathetic fellow creatures, beings for whom honesty, fidelity, constancy and sincerity are constitutive.

Reciprocity ought to be effortless in a world where I can be sure that all others are just like me. Among the earliest articulations of this possibility is the mythic prehistory evoked in the first *Discourse*: 'How sweet it would be to live among us if outer appearances were always the likeness of the heart's dispositions', for then 'men found their safety in the ease with which they saw through each other'.[5] Clear perception of the other's heart makes life among others safe; what makes such a life sweet, however, is the unarticulated assumption that the 'heart's dispositions' will accord not only with 'outer appearances', but also with the dispositions of all other hearts. Intersubjective transparency seems always already to entail a harmony of sentiments in Rousseau, a likeness that is not the condition for the identification upon which sympathy depends, but one so complete as to make identification itself seem a mediated form of knowledge. The conjectural past of the first discourse is the fantastic other world Rousseau recollects in the *Confessions* (comp. 1770) as the conceptual inspiration for *La Nouvelle Héloïse*:

> The impossibility of attaining the real persons precipitated me into the land of chimeras; and seeing nothing that existed worthy of my exalted feelings, I fostered them in an ideal world which my creative imagination soon peopled with beings after my own heart ... Altogether ignoring the human race, I created for myself societies of perfect creatures celestial in their virtue and beauty, and of reliable, tender and faithful friends such as I had never found here below.[6]

'Reliable, tender and faithful friends' prove impossible to find 'here below' because the social world Rousseau describes and laments is one in which individual survival involves a set of adaptive traits designed to exploit the inherent empirical limits of intersubjectivity. The evolution and pursuit of private interests, desires and motives, the advantages of suspicion, deliberate misrepresentation: such cultivation of inner depth makes use of a reciprocal opacity and, in so doing, engenders differences that destroy the basis of sympathetic recognition. The powerful social criticism of Rousseau's earliest writings is succeeded by a series of works unified by the task of imagining conditions under which human beings would be shaped by altogether different adaptations to the inherent insecurity of intersubjective knowledge. Commitment to shared interests and a common good, participation in public surveillance and spectacle, uninhibited candor: the social relations described in the *Letter to d'Alembert* (1758), *La Nouvelle Héloïse* (1761), *Emile* (1762) and the *Social Contract* (1762) offer no space for the cultivation of privacy and, in so doing, foster and sustain similarity and equality. Individuals are liberated from suspicion and anxiety because they can be confident of dwelling among 'beings after my own heart'. Sympathetic recognition, based on utter transparency, is ensured because there are no unknowable depths to the other, no hidden difference between my self and the other's self.

From the intimacy of romance to the civic space of the polity, Rousseau's middle works indulge a fantasy about expunging the unknowable in others by imagining them to be self-evidently the same, absolutely exposed and therefore fully predictable. In *Emile*, this aspiration is articulated as a longing to give human relations the same 'inflexibility' as laws of nature, so that 'dependence on men would then become dependence on things'.[7] The preceptor thus shapes Emile into a wholly knowable object: 'he ought not to take a step without your having foreseen it' and 'ought not to open his mouth without your knowing what he is going to say'.[8] The foresight is consonant with the law of constant disclosure that governs Clarens in *La Nouvelle Héloïse*: 'A single precept of morality can do for all the others', Julie explains, 'Never do or say anything that thou dost not wish everyone to see and hear'.[9]

Tensions between coerciveness and freedom, oppression and fulfillment, constraint and virtue unavoidably arise in Rousseau's 'societies of perfect creatures'. Transparency is achieved, but under conditions which so restrict the unpredictable play of passions and personalities as to make one wonder whether the epistemic limits that make our commitments so vulnerable are not, somehow, constitutive of ethical life rather than the underlying cause of moral failing.

The balance of this essay explores Rousseau's efforts to imagine epistemic security as the basis and necessary condition for fidelity, trust and constancy-virtues that in the eighteenth century are more familiarly associated with and derived from the moral sentiments in general, and from sympathy in particular. The inextricability of transparency and sympathy entails a critical revision of sentimentalist hypotheses about the origins of the affections devastating in its implications, for even as Rousseau insists on the primacy of feeling in moral experience he erodes the 'natural' grounding of feeling assumed by his predecessors. The aspirations and unavoidable failings of this effort to align the intersubjective confidence of sentimentalism with epistemic certainty are bound up with, but not reducible to, the articulation of sexual difference that marks Rousseau's fictional and theoretical accounts of marriage. In Rousseau's efforts to imagine marriage as the secure foundation for broader forms of social organization, coherently elaborated schemes for the eradication of unpredictability abruptly collapse, thereby allowing the fundamental questions about intersubjective knowledge they were intended to foreclose to re-emerge as affectively charged ethical challenges. Abstract conceptions of the moral possibilities of community are both determined and troubled by the vulnerabilities and risks of intimacy.

Julie's Fall

Let us begin with the deliberate coincidence of irresistible maternal sentiment and debilitating anxiety about conjugal fidelity that determine the heroine's fate in *La Nouvelle Héloïse*. A child stumbles, loses his footing, and falls into the deep waters of Lake Geneva. His mother flies after him without a moment's hesitation, plunges into the lake and, in saving him, contracts a fever from which she will not recover. This over-determined accident is the immediate cause of Julie's death, affirming the heroine's status as a model *materfamilias* in an act of self-sacrifice perfectly exemplifying the 'natural sympathy' philosophers of moral sentiment such as Hume identify as the foundation of the 'social virtues of humanity and benevolence'. The 'parent fly[ing] to the relief of his child, transported by that natural sympathy which actuates him', writes Hume in *An Enquiry Concerning the Principles of Morals* (1751), is irresistibly driven by 'beneficent affections' that have the force of instinct.[10] It is not the child who occupies Julie's heart and mind in her final hours, however. The last words ascribed to her in the novel suggest that it is her own life she imagines having saved with her fatal plunge, specifically her life as a wife whose conscience is untroubled: 'virtue remains to me without spot, and love has remained to me without remorse'.[11] The fall into the icy waters spares 'the most virtuous of wives' from the more destructive vertiginous fall she has feared.[12] 'Who knows whether seeing myself so near the abyss, I would not have been drawn into it?' she asks St Preux in her final letter, expressing relief that the potential calamity of their permanent reunion in her household, where he was about to take up the role of preceptor to her children, has been irrevocably averted: 'I dare pride myself in the past, but who could have answered to me for the future? One day more, perhaps, and I was a criminal! How about a whole life spent with you? What dangers I have run unawares!'[13]

For those with whom Julie is intimately involved, the agitating preoccupation with the perilous fragility of her virtue seems an unwarranted, even self-indulgent preoccupation belied by her evident fulfilment in the role of devoted wife and mother. Her cousin and confidante Claire would seem to be entirely justified in asserting that 'the circumspection that you base on your past faults is insulting to your present state'.[14] 'The only failing I find in you is your inability to regain the confidence you owe yourself', Wolmar observes, adding that 'it is not enough for me that [my wife] keep her faith; I am offended that she doubts it'.[15] But it is not simply that for Rousseau's protagonist the past inappropriately impinges on the present. Julie herself acknowledges what her loved ones know: 'the more I try to sound my soul's present state, the more I find in it to reassure me'. But such introspection gives her no relief. After all, her anxieties are prospective rather than retrospective (only an 'excess of confidence ... makes us gauge the future by the present', she reasons) so that the self-certainty of the present might itself be taken as cause for doubt: 'We feel steady for a moment and assume we will never be shaken', she concludes in a letter to St Preux, justifying her insistence that 'one must constantly be on one's guard'.[16] Recognizing the irresolvable form of Julie's worries, St Preux dismisses them as the 'scruples of a timorous soul that considers it a duty to take fright, and believes one must fear everything so as to protect oneself from everything'.[17] He warns that 'extreme timidity has its danger just as an excessive confidence does. By constantly pointing out monsters to us where there are none, it exhausts us in tilting against phantasms.'[18] However, like the doubts of the suspicion-driven sceptic, or the inconsolably jealous lover, those that plague Julie appear gratuitous and self-perpetuating precisely to the degree that they are inexorably rational. 'Is it enough for my heart to reassure me, when reason should alarm me?' she asks, 'Who can promise me that my confidence is not again an illusion of vice? How can I trust sentiments that have so many times deluded me?'[19]

Julie's unease is clearly a self-inflicted and powerful introjection of an uncertainty that ought properly to torment her husband and while it is intriguing that Rousseau effects this transference of anxiety on to the wife he typically tasks with the duty of assuaging it, the most remarkable feature of this *self*-doubt may well be how little it seems to differ from doubts about the constancy of persons or even objects in the external world. Indeed Julie's despairing inability to 'trust anything I see or feel' itself suggests a strange similitude between destabilizing doubt of her (inner) sentiments and the more philosophically familiar doubt cast on the (outer) world of persons and things.[20]

It is no accident that Julie's fatal plunge occurs immediately after the definitive rejection of her proposals to unite St Preux with Claire so that, becoming 'simply sisters and brothers to each other', the former lovers might finally live together 'without danger', their 'tenderest sentiments' legitimized and therefore 'dangerous no longer'.[21] These proposals are motivated, as Julie herself recognizes, by the ever-present fear for her own future fidelity: 'No doubt I felt for myself the perils I thought I was feeling for you', she concedes in that final letter.[22] In spite of ever more vigilant efforts to secure her virtue, the comfort she ultimately takes in the notion that death will safeguard her against a perilous intimacy with St Preux follows a conclusion that turns her fear for herself into a final certainty about the illusions of her own feeling: 'I have long deluded myself', she decides, 'You have long believed I was cured, and I thought I was'.[23] To read Julie's demise as a surrender to fatally ineradicable self-doubt is to say that *La Nouvelle Héloïse* undoes the narrative of the heroine's definitive conversion at the altar quite as effectively as that conversion undoes the romance of the first half of the novel. It is also to emphasize a peculiar conjunction in Rousseau's work: the sudden collapse of marriages apparently conceived and presented as ideal models of secure, untroubled unions.

In a more overt, under-motivated and unexpected undermining of marital stability, Rousseau begins the unfinished sequel to *Emile* with the revelation that Sophie – imagined in the first book as a woman who 'will be chaste and decent until her last breath' – has irredeemably violated her marriage: 'Another has defiled your bed', she confesses, 'I am with child – our persons shall never be united' (*Je suis enceinte; vous ne me toucherez de ma vie*).[24] The elaborately contrived education designed to ensure that this wife provide 'evidence of her virtue to the eyes of others as well as to her own conscience' and thereby give her husband 'the confidence to call [her children] his own' fails under sketchily described circumstances of estrangement that do not, in any case, prepare Emile for Sophie's confession.[25] He is struck 'motionless', 'benumbed', 'annihilated' by a shockingly unanticipated betrayal. In formal terms, the novel emphasizes this abrupt reversal of fate, opening with the revelation that 'All is vanished like a dream ... I have lost all that was dear to me – wife – children – friends, everything, in short, even the intercourse of men [*commerce de mes semblables*]', an unexpected and alarming reintroduction to a character Rousseau had left happily married and on the brink of fatherhood in *Emile*.[26] The preceptor had introduced Sophie to his pupil as one whose 'expression gives promise of a soul and does not lie', a certainty Emile directly overturns in the sequel: 'My friend you think you knew this enchanting girl. O how you have been mistaken!'[27]

And though love itself might recover, nothing will ever restore that 'confidence without which regret, disgust and despair are the inseparable attendants of the marriage state'.[28] Given her betrayal, Sophie's singular formation for fidelity seems to undermine the possibility of any secure interpersonal bond as Emile's despair radiates inexorably outward from the collapse of his marriage: 'Every tie broken ... every relation altered'.[29]

These Rousseauvian contributions to anxieties about feminine fidelity and chastity, while clearly taking a part in debates about natural virtues and sympathy, need to be understood as especially compelling and dramatic elaborations of unresolved epistemological tensions in eighteenth-century sentimentalism. The fate of Rousseau's heroines engages moral theories about the source of fellow feeling on the way towards taking on fundamental questions about intersubjective knowledge.

Lovers and Parents: The Origins of Affiliation

The bare fact of filial attachment – the instinctual love of parents for their children – is repeatedly invoked as the foundation of natural affections, the model and origin for more complex emotional and social bonds. In Shaftesbury, Hutcheson, Hume and others, sympathy, fellow-feeling and even benevolence are all ultimately derived from an imagination of the irresistible bonds of feeling engendered by the fact and through the experience of sexual partnership and parenting. Shaftesbury, for example, argues that the 'long and helpless infancy' of human creatures ensures that 'union and strict society is required between the sexes to preserve and nurse their growing offspring' and, therefore, to 'pair and live in love and fellowship with ... partner and offspring' inevitably leads to the formation of tribes and nations. 'Conjugal affection and natural affection to parents' evolve unproblematically into civic 'love of a common city, community or country'.[30] Hume does not go so far; indeed the potential conflict between love for our relations and 'extensive concern for society' or 'universal affection for mankind' is central to his ethics. Nevertheless he too locates our 'first and most natural sentiment of morals' in the 'concern for offspring' that 'unites' the two sexes.[31]

Given the long tradition on which he might have drawn, it is notable that for Rousseau, the notion that 'the most natural of all societies and the only natural one, is that of the family'[32] has no necessary implications for moral psychology. Rousseau's insistence on the conceptual factitiousness of 'nature' necessarily complicates our understanding of claims based on that category. Family might be the 'most natural' of all societies, but no form of social life is natural in the sense of given, or inevitable for Rousseau.[33] His argument that there is no obvious relation between sexual intercourse, pregnancy and prolonged union between the sexes is bound to expose the epistemological presuppositions at work in the arguments of his predecessors. In the state of nature, 'once the sexual appetite is satisfied, the man no longer needs the woman, nor the woman [the] man' and because neither has the 'least idea of the consequences of [their] action. One goes off in one direction, and the other in that, and there is no likelihood that at the end of nine months they will remember ever having known each other.'[34] Why would the sexes remain united to rear a child whose birth neither willed nor foresaw? Human beings move from solitude and independence to dependence and affiliation by force of accident rather than necessity in the philosophical narrative of the second *Discourse*. For all that 'conjugal love and paternal love' become the 'sweetest sentiments known to man', they arise from the acquired 'habit of living together' that comes about only through a 'concatenation of extraordinary circumstances', not inevitable, natural evolution.[35] The 'first developments of the heart' originate within the family and are the basis for wider forms of social association but Rousseau does not attribute these feelings to 'nature'. To do so would be to evade the critical work of providing groundwork for that which is necessary but not given: affectionate attachment and reliable association. The opening assertion about the familial origins of communal life in the *Social Contract* is immediately qualified: the prolonged union of persons we call a family is not 'natural, but voluntar[y], and the family maintains itself only by means of convention'.[36] And yet no more and no less that the constitution of civil, political and moral life rests on that mere convention. Not natural, yet essential: it is a troubling but characteristic paradox.

The physical fact of kinship provided earlier theorists with a powerful metaphor for the irresistible workings of impassioned care, parent and child serving as the exemplary two-person model for an inherent sympathetic relation that could be assumed, without explanation, without need for foundation. In so far as these arguments arise in response to Hobbes's view of natural egotism, they assume a benign form of interdependence that Hobbes does not grant even to the relationship between mother and child. Reasoning that 'it cannot be understood that any man hath ... afforded life to another, that he might both get strength by his years, and at once become an enemy', Hobbes concludes that 'every woman that bears children [in the state of nature] becomes both a mother and a lord' because a mother will only 'breed up' her child on the condition that he obey her when full-grown.[37] Love does not motivate motherhood, nor does instinct drive mothers to benevolent caretaking. The earlier philosopher's imagination of an implicit, mutually self-interested contract between parent and offspring is a reminder both of the basic disagreement over the natural inclinations of human beings that are always in the background of eighteenth-century discussions of sympathy, and of the weakness of examples intended to preclude explanation in moral philosophy of the period. Presumably the image of a mother nourishing her child would not serve Hobbes as an illustration of innate moral sense. The physical fact of filiation does not necessarily correspond to an emotional or sentimental fact about human experience, nor does it provide a basis for a moral psychology. Mother and child are related, but what they feel for one another, or what they ought to be to one another remains undetermined.

'The child ought to love his mother before knowing that he ought to', writes Rousseau in *Emile*, but 'if the voice of blood is not strengthened by habit and care, it is extinguished in the first years, and the heart dies, so to speak, before being born'.[38] Without assuming a natural egotism in need of constraint, Rousseau nevertheless insists that even filial love requires prolonged cultivation, thus raising the question of what ensures endurance and constancy in human associations. Rousseau's complaint at the beginning of *Emile* is telling: 'There are no longer fathers, mothers, children, brothers, or sisters. They all hardly know each other. How could they love each other?'[39] The remark appears in the midst of an attack on the practice of wet-nursing ('let mothers deign to nurse their children, morals will reform themselves, nature's sentiments will be awakened in every heart') where breastfeeding serves as a metonym for the larger idea that 'peaceful care of the family and the home are [women's] lot'.[40] What Rousseau promises the devoted mother ('solid and constant attachment on the part of their husbands, a truly filial tenderness on the part of their children') is the *cultivation* of the very sentiments and loyalties that earlier theorists had assumed to naturally link members of a family. Paradoxically, the 'natural sentiments' to be awakened arise from rather than underlie cultural practices and convention. 'Let women once again become mothers', Rousseau urges, 'men will soon become fathers and husbands again' rather than being solitary cohabitants who 'all hardly know each other'.[41]

It is by no means clear in what sense the members of a family can be said to be unknown to one another, but the implications of Rousseau's lament are intriguing. The very identification of individuals as belonging to a family (mothers, husbands, fathers) is withheld from those who do not know one another, and loving in this formulation is contingent upon knowing: 'They all hardly know each other. How could they love each other?' The conjunction between knowing, loving and being related or affiliated is both critical to Rousseau's imagination of stable social relations and marks a significant divergence from the moral psychology of his immediate predecessors. When, in *Julie* (and other works of the same period such as *Emile* and the *Letter to d'Alembert*), Rousseau writes of marriage rather than family as the 'root of all social order', the association he elects to treat as foundational is one in which neither love nor trust can be taken for granted. In the context of sentimentalist claims for the moral feelings evinced by familial ties, Rousseau's emphasis on marriage, the two person union that is, after all, the necessary condition for the formation of family, is not so much an explicit rejection of the idea of natural affections as it is a methodological return to the work of establishing a secure foundation for the relationship from which intersubjective, social and political possibilities are to be derived. The conjugal relation in particular is an especially appropriate site for the incursion of episte-mological anxieties within the heart, as it were, of sentimental certainty about the natural affections – precisely the anxieties that hypotheses of natural sympathy fail to dispel.

The turn away from sentimental assurance to anxious uncertainty is perhaps nowhere more apparent than in the obsessive evocations of sexual betrayal and illegitimacy that persistently arise in Rousseau's discussions of marital union. Although ignorance of the relationship between intercourse and birth is among the reasons that the independent male and female described in the second *Discourse* reproduce but form no families, the question 'why will he help her raise a child that he does not know belongs to him alone?' remains both pressing and unanswerable outside the state of nature, after the 'habit' of living together has been established. Rousseau's formulation in the first draft of the *Social Contract* is concise and straightforward on this point: 'it is important to [the husband] that the children he is forced to recognize do not belong to anyone other then himself'.[42] It is no accident that Rousseau's most important, prescriptive work in political theory is written during the same period as the works on culture and education in which he proposes an ideal of female conduct designed to ensure that men live free from doubt about their paternity. 'All the austere duties of the woman [are] derived from the single fact that a child ought to have a father', explains Rousseau in the *Letter to d'Alembert* (1758).[43] Although generally treated as part of Rousseau's elaboration of the 'moral difference' between the sexes, the specter of sexual betrayal is not simply or only a justification for turning female 'virtues' of chastity, modesty and obedience into severe 'duties'. It is continuous with and derivative of anxieties that Rousseau finds endemic to all forms of intersubjective relationship. The 'unhappy father' who 'wonders, in embracing his child, whether he is embracing another' suffers the same insecurity as the weak member of a society ungoverned by a social contract who 'finally perishes as a victim of the deceptive union from which he expected happiness'.[44]

To claim that the 'unfaithful woman ... dissolves the family and breaks all the bonds of nature', creating a 'society of secret enemies' condemned to dwell with one another in a state of unrelieved mistrust might provide a rationale for sexual inequality, but it also connects the 'sweetest sentiments of [the] heart' to a confidence in the other that love cannot secure and for which mere faith is insufficient. Rousseau's insistence on female fidelity appears as something deeper and more gravely insidious than a patriarchal sexual contract when seen in the broader context of sentimental assurance about natural feeling. 'Who will give a father confidence in the sentiment of nature when he embraces his own child?': the question explicitly conjures up uncertainty where Shaftesbury would find untroubled necessity, making a sentiment as 'natural' as parental love conditional upon the kind of confidence that can easily be shaken.[45] But in assuming that a father cannot help but feel stirrings of sentiment, Rousseau also evokes a longing for attachment that would never trouble Hobbesian reasoning about paternity. Rousseau's man is vulnerable precisely because he is irresistibly inclined to love his wife and her child. Love (for the child) is inextricably bound up with and entirely dependent upon confidence (in the wife). What painful upheavals of sentiment would follow from loss of confidence? There is no more 'frightful condition in the world', Rousseau writes in *Emile* than 'that of the unhappy father who, lacking confidence in his wife, does not dare yield to the sweetest sentiments of his heart, who wonders, in embracing his child, whether he is embracing another's'.[46] In so far as it represents an anxious recognition that the feelings which bind persons in relation to one another both require and lack epistemological grounding, the doubt about paternity, with all its troublesome implications for the 'natural affections' of conjugal and filial love, may be seen as a distillation of Rousseau's fundamental insight and revisionary contribution to eighteenth-century sentimentalism: that we must know the other before being obliged to love the other.

Can Julie Be Trusted?

The centrality of marriage is frequently and forcefully declared in Rousseau's great and varied sequence of mid-career works devoted to the imagination of political justice and communal harmony. But when set in the context of the particular threats to social unity envisioned in the *Social Contract*, the *Letter to d'Alembert, Julie* and *Emile*, Rousseau's repeated insistence that 'the first and holiest of all the bonds of Society is marriage' is most properly understood as an anxiously prescriptive statement of necessary conditions rather than a confident description of a given state of affairs.[47] Julie's avowal that 'Nothing can subsist in the legitimate order of human things' without the 'public and sacred faith of marriage' is phrased as a conclusive discovery, but it comes at that awkward moment in the novel when the promise of fidelity made to Wolmar is most clearly also the breaking of a promise to St Preux. Indeed Julie's turn from resolutely resisting paternal command to willingly embracing the duties of daughter and wife is presented with deliberate abruptness. The tersely delivered pronouncement that St Preux's 'lover is no more ... Julie is married' is followed by a long letter tracing a series of events and realizations which might have been allowed to unfold gradually, the outcome left uncertain, instead of being presented as a *fait accompli*.[48] The suddenness of the announcement hastily dispels the drama of Julie's conflict, or rather narrative suspense is surrendered while philosophical tension is heightened by the emphatic coincidence of rupture and commitment at this point in the novel.

Julie's conversion is meant to be irreversible, her revelations of conjugal virtue deepened and confirmed by her experiences and achievements as Madame de Wolmar. But the idea that one marries 'in order to fulfill conjointly the duties of civil life', however definitely asserted, remains as liable to revision as the idea it so suddenly displaces, that a 'union of hearts' is the 'freest' of engagements 'subject neither to sovereign power nor to paternal authority'.[49] 'I am weary of serving an illusory virtue at the expense of justice', writes Julie in her last letter to St Preux as an unmarried woman, placing justice and duty on the side of the commitment she has made to her lover in private exchanges and intimate acts over and against their misleading articulations in the social order represented by her father's promise and his power to command her obedience.[50] Her next letter reverses this understanding, identifying the *illusions* of virtue in cherishing love, over and against the 'chaste and sublime duties' she recognizes in her marriage.[51] 'I will be faithful because that is the first duty which binds the family and all of society. I will be chaste because that is the first virtue which nurtures all the others': thus Julie vows 'obedience and absolute fidelity' to Wolmar, assuring St Preux (and the readers of their correspondence) that 'my mouth and my heart made the promise'.[52] But Julie's sincerity cannot itself make self-evident the principles she espouses upon marrying, nor does her apparent resolution make the vows she utters more binding than her promises to St Preux. Indeed the gravity of all that depends on her marriage vows (the binding up of 'the family and all of society', the cradle of all the virtues) is only more pronounced for appearing so precariously, in the middle of a letter that reinterprets and overturns prior sincere and impassioned vows of faithful attachment. The deliberate juxtaposition anticipates doubts about the endurance of attachment which become the heroine's singular preoccupation and which can be seen, more broadly, to both motivate and recurrently undermine the ameliorative political and cultural projects of Rousseau's utopian works.

If this moment of whole-hearted commitment is ultimately no more secure than any other why is it supposed to be different, no more and no less than a 'revolution' in Julie's being? First among Julie's explanations is one that deepens rather than dispels the mystery of her conversion given the romantic love plot to which the entire novel has been devoted up to this point. Questioning and revaluating her commitment to St Preux, Julie differentiates between the attachment of lovers and the bond of spouses, attributing the fragility of the former, paradoxically enough, to the power of the passions aroused, and the solidity of the latter to the relative absence of intense feeling.

Honest, virtue, certain conformities ... of character and humor suffice between husband and wife; that does not prevent a very tender attachment from emerging from
this union which, without exactly being love, is nonetheless sweet and for that only
the more lasting. Love is accompanied by a continual anxiety of jealousy or depriva-
tion, ill-suited to marriage.[53]

The key distinction here, for Rousseau if not for Julie, is not between the agitation of love and the tranquil sweetness of conjugal compatibility, but between
the presence and absence of anxiety about the authenticity and continuity of
attachment. In *Emile*, where the same distinction between the 'sweet habit' of
marital affection and passion is drawn, the lover's anxiety is defined in terms of
epistemic vulnerability: 'unbridled ardor ... intoxicates him with the chimeri-
cal attractions of an object which he no longer sees as it really is'.[54] Conversely,
Julie boasts of her union with Wolmar that 'we see each other as we are' even
though, or perhaps precisely because, the 'sentiment that joins us is not the blind
transport of passionate hearts'.[55] Passion does not itself blind the lover, however,
but rather makes him liable to feel as strongly both extremes – either utter confidence or deep suspicion. Passion is 'credulous', 'easy to persuade' and thus 'love
is anxious'.[56] In the *Letter to d'Alembert*, Rousseau proposes that poets 'teach the
young to distrust the illusions of love, to flee the error of a blind penchant ...
and to be afraid of confiding a virtuous heart to an object that is sometimes
unworthy', but it would be a mistake to see impassioned romantics as alone in
a vulnerability that they only demonstrate more vividly.[57] Rousseau finds the
same misgivings and insecurities inherent in all social life. The illusion and
error distorting the lover's perception of his object is not essentially different
from illusions and errors afflicting friendships, partnerships and civic affiliation. 'Everything you tell me about the advantages of the social law would be
fine, if while I were scrupulously observing it toward others, I were sure that all
of them would observe it toward me', objects an imaginary interlocutor in the
'Geneva Manuscript', interrupting the reasonings of the social contract theorist,
'But what assurance [*sureté*] of this can you give me?'[58] Characteristically in *La
Nouvelle Héloïse*, Julie's sense of this vulnerability is self-reflexive, originating in
and directed at herself: 'What assurance [*sureté*] had I of loving you alone in
the world', she asks St Preux, 'except for an inner sentiment all lovers think they
have, when they pledge everlasting constancy to each other?'[59] Like the corro-
sive self-doubt that will afflict her throughout her marriage, this alarm about the
certainty of her own 'inner sentiments' is an introjection of disquiet that more
properly belongs to those who count on her constancy. Here Julie is not saying
'I am not sure I love you', but something simultaneously more banal and more
incoherent. The 'inner sentiment all lovers think they have' is no more and no less
than the feeling of being in love ('loving you alone in the world'); one does not
generally need further assurance of one's own feeling (any more than one needs

assurance of other inner states: pain, for example, or curiosity, or fear). To pledge 'everlasting constancy' in the grip of that passion is, perhaps, simply another way saying 'I love you alone', and so Julie's doubt confuses a familiar sense of wonder about love (the banal 'is this really love?') with a troubling question about the security of commitment that might equally be asked of the companionate marriage. 'Inner sentiment', be it love or mere tenderness, is in fact irrelevant to the '*sureté*' of a pledged attachment, so while Julie claims that unreliable passions are insufficient guarantee of future constancy, it is not yet clear what provides that assurance for her union with Wolmar. If Rousseau stakes the possibility for secure union on the capacity to see the other as '(s)he really is', then one question which inevitably arises is whether certainty altogether displaces passion as the grounds of attachment, whether, in aiming to eradicate anxiety, other 'inner sentiments' that bind and separate individuals (love, hatred, resentment, indifference, antipathy) are also necessarily precluded.

It bears emphasizing that a truer or more genuine 'inner sentiment' would not suffice to provide the certainty Julie calls for. This is especially important because it often seems as though Rousseau is principally concerned with the unstable relations created by deceptive *appearances*. In *Emile*, for example, the lover's difficulty of seeing the other as she 'really is' is compounded by corrupt social forms that 'have made women so dissembling ... that one can hardly count on their most proved attachment', a complaint that returns to the opening protest of Rousseau's earliest social criticism: 'One never really knows with whom one is dealing' because hatred, fear, offense and betrayal are all always 'hidden under a uniform and deceitful veil of politeness'.[60] The world Rousseau describes in the first *Discourse* is precisely that in which he found his first real lover, Madame de Warens, a woman who 'loathed duplicity and lying' but could nevertheless adopt and act on the view that 'marital fidelity need only be kept up in appearance, its moral importance being confined to its effect on public opinion'.[61] If, in a world of deceptive semblances of affection, relationships of love and friendship are vulnerable to betrayal, disappointment and rupture, then marriage is an especially troubled association in Rousseau precisely because he imagines it to be the foundation of broader social structures.

The insidious possibility that appearance might substitute for real fidelity – that, in Madame de Warens' reasoning 'every woman who appeared virtuous by that mere fact became so' – complicates the insistence that maintaining the 'appearance' of fidelity and chastity is among the most important duties of the married woman:[62]

> It is important, then, not only that a woman be faithful, but that she be judged to be faithful by her husband, by those near her, by everyone ... that she give evidence of her virtue to the eyes of others as well as to her own conscience. If it is important that a father love his children, it is important that he esteem their mother. These are the

reasons which put even appearances among the duties of women, and make honor and reputation no less indispensable to them than chastity.[63]

Mary Wollstonecraft famously criticizes this Rousseauvian prescription by cautioning husbands to 'beware of trusting too implicitly to ... servile appearance' and warning that 'winning sweetness' might itself be 'preparation for adultery.'[64] Effectively turning the appearance of fidelity into grounds for suspicion rather than reassurance, Wollstonecraft revives doubts that Rousseau hopes to dispel, but also points to dangers that Rousseau himself recognizes even as he issues these strictures on female conduct. The need to secure reliable 'evidence' for the other's faithful attachment is occasionally confounded with and discussed in the same context as the problem of masks, inscrutability and other forms of deliberate, conventional concealment, but is not ultimately reducible to that problem.

Before turning to the question of what might assure attachment if not genuine and sincere 'inner sentiment', it is worth asking under what conditions Rousseau imagines that (external) appearances could be counted upon as 'evidence of virtue'. Certainly a world in which the duty of appearing faithful reliably coheres with fidelity is one in which possibilities for the kind of concealment that cleaves 'inner sentiment' from outward bearing have been eliminated. How is this possible?

Dispassionate Subjects and Unpredictable Objects

Describing the elaborately rigid divisions of labor, space and time at Clarens, St Preux observes that the 'ordering of a house must begin' with the inclusion of 'only honest folk who do not bring in the secret desire to upset that order'. As such persons do not exist in the world, 'to have them one must not look for them, but make them'.[65] The 'making' of 'honest folk' (or of what Rousseau calls a 'people' in the *Social Contract*) involves a radical reconstruction of persons that effectively eliminates the pernicious individuation of interiority.

In a small and peaceable world where 'several men together consider themselves to be a single body' with 'but a single will', neither distance nor difference separate minds and hearts, and 'the common good is clearly apparent [*se montre*] everywhere, demanding only good sense in order to be perceived [*être apercus*]'. To speak in such a world is 'merely [to] sa[y] what everybody has already felt'.[66] 'The whole charm of the relationship that prevailed among us', explains Julie, 'lies in the openness of the heart that places all sentiments, all thoughts in common, and makes it so that each one, feeling he is what he ought to be, reveals himself to all such as he is'.[67] This effortless self-revelation only affirms that all thoughts and feelings are public in the sense of shared, held in common. To say that the charm of this openness would be destroyed by concealment ('Imagine for a moment some secret intrigue, some liaison that had to be hid, some reason for reserve and secrecy: instantly the whole pleasure of being together [*de se voir*] vanishes') is simply to reason in a circle unless it is understood that secrecy implies the presence of the not-shared, the uncommon, the different.[68]

'Good social institutions are those that best know how to denature man', writes Rousseau in *Emile*, a reformation that 'transport[s] the I into the common unity ... with the result that the individual ... no longer feels except with the whole'.[69] The eradication of privacy and cultivation of conformity in the utopian works are designed to re-create human beings as fully knowable objects and so to secure human association on the firm basis of an identificatory unity. These communities engender beings who behave with the dependable consistency of objects and can therefore certainly be counted on to keep their mutual commitments. Consider the courtship balls described in both *La Nouvelle Héloïse* and the *Letter to d'Alembert*. These 'occasions for gathering in order to form unions and for arranging the establishment of families' make a public matter of the couplings upon which the order and continuity of the larger civic association depend: 'from the bosom of joy and pleasures would be born preservation, the concord, and the prosperity of the Republic'.[70] Regular dances allow marriageable men and women 'to get a taste for one another and to see one another' in a space where 'the eyes of the public are constantly open and upon them'. Rousseau identifies the superlative advantage of these 'entertainments' in achievement of clear knowledge of the other: 'Can a more decent way of not deceiving one another ... be imagined?' he asks, or a better way of 'show[ing] themselves off ... to the people whose interest it is to know them well before being obliged to love them?'[71] Knowledge as the precondition of love: it is tempting to suggest that the epistemological ideal of grounding relations upon a secure basis of knowledge underlies or precedes the moral aspiration of commitment to a decent way of not deceiving others. But knowledge substitutes for and displaces love in these worlds of publicly formed beings.

It is particularly telling that the denaturing alteration of the human constitution Rousseau describes can only be achieved through the intercession of figures who are not themselves subject to the specific human vulnerability they will remedy. In the *Social Contract*, the lawgiver who 'discover[s] the rules of society' is one who 'beholds all the passions of men without feeling any of them'. This 'superior intelligence' is not merely dispassionate and disinterested, but all-knowing precisely to the extent that he is devoid of human passions and interests: he has 'no affinity with our nature, yet knows it through and through'.[72] In *La Nouvelle Héloïse*, Wolmar describes himself as 'a tranquil soul with a cold heart', and it is precisely this curious freedom from feeling that he credits for an unerring ability to 'read what is in men's hearts'.[73] The emotions that neither distort nor inform Wolmar's observations are precisely those of moral sentiment: 'interest and humanity', 'pity', 'pain'. Julie reports that he is ungoverned by passion, and that his attachment to her is an even-tempered rational form of love. This dispassion makes him 'superior to all us people of sentiment', Julie explains, because he is invulnerable to deception: 'the heart deceives us in a thousand ways and acts only on a principle that is always suspect; but reason has no end save what is good'.[74] Wolmar is not only a proto-Kantian figure of disinterested judgment, but also a figure of intersubjective omniscience whose invulnerability to deceit is inextricably bound up with an absence of emotions. While Julie appears to aspire to this state of dispassionate, knowing guardianship over others, she (and the novel) also appropriately, ultimately, identify this condition with death. A soul separated from the body might dwell 'near those it cherished', she conjectures in her final hours, 'to learn for itself what we are thinking and feeling, through a direct communication, comparable to that by which God reads our thoughts'.[75]

I have argued that the anxious effort to secure marital union in Rousseau's utopian works involves questions of intersubjective transparency and confidence that are not only deeply connected to his works of social criticism and political theory, but that also point directly to unresolved epistemological tensions within eighteenth-century moral sentimentalism. To stake the possibility of broader forms of social association on conjugal union is, at one and the same time, to reject the notion that feelings of attachment are the natural foundation for social bonds while still maintaining the centrality of those feelings and the relationships they engender to a social world Rousseau envisions as ideally one of shared pleasures, projects and concerns. His imagined communities of mutually transparent, like-minded, open-hearted persons make possible an epistemic security that results in ethical achievements such as honesty, fidelity and esteem. Sympathetic correspondence and identificatory unity are ensured among beings who appear just as they are, and who are all deeply similar. Whether the utter unity and conformity Rousseau imagines ought to be understood as anticipating Kant in the vision of individuals participating in a kingdom of ends, or as an unrealistically oppressive eradication of individual experience remains an open question.[76] It is nevertheless clear that Rousseauvian transparency entails a radical alteration of the human constitution aimed at the formation of individuals who behave towards one another with an untroubling predictability.

The establishment of a 'people' in the *Social Contract* requires a lawgiver who will 'alter [*altérer*] man's constitution in order to strengthen it'. But this is a well-known revision of the earlier, bolder formulation the philosopher sets down in the 'Geneva manuscript': 'He must, in a sense, mutilate [*mutile*] man's constitution'.[77] The revision is emblematic of arresting contradictions in Rousseau's imagination of societies of perfect creatures – between amelioration and deformation of human 'nature', liberation and constraint, manipulation and guardianship, carefree disinhibition and oppressive surveillance. I now want to suggest that the apparent ambivalence of Rousseau's presentation of this project keeps open the possibility that unknowability might be intrinsic to valuation of others, that the very idea of knowing others before being obliged to love them entails loss of precisely that which makes others loveable. The tragic and unanticipated endings he contrives for the ideal marriages he constructs in *Emile* and *La Nouvelle Héloïse* are flagrant reassertions of the unpredictable and unknowable. The relentless self-doubt rejected by all who know Julie, her own insistence on the 'triumph of virtue' in transforming illicit love into honourable friendship, her final avowal to Wolmar that 'I die as I have lived, worthy of being your spouse' – all these assurances of conjugal devotion and fidelity make the posthumous professions of emotional conflict and renascent love for St Preux as abrupt and shocking as was her sudden, whole-hearted renunciation of St Preux and commitment to married life.[78]

Certainly the unforeseen disintegrations of carefully conceived and idealized unions suggest an exhaustion of the idea that knowledge could secure love or constancy. But in so doing they leave open the possibility that vulnerability itself might be what binds us anxiously together. Emile implies as much when he laments that 'fidelity, virtue, love, everything may return except that unbounded *confidence* without which regret, disgust and despair are the inseparable attendants of the marriage state'.[79] If Rousseau's protagonists cannot live among others without that unbounded confidence, the tragic insecurity to which even their idealized attachments succumb compels imagination of just how fidelity, virtue and love might unite individuals who can never be sure of seeing one another as they really are.

12 AFTER THE SUMMUM BONUM: NOVELS, TREATISES AND THE ENQUIRY AFTER HAPPINESS

Brian Michael Norton

Perhaps no philosophical problem in the eighteenth century enjoyed more popular appeal than the problem of happiness. The question was taken up in a wide
range of texts, including philosophical treatises, periodical essays, sermons, epis-
tles, dramatic poems, letters, journals, allegories and prose fiction. More than one
historian has deemed happiness an 'obsession' of the age.[1] While this scholarship
has tended to focus on France, a casual search of the British Library catalogue
suggests that the literature on happiness was equally vast on this side of the
Channel.[2] With titles such as *An Enquiry after Happiness*, *An Essay on Happiness*
and *The Way to Happiness*, these works could run to three and four volumes and
go through as many as fourteen reprints. So abundant was this literature that by
the latter half of the century some writers acknowledged that their reader might
be 'impatient to know ... what can be added to the many treatises, ancient and
modern, that have been wrote upon it'.[3] But no one doubted that the culture's
appetite for such works remained undiminished. When Samuel Johnson needed
to write a money-maker, he knew exactly what he was doing when he selected
happiness as his theme in *Rasselas*.

Fred Parker reminds us that 'philosophy and literature were often on unusually friendly terms' during the period, and that 'any line of demarcation between
them sometimes disappeared altogether'.[4] This is especially true of writings on
happiness. Not only did eighteenth-century enquiries after happiness assume a
wide variety of forms, but individual works themselves were often generically
unstable or hybrid in nature. Henry MacKenzie's 'The Pursuits of Happiness'
(1771), for example, takes the form of a verse epistle addressed to a friend, and as
such it belongs comfortably to the world of literature. At the same time, however,
it is steeped in the philosophy of the Scottish Enlightenment and enters into a
dialogue with more theoretical accounts of happiness – such as the 'doubts deis-
tical' he finds in the writings of 'Father Chubb' – as if demanding to be read as a
work of philosophy in its own right. John Norris's *An Idea of Happiness* (1684),

to approach the matter from the other direction, is clearly a work of religious and philosophical speculation. But this early critic of Locke and disciple of the Cambridge Platonists employs such a rhetorically-charged and figurative style of writing that the text is equally at home in the world of polite letters. Taken together, writings on happiness formed a kind of popular philosophy, a discourse deeply rooted in ancient moral philosophy, but one that eagerly sought advantage in the literary marketplace. And it was a subject which seemed to invite commentary from the widest range of perspectives: Anglicans, Catholics, theists, deists, hedonists, moralists, empiricists and classicists all had something to say about the nature of happiness and the means of attaining it. Everyone was a philosopher in this sense. As Shaftesbury famously put it: 'If Philosophy be, as we take it, *the study of happiness*, must not everyone ... philosophize?'[5]

It is in this context that what we now call the 'novel' emerged as a new genre and began to consolidate a poetics of its own, however loosely and provisionally we may understand the latter. And novels, to be sure, showed a deep interest in the question of happiness. Robinson Crusoe's adventures begin when he disregards his father's advice to stay put in the 'upper Station of Low Life', something experience had taught him is 'the most suited to human Happiness'.[6] Pamela shows a similar difficulty in heeding her father's warnings about Mr B., even though her 'everlasting Happiness in this World and the next' is at stake.[7] Emma Courtney too, to cite a final example, is admonished by her mother to check her 'ardent and impetuous sensations', because they 'fill me with apprehension for the virtue, for the happiness of my child'.[8] Such examples could be enumerated at great length. Indeed, in some sense all novels unfold against the backdrop of happiness, with its characters eagerly seeking their own well-being. One of the aspects of the novel's rejection of traditional plots and historical actors, which scholars from Watt to Hunter and Richetti have seen as central to the new form, is that its narratives focus instead on the more prosaic struggles of everyday life. It is tempting to even think of this as definitional of the genre: whereas epic and romance trade in the heroic exploits of great figures, novels dramatize the search by ordinary individuals after simple fulfillment.

But to fully appreciate the novel's involvement with eighteenth-century ideas of happiness, it is necessary to take a closer look at those ideas themselves. Guided by Charles Taylor's suggestion that there is a historical connection between a culture's 'understandings of good' and its 'modes of narrativity', this essay seeks to highlight the special affinities between emerging ideas of happiness and the developing novel.[9] In what follows, I will demonstrate that the early modern period gave rise to new subjective and psychological ideas of happiness that could only uneasily be contained within the *eudaimonist* framework of classical ethics. This raised a number of conceptual and moral concerns about the potential forms a happy life might take. Keeping this in mind, treatises and novels can be read as two exemplary, and contrasting, eighteenth-century responses to these challenges. While treatises theorized the conditions that make happiness possible in general, novels offered an unprecedented way of interrogating the problem on the level of the particular, in the details of single individual's character and unique circumstances. This paper concludes with a reading of *Rasselas*, that most famous of eighteenth-century works on happiness. With its trenchant critique of abstract accounts of happiness, and its steady privileging of practice over theory, Johnson's tale exposes the limitations of treatises and, in doing so, it highlights some of the methodological advantages of novelistic discourse.

Early modern theories of the good life disarticulate the concept of happiness from that of the *summum bonum*. Aristotle offers a nice point of contrast. He begins the *Nichomachean Ethics* by inquiring into the final end to which all our various aims and projects are directed. 'What', he asks, 'is the highest of all goods pursued in action?'[10] His answer is revealing: 'As far as the name goes, most people virtually agree [about what the good is], since both the many and the cultivated call it happiness, and suppose that living well and doing well are the same as being happy'.[11] If this is the starting point for ancient reflections on the good life, as Julia Annas and others have demonstrated, then we might usefully periodize the emergence of modern ideas of happiness at the moment when this equation is no longer taken for granted. For modern thinkers, there is no assumed identity between the moral quality of a person's life and his or her subjective state of mind. With Descartes, for example, we see a clear distinction between these concepts, as well as some impatience on the philosopher's part that Seneca would allow them to be conflated: 'My first observation is that there is a difference between happiness, the supreme good, and the final end or goal towards which our actions ought to tend. For happiness is not the supreme good, but presupposes it, being the contentment or satisfaction of the mind which results from possessing it.'[12] This distinction – and the corresponding critique of the ancients – would become commonplace in the eighteenth century. The *Encyclopédie* entry on 'Bonheur' observes that what Aristotle defined as happiness was in fact 'only the basis of happiness', and it chides the Stoics for confusing the 'possession of wisdom' with the '*inner satisfaction* which they gained from this wisdom'. Philips Glover, the author of *An Inquiry Concerning Virtue and Happiness* (1751), similarly explains that the 'mistake' of the 'old philosophers' was that 'they did not distinguish between natural and moral good and evil; for them the *summum bonum* was happiness'.[13] The moderns, to be sure, continued to view the moral quality of one's life and one's subjective well-being as standing in some kind of complex and intimate relation. Countless moralists and most philosophers (at least until Kant) were dedicated to establishing and specifying these very links. But this is the difference: the relationship between 'living well' and 'being happy' now *needed* to be demonstrated. The 'many and the cultivated' no longer took them to be the same thing.

As the concept of happiness came to be dissevered from that of the *summum bonum*, a number of Enlightenment thinkers saw the latter term as irreparably outdated. Thomas Hobbes, for example, flatly rejects this time-honoured staple of traditional ethics: 'There is no such *finis ultimus*, utmost aim, nor *summum bonum*, greatest good, as is spoken of in the books of the old moral philosophers'.[14] Hobbes was reluctant to identify happiness with possessing the highest good, however the latter may be defined, because it contradicted a fundamental fact of human desire: the attainment of any object, as Hobbes saw it, did not produce contentment but only fresh desires for further objects. What is more significant for our purposes here than Hobbes's specific theory of power is the way his discussion of happiness shifts the emphasis from the good being sought to the subject doing the seeking. As John Locke would later observe, 'All pursue Good, [but] the same thing is not good to every Man alike'. Given the great diversity of human desires and appetites, Locke was sceptical that a single model of life could hold valid for all. Indeed, he subjects the idea to withering satire: 'Philosophers of old did in vain enquire, whether *summum bonum* consisted in riches, or bodily delights, or virtue or contemplation: and they might have as reasonably disputed whether the best relish were to be found in apples, plumbs, or nuts; and have divided themselves into sects upon it'.[15] The ripples of this action could be felt on the other side of the Channel. Voltaire would follow the lead of the British empiricists in jettisoning the concept. 'The Sovereign Good!' he declares with similar exasperation. 'What a word! You might just as well have asked what is the sovereign blue or the sovereign stew, sovereign walking, sovereign reading, etc.'[16]

Modern theories of the good life move the problem of happiness inward, psychologizing it. Descartes, as we saw, describes happiness as 'contentment or satisfaction of the mind'. In Samuel Johnson's well-known, but rather enigmatic expression, 'happiness consists in the multiplicity of agreeable consciousness'.[17] So decisive are these internal impressions that some argued that one could even have the external facts about one's life wrong and still be happy. As John Norris explains, 'it matters not to the reality of my happiness, whether the object of it be really good or only apprehended so, since it were never so real, it pleases only as apparent. The fool has his Paradice as well as the wise-man.'[18] Happiness is a 'sensation of ease or joy', Glover writes, 'it is a perception of the mind, and nothing else'.[19] This sensationist view of happiness, drawing support from Enlightenment psychology, identified happiness as an 'agreeable sensation'.[20] Lévesque de Pouilly had popularized this term with his *Theorie des sentiments agréables* (1747), an influential work that informed the *Encylopédie* entries on 'Passion' and 'Plaisir' and which was quickly translated into English. Glover draws on the concept in his axiomatic claim that 'the happiness of any being is neither more nor less than its agreeable sensations'. Whereas Aristotle regarded happiness to be a kind of action, for the moderns, happiness is decidedly something that is *felt*.[21]

Indeed, it is important to appreciate how far modern conceptions of happiness depart from their classical forebears.[22] In ancient philosophy happiness represented a largely objective problem that referred to the way one's life as a whole unfolded. As Cicero explains, 'for we usually speak of a life as a happy one not in reference to a part of it, but to the whole of a life-time; indeed "a life" means a finished and complete life'.[23] Because this could not be grasped in its entirety until it stopped changing, the ancient Greeks maintained that an individual should not be judged happy until he is dead. The idea may sound counterintuitive to us, being heirs to the modern views I have been sketching here. But as the classicist A. A. Long explains, the ancient concept of happiness was irreducible to the feelings or attitude one has toward life: 'The happiness of the Greek philosophical ideal is not an everyday state of mind, which comes and goes like moods and feelings as one's reaction to circumstances changes, and it has nothing to do with our modern interests in excitement, ecstasy, or simple domestic comfort'.[24] 'To call someone eudaimon', Long writes elsewhere, 'is to describe a person whose whole life is flourishing to the greatest extent available to a human being'.[25] It is this objective component that is decisive. So although 'the happy life certainly had to be pleasant or enjoyable', Gisela Striker explains, 'they did not think that happiness itself consisted in being pleased with one's life'.[26] This, as we have seen, is precisely what the moderns came to insist. In Montaigne's bold formulation: 'Each man is as well or as badly off as he thinks he is. Not the man of whom it is thought, but the one who thinks it of himself, is happy. And by just this fact belief gains reality and truth.'[27]

Highlighting this new emphasis on the subject – indeed, on the subjective – is the frequency with which modern discussions of happiness are couched in gustatory terms.[28] Happiness is a matter of satisfying one's 'appetites'. The 'relish' of any good – ethical no less than gastronomical – must be determined by the 'taste' of the person in question. Montaigne tropes on this idea in the title of the essay cited above, 'That the taste [le goust] of good and evil depends in large part on the opinion we have of them'. Locke employs the rhetoric to devastating effect when he suggests that the search for the sovereign good was about as reasonable as debating the superiority of fruits or nuts, a critique Voltaire takes over with his mockery of the 'sovereign stew'.[29] John Norris too declares that it is not the 'circumstances' of life that determine happiness, but the 'opinion' that gives 'the relish'.[30] It is in this context, I believe, that we are to read Sterne's famous translation of the Latin tag: 'De gustibus non est disputandum;–that is, there is no disputing against Hobby-Horses'.

While these subjective models of happiness promised a richer variety of sources of satisfaction, they also raised a number of concerns. The notion that happiness depends ultimately on nothing firmer or more reliable than an individual's private 'tastes', implied that the good life was considerably more variable and conceptually elusive than traditional ethicists had supposed. And for all their didactic bravado, one detects in the modern literature on happiness more than a little embarrassment in trying to pin happiness down. In his *Sermons on Happiness* (1760), Thomas Newman proffers, rather awkwardly, that he 'need not enter into a definition of the thing which probably we have all a better idea of than words can convey'.[31] Philips Glover has an even harder time of it: 'happiness, or pleasure, which is the same, can hardly be defined so that a more adequate idea of it may be got, than the words themselves are used to give us'. Happiness, in some sense, was simply thought to be too self-evident to demand explanation, a notion immortalized in Pope's tautology: 'Who thus define it say they more or less / Than this, that happiness is happiness'. But the real difficulty, as John Norris and so many after him point out, did not lie in the 'general' but in specifying the 'particular wherein it consists'. Many suspected that these particulars were too numerous and too varied to ever lend themselves to universal demonstration. Consider, for example, a letter reprinted in the *Gentleman's Magazine* describing a fashionable scene in which the 'Nature of Happiness' is debated. After the party proposes as many different notions of happiness as there are individuals present, one of the members offers this explanation of their difficulty:

> I think none of you have hit the Case we are upon: for you will never be able to give such a Definition of Happiness, and prescribe such a certain Means of attaining it, as to make it reasonable for all to agree in the same Notion of it, and to pursue the same Tract to arrive at it. Happiness is a relative Thing, and varies as much as every Individual of the human Species from each other. It depends upon Constitution, Temper, Education, and a thousand other Circumstances.[32]

As a 'relative thing', it seemed increasingly unlikely that happiness could be generalized or brought to bear under uniform laws.[33]

Given the history of happiness, the implications were ethical as well as conceptual. Eighteenth-century ideas of happiness were profoundly shaped by the concerns and conceptual frameworks of the classical moral philosophy from which it descended. Adam Potkay has even suggested that the very term 'does not fully take wing until the eighteenth century, as a translation of philosophical *eudaimonia*'.[34] But modern happiness would always be morally problematic. By dissolving the theory of the good life into two distinct concepts – the moral good, on the one hand and subjective well-being, on the other – modern ideas of happiness raise the possibility that happiness might be sought *in place* of virtue.

The seeds of this problem are already evident in Descartes, who, immediately after clarifying Seneca's terms, seems to recognize this new difficulty:

> The end of our actions, however, can be understood to be one or the other; for the supreme good [which Descartes takes to consist in the 'exercise of virtue'] is undoubtedly the thing we ought to set ourselves as the goal of all our actions, and the resulting contentment of the mind is also rightly called our end, since it is the attraction which makes us seek the supreme good.[35]

The normative power of happiness would become consolidated during the Enlightenment. When Pope, for example, calls happiness 'our being's end and aim', he is not just describing what we in fact pursue, but what we *ought* to pursue. Locke before him had claimed that 'the highest perfection of intellectual nature, lies in a careful and constant pursuit of true and solid happiness',[36] and Johnson would later counsel Boswell that 'the business of the wise man is to be happy'.[37] If we were created (by God or nature) for happiness, then this pursuit is not only a right – it might also be a kind of obligation.[38] The *Encyclopédie* refers to happiness as 'a law of our being', and it is perhaps this law above all others that must be obeyed. 'There is', Diderot affirmed, 'but one duty; it is to be happy.'

With the rise of subjectivist ideas of happiness, however, there no longer seemed to be any a priori guarantee that this happiness was consistent with a moral life. While Descartes was careful to specify that happiness 'presupposes' virtue, the growing belief that happiness comes down to one's personal 'tastes' implied other possibilities. Using Julia Annas's work on ancient happiness as a point of contrast we can bring into focus the moral challenges unique to modern happiness. Annas claims that what is more distinctive about classical 'happiness' than its degree of objectivity is the term's vagueness. According to Annas, rather than coming to ethics with a concrete and well-defined idea of happiness in mind, 'Happiness in ancient theory is given its sense by the role it plays; and the most important role it plays is that of an obvious, but thin, specification of the final end'.[39] Aristotle could assume that 'living well' was the same as 'being happy' because, as Annas explains, 'in saying that the final good is happiness we are ... adding very little'.[40] Indeed, the concept was thin enough that the Stoics could use it, controversially but not implausibly, to describe the life of a virtuous man on the rack. Extending Annas's line of reasoning, I would argue that the thicker, more determinate idea of happiness we find coalescing in the modern period is not so easily reconciled with virtue. Happiness here is not an empty signifier that acquires meaning in the course of investigating our 'final end'. It is already a highly particularized concept, intimately tied to one's individual penchants and appetites. Like the enjoyment of a piece of fruit, modern happiness is palpable. Its precise relation to virtue would be the subject of anxious speculation.

Indeed, I would even suggest that this anxiety is part of the reason we see so much attention paid to happiness in this period. Interest in happiness is not simply an expression of Enlightenment optimism; it also speaks of a larger cultural need to come to terms with the seemingly anarchic, and possibly amoral, nature of subjective well-being. The treatises of the period make this fact abundantly clear. For all their differences in intellectual and religious orientation, and despite their formal variety, all treatises ultimately make the same argument: there can be no happiness without virtue. The fall of the *summum bonum* thus had the paradoxical effect of bringing new urgency to the specifically moral side of this ancient project: now that happiness and virtue were rigorously distinguished on a conceptual level, moralists were more determined than ever to prove that they still entailed each other in practice.

Treatise writers elaborated countless arguments to support this position. Some of these involve subtly challenging the subjectivism so central to modern happiness. Samuel Gott's *An Essay of the True Happiness of Man* (1650), for example, maintains that while happiness may appear to be a subjective matter, it is in fact rooted in objective truth: 'True happiness consists both in the true taste of the soul, and also in the truth of the thing itself'.[41] This vaguely Socratic idea contradicts Montaigne and Norris's claim that believing oneself happy is in fact to be happy, and indeed, it stands counter to the main intellectual currents we have been discussing here. Much the same can be said about James Harris's remarkably erudite, but ultimately unconvincing *Three Treatises* (1744). In this neo-Stoic text, Harris creates an intentional slippage between 'happiness' and the 'sovereign good', and much as Annas describes of ancient ethics, he defines the former in terms of the latter. Ultimately, Harris is able to conclude that well-being is completely in one's own keeping because it is not the 'event' of one's actions that matters, but the 'rectitude' of the conduct.[42] This effort, in effect to rejoin what Descartes had carefully distinguished, was not fully successful. As John Bethune would observe of Harris's treatise, 'there are many reasons for considering this [rectitude] rather as a mean or qualification necessary to happiness, than as happiness itself'.[43]

A more effective strategy accepted the subjectivism of modern happiness but sought to argue, in pragmatic and even hedonistic terms, that one could maximize happiness through virtue. It was widely accepted – or at least professed – that the greatest pleasures were to be found in virtuous action and benevolence. John Norris writes, 'I confess, the practice of vertue is a very great instrument of happiness, and that there is a great deal more true satisfaction and solid content to be found in a constant course of well living, than in all the soft caresses of the most studied luxury, or the voluptuousness of a Seraglio'.[44] It was this promise of greater happiness, rather than mere moralizing, that could bring about a rake's reformation. As the rehabilitated Mr B. exclaims, 'What joys, what true joys, flow from virtuous love! Joys which the narrow soul of the libertine cannot take in, nor his thought conceive!'[45] This argument was especially powerful when formulated negatively. Virtue may not guarantee happiness, as James Harris claimed, but vice made it impossible. There was almost universal agreement that, whatever else it might be, happiness required a certain level of tranquility or repose, inner harmony among one's memories, desires and values, and outer harmony with the immediate social world. What all treatises argue, in one way or another, is that the pleasures of an immoral life are too fleeting, precarious, unhealthy, easily exhausted and, above all, too liable to feelings of remorse to ever satisfy these conditions.

We have already noted the novel's interest in happiness. But we can now understand this concept in the historically-specific sense I have been describing here. What characters in novels seek is not happiness in general but their own particular good. This attention to particularity, as John Richetti notes, has in fact become central to our understanding of what a novel is: 'We now recognize that the novel adds up in the long run (and retrospectively) to an unprecedented attempt to project a new sort of particularized presence, and to imagine persons speaking about themselves in their singularity, asserting themselves as unique individuals and thereby breaking with those generalized types and with those communal affiliations that had long served as the primary markers of identity'.[46] While Richetti is speaking specifically here about personal identity, his comments apply equally well to emerging ideas about subjective well-being. Indeed, one of the most basic eighteenth-century plots originates when a protagonist rejects – or at least questions – the 'official' happiness prescribed by her parents, guardians or society in order to search out a more individual form of happiness for herself. Such is the case with Robinson Crusoe, Pamela and Emma Courtney. The happiness these characters seek is explicitly not the one that their guardians have in mind for them.

Novelists, to be sure, were also deeply concerned with the ethical challenges presented by the new understanding of happiness. This too is evident in the above examples. Robinson Crusoe comes to see his rejection of his father's happiness as his 'Original Sin'. Goodman Andrew's fears for his daughter's happiness are indistinguishable from his fears for 'that Jewel', her 'virtue'. And the maternal warnings of *Emma Courtney* explicitly conflate virtue and happiness. Throughout the eighteenth century, novelistic explorations of happiness are simultaneously, and necessarily, ethical explorations. The novel's treatment of this problem thus cannot be understood simply as a question of 'poetic justice'. Rather, it is more useful to understand the genre itself as an active participant in the broader cultural enquiry into the nature and significance of modern happiness.

But novels provided a very different means of exploring this problem. Following John Bender, we can see novels as 'cognitive instruments' characterized by a 'fine, observationally ordered, materially exhaustive grid of representation'. Rather than identifying the general conditions of happiness, as treatises did, novels examined happiness one case at a time, offering an extraordinarily fine-tuned and detailed way of looking at the problem. And indeed, novels excelled at dealing with the very details the sceptic in the above letter cited as making the study of happiness so impracticable: the specifics of one's unique 'constitution, temper, education, and a thousand other circumstances'. In recent years, philosophers such as Martha Nussbaum and Richard Rorty have highlighted the ethical advantages of such fine-tuned attention to particularity, emotion, context and contingency. But in a sense, Nussbaum and Rorty have only rediscovered what was evident to a number of eighteenth-century writers. Henry Fielding, for example, claims that by 'observing minutely' the subtle forces and connections playing out around us 'we shall best be instructed in this most useful of all arts ... the Art of Life'.[47] And Mary Hays, in a passage whose author could easily be mistaken for Nussbaum, writes that what distinguishes the novel from romance is 'an attentive observance of mankind, acute discernment, exquisite moral sensibility, and an intimate acquaintance with human passions and powers'.[48] Unlike other modes of ethical discourse, novels put moral ideas into 'practice'.[49]

Curiously, the contrast between treatises and novels can best be seen in an eighteenth-century text that does not fit neatly into either category: Samuel Johnson's *Rasselas*. While Johnson's narrative is rarely cited as a classic example of the novel form, lacking as it does the particularity Richetti identifies with the genre, its unsparing critique of the contemporary discourse on happiness highlights the blind-spots of treatises, and in doing so, it points to the direction taken by the developing novel.[50] What Johnson objects to in this literature, in the simplest terms, is that it does not fully appreciate the difference between theorizing happiness and living a happy life.

Johnson's critique is already evident in his characterization of the 'Happy Valley', the idyllic retreat where the royal children of Abissinia are sequestered from the hurly-burly of the outside world. As its name suggests, the sanctuary was designed to provide the highest form of happiness this life affords, with nature furnishing its necessities and art its luxuries. Life passes here, in the narrator's felicitous phrase, in the 'soft vicissitudes of pleasure and repose'. It has been suggested, most persuasively by Nicholas Hudson, that this portion of Johnson's narrative is concerned solely with sensual happiness.[51] Johnson's foregrounding of 'pleasure' and 'repose' – privileged terms in the lexicon of Epicurean moral philosophy – would appear to support this case. But I would argue instead that Johnson's target here is more general, and cannot be restricted to the neo-Epicureans, materialists and modern hedonists. Indeed, he will examine this mode of life in a later chapter on the 'young men of spirit and gaiety'. What Johnson is engaging in the Happy Valley is not a specific form of happiness, but what thinkers of the period regarded to the be conditions of happiness as such: that it be pleasant, an 'agreeable sensation' in the eighteenth-century terminology; and that it be durable, lasting, and free from worry. John Norris, for example, had defined happiness as that state 'In which there is no Evil you can fear, no Good which you desire and have not; that which fully and constantly satisfies the Demand of every Appetite'.[52] And Philips Glover similarly explained that 'Happiness, or Pleasure, which is the same ... is a Sensation of Ease or Joy, let the Occasion or Subject be what it will'.[53]

The problem with the Happy Valley, then, is not its hedonism but with its static and purely formal conception of happiness. Bearing out D. A. Miller's conjecture that happiness is one of the quintessential 'nonnarratable' states, Johnson does not narrate the first chapter, but gives us instead a 'description' of its flora and fauna, customs and routines.[54] By collapsing the temporal gap between desire and satisfaction ('Every desire was immediately granted') the chapter presents us with a happiness that exists nowhere in time and is untroubled by the temporal dimensions of the problem. Furthermore, as in most treatises, this is a happiness without a person attached: *Whose* desire? And desire for *what*? It is only with the appearance of Rasselas in the second chapter, the first concrete individual we meet in the story, that description erupts into narrative and the problem of *living* a happy life comes to the fore. 'Possessing all that I can want, I find one day and one hour exactly like another, except that the latter is still more tedious than the former ... I have already enjoyed too much; give me something to desire.'[55] Even where the formal conditions of happiness are met, something slips away. Like so many other eighteenth-century protagonists, Rasselas rejects the official happiness that is intended for him in order to search out an elusive happiness of his own.

Johnson's critique of the literature on happiness becomes even more pointed once his characters' search for happiness has taken them out of the Happy Valley. Adopting a common practice in treatises, Johnson goes on to perform a broad and rapid survey of various modes of living: a life of pleasure and a life of reason, public life and private life, urban life and a life of solitude, etc. These taxonomies varied from one treatise to the next. John Bethune's *Essay and Dissertations on Various Subjects, Relating to Human Life and Happiness* (1771), for example, examines consecutively the 'sensual pleasures', including those of 'riches', 'honour' and 'fame', the 'speculative pleasures' and the 'pleasures of the imagination'. An anonymous *Enquiry after Happiness* (1747) investigates the pleasures of 'imagination', 'friendship', 'love', 'learning and knowledge' and 'honour and riches'. James Harris reduces this diversity to two basic kinds of life, 'business' and 'leisure', each having two subdivisions: the life of business centers on either 'power' or 'wealth'; and the life of leisure on 'pleasure' or 'contemplation'. Despite these differences, the method of argument is always the same. Rapidly working through the different ways of living and the pleasures they afford, treatises reject them one by one until, through a process of elimination, they arrive at the one life that could produce a solid and lasting happiness: invariably, this is a life of virtue or religion or some combination of the two. Johnson employs the same technique in his text, revealing each of the lifestyles he surveys to fall short of the happiness it seemed to promise. What distinguishes Johnson's enquiry, however, is that it ends – rather perversely given the precedent established by treatises – with a 'conclusion, in which nothing is concluded'. By resisting the closure readers of treatises would have come to expect, Johnson suggests that the project is rather more difficult than it is usually taken to be.[56] This inconclusiveness, however, has as much to say about the methods of the enquirers as it does about the nature of happiness.

Like enquirers in a treatise (and quite unlike most literary protagonists) the travellers have a purely spectatorial attitude toward life: they are only tenuously implicated in the events of these chapters, no discernible plot comes into focus, and whatever conflict arises belongs less to them than to those they survey. In fact, in their detachment, they resemble the 'pendent spectator' imagined by the artist of flight, soaring above the world, looking on its 'marts of trade' and 'fields of battle' with blithe indifference. In a text that so consistently privileges practice over theory, we might have expected Johnson to test the travellers' idea against the hard realities of life, a formula he employs with the artist of flight, the young Imlac, and, most memorably, the would-be Stoic who is devastated by the news of his daughter's death.[57] But the travellers themselves are spared from such tests. Leopold Damrosch wryly notes that despite Imlac's warnings about the 'waves of violence' and 'rocks of treachery', 'The prince and princess founder on no rocks'.[58] By thus insulating his characters from their own search, Johnson highlights the absurdity of pursuing happiness without reference to the social world of commitments and responsibilities, or to one's own unique desires and attachments. Like enquirers in a treatise, Johnson's characters pursue happiness in a conceptual vacuum. It is no wonder that their search is inconclusive.

According to Anna Laetitia Barbauld, in fact, this is the very 'moral' of Johnson's philosophical tale. In her preface to *Rasselas* for the *British Novelists* (1811), Barbauld writes,

> The proper moral to be drawn from Rasselas is ... not that goods and evils are so balanced against each other that no unmixed happiness is to be found in life, – a deduction equally trite and obvious; nor yet that a reasoning man can make no choice, – but rather that a *merely* reasoning man will be likely to make no choice.[59]

The 'choice of life', Barbauld argues, cannot be made without reference to one's 'particular position', 'honest partialities', 'individual propensities' and 'early associations' – the very things that novels excelled at examining. That Barbauld would take it as self-evident that these details are essential for happiness suggests the extent to which the new particularized understanding of happiness had become part of the new orthodoxy. It might also hint at the role novels may have played in shaping the way the culture viewed the problem of living a happy life. Barbauld, as it were, sees the problem of happiness through the dense representational field of a novel, and she is rather perplexed that *Rasselas* would characterize it otherwise:

> If we choose to imagine an insulated being, detached from all connexions and all duties, it may be difficult for mere reason to direct his choice; but no man is so insulated: we are woven into the web of society, and to each individual it is seldom dubious what *he* shall do. Very different is the search after abstract good, and the pursuit of what a being born and nurtured amidst innumerable ties of kindred and companionship, feeling his own wants, impelled by his own passions, and influenced by his own peculiar associations, finds best for *him*.[60]

For Barbauld and Johnson, and indeed, for most novelists, abstract treatments of happiness will always miss something essential.

To read the novel alongside contemporary treatises on happiness is to see it as a participant in a broader cultural enquiry into the question of what it means to live a good life in the modern world. Further, it provides insight into the conceptual and moral problems that attend one of the genre's most fundamental plots. And it challenges us to consider the part novels played in the development of our own understanding of the difficulties of living a happy life. But to see the novel as a participant in these ethical enquiries is perhaps also to rethink the assumption that the Enlightenment bequeathed to modernity an 'impoverished' conception of moral selfhood.[61] As Barbauld's reading of *Rasselas* makes clear, eighteenth-century thinkers could be as critical of 'disembodied' and 'disembedded' forms of theorizing as the communitarians of our own day. It is the novel, more than any other form of writing, that promoted this way of reflecting on moral problems. Perhaps alongside Kantianism and utilitarianism, we might see the novel itself as one of the Enlightenment's most enduring ethical inventions.[62]

13 MUSIC VS CONSCIENCE IN WORDSWORTH'S POETRY

Adam Potkay

Judging by literary accounts, it was not uncommon in the later eighteenth century to withdraw to rural solitude to better hear the 'still, small voice' of conscience. This faculty could be understood (especially by evangelical Christians) as God's guiding voice, and not simply his scourge. But Wordsworth, in his verse of the 1790s and early 1800s, depicted something quite novel: withdrawing to hear not conscience but rather *music*. The nature of Wordsworth's 'music' is complex: in various contexts, it might mean either actual music or the harmonious sounds of natural surroundings; alternatively, receptivity to music might figure receptivity to nature, including human nature. In any case, whether listening to music or acting as though one were listening to music, something very different is happening than being guided by voices. Music prompts an affective state that we may call, with Alexander Gerard, 'a pleasant disposition of soul' that 'renders us prone to every agreeable affection',[1] but it is not, like conscience, directive: it does not tell us what to think, feel, or do. Thus to suggest, as Wordsworth does, that moral response begins either in music or on the model of our response to music is to challenge a logocentric ethics of obedience, a challenge that, especially in the 1790s, evidently has political as well as theological implications. That Wordsworth was aware of these is, I believe, strongly implied by his adoption of a more or less Christian conscience as his supreme value in *The Excursion*, a value that even the often-contrary Solitary does not contest. Wordsworth's turn to conscience in his later poetry highlights, in his career, his earlier avoidance or eschewal of it, setting conscience in dialectical opposition to his tentative assays at an ethical subject shaped by music.

Conscience

To appreciate Wordsworth's turn from and back to conscience requires our having some historical sense of what the term meant or could mean in the early Romantic era. It is, primarily, the English version of the Vulgate Bible's *conscientia*, itself a rendering of St Paul's Greek concept-word *syneidēsis*: the law written in the heart of the Gentiles, the moral code that all humans possess independently of revelation.[2] But in Pauline Christianity, references to conscience commonly stress what it *dis*approves. *Syneidēsis* is, in Greek, 'an index of moral failings or ... a moral dissuasive: on this view it never gives positive encouragement: a good conscience [Paul's *syneidēsis agathē*] is a quiet conscience'.[3] Theologians have at times construed *conscientia* in a more positive sense – some twelfth-century commentators, for example, equated it with the 'image and likeness of God' of Genesis 1:26[4] – but in the sermon and literary traditions Wordsworth knew, 'conscience' appears most often in its minatory or punitive aspects. Thus an eighteenth-century English translation of Montaigne's essay 'Of Conscience' is rife with references to unforgiving conscience: 'Conscience, the Soul's Tormentor'; 'the revengeful Furies of ... Conscience'; 'Conscience ... [that] tortures us sleeping and waking with many racking Thoughts'.[5] Francis Atterbury (1662–1732) preached a sermon on 'The Terrors of Conscience', defining this faculty as 'the Avenging Principle within us'.[6] Even the irenic Hugh Blair, whose *Sermons* remained a transatlantic model for moderate clergy well into the nineteenth century, defines 'the power of conscience' negatively: 'it produces an apprehension of merited punishment, when we have committed evil'.[7] It is not surprising, then, to find this notion of conscience in a broadside ballad such as 'The Children in the Wood', a poem Wordsworth much admired: 'And now the heavy wrathe of God / Upon their uncle fell; / Yea, fearfull fiends did haunt his house, / His conscience felt a hell'.[8]

Yet in another context, which Wordsworth also may have known, conscience features not (only) as a ministry of pain but, more positively, as the approbative voice of God. Offering the eighteenth century's most significant philosophical elaboration on conscience, Joseph Butler displays a special (we may call it an enlightened) decorum when he speaks of it as a faculty of approbation, man's 'rule of right within himself' which entails the obligation to follow it:

> Your obligation to obey this law, is its being the law of your nature. That your conscience approves of and attests to such a course of action, is itself alone an obligation. Conscience does not only offer itself to show us the way we should walk in, but it likewise carries its own authority with it, that it is our natural guide; the guide assigned us by the Author of our nature: it therefore belongs to our condition of being.[9]

Conscience can hasten as well as chasten, and it is in this double sense sometimes associated with the 'still small voice' of 1 Kings 19:11–12 that subdues the fire-eating prophet Elijah, rendering him serviceable to God's designs. Conscience becomes, particularly among evangelicals, the 'still small voice' of enlightenment for which the Christian should listen in composure and silence, outside the din of the public world and particularly of England's *ancien régime*. Conscience so construed is the only source of natural morality. Thus Cowper satirizes the ethics

of the third earl of Shaftesbury, which equate the moral sense and the sense of
beauty, as 'tinkling cymbal and high sounding brass / Smitten in vain!'; for 'such
music cannot charm' the soul where 'The STILL, SMALL VOICE is wanted'.[10]
For William Wilberforce, that voice is the bliss of solitude, and prepares the true
(as opposed to merely nominal) Christian for virtuous public activity:

> Rise on the wings of contemplation, until the praises and the censures of men die
> away upon the ear, and the still small voice of conscience is no longer drowned by the
> din of this nether world ... Thus, at chosen seasons, the Christian exercises himself;
> and when, from this elevated region he descends into the plain below, and mixes in
> the bustle of life, he still retains the impression of his more retired hours.[11]

Similarly, Vicesimus Knox asked rhetorically, within a larger satire on the pernicious moral example of 'lords, dukes, and East India nabobs': 'Can the still
small voice of conscience be heard by those who live in the noise and tumult
of pleasurable pursuits?'[12] Both 'the world' in its widest Johannine sense, and
the particular social world of 'the higher and middle classes of this country', as
Wilberforce put it, are what the Christian must be periodically escape in order
that he might return to the practice of charity within them. In William Crowe's
poem *Lewesdon Hill* (1788) the awe-inspiring voice of conscience is what turns
the Christian back from retirement. One would never descend the mount of
contemplation for 'the noisy world', writes Crowe, were it not for 'conscience,
which still censures on our acts, / That awful voice within us, and the sense / Of
an hereafter', which rouse us 'to remove, according to our power, / The wants and
evils of our brother's state'.[13]

More could be said on the career of 'conscience' in the 1790s, but suffice it here
to say that the concept was a vital and polyvalent one, and that Wordsworth, in
his poetry before *The Excursion*, almost entirely avoided it. What makes this surprising is his sustained exploration, especially through 1798, of the psychology
of crime, guilt and sorrow,[14] themes that, before and after Wordsworth – from,
say, 'The Children in the Wood' to Gaskell's *Mary Barton* – typically involve a
greater or lesser engagement with conscience. In the two cases in which Wordsworth uses 'conscience' in the 1790s, he does so with qualifying irony. In the
early version of *The Borderers* (1797–9) conscience is a concept that only Rivers,
the Iago-like villain, invokes, and he does so with patently evil intention. In Act
2, Scene 3, when Herbert innocently wakes in the night, impeding Rivers's plan
to inveigle Mortimer into murdering him in his sleep, Rivers puts this appearance in a bad light, commenting to Mortimer in an aside: 'how comes he here?
The night-mare, conscience / Has driven him out of harbour?'[15] The appeal to
conscience, the soul's tormentor, is reduced to a conman's trick. In 'The Convict'
from the 1798 *Lyrical Ballads*, conscience appears as a *bona fide* torment, but as
one that might be assuaged by transportation (presumably to Australia) and a

moral reformation in nature. The convict's conscience is less consistently tortur-
ing than his cell, 'the comfortless vault of disease';[16] the poem's speaker offers the
convict, in closing, this impotent blessing: 'My care, if the arm of the mighty
were mine, / Would plant thee where yet thou might'st blossom again'.[17]

Music in Lieu of Conscience

Among Wordsworth's greatest innovations as a (semi-) secularizing poet in the
Alfoxden and Grasmere years was his transformation of logocentric conscience,
'the soul's tormentor' and the 'still small voice', into inarticulate and non-direc-
tive 'music'. This is sometimes the music or blended sounds of outer nature: e.g.
'th' aëreal music of the hill' of *An Evening Walk*,[18] or the 'soothing melody' that
begins and ends *The Ruined Cottage*, Ms. D.[19] Alternatively, this music may be
an emanation or abstraction from human nature, 'the still, sad music of humanity'. Thus, in the poem that follows 'The Convict' in the 1798 *Lyrical Ballads*,
'Tintern Abbey', the tortures of the prisoner's conscience become, in the open
air, 'The still, sad music of humanity, / Not harsh nor grating, though of ample
power / To chasten and subdue'. To read this music as a humanized version of
conscience is to understand why it is not harsh nor punitive (as conscience was
popularly held to be), but nonetheless chastens by putting one into an ethically-
receptive mood, an orientation of responsiveness towards the Other, outside of a
Christian (or monarchist) ethics of obedience or, as Wordsworth called it in an
Alfoxden fragment, 'negative morality'.[20]

An important feature of this music, characteristic of Wordsworth's sense of
music in general, is that even when 'sad' it does not sadden. As music, it does
not even *express* sadness but, to use the philosopher Peter Kivy's distinction, is
rather *expressive of* sadness, in the way that a St Bernard's face may be said, quite
apart from any inference about its emotional state, to 'look sad'.[21] The aesthetic
response to music is arguably never sadness, but always some type of pleasure or
exhilaration. Coleridge suggests the argument that Kivy will develop: 'If we sink
into music ... we feel ourselves moved so deeply as no object in mortal life can
move us except by anguish, and here it is present with Joy. It is in all its forms
still Joy.'[22] Kivy argues, similarly, that the emotions (e.g. anguish) we hear in
pure music do not excite corresponding emotions in us, but rather always arouse
excitement, wonder or awe.[23] The sound of sorrow, or sorrow understood as a
sound, pleases not because of any theodicy, any belief in providence or in the
invulnerability of rationality, but simply because it partakes of music. 'It is only
through the spirit of music that we can understand the joy involved in the annihilation of the individual'.[24] Nietzsche wrote this in light of Schopenhauer, but
he might have done so in response to 'Tintern Abbey' or *The Ruined Cottage*.

Wordsworth, after venturing in these works beyond Protestant conscience, returned to it as with a vengeance in *The Excursion*, where the term features eleven times in solemn usage, beginning with the introductory 'Prospectus to *The Recluse*': 'subject there [in retirement] / To Conscience only, and the law supreme / Of that Intelligence which governs all'.[25] Significantly, this substitutes for the very different lines in *Home at Grasmere*, Ms. B – retirement 'consists/ With being limitless the one great Life' – and its prelusive strain, 'On Man, on Nature, and on human Life, / Thinking in solitude, from time to time / I feel sweet passions traversing my Soul / Like Music'.[26]

The Music of Things

Non-rational (or un-conscientious) things have song, melody, even 'language' – just not, in Wordsworth's phrase, 'articulate language'. Wordsworth makes a fundamental distinction between human language and the language of all things, and he tends in his early poetry to emphasize attentiveness to the latter as a crucial step in moral education, as well as an abiding source of pleasure. This is the burden of an Alfoxden Notebook entry from January-February 1798, arguably written with *The Ruined Cottage* in mind:

> Why is it we feel
> So little for each other but for this
> That we with nature have no sympathy
> Or with such idle objects as have no power to hold
> Articulate language.[27]

Before we can be ethically open to other humans, we need first to open ourselves to the ethical demands that all things make, rational and non-rational alike, and to do this we need to be attuned to languages that are not 'articulate', that is, literally, composed of distinctive, serial sounds. Johnson's 1755 *Dictionary* defines 'articulate' as 'distinct ... not continued in one tone ... that is, sounds varied and changed at proper pauses, in opposition to the voice of animals, which admit no such variety'. The voices of animals; the sounds generated by the actions and reactions of wind, water, rock, wood; the sound of fiddle music (as in Wordsworth's 'The Power of Music' from the 1807 *Poems, in Two Volumes*): all these inarticulate languages have a moral claim to our attention, Wordsworth suggests, and moreover this tendering of attention, or tenderness, is the foundation of all ethics, the prerequisite to a proper attitude towards other rational beings. Hearing these languages is not distinct from hearing music: thus, 'I heard a Stock-dove *sing* or *say* / His homely tale, this very day' (emphasis added).[28]

That a musical language abides with birds may not be a novel insight in the canons of poetry, but Wordsworth grants voice to other inarticulate beings and inanimate objects in remarkable ways. In *An Evening Walk* (1793), the elements of nature (are said to) sing to each other, claim one another's attention, give each other pleasure: 'While music stealing round the glimmering deeps, / Charms the tall circle of th'enchanted steeps'.[29] 'All air is, as the sleeping water, still, / List'ning th'aëreal music of the hill'.[30] Humans have no privileged place in the call and response of *Descriptive Sketches* (1793):

> – And sure there is a secret Power that reigns
> Here, where no trace of man the spot profanes ...
> How still! no irreligious sound or sight
> Rouzes the soul from her severe delight.
> An idle voice the sabbath region fills
> Of Deep that calls to Deep across the hills,
> Broke only by the melancholy sound
> Of drowsy bells for ever tinkling round;
> Faint wail of eagle melting into blue
> Beneath the cliffs, and pine-woods steady sugh;
> The solitary heifer's deepn'd low;
> Or rumbling heard remote of falling snow.[31]

Wordsworth rounded off this soundscape in his revised poem: 'All motions, sounds, and voices, far and nigh, / Blend in a music of tranquility'.[32] This tranquility is akin to that coveted by Crowe in his ascent of Lewesdon Hill, the mount of contemplation – it too is tonic for a soul that has transcended the irreligious world – but Wordsworth's lines differ from Crowe's in their de-centering not just of the world apart from contemplative consciousness, but that consciousness itself in the accumulation of particular sounds conveyed as though for their own sake. In the 'Deep that calls to Deep across the hills', the *basso continuo* over which play an array of 'melancholy' (but not saddening) sounds, Wordsworth recalls the first line of Psalm 42:7 – 'Deep calleth unto deep at the noise of thy waterspouts [cataracts]' – while signally omitting its second line, in which the sound of ravines becomes a vehicle for the speaker's spiritual dejection: 'All thy waves and thy billows are gone over me'. In Wordsworth's lines inner landscape gives way to outer: the deeps are those of nature, not of spirit. The deeps call, but not to us, the speaker's witness notwithstanding. Similarly, *The Prelude* depicts human presence among inarticulate languages we cannot, or cannot fully, understand: 'the ghostly language of the ancient earth';[33] the dry wind that blows 'with what strange utterance';[34] 'the voice of mountain torrents' carried far into the Boy of Winander's heart;[35] the rocks of Simplon Pass that 'muttered close', while 'black drizzling crags ... spake ... / As if a voice were in them'.[36] It is indeed a 'mighty sum / Of things for ever speaking' ('Expostulation and Reply'), but they are not speaking wholly, or solely, to us.

Natural music participates in the economy of interchange or gift that, as Alex Dick argues, also characterizes poetry, charity and Wordsworth's sense of them:

they all are more or less useless expenditures that can only be partially recuperated into a system of mutual obligation.[37] The poet's song, like the bird's, is
in one light always a 'waste': and yet, to quote James Thomson's fine line on
springtime birdsong, 'This waste of music is the voice of love'.[38] Song is one
of the acts of giving that constitutes (natural) community. From the auditor's
point of view, it provides as well a model of ethics grounded not in reciprocity,
justice, or any rational imperative but, rather, on attending to the inarticulate
language of other things, including the non-human Other, and responding to
the Other's very alterity as though it were a gift.[39]

That ethical relations must begin with 'idle objects as have no power to
hold / Articulate language' is due in large part to the 'strife of phrase' that
too often divides articulate speakers especially when, as in 'Expostulation and
Reply' and 'The Tables Turned', the topic is books (here, implicitly, of moral
philosophy). 'Books! 'tis a dull and endless strife, / Come, hear the woodland
linnet, / How sweet his music; on my life / There's more of wisdom in it.' In
The Prelude, Wordsworth inveighs, 'how vain / A correspondence with the
talking world / Proves to the most', and proceeds to hoist eloquent speakers
with the petard of (their own) Popean rhetoric:

> ... men adroit
> In speech and for communion with the world
> Accomplished, minds whose faculties are then
> Most active when they are most eloquent,
> And elevated most when most admired.[40]

Wordsworth's final two lines are garnished with rhetorical figures – the par-
allelism of the one line flipping into the chiasmus of the next, with zeugma
underlying the whole – designed to garner the esteem of others: for *amour
propre* is the greatest good of the conversable world. Yet for Wordsworth,
at this stage, verbal facility is in reality the menace of ethics. Wordsworth
offers as his ideal silent poets: 'men for contemplation framed / Shy, and
unpracticed in the strife of phrase'. 'Theirs is the language of the heavens', he
concludes with sublime indistinctness, 'the power, / The thought, the image,
and the silent joy'.[41]

Writing for or as one of such socially silent men, Wordsworth lays claim
to the poetic theme of a sadness that pleases: 'Sorrow that is not sorrow but
delight, / And miserable love that is not pain / To hear of'.[42] 'To hear of' is
key: for Wordsworth, whatever is or may be heard as music can only be received
with joy.

The Music of Humanity

'The still, sad music of humanity' is, of all of Wordsworth's enigmatic phrases, perhaps the most enigmatic, as well as the most provocative. It arrives in 'Tintern Abbey' where conscience might have featured in a more conventional poem. It's something the speaker conjures hearing where 'the still, small voice' might be – indeed Wordsworth's phrase seems deliberately to evoke this Biblical locution – except instead of Wilberforce's concluding 'of conscience' we find 'of humanity'. 'Humanity' is a complex word: according to Johnson's *Dictionary*, it means 'the nature of man'; 'the collective body of mankind'; or 'benevolence, tenderness'. The 'music *of* humanity' is a strange utterance, not only because of the ambiguities of 'humanity' but also because 'of' is here, as Christopher Ricks has shown it so often is in Wordsworth's verse, a 'busy preposition'.[43] The music the speaker of 'Tintern Abbey' hears could be *about* humanity, or somehow emanating *from* humanity, or be itself 'humane music'. How he 'hears' it is another question: it could be with 'the fleshly ear', as he puts it in *The Prelude*, but it might also, as with the 'one song' of nature there, be 'most audible then when the fleshly ear ... / Forgot its functions and slept undisturbed'.[44] One possibility that can, I think, be discounted is that this is a music *made* by human hands, 'music' in its ordinary sense: man-made music would be the music 'of (particular) humans', not of mankind as a whole, or tenderness as a quality. Still less is this music, as David Bromwich ventures, 'the cry of human suffering and human need'.[45] Music by its very nature is not a cry or an appeal. Bromwich himself concedes as much when he adds that the music of humanity chastens the grand rhetorical aims of the French Revolution: 'music, we know, is to be listened to, and not taken as a guide to action'.[46] Accordingly, we cannot respond to it as we would to a cry for help. We can only listen to it; find in it pleasure or displeasure, agitation or comfort; judge it to be beautiful, or not.

What we cannot do, however, is be saddened by it, even if it is 'still, sad music'. Wordsworth here relies, I think, on a reader's knowing something about the philosophy of music as it was known in his day – which is, by a happy coincidence, proximate to the philosophy of music in our own day, in so far as one of its leading practitioners, Peter Kivy, worked out his ideas in dialogue with the musical theory of seventeenth- and eighteenth-century Europe.[47] For Wordsworth, then, as for Kivy, being moved by sadness in music is not being moved to sadness. It is being moved to pleasure, to a general feeling of excitement, by the formal beauty of a music that is expressive of sadness. Music that we perceive as being sad – and, in Wordsworth's case, human conditions or qualities that we perceive as or akin to sad music – do not make us sad, but may offer us both pleasure and a finer moral sensibility. To recur to the Alexander Gerard sentence with which I began this essay, 'Music, producing by its harmony a pleasant disposition of soul, renders us prone to every agreeable affection'. Wordsworth, extending these affections to the entire sphere of 'things' (animals, inanimate objects, events), lauded the power of musical harmony: 'while with an eye made quiet by the power/ Of harmony, and the deep power of joy, / We see into the life of things'.

In his poetry through 1807, Wordsworth strongly implies that music, even sad music, never saddens; it only enlivens. The speaker of 'The Solitary Reaper', for example, overhears a song in a foreign tongue that seems expressive of sadness ('some natural sorrow, loss, or pain'), but it excites in the speaker nothing but excitement, wonder and pleasure. Another example comes from Wordsworth's translations from Virgil's *Georgics* (29 BC), dating back to his Cambridge years, and including portions of the Orpheus and Eurydice story.[48] Wordsworth adds to his translation of the Orpheus story a detail not in Virgil or in Virgil's pre-eminent poetic translator, Dryden: in Wordsworth alone, when Orpheus sings his 'tale of sorrow' for the doubly-lost Euridyce, all the forest rejoices. The line in which Virgil expresses Orpheus's power over brutes and the wilderness – he mourns, *mulcentem tigris et agentem carmine quercus,* 'charming the tigers and moving the oaks with song' – is rendered by Wordsworth freely as 'the solemn forest ... / Had ears to joy':

> For sev'n long moons he sat by [S]trymon's shore
> And sung the [tale] of sorrow o'er and o'er
> High o'er his head as sad the mourner sung
> Aerial rocks in shaggy prospect hung
> The solemn forest at the magic song
> Had ears to joy – and slowly moved along.[49]

What beautiful music or poetry inspires in the listener is wonder or pleasure: the power of music is, for Wordsworth, always halcyon or harmonizing.[50] Its difference from conscience is underscored by the last line of Wordsworth's Orpheus translation, in which the poet's dying cry echoes along the river banks, 'from [s]till small voices heard on every side'.[51] Unlike the still, small voice of conscience they evoke, these voices are not directive, but rather commemorative, communal and quietly joyous.

And so is the voice that speaks 'the still sad music of humanity', a sentiment itself part echo, and not fully distinct from the music that conveys it. '*All art constantly aspires towards the condition of music.* For while in all other works of art it is possible to distinguish the matter from the form, and the understanding can always make this distinction, yet it is the constant effort of art to obliterate it.'[52] Wordsworth may not have agreed whole-heartedly with this judgment of Pater's, but he would at least have understood it – and he may have been the first poet in English to be able to do so. To be sure, 'Tintern Abbey' has subject matter and morality; it is not defined wholly, like pure music, by its structural and sensual properties. But the poem's subject matter is, at crucial moments, and especially in his lines on 'the still, sad music of humanity', left indefinite and subordinate to the rhythms, alliteration and vowel music of verse. By the 1830s, this aspect of Wordsworth's poetry was recognized and prized, particularly in America. An anonymous essayist on Wordsworth in Richmond, VA's *Southern Literary Messenger* (1837) praises Wordsworth's 'eminently lyrical' genius: 'There is no poet who seems to have a more exquisite ear for the musical qualities of language, which he selects and combines for his varied purposes, with an instinctive sense of melody and harmony truly admirable'.[53] Seven years later Edwin Percy Whipple wrote of Wordsworth for the *North American Review*:

> The vagueness and indistinctness of the impression which the most beautiful and sublime passages of his works leave upon the mind is similar to that which is conveyed by the most exquisite music ... His description of indefinite emotions and subtle ideas is so expressed as to be heard by the soul, rather than seen by mental vision.[54]

Wordsworth's 'music of humanity' may include, finally, a self-reflexive glance at the humane music of his own verse.

That is, the music of humanity is not only described but embodied by Wordsworth's lines: they, too, may chasten and subdue, even while giving the pleasure that music gives. Indeed, chastening and subduing, making us tender or humane, would seem to be precisely the ethical aim or 'worthy *purpose*' of Wordsworth's most sublime and beautiful verse, and 'Tintern Abbey' in particular.[55] Here, by transforming conscience into music, Wordsworth turns an ethics of obedience (thou shalt/thou shalt not) into a less structured responsiveness to the human and non-human other, an attitude of beneficence.

The morality of conscience was typically, we have seen, a negative one: conscience served as deterrence from, and punishment of, evil acts and intentions. Wordsworth rid his early poetry of its terrors, and offered instead music, along with aesthetic response more generally, as a source of uplift and consolation. Consolation will always be necessary as long as there are evil and death, and Wordsworth's early poetry abounds in both of these, from the nearly-motiveless malignity of Rivers in *The Borderers* through to the evil at the edges of 'Tintern Abbey': those 'evils tongues', 'rash judgments', 'sneers of selfish men' and 'greetings where no kindness is' that the speaker holds up to Dorothy in the poem's final movement. But here, as more prominently in *The Ruined Cottage*, critics have been too quick to assume that Wordsworth's consolations for suffering and death are Stoical, or constitute a theodicy. Cleanth Brooks set a ball rolling when he wrote that sufferings were presented by Wordsworth as, at least in part, 'a necessary part of a total pattern, rich and various and finally harmonious'.[56] However, neither *The Ruined Cottage* nor 'Tintern Abbey' invoke any such pattern: in the former, Armytage simply speaks, in passing, of 'the passing shews of being', and then he and the narrator feel the sun and hear birds sing. The music of things delights, and if there is a consolation here beyond delight itself it lies in the very proximity of music to the motion and force of life itself, beneath and apart from individual lives. As Keats addressed his singing nightingale, 'Thou wast not born for death, immortal bird!': neither, in this limited sense, are we. From this insight, later Romantics would elaborate a metaphysics of music, from Schopenahauer, for whom the motions of music are an index to the motions of the 'will' or sexualized life force that underlies all passing phenomena, to Nietzsche, who claimed that 'It is only through the spirit of music that we can understand the joy involved in the annihilation of the individual'.[57] Through music we rejoice in the will or Dionysian life force that undergirds all phenomenal beings and periodically reclaims them. Although Wordsworth in the 1790s would not have gone so far as this, he is closer to Nietzsche and Yeats than he is to the neo-Stoic theodicies of Leibniz and Pope.

The Return to Conscience in and after *The Excursion*

The 'Prospectus to *The Recluse*' that prefaces *The Excursion* introduces a new note in Wordsworth's poetry: a clear and ringing endorsement of conscience and divine law. The poet is subject in retirement 'To Conscience only, and the law supreme / Of that Intelligence which governs all'.[58] In *The Excursion* itself, the characters of the Wanderer (the poem's 'philosophical orator') and the sceptical, inconsolable Solitary do not agree on much, but they do agree on the power and importance of conscience.[59] In practice, however, they again differ, as the Solitary attests to conscience as a punitive force, while the Wanderer assumes a more exalted view of it as the image and likeness of God in humanity. The Solitary recalls the torment of conscience when, having outlived his children, wife, and zealous hopes in the French Revolution, he set off for America:

> O, never let the Wretched, if a choice
> Be left him, trust the freight of his distress
> To a long voyage on the silent deep!
> For, like a plague, will memory break out;
> And, in the blank and solitude of things,
> Upon his spirit, with a fever's strength,
> Will conscience prey.[60]

Conscience similarly rears its head in one of Pastor's obituaries of former parishioners (Book 6): Wilfred Armathwaite, who 'against his conscience rose in arms, and braving / Divine displeasure, broke the marriage vow'; 'stung by his inward thoughts, and by the smiles / Of wife and children stung to agony', 'through remorse and grief he died'.[61] In these cases conscience seems implacable, though elsewhere the Solitary suggests that it can sometimes be tricked or too easily assuaged, as it is with the daleswoman who has sent her old lodger to what turns out to be his death in a winter storm: on finding him returned not (yet) dead, 'Great show of joy the housewife made, and truly / Was glad to find her conscience set at ease'.[62] The Puritan minister Joseph Alleine earlier stressed the imperfection of conscience without conversion: 'Whilst conscience holds the whip over them, many will pray, hear, read, and forbear their delightful sins; but no sooner is the lion asleep, but they are at their vomit again'.[63]

The Wanderer, in his discourse designed (ineffectually) to correct the Solitary's despondency, offers a more attractive conception of conscience, one ultimately derived from medieval commentary on Genesis 1:26 (man made in the 'image and likeness' of God):

> But, above all, the victory [over despondency] is most sure
> For him, who, seeking faith by virtue, strives
> To yield entire submission to the law
> Of conscience – conscience reverenced and obeyed,
> As God's most intimate presence in the soul,
> And His most perfect image in the world.[64]

Presented in this way, conscience appears an ennobling faculty, the point of divine similitude: humans either follow the same law that God obeys, or legislate for themselves in the manner that God does. It is indeed a remnant of Paradise, where man 'heard, borne on the wind, the articulate voice / Of God'.[65]

Note how completely, in the Wanderer's discourse, the logocentrism of conscience has replaced Wordsworth's earlier experiments with an ethics modeled on the response to music: whereas earlier the reader was told that sympathy with 'inarticulate language' was fundamental to moral development, here the originary moral mode is 'the articulate voice' of a law-revealing God. Finally, the Wanderer's own articulate voice, the voice of philosophical oratory, is now described, as though in renunciation of Wordsworth's earlier ethic, as 'listened [to] with readier patience than to strain / Of music, lute or harp'.[66] These lines serve as prelude to the Wanderer's climactic speech in Book 9, a speech that begins with a Christianized revision of the 1798 fragment on the 'active principle alive in all things', shorn of its critique of 'negative morality'. With *The Excursion*, Wordsworth not only admits logocentrism, but also largely leaves behind the musicality of his own best verse, as Whipple understood it, becoming more rhetorical or conventionally eloquent.[67] Subject matter artfully arranged assumes pride of place over the structural and sensual elements, the music, of verse. Wordsworth not only joins the conversable world he earlier satirized, but has his several interlocutors variously direct us on how to view life. The Wanderer, hoping to convert the Solitary, does not shy from unitary claims – 'One adequate support / For the calamities of mortal life / Exists', namely, belief in divine providence – but the Solitary is no less didactic in his despondency: thus a spent bonfire is for him, near the poem's end, 'an emblem ... / Of one day's pleasure, and all mortal joys'.[68]

Having raised the banner of conscience and the Word in *The Excursion*, Wordsworth extends their dominion into his revisions of the unpublished poetry begun in the 1790s. In the late version of *The Borderers* (1842), the power of conscience earlier only proposed, slyly, by Rivers (here re-named Oswald), is now witnessed by a repentant woman beggar: 'Pity me, I am haunted; – thrice this day / My conscience made me wish to be struck blind; / And then I would have prayed, and had no voice'.[69] In the early 1790s Wordsworth developed *Salisbury Plain* into *Adventures on Salisbury Plain* by adding to the female vagrant's tale the story of the discharged sailor who robbed and killed a man to feed his family; in *Adventures*, the sailor knows fear and guilt, but only in Wordsworth's later re-working, *Guilt and Sorrow* (1842), does 'conscience' explicitly prompt his confession: '"O welcome sentence which will end though late," / He said, "the pangs that to my conscience came / Out of that deed. My trust, Saviour! is in thy name!"'.[70]

But the acme of Wordsworth's rewriting of his earlier ethic, and the final triumph of the logocentric conscience over music, comes in the late 'On the Power of Sound' (1835), where the effect of music is now analogous to that of punitive conscience. Both offer a traumatic access to 'reason', a divine light so hard it punishes those, like evil-doers and idiots, who have acted in its absence:

> As Conscience, to the centre
> Of being, smites with irresistible pain,
> So shall a solemn cadence, if it enter
> The mouldy vaults of the dull idiot's brain,
> Transmute him to a wretch from quiet hurled –
> Convulsed as by a jarring din;
> And then aghast, as at the world
> Of reason partly let in
> By concords winding with a sway
> Terrible for sense and soul![71]

In this stunning passage, music no longer chastens and consoles, but rather, like conscience, reveals in a flash the terrible chasm between the logos and any mind habituated to moral or intellectual darkness. Wordsworth has wandered far from his earlier adventures in proto-post-modern ethics, not to mention from the anarchic glee of his early poem 'The Idiot Boy'.

As 'On the Power of Sound' continues, the music of things is yoked as well to praise of the divine: Wordsworth revisits the 'Deep that calls to Deep across the hills' of *Descriptive Sketches*, and turns it into a similitude for the universal praise of God:

As Deep to Deep
Shouting through one valley calls,
All worlds, all natures, mood and measure keep
For praise and ceaseless gratulation, poured
Into the ear of God, their Lord![72]

The ode's last and most striking revision is of Wordsworth's well-known *Ode: Intimations of Immortality*.[73] Whereas the earlier poem tentatively played with 'the eternal Silence' as the deeper reality beneath the passing show of phenomenal being, 'On the Power of Sound' ends with a ringing endorsement of the Word that sustains and will survive the passing world: 'O Silence! are Man's noisy years / Nor more than moments of thy life?' 'No!', the speaker emphatically answers, concluding that 'Harmony' is inextricable from the divine Logos: 'though earth be dust / And vanish, though the heavens dissolve, her [Harmony's] stay / Is in the WORD, that shall not pass away'.[74]

Not to give the older Wordsworth the last word, I will close with a brief reflection on the poet's reception in the Victorian novel. His quondam transformation of 'still small voice' into the music of nature was not lost on astute Victorian readers. In Elizabeth Gaskell's *Mary Barton* (1848), the conventional image of conscience as the punitive law inside us is balanced or offset by an earlier Wordsworthian sense that the music of things can both shape an ethical subject and console those who suffer or bear witness to suffering. Gaskell's narrator evidently takes pleasure in dramatizing the effect of 'the Destroyer, Conscience' on John Barton, Mary's trade-unionist father who has committed a murder.[75] But, at one remarkable point in her narration, Gaskell's narrator distinguishes herself from her titular protagonist through her fortunate attendance to nature's healing music. Mary, living in Manchester, can find little solace for her suffering in 'the outward scene' of 'hard, square outlines'. The narrator, by contrast, can both sympathize with Mary's plight and find solace for her own uneasiness because she's writing 'this lovely night in the country', where

the nearer trees sway gently to and fro in the night-wind with something of almost human motion; and the rustling air makes music among their branches, as if speaking soothingly to the weary ones, who lie awake in heaviness of heart. The sights and sounds of such a night lull pain and grief to rest.[76]

NOTES

Lupton and Dick, 'Introduction'

1. D. Hume, *A Treatise of Human Nature*, ed. L. A. Selby-Bigge and P. H. Nidditch, 2nd edn (Oxford: Clarendon Press, 1978), p. 196.
2. C. Siskin, *Work of Writing: Literature and Social Change in Britain 1700–1830* (Baltimore, MD, and London: Johns Hopkins University Press).
3. J. Locke, *An Essay Concerning Human Understanding*, ed. P. H. Nidditch (Oxford: Oxford University Press, 1975), p. 407.
4. Hume, *Treatise of Human Nature* (1978 edn), p. 490.
5. F. Parker, *Scepticism and Literature: An Essay on Pope, Hume, Sterne, and Johnson* (Oxford: Oxford University Press, 2003), p. 231.
6. I. Armstrong, *The Radical Aesthetic* (Oxford: Blackwell, 2000), p. 55. Armstrong's full point about de Man and Derrida is that 'they make just the aesthetic move – an exemption from the constraints of propositionality – which they attribute to the texts they critique'.
7. *Letters of David Hume to William Strahan*, ed. B. Hill (Oxford: Clarendon Press, 1888). See, for instance, pp. 256, 182, 342.
8. J. Christensen, *Practicing Enlightenment: Hume and the Formation of a Literary Career* (Madison, WI: University of Wisconsin Press, 1987), p. 14.
9. J. Richetti, *Philosophical Writing: Locke, Berkeley, Hume* (Cambridge, MA: Harvard University Press, 1983), p. 222.
10. L. Damrosch, *Fictions of Reality in the Age of Hume and Johnson* (Madison, WI: University of Wisconsin Press, 1989), p. 3.
11. F. Hutcheson. *An Inquiry into the Original of our Ideas of Beauty and Virtue in Two Treatises*, ed. W. Leidhold (Indianapolis, IN: Liberty Fund, 2004), p. 9.
12. Ibid., p. 65.

1 Hudson, 'Philosophy/Non-Philosophy'

1. J. Greene, 'Hors D'Œuvre', *Eighteenth-Century Studies*, 40 (2007), pp. 367–79. This is the opening essay in a special issue of *Eighteenth-Century Studies* devoted to Derrida and the eighteenth century. Other essays in this volume will be cited in the course of the following essay.

2. J. Derrida, 'Violence and Metaphysics: An Essay on the Thought of Emmanuel Levinas', in *Writing and Difference*, trans. A. Bass (London, Melbourne and Henley: Routledge & Kegan Paul, 1978), pp. 79–153; p. 152.
3. Derrida, 'Violence and Metaphysics', p. 151.
4. J. Derrida, *Of Grammatology*, trans. G. C. Spivak (London and Baltimore, MD: Johns Hopkins University Press, 1974), p. 49.
5. J. Derrida, *Speech and Phenomena and the Essay on Husserl's Theory of Signs*, trans. D. B. Allison (Evaston, IL: Northwestern University Press, 1973), pp. 45–6, n. 4. See J. Barnouw, 'Peirce and Derrida: "Natural Signs" Empiricism versus "Originary Trace" Deconstruction', *Poetics Today*, 7 (1986), pp. 73–94. See also Derrida, *Of Grammmatology*, p. 50.
6. Derrida, *Speech and Phenomena*, p. 43.
7. R. Rorty considered Derrida's rejection of empiricism as one of the major differences between deconstruction and pragmaticism. See R. Rorty, 'Remarks on Deconstruction and Pragmatism', in C. Mouffe (ed.), *Deconstruction and Pragmatism* (London and New York: Routledge, 1996), pp. 13–18; p. 16. For a rather different point of view – that Derrida ignores the role of *différance* in Husserl's philosophy, and that Derrida himself is an 'empirical realist' – see T. Mooney, 'Derrida's Empirical Realism', *Philosophy & Social Criticism*, 25 (1999), pp. 33–56.
8. E. Levinas, *Totality and Infinity: An Essay on Exteriority*, trans. A. Lingis (The Hague, Boston, MA, and London: Martinus Nijhoff, 1979), p. 44.
9. Ibid., p. 76.
10. Derrida, 'Violence and Metaphysics', p. 95.
11. Ibid., pp. 101–2.
12. Ibid., p. 130.
13. Ibid., p. 136.
14. Ibid., p. 138.
15. Ibid., pp. 151–2.
16. Ibid., p. 139.
17. Ibid., p. 131.
18. Modern scholars of the eighteenth century remain sadly misled by Michel Foucault's *The Order of Things* (1966; trans. 1970). For refutations of Foucault, and more reliable accounts of eighteenth-century language theory, see H. Aarsleff, *From Locke to Saussure: Essays on the Study of Language and Intellectual History* (Minneapolis, MN: University of Minnesota Press, 1982); L. Formigari, *Signs, Science and Politics: Philosophies of Language in Europe 1700–1830*, trans. W. Dodd (Amsterdam and Philadelphia, PA: John Benjamins, 1993); U. Ricken, *Linguistics, Anthropology and Philosophy in the French Enlightenment*, trans. R. W. Norton (London and New York: Routledge, 1994); N. Hudson, 'Theories of Language', in *The Cambridge History of Literary Criticism: Vol. 4, The Eighteenth Century*, ed. H. B. Nisbet and C. Rawson (Cambridge: Cambridge University Press, 1997), pp. 335–48.
19. See Derrida, *Of Grammatology*, pp. 75–81.
20. Ibid., pp. 98–9.
21. Locke, *Essay Concerning Human Understanding* (1975 edn), p. 372 (bk 2, ch. 30).
22. Ibid., p. 502.
23. Ibid., p. 458.
24. Ibid., p. 453.
25. Ibid., p. 500.

26. Ibid., p. 335.
27. G. Berkeley, *A Treatise Concerning the Principles of Human Understanding*, in *Works of George Berkeley*, ed. A. C. Fraser, 4 vols (Oxford: Clarendon Press, 1901), vol. 1, pp. 211–347; p. 245.
28. G. Berkeley, *A New Theory of Vision*, in *Works of George Berkeley*, vol. 1, pp. 93–210; p. 200.
29. Ibid., p. 200.
30. Ibid., p. 258.
31. Ibid.
32. Hume, *Treatise of Human Nature* (1978 edn), p. 254.
33. Ibid., p. 17.
34. P. L. M. de Maupertuis, *Réflexions philosophiques sur l'origine des langues et la signification des mots*, in *Œuvres de Maupertuis*, 2nd edn, 4 vols (Lyons: Jean Marie Bruyset, 1768), vol. 1, pp. 259–309; pp. 272–3.
35. Ibid., pp. 265–6.
36. Ibid., pp. 278–9.
37. 'That which we call our sciences depends so intimately on the ways which we use to designate perceptions that it seems to me that questions and propositions would be totally different if we had established orders for our first perceptions.' Ibid., p. 268.
38. Besides the work of Locke, Berkeley, Hume and Maupertuis, 'constitutive' understandings of the relationship between mind and language were developed by D. Diderot in *Lettre sur les sourds et muets* (Paris: n.p., 1751), E. Burke in part 5 of *A Philosophical Enquiry into the Origin of our Ideas of the Sublime and Beautiful* (London: R. and J. Dodsley, 1757), and A. Smith in *Considerations Concerning the First Formation of Languages* (Edinburgh, 1767).
39. J. Derrida, *The Archeology of the Frivolous*, trans. J. P. Leavey, Jr (Lincoln, NE, and London: University of Nebraska Press, 1980), p. 94.
40. Ibid., p. 100.
41. Ibid., p. 112.
42. Ibid., p. 71.
43. Stewart refers to Smith's *Considerations Concerning the First Formation of Languages* in *An Account of the Life and Writings of Adam Smith* (1794), reprinted in A. Smith, *Essays on Philosophical Subjects*, ed. W. P. D. Wightman, J. C. Bryce and I. S. Ross, in *The Glasgow Edition of the Works and Correspondence of Adam Smith*, 6 vols (Oxford: Clarendon Press, 1976–83), vol. 3, p. 293.
44. See E. B. de Condillac, *An Essay on the Origin of Human Knowledge*, trans. T. Nugent (London, 1756; repr. Gainesville, FL: Scholars' Facsmilies & Reprints, 1971), pp. 30–1.
45. Ibid., p. 132.
46. Ibid., pp. 140–1.
47. Ibid., pp. 141.
48. Derrida, *Archeology of the Frivolous*, pp. 97–8. See also Derrida's note on these pages.
49. Condillac, *Essay on the Origin of Human Knowledge*, p. 38.
50. Ibid., p. 284.
51. Ibid., pp. 283–300.
52. Ibid., p. 293.
53. Ibid., p. 296.
54. G. Bennington, 'Derrida's "Eighteenth Century"', *Eighteenth-Century Studies*, 40 (2007), pp. 381–93; p. 382; see also J. Candler Hayes, 'Unconditional Translation: Derrida's Enlightenment-To-Come', *Eighteenth-Century Studies*, 40 (2007), pp. 443–55; p. 443.
55. Condillac, *Essay on the Origin of Human Knowledge*, pp. 273–83.

56. J. Derrida, 'Signature, Event, Context', in *Margins of Philosophy*, ed. A. Bass (Chicago, IL: University of Chicago Press, 1982), pp. 308–30; p. 311. This essay was originally published in *Glyph*, 1 (1977), pp. 172–97.

57. See J. R. Searle, 'Reiterating the Differences: A Reply to Derrida', *Glyph*, 1 (1977), pp. 198–208; p. 202.

58. Derrida, *Archeology of the Frivolous*, p. 126.

59. '[F]ormed and perfected tongues.' Condillac, *Grammaire* in *Œuvres philosophiques*, ed. G. le Rou (Paris: Presses Universitaires de France, 1947), p. 447. Condillac is referring to a prose passage by Corneille in terms of its punctuation and paragraph structure.

60. Condillac, *Essay on the Origin of Human Knowledge*, p. 308.

61. Ibid., p. 288. For a lengthy declaration of the same principle, see *Cours d'études pour l'instruction du prince de Parme*, in *Œuvres philosophiques*, p. 404.

62. D. Hartley, *Observations on Man* (London: James Leake and Wm. Frederick, 1749), p. 44. See also G. Vico, *La scienza nuova* (Naples, 1725–44); J. Wachter, *Naturæ et scripturæ concordia* (Lipsiæ et Hafniæ, 1752); R. Jones, *Hieroglyphic: or, a Grammatical Introduction to an Universal Hieroglyphic Language* (London: John Hughs, 1768); A. Court de Gébelin, *Monde primtif, analysé et comparé avec le monde moderne*, 9 vols (Paris, 1771–83), vol. 3.

63. For detailed discussion of all these points, see N. Hudson, *Writing and European Thought, 1600–1830* (Cambridge: Cambridge University Press, 1994), esp. pp. 55–142.

64. 'The art of speaking, the art of reasoning, and the art of thinking are, at bottom, one and the same art.' Condillac, *Cours d'études pour l'instruction du prince de Parme*, in *Œuvres philosophiques*, p. 403.

65. W. Warburton, *The Divine Legation of Moses*, 4 vols (London: Fletcher Gyles, 1738–41), vol. 4, p. 156.

66. Ibid., p. 81.

67. J. Derrida, 'Scribble (Writing-Power)', trans. C. Plotkin, *Yale French Studies*, 58 (1979), pp. 116–47; p. 123.

68. Ibid., p. 133.

69. Warburton, *Divine Legation of Moses*, vol. 2, pp. 138–9.

70. Derrida, 'Scribble', p. 129.

71. For the case that Derrida *is* arguing 'in some sense in the interests of history', despite his claims against the historicism of Foucault and others, see Bennington, 'Derrida's "Eighteenth Century"', p. 390.

72. Derrida, *Of Grammmatology*, pp. 162–3.

73. Ibid., p. 162.

74. Ibid., p. 237.

75. Derrida, 'Scribble', p. 144.

76. J. J. Rousseau, *A Discourse on Inequality*, trans. M. Cranston (Harmondsworth: Penguin, 1984), p. 91.

77. Ibid., p. 93.

78. Derrida, *Of Grammmatology*, p. 211.

79. Ibid., p. 213.

80. J. J. Rousseau, *Essay on the Origin of Languages* in *On the Origin of Language*, trans. J. H. Moran and A. Gode (Chicago, IL, and London: University of Chicago Press, 1966), p. 58.

81. Ibid., p. 15.

82. Ibid.

83. Ibid., p. 28.

84. Ibid., p. 21.
85. Derrida, *Of Grammmatology*, p. 159.
86. Ibid., p. 166.

2 Kramnick, 'Locke's Desire'

1. B. Mandeville, *The Fable of the Bees*, 2 vols, ed. F. B. Kaye (Indianapolis, IN: Liberty Classics, 1988), vol. 1, p. 344.
2. Ibid., p. 350.
3. Locke makes his own position clear on this matter in the closing section of the *Essay*, which discusses the 'division of the sciences'. The equating of modernity with societal' differentiation' – or the multiform division of knowledge and division of labour – is made early on in the *Essay* when Locke states that what he is doing is working as an 'under-labourer' for 'science' (J. Locke, *An Essay Concerning Human Understanding*, 1st edn (London: T. Basset, 1690, p. 4). In other words, 'philosophy' is a separate practice from experimental 'science' – a novel and, obviously enough, prescient claim to make.
4. The examples are many (consider Book 3 of *Gulliver's Travels*) and take recognizable form in the Enlightenment's stock character of the 'pedant', whose expertise is a condition of his futility.
5. My sense of the tensions placed on intimate culture by the 'differentiation of society' is informed by the insights of N. Luhmann's *Love as Passion: The Codification of Intimacy*, trans. J Gaines and D. Jones (Cambridge, MA: Harvard University Press, 1988), which analyses how erotic life changes along with the transformation from a 'stratified' (traditional, religious, and hierarchical) society to a 'functional' (modern, secular, and liberal) society.
6. Locke reflects on the dilemmas of expertise most explicitly in Book II of the *Essay*, which attempts to define terms that could mediate the necessary difficulty of technical language. The effort is to find precise terms that do not wall off the new disciplines from each other or from the sociable idioms of civil society. The making of disciplines is simultaneous with their wished-for transcendence. Three centuries later this same desire structures the purported 'deconstruction' of Locke's linguistics by P. de Man in 'The Epistemology of Metaphor', *Critical Inquiry*, 5:1 (1978), pp. 13–30. On this account, Locke's attempt to 'control figuration ... stands behind the recurrent efforts to map out the distinctions between philosophical, scientific, theological, and poetic discourse and informs such institutional questions as the departmental structure of schools and universities' (p. 14). The deconstructive insight that figuration cannot be controlled in turn stands behind the effort to overcome disciplinary specialization by means of rigorous, rhetorical reading. Whatever one makes of this effort – surely now something of a museum piece of the intellectual culture of the 1970s – it is far closer to the designs of Locke than it wants to admit.
7. The chapter is typically discussed by Locke scholars as either a question of his ethics, which I will take up below, or his position on free will versus determinism. Most helpful in this regard have been M. Ayers, *Locke: Epistemology and Ontology*, 2 vols (New York: Routledge, 1991), vol. 2, pp. 184–202; S. Darnwall, *The British Moralists and the Internal 'Ought'* (Cambridge: Cambridge University Press, 1995), pp. 149–75; R. Polin, 'John Locke's Conception of Freedom', in J. Yolton (ed.), *John Locke: Problems and Perspectives* (Cambridge: Cambridge University Press, 1969), pp. 1–18; and P. Schouls, *Reasoned Freedom: John Locke and Enlightenment* (Ithaca, NY: Cornell University Press,

1992), pp. 117–72. My understanding of Locke's position – as reflexive – is closest to that advanced by V. Chappel in 'Locke on Freedom of the Will', in G. A. J. Rogers (ed.), *Locke's Philosophy: Content and Context* (Oxford: Clarendon Press, 1994), pp. 101–21.

8. Locke, *Essay Concerning Human Understanding* (1690 edn), p. 119, original emphasis.
9. Ibid., p. 119.
10. Ibid., p. 119.
11. Ibid., p. 119.
12. Ibid., p. 123.
13. Ibid., p. 121, original emphasis.
14. Ibid., p. 124.
15. Ibid., p. 124.
16. Ibid., p. 124.
17. Ibid., p. 124.
18. The canonical statement on these matters was *A Practical Discourse Concerning a Future Judgment* (London: W. Rogers, 1692), written by W. Sherlock, Dean of St Paul's, and reprinted in seven editions over the next fifty years. Sherlock's book shows how the dominant strains of ecclesiastical thought presented, in language stripped of the overweening 'enthusiasm' of Puritan rhetoric, knowledge of the everlasting as the guarantor of subjective volition:

    > a wise being will take care to govern the creatures which he makes and to govern them in such a way as is agreeable to the natures he has given them; and since man, who is a free agent, can be governed only by hopes and fears, God would never have made man, had he not intended to judge him; that is, he would never have made such a creature as can be governed only by the hope of rewards and by the fear of punishments, had he not resolved to lay these restraints upon him, to reward and punish him according to his works. (p. 10)

19. Locke, *Essay Concerning Human Understanding* (1690 edn), p. 127.
20. Ibid., p. 127.
21. Ibid., p. 128.
22. See, for example, G. Cragg, *Reason and Authority in the Eighteenth Century* (Cambridge: Cambridge University Press, 1964), pp. 1–28.
23. H. More, *The Immortality of the Soul* (London: William Morden, 1659), p. 14.
24. The concept of incorporeal substance was essential to the doctrine of the immortality of the soul, which More argues for, against what he takes to be Hobbes's materialism (52–6 and passim): 'We have discovered out of the simple phaenomenon of motion the necessity of the existence of some incorporeal essence distinct from matter' (More, *Immortality*, p. 66).
25. Ibid., pp. 56, 169.
26. Ibid., p. 88.
27. Other examples include R. Cudworth, whose *True Intellectual System of the Universe* (London: Richard Royston, 1678) argued we know that 'there is some such absolutely perfect being, which though not inconceivable, yet is incomprehensible to our finite understandings; by certain passions which it hath implanted in us, that otherwise would want an object to display themselves upon' (p. 640).
28. Norris responds to the *Essay* in *Cursory Reflections on a Book Call'd An Essay Concerning Human Understanding* (London, 1690). Locke declines to respond to Norris in print, although he does deride him in correspondence. The official 'Lockean' response to Norris came, rather, from his friend L. D. Masham in *A Discourse Concerning the Love of God*

(London: Awnsham and John Churchil, 1696). For the intellectual context of Norris's thought, see C. McCracken, *Malebranche and the British Philosophy* (Oxford: Oxford University Press, 1983).

29. J. Norris, *The Theory and Regulation of Love: A Moral Essay* (Oxford, 1688), p. 10.
30. Ibid., p. 11.
31. Ibid., p. 20.
32. Ibid., p. 38.
33. Ibid., p. 28.
34. Quoted in M. Cranston, *John Locke, a Biography* (London: Longmans, 1957), p. 359. Scholars of the history of philosophy will recall Molyneux's importance to Locke's account of vision, especially after he posed the familiar riddle, would a blind man, familiar with the properties of a cube and sphere from touch and suddenly possessed of sight, be able to discern the difference between the two shapes at a distance? Locke and Molyneux both respond in the negative.
35. *The Correspondence of John Locke*, ed. E. S. De Beer, 7 vols (Oxford: Clarendon Press, 1979), vol. 4, pp. 479, 508.
36. For a cogent reflection on the antinomies of early-modern friendship, see A. Bray, 'Homosexuality and the Signs of Male Friendship in Elizabethan England', in J. Goldberg (ed.), *Queering the Renaissance* (Durham, NC: Duke University Press, 1993), pp. 40–61. Bray presents the 'friend' and the 'sodomite' as twin figures of honour and abuse; importantly for the present essay, he also points to the erotic relations of friendship that were enabled by their not being perceived as sodomy.
37. Cranston, *John Locke*, p. 360.
38. *Correspondence of John Locke*, vol. 4, p. 522.
39. Ibid., pp. 524–5.
40. Ibid., p. 522. The two had noted in their first letters that they were in Holland at the same time but had not met.
41. On 'transparency' as the desired end of modern intimacy, see Luhmann, *Love as Passion*, esp. pp. 173–8.
42. *Correspondence of John Locke*, vol. 4, p. 609.
43. Literary critics will be most accustomed to this as the argument of B. Anderson's widely-influential study, *Imagined Communities: Reflections on the Origin and Spread of Nationalism*, rev. edn (London: Verso, 1991). On disembedding as a social process characteristic of 'modernity', see A. Giddens, *The Consequences of Modernity* (Stanford, CA: Stanford University Press, 1990) and C. Taylor, *Modern Social Imaginaries* (Durham, NC: Duke University Press, 2004), pp. 49–68.
44. *Correspondence of John Locke*, vol. 4, p. 664.
45. Ibid.
46. As for the former, witness the scene which Locke presents as the very genesis of the *Essay* at the beginning of the essay: 'Were it fit to trouble thee with the history of this *Essay*, I would tell thee that five or six friends meeting at my chamber, and discoursing on a subject very remote from this, found themselves quickly at a stand, by the difficulties that rose on every side' (1st and 2nd edn, p. b2). A copy of the 1690 edition in the British Museum sheds light on this moment. In it, Locke's friend William Tyrell writes in the margins: 'This was in winter 1673 as I remember: being myself one of those that then met there when the discourse began about the principles of morality, and revealed religion'.

47. By this I mean disclosure in the published form of Locke's work. Yet it is not without irony in this case that the Locke–Molyneux correspondence would itself be published, posthumously, as *Some Familiar Letters Between Mr. Locke and His Friends* (London: A. and J. Churchill, 1708).
48. *Correspondence of John Locke*, vol. 4, p. 665.
49. Ibid., p. 601.
50. Ibid., p. 602.
51. E.g., 15 October 1692: 'I am wonderfully pleased that you give me hopes of seeing a moral essay from your hand, which I assure you sir with all sincerity is highly respected by ...' (ibid., p. 533). This unrequited plea is repeated in virtually every letter; here is 2 March 1693: 'On this consideration of usefulness to mankind, I will presume again to remind you of your discourse of morality; And I shall think my self very happy, if by putting you on the thought, I should be the least occasion of so great good to the world' (ibid., p. 649).
52. Ibid., p. 602.
53. Molyneux repeatedly chides Locke for having mentioned, in an aside, that morals are 'demonstrable according to Mathematical formula' (ibid., p. 508).
54. Ibid., p. 700.
55. Ibid., p. 700.
56. Molyneux's words for Norris and others he decrees as 'Platonists' are merciless:
    > I look upon [Nicolas] Malbranches notions, or rather Platos, [as] perfectly unintelligible; And if you will ingage in a philosophick controversy, you cannot do it with more advantage than in this matter. What you lay down concerning our ideas and knowledge is founded and confirmed by experiment, and observation, that any man may make in himself, or the children he converses with; wherein he may note the gradual steps that we make in knowledge. But Plato's fancy has no foundation in nature, but is merely the product of his own brain (ibid., p. 688).
57. See the enumeration of the sub-sections of the chapter in the letter dated 15 July 1693 (ibid., pp. 700–1) and the synopsis of the argument in the letter dated 23 August 1693 (ibid., pp. 722–3).
58. Ibid., p. 700.
59. Haywood's widely popular first novel *Love in Excess* (1719–20) uses the term frequently, as a description of desire. Mandeville's notorious *Fable of the Bees* (especially its important chapter on charity-schools) finds 'uneasiness' to be the motive of all action, 'virtuous' or otherwise.
60. *Correspondence of John Locke*, vol. 4, p. 722.
61. Locke, *Essay Concerning Human Understanding* (1690 edn), p. 117.
62. J. Locke, *An Essay Concerning Human Understanding*, 2nd edn (London: Awnsham and John Churchil; and Samuel Manship, 1694), p. 125.
63. Ibid., pp. 125–6.
64. Ibid., p. 133.
65. Ibid.
66. Ibid., p. 134.
67. Ibid., pp. 134–5.
68. Ibid., p. 135.
69. See, respectively, S. Shapin, *The Social History of Truth: Civility and Science in Seventeenth-Century England* (Chicago, IL: University of Chicago Press, 1994); J. Kramnick, *Making the English Canon* (Cambridge: Cambridge University Press, 1999); and J. Hab-

ermas, *The Structural Transformation of the Public Sphere*, trans. T. Burger (Cambridge: MIT Press, 1989).

70. Locke, *Essay Concerning Human Understanding* (1690 edn), p. 124.
71. Locke, *Essay Concerning Human Understanding* (1694 edn), p. 124.
72. For an incisive discussion of Locke's nominalism, see N. Hudson, 'John Locke and the Tradition of Nominalism', in H. Keiper, C. Bode and R. J. Utz (eds), *Nominalism and Literary Discourse: New Perspectives* (Amsterdam: Rodopi, 1997), pp. 283–300.
73. Locke, *Essay Concerning Human Understanding* (1690 edn), p. 131; Locke, *Essay Concerning Human Understanding* (1694 edn), p. 152.
74. Locke, *An Essay Concerning Human Understanding* (1694 edn), p. 140.
75. For the classic statement by Freud, see 'Mourning and Melancholia', in *The Standard Edition of the Complete Psychological Works of Sigmund Freud*, ed. and trans. J. Strachey et al., 24 vols (London: Hogarth, 1953–74), vol. 14; for the now canonical deconstruction of this statement see J. Butler, *The Psychic Life of Power* (Stanford, CA: Stanford University Press, 1997), pp. 167–98.
76. This dialectic may be found, too, in the linguistic programme of the *Essay*, which attempts to build a language that has both a 'civil' and 'philosophical' use, one that 'may serve for the upholding common conversation and commerce, about the ordinary affairs and conveniences of civil life, in the societies of men, on amongst another' and at the same time 'may serve to convey the precise notions of things, and to express, in general propositions, certain and undoubted truths, which the mind may rest upon, and be satisfied with, in its search after true knowledge' (Locke, *Essay Concerning Human Understanding* (1690 edn), p. 231; Locke, *Essay Concerning Human Understanding* (1694 edn), pp. 268–9).
77. Locke, *Essay Concerning Human Understanding* (1690 edn), p. 138.
78. Ibid., p. 140.
79. Ibid., p. 135.
80. The most vivid example of this dynamic in the *Essay* is the rather unassuming case of a man crippled with gout who wants relief from his several pains but fears that any one satiation will reproduce the pain elsewhere (ibid., p. 250).
81. Ibid., p. 141.
82. J. Locke, *An Essay Concerning Human Understanding*, 5th edn (London: Awnsham and John Churchill; and Samuel Manship, 1706), pp. 171–2.
83. J. Habermas, *The Philosophical Discourse of Modernity* (Cambridge, MA: MIT Press, 1987), p. 20. Habermas places against this one-sided development of reason – in science, bureaucracy, capital – the potential for intersubjective communication as the 'unfinished project' of the Enlightenment.
84. This is a position often attributed to Foucault, who actually had a very different sense of the Enlightenment as the process of experimental self-making. See 'What is Critique?', in S. Schmidt (ed.), *What is Enlightenment?* (Berkeley, CA: University of California Press, 1995), pp. 182–204. It is closer, though, to F. Lyotard, who assigned the Enlightenment to the same burial as all other so-called 'narratives of progress'; see *The Postmodern Condition: A Report on Knowledge* (Minneapolis, MN: University of Minnesota Press, 1984).
85. The most tireless exponent of the 'point of origin' argument has certainly been R. Trumbach, whose many essays culminated in *Sex and the Gender Revolution 1: Heterosexuality and the Third Gender in Enlightenment London* (Chicago, IL: University of Chicago Press, 1998). Where Trumbach looks to eighteenth-century England to see the beginnings of a homosexual identity (first for men, later for women) evidently drawn from the present – an early essay located in the Enlightenment the 'birth of the queen' – other

scholars have looked to the period for 'queer' transgression or subversiveness (see C. McFarlane's *The Sodomite in Fiction and Satire, 1660–1750* (New York: Columbia, 1997) or K. Straub, *Sexual Suspects: Eighteenth-Century Players and Sexual Ideology* (Princeton, NJ: Princeton University Press, 1992)). In either case, a particular version of the present is read into the past: the eighteenth century produces identities, as in, say, Trumbach's inventory of types (the 'molly', the 'sapphist', etc.), or it subverts and renders 'performative' these identities.

3 Chaves, 'Philosophy and Politeness'

1. A. A. Cooper, third Earl of Shaftesbury, *Characteristics of Men, Manners, Opinions, Times*, ed. L. E. Klein (Cambridge and New York: Cambridge University Press, 1999), pp. 148–9, n. 82.
2. Ibid., pp. 232, 148–9, n. 82, p. 232; L. E. Klein, *Shaftesbury and the Culture of Politeness: Moral Discourse and the Cultural Politics of Early Eighteenth-Century England* (New York: Cambridge University Press, 1994), p. 37.
3. Shaftesbury, *Characteristics*, p. 233.
4. Ibid., p. 125.
5. Ibid., pp. 151–3, 52; For example, R. Paulson suggests that, in the *Characteristics*, the 'potential for sensual enjoyment is rigidly and consistently held in abeyance'. Paulson argues that pleasure is a key term for Shaftesbury, but also that he 'refines it out of a physical into a mental state, distinguishing pleasures qualitatively'. R. Paulson, *Breaking and Remaking: Aesthetic Practice in England, 1700–1820* (New Brunswick, NJ: Rutgers University Press, 1989), pp. 24–5.
6. Shaftesbury, *Characteristics*, p. 233.
7. See R. Tierney-Hynes, 'Shaftesbury's Soliloquy: Authorship and the Psychology of Romance', *Eighteenth-Century Studies*, 38:4 (2005), pp. 605–21.
8. J. Barrell, *English Literature in History 1730–80: An Equal, Wide Survey* (London: Hutchinson, 1983), pp. 26–39.
9. See Paulson, *Breaking and Remaking*, pp. 1–4, 24. For another take on Shaftesbury in this vein, see R. Markley, 'Sentimentality as Performance: Shaftesbury, Sterne, and the Theatrics of Virtue', in F. Nussbaum and L. Brown (eds), *The New Eighteenth Century* (New York and London: Methuen, 1987), pp. 210–30.
10. Klein, *Shaftesbury and the Culture of Politeness*, p. 21.
11. M. B. Prince, *Philosophical Dialogue in the British Enlightenment: Theology, Aesthetics, and the Novel* (Cambridge: Cambridge University Press, 1996), pp. 37–8.
12. Shaftesbury, *Characteristics*, p. 407.
13. L. E. Klein, 'The Third Earl of Shaftesbury and the Progress of Politeness', *Eighteenth-Century Studies*, 18:2 (1984–5), pp. 185–214.
14. Shaftesbury, *Characteristics*, p. 150.
15. Ibid., p. 37.
16. Ibid., p. 33; Shapin, *Social History of Truth*, p. 66.
17. Shaftesbury, *Characteristics*, p. 33.
18. L. E. Klein, 'Enlightenment as Conversation', in K. M. Baker and P. Hanns Reill (eds), *What's Left of Enlightenment? A Postmodern Question* (Stanford, CA: Stanford University Press, 2001), p. 157.
19. Shaftesbury, *Characteristics*, p. 33.
20. Ibid., p. 33.

21. Ibid., pp. 29–30.
22. Ibid.
23. Ibid., p. 31.
24. Ibid., p. 94.
25. Ibid., pp. 35, 119.
26. Ibid., p. 59. For Starobinski, 'la différence se reduit au point de n'être plus génératrice de conflit mais du jeu'. Quoted in E. Goldsmith, *Exclusive Conversations: The Art of Interaction in Seventeenth-Century France* (Philadelphia, PA: University of Philadelphia Press, 1989), p. 13.
27. Shaftesbury, *Characteristics*, pp. 30–3.
28. Ibid., p. 147.
29. Ibid., p. 353.
30. Ibid., p. 422. See also p. 410: 'Equipages, titles, precedencies, staffs, ribbons and other such glittering ware are taken in exchange for inward merit, honour and a character.'
31. Ibid., pp. 57, 64.
32. Ibid., p. 422.
33. M. Price, *To the Palace of Wisdom: Studies in Order and Energy from Dryden to Blake* (New York: Doubleday & Co., 1964), p. 94.
34. H. Caygill, *Art of Judgment* (Oxford: Blackwell, 1989), p. 48.
35. Shaftesbury, *Characteristics*, p. 191.
36. J. Guillory, *Cultural Capital: The Problem of Literary Canon Formation* (Chicago, IL: Chicago University Press, 1993), p. 305.
37. Shaftesbury, *Characteristics*, pp. 93, 148.
38. For Gadamer, Shaftesbury's *sensus communis* 'already embraces a sum of judgments and criteria for judgment that determine its contents'. H.-G. Gadamer, *Truth and Method*, trans. J. Weinsheimer and D. G. Marshall (New York: Crossroad, 1989), pp. 21–35.
39. Caygill, *Art of Judgment*, p. 49.
40. B. Mandeville, *The Fable of the Bees: or, Private Vices, Publick Benefits* and *The Fable of the Bees, Part II*, ed. F. B. Kaye, 2 vols (Oxford: Clarendon Press, 1924), vol. 2, pp. 39–57. See also Caygill, *Art of Judgment*, pp. 48–53.
41. Guillory, *Cultural Capital*, p. 305.
42. Shaftesbury, *Characteristics*, p. 408.
43. Ibid., p. 255.
44. I borrow this way of expressing the distinction from G. J. Barker-Benfield, who criticizes Shaftesbury for conflating the two. G. J. Barker-Benfield, *The Culture of Sensibility: Sex and Society in Eighteenth-Century Britain* (Chicago, IL: University of Chicago Press, 1992), p. 108.
45. For Shaftesbury, as C. Taylor observes, 'our natural affections would carry beyond our immediate family and entourage to a disinterested love of all mankind, if we rightly understood our situation'. C. Taylor, *Sources of the Self: The Making of Modern Identity* (Cambridge, MA: Harvard University Press, 1989), p. 255.
46. Shaftesbury, *Characteristics*, pp. 243–4.
47. Ibid., p. 52.
48. Ibid., p. 52.
49. Ibid., pp. 326–7.
50. 'All is revolution in us. We are no more the self-same matter or system of matter from one day to another' (ibid., p. 254). The subject's presumptive 'independency and freedom' are 'mere glosses and resolution, a nose of wax. For let will be ever so free, humour and fancy,

we see, govern it. And these, as free as we suppose them, are often changed we know not how, without asking our consent or giving us any account' (ibid., p. 83).

51. Ibid., p. 244. On the manner in which Shaftesbury's discipline of 'self-converse', the topic of the next section, conflicts with the assertion of a capacity for spontaneous moral judgment, see R. Marsh, 'Shaftesbury's Theory of Poetry: The Importance of the Inward Colloquy', *English Literary History*, 28 (1961), pp. 54–69.

52. Shaftesbury, *Characteristics*, p. 129.

53. Ibid., p. 405.

54. Ibid., p. 131.

55. Ibid., p. 126.

56. Ibid., p. 79.

57. Ibid., p. 79.

58. Ibid., p. 132.

59. Ibid., pp. 404–5.

60. Ibid., p. 94.

61. Ibid., p. 88.

62. Ibid., pp. 88, 83.

63. Ibid., p. 87.

64. Ibid., pp. 78, 84.

65. Ibid., p. 78.

66. Ibid., pp. 139, 84.

67. Klein, *Shaftesbury and the Culture of Politeness*, pp. 87–9.

68. Shaftesbury, *Characteristics*, p. 72.

69. Ibid., p. 79.

70. Klein, *Shaftesbury and the Culture of Politeness*, p. 87–9.

71. See also Shaftesbury, *Characteristics*, p. 84.

72. Ibid., p. 34.

73. Ibid., p. 84. Similarly, 'Nor is there any thing un-galante in the manner of thus questioning the *Lady-Fancys*, which present themselves as charmingly dress'd as possible to solicit their Cause' (ibid., p. 139).

74. Ibid., pp. 396, 417, 136, 379.

75. Ibid., pp. 347–9.

76. Ibid., p. 54.

77. Ibid., p. 419.

78. See R. Voitle, *The Third Earl of Shaftesbury, 1671–1713* (Baton Rouge, LA, and London: Louisiana State University Press, 1984), pp. 338–9, as well as C. McIntosh, *The Evolution of English Prose, 1700–1800: Style, Politeness and Print Culture* (Cambridge: Cambridge University Press, 1998), pp. 68–75.

79. Prince, *Philosophical Dialogue in the British Enlightenment*, p. 28.

80. Shaftesbury, *Characteristics*, p. 342.

81. Ibid., pp. 399, 342.

82. Ibid., p. 433.

83. Ibid., pp. 342, 433, 342.

84. Ibid., p. 433.

85. Ibid., p. 380.

86. Ibid.

87. Ibid., p. 420.

88. Ibid., p. 339.

89. Ibid., p. 35.
90. Ibid., p. 70; Persius, *Satires* I.7.

4 Dick, 'Reid, Writing and the Mechanics of Common Sense'

1. P. Keen. 'The "Balloonomania": Science and Spectacle in 1780s England', *Eighteenth-Century Studies*, 39 (2006), pp. 507–35; J. Park, 'Pains and Pleasures of the Automaton: Frances Burney's Mechanics of Coming Out', *Eighteenth-Century Studies*, 40 (2006), pp. 23–49.

2. W. Wordsworth, 'Steamboat, Viaducts, and Railways', in G. Jackson (ed.), *Sonnet Series and Itinerary Poems 1820–1845* (Ithaca, NY: Cornell University Press, 2004), p. 604.

3. J. D. Bolter and R. Grusin, *Remediation: Understanding New Media* (Cambridge: MIT Press, 2002), p. 59.

4. See O. Mayr, *Authority, Liberty and Automatic Machinery in Early Modern Europe* (Baltimore, MD, and London: Johns Hopkins University Press, 1986) and S. Schaffer, 'Enlightened Automata', in W. Clark, J. Golinski and S. Schaffer (eds), *The Sciences in Enlightened Europe* (Chicago, IL: University of Chicago Press, 1999), pp. 126–65.

5. For the relationship between mechanical spectacles and consumer culture see especially B. Benedict, *Curiosity: A Cultural History of Early Modern Inquiry* (Chicago, IL: University of Chicago Press, 2001). The way this nexus was depicted and to a great extent resisted in eighteenth-century literature is considered in L. Brown, *Fables of Modernity: Literature and Culture in the English Eighteenth Century* (Ithaca, NY: Cornell University Press, 2001) and D. S. Lynch, *The Economy of Character: Novels, Market Culture, and the Business of Inner Meaning* (Chicago, IL: University of Chicago Press, 1998).

6. To date, Reid has played next to no part in historical discussions of Enlightenment engineering or its ideological significance. There is more than one reason for this. His reputation as a rather plodding, dowdy realist, not to mention his critique of the doctrine of ideas, has largely precluded him from literary discussions of eighteenth-century philosophy which tend to favor the sceptical and elegant empiricisms of Locke and Hume. More importantly, historians of science who have written on Reid's expertise in mathematics, chemistry and botany and its influence on his epistemology and politics have tended to interpret his ideological position as 'anti-mechanist'. See especially H. Maas, 'Where Mechanism Ends: Thomas Reid on the Moral and the Animal Oeconomy', *History of Political Economy*, 35 (2003), pp. 338–60.

7. The standard line on Reid dates back to Kant's dismissal of the common sense school in the *Prolegomena to Any Future Metaphysics*, trans. P. G. Lucas and G. Zöller (Oxford: Oxford University Press, 2004), p. 66. But see also J. Priestley, *An Examination of Dr. Reid's Inquiry into the Human Mind on the Principles of Common Sense, Dr. Beattie's Essay on the Nature and Immutability of Truth, and Dr. Oswald's Appeal to Common Sense in Behalf of Religion* (London: J. Johnson, 1774) for a full critique of Reid on materialist grounds. Reid's own notes on Priestley's attack can be found in P. Wood (ed.), *Thomas Reid on the Animate Creation: Papers Related to the Life Science* (Edinburgh: Edinburgh University Press, 1995).

8. K. Lehrer, *Thomas Reid* (London: Routledge, 1989); R. Copenhaver, 'A Realism for Reid: Mediated But Direct', *British Journal for the History of Philosophy*, 12 (2004), pp. 61–74.

9. J. Houston, 'Reading Reid', in J. Houston (ed.), *Thomas Reid: Context, Influence, and Significance* (Edinburgh: Dunedin Academic Press, 2004), pp. 1–7; p. 5.

10. T. Reid, *An Inquiry into the Human Mind, on the Principles of Common Sense* (London: A. Millar; Edinburgh: A. Kincaid & J. Bell, 1764), pp. 29–30.

11. Ibid.

12. See B. Stafford, *Artful Science: Enlightenment Education and the Eclipse of Visual Entertainment* (Cambridge, MA: MIT Press, 1994) and L. Stewart, *The Rise of Public Science: Rhetoric, Technology, and Natural Philosophy in Newtonian Britain, 1660–1750* (Cambridge: Cambridge University Press, 1992).

13. Cited in Stafford, *Artful Science*, p. 23.

14. Stafford uses Hume as an example of a Protestant iconoclast in the fight against the Catholicity of visual education (ibid., p. 123).

15. D. Hume, 'Of Essay Writing', in *Essays: Moral, Political, and Literary*, ed. E. F. Miller (Indianapolis, IN: Liberty Classics, 1985), pp. 533–7; p. 534.

16. Ibid., p. 535.

17. Reid, *Inquiry into the Human Mind*, p. 59.

18. The thermometer is a good example of a fixed point system: no change in temperature can alter the scale of temperature as such.

19. For an illuminating discussion of the relation between the vanishing point thesis and the rise of Protestantism, see B. Rotman, *Signifying Nothing: The Semiotics of Zero* (Stanford, CA: Stanford University Press, 1987), pp. 32–46.

20. *The Correspondence of Thomas Reid*, ed. P. Wood (University Park, PA: Pennsylvania State University Press, 2002), p. 42.

21. See A. Mellanby, *James Watt: Mathematical Instrument Maker to the University of Glasgow* (Glasgow: Jackson and Son, 1936).

22. The most important of these was Dubreuil's *La Perspective Practique* (Paris, 1642–9) translated into English by E. Chambers as *Practical Perspective* (c. 1730). Other examples include H. Ditton, *A Treatise of Perspective Demonstrative and Practical* (London: B. Tooke, 1712), B. Taylor, *Principles in Linear Perspective* (London: R. Knaplock, 1715), and H. Clarke, *Practical Perspective* (London: for the author, 1781).

23. Several works devoted to the art of perspective drawing and its technology had been translated into English, many stressing just how easy it was for anyone to be an artist by learning basic drawing and measuring techniques and especially by using perspective machines. See for instance, W. Halfpenny, *Perspective Made Easy, or a New Method of Practical Perspective* (London: John Oswald, 1731). Halfpenny's book contains a design for his 'New Invented Senographical Protractor' a machine which, he claims on the title page, is 'so easy, that a person, tho' an entire stranger to PERSPECTIVE, may, by Reading a few Lines, become Master of the Instrument, without the help of a Master'. Chambers's translation of Dubreuil contains several chapters on machines with titles such as 'A very curious Method of drawing all Perspectives in a manner most Natural without observing the Rules' and 'Another elegant Manner of Practicing Perspective, without understanding it' (pp. 120–1). These titles all point to a conjunction between machine drawing and the general principle of common sense.

24. *Correspondence of Thomas Reid*, p. 43.

25. Reid, *Inquiry into the Human Mind*, p. 168.

26. T. Reid, *Essays on the Intellectual Powers of Man* (London: G. G. J. and J. Robinson, 1785), p. 78.

27. Ibid., p. 95.

28. Ibid., p. 413.

29. Ibid.

30. T. Reid, *Essays on the Active Powers of Man* (London: G. G. J. and J. Robinson, 1788), p. 49.
31. The question is taken up in one of Reid's last essays, published recently as 'An Essay by Thomas Reid on the Conception of Power', *Philosophical Quarterly*, 51 (2001), pp. 1–12. See also N. Wolterstorff, 'God and Darkness in Reid', in Houston (ed.), *Thomas Reid*, pp. 77–102.
32. Reid, *Inquiry into the Human Mind*, p. 422.
33. Ibid., p. 423.
34. Ibid., p. 424.
35. Reid, *Intellectual Powers*, p. 674.
36. Ibid., p. 745.
37. The reason why the mechanic can illustrate aesthetic taste is because Reid's aesthetics is essentially utilitarian. See P. Kivy, '"Lectures on the Fine Arts": An Unpublished Manuscript of Thomas Reid's', *Journal of the History of Ideas*, 31 (1970), pp. 17–31. But D. Townsend argues that Reid's theory of taste presumes the exclusivity of these judgements: only those who are equipped to recognize the beauty that objects 'exhibit' can be counted as proper judges. See 'Thomas Reid and the Theory of Taste', *Journal of Aesthetics and Art Criticism*, 61 (2003), pp. 341–51.
38. Reid, *Intellectual Powers*, p. 674.
39. T. Reid, 'An Essay on Quantity, Occasioned by Reading a Treatise in which Simple and Compound Ratio's Are Applied to Virtue and Merit', *Philosophical Transactions*, 45 (1748), pp. 505–20; p. 508.
40. Ibid., p. 510.
41. T. Reid, *Philosophical Orations of Thomas Reid: Delivered at Graduation Ceremonies at King's College, Aberdeen in 1753, 1756, 1759, 1762*, trans. S. Darcus Sullivan, ed. D. D. Todd (Carbondale, IL: Southern Illinois University Press, 1989), p. 36.
42. Reid, *Philosophical Orations*, p. 36.
43. Reid, *Inquiry into the Human Mind*, p. 104.
44. See A. Broadie, 'George Campbell, Thomas Reid, and Universals of Language', in P. Wood (ed.), *The Scottish Enlightenment: Essays in Reinterpretation* (Rochester, NY: University of Rochester Press, 2000), pp. 351–71.
45. Reid, *Inquiry into the Human Mind*, p. 84.
46. Ibid., pp. 108–9.
47. Reid, *Intellectual Powers*, p. 459.
48. Reid, *Inquiry into the Human Mind*, p. 71.
49. Ibid., p. 72.
50. Reid, *Active Powers*, p. 463. See A. Esterhammer, *The Romantic Performative: Language and Action in British and German Romanticism* (Stanford, CA: Stanford University Press, 2000), pp. 33–41.
51. *Correspondence of Thomas Reid*, pp. 191–2.
52. Ibid., pp. 192–3.

5 Blackwell, 'Preposterous Hume'

1. G. Puttenham, *The Arte of English Poesie*, ed. G. D. Willcock and A. Walker (Cambridge: Cambridge University Press, 1936), p. 170.

2. L. Sterne, *The Life and Opinions of Tristram Shandy, Gentleman* (1759–67), ed. M. New and J. New, vols 1–3 of *The Florida Edition of the Works of Laurence Sterne* (Gainesville, FL: University Presses of Florida, 1978–84), vol. 2, p. 672.
3. Richetti, *Philosophical Writing*, p. 15.
4. Ibid., pp. 43, 184.
5. Ibid., pp. 188, 189, 191.
6. Ibid., pp. 87, 194.
7. Ibid., p. 191.
8. D. Hume, 'Of Eloquence', in *Essays: Moral, Political, and Literary*, ed. E. F. Miller, rev. edn (Indianapolis, IN: Liberty Classics, 1987), pp. 97–110; p. 104.
9. Ibid., p. 108.
10. J. Altman contends that, in *Othello*, hysteron proteron 'is not simply a verbal scheme but a way of knowing, of behaving, and of representing' ('"Preposterous Conclusions": Eros, *Enargeia*, and the Composition of *Othello*', *Representations*, 18 (1987), pp. 129–57; p. 134). In an interesting parallel to my discussion of Hume, Altman sees Shakespeare's use of the figure as a means of responding to the growing importance of probability – in particular, to the complicated relationship between two different 'arts of the probable': the philosophical discipline of dialectic, aimed at determining the truth, and the rhetorical art of persuasion (p. 151).
11. Though I focus in this essay on the *Treatise*, other of Hume's works likewise display his penchant for the figure of the preposterous. For instance, J. Christensen characterizes 'My Own Life' as a work in which 'The last is made first' and describes Hume's demand that this autobiographical sketch preface his collected works as a desire to see his work 'Prefixed by a postscript' (*Practicing Enlightenment*, p. 49).
12. S. Johnson, *A Dictionary of the English Language*, 2 vols (London: J. and P. Knapton, 1755).
13. Puttenham, *Arte of Poesie*, pp. 168, 170.
14. Ibid., p. 171.
15. A. Preminger and T. V. F. Brogan (eds), *The New Princeton Encyclopedia of Poetry and Poetics* (New York: MJF Books, 1993), p. 545.
16. Ibid., p. 547.
17. N. Bailey, *An Universal Etymological English Dictionary*, 3rd edn (London: J. Darby. A. Bettesworth, F. Fayram, J. Pemberton, J. Hooke et al., 1726).
18. See, for instance, M. Bal, *Narratology: Introduction to the Theory of Narrative*, 2nd edn (Toronto, ON: University of Toronto Press, 1997), p. 83 ff.
19. K. K. Ruthven, 'Preposterous Chatterton', *ELH*, 71:2 (2004), pp. 345–75; p. 345.
20. Altman, '"Preposterous Conclusions"', p. 133.
21. Hume, *Treatise of Human Nature* (1978 edn), pp. 118–19. M. Bal suggests that 'deviations in sequential ordering' 'forc[e] the reader to read more intensively' (*Narratology*, p. 82).
22. *Dionysius Longinus on the Sublime*, trans. W. Smith (London: W. Innys and R. Manby, 1739), pp. 57, 59–60.
23. I have in mind N. K. Hayles's definition of materiality as something that 'emerges from interactions between physical properties and a work's artistic strategies ... materiality depends on how the work mobilizes its resources as a physical artifact as well as on the user's interactions with the work and the interpretive strategies she develops' (*Writing Machines* (Cambridge, MA: MIT Press, 2002), p. 33). Also see her 'Translating Media: Why We Should Rethink Textuality', *Yale Journal of Criticism*, 16:2 (2003), pp. 263–90:

'the text creates possibilities to create or pursue meaning by mobilizing certain aspects of its physicality' (p. 276).

24. R. Hurd, 'Post-script' to *Moral and Political Dialogues* (London, 1761), quoted in E. C. Mossner, *The Life of David Hume*, 2nd edn (Oxford: Clarendon Press, 1980), p. 302.

25. N. K. Smith, *The Philosophy of David Hume: A Critical Study of its Origins and Central Doctrines* (London: Macmillan, 1941), p. 12. For the external evidence in support of Smith's contention, see p. 14 ff.

26. Ibid., p. vi. J. Sitter raises similar questions about the *Treatise*'s order of composition (*Literary Loneliness in Mid-Eighteenth-Century England* (Ithaca, NY: Cornell University Press, 1982), p. 33).

27. Hume, *Treatise of Human Nature* (1978 edn), pp. 74–6.

28. G. Deleuze, *Empiricism and Subjectivity: An Essay on Hume's Theory of Human Nature*, trans. C. V. Boundas (New York: Columbia University Press, 1991), p. 21. Deleuze continues, 'one must be a moralist, sociologist, or historian *before* being a psychologist, *in order to* be a psychologist' (p. 22).

29. Hume, *Treatise of Human Nature* (1978 edn), p. 633.

30. Ibid., p. 665.

31. I am indebted to Tina Lupton for this suggestion.

32. Hayles, *Writing Machines*, p. 25.

33. J. Bolter, *Writing Space: The Computer, Hypertext, and the History of Writing* (Hillsdale, NJ: Lawrence Erlbaum Associates, 1991), pp. 22–3, 112–13.

34. Ibid., p. 115.

35. Hume, *Treatise of Human Nature* (1978 edn), p. 5.

36. Ibid., p. 8.

37. Ibid., p. 8.

38. Ibid., pp. 9, 10.

39. Ibid., p. 9.

40. Altman, '"Preposterous Conclusions"', p. 133.

41. Hume, *Treatise of Human Nature* (1978 edn), pp. 74–5.

42. Ibid., pp. 77–8. Richetti rightly notes that 'Hume seems to control such ironic reversals' and that his rhetoric quite deliberately 'balances instability against the formulas and patterns of recurrence and inevitability' (*Philosophical Writing*, pp. 43, 206–7).

43. Hume, *Treatise of Human Nature* (1978 edn), p. 273.

44. Ibid., p. 87.

45. *Dionysius Longinus on the Sublime*, p. 56.

46. Hume, *Treatise of Human Nature* (1978 edn), p. 88.

47. Ibid., pp. 165, 167.

48. Ibid., p. 169.

49. 'In logic', K. K. Ruthven notes, '*hysteron proteron* names a type of fallacy in which the conclusion is said to antecede the premises because one of them already assumes the proof for it' ('Preposterous Chatterton', p. 346).

50. Rick Bogel first drew my attention to the curious syntax of this sentence.

51. Recall Horkheimer and Adorno on Odysseus as harbinger of the Enlightenment: 'Odysseus loses himself in order to find himself' (*The Dialectic of Enlightenment*, trans. J. Cumming (New York: Continuum, 1972), p. 48).

52. Hume, *Treatise of Human Nature* (1978 edn), p. 97, n. 1.

53. Ibid., p. 110.

54. Ibid., p. 77.

55. Thus causation is logically precedent but temporally subsequent to inference. Inference proceeds 1 > 2; causality proceeds 1 > 3 > 2, where 3 is the relation that we call causation.
56. Hume, *Treatise of Human Nature* (1978 edn), p. 156.
57. W. Wordsworth, *The Prelude 1799, 1805, 1850*, ed. J. Wordsworth, M. H. Abrams and S. Gill (New York: Norton, 1979), p. 217 (1850 version).
58. See J. F. Lyotard, 'The Sublime and the Avant-Garde', in *The Lyotard Reader*, ed. A. Benjamin (New York: Blackwell, 1989), p. 197, on the sublime 'now' or 'happening' or 'occurrence' as 'what consciousness forgets in order to formulate itself'.
59. N. Capaldi sees the same structure of retrospection at work in Hume's treatment of the self: 'we do have an idea of self, a complex idea, but the complex idea of the self is apprehended only in retrospect' ('The Dogmatic Slumber of Hume Scholarship', *Hume Studies*, 18:2 (1992), pp. 117–35; p. 127).
60. Hume, *Treatise of Human Nature* (1978 edn), p. 250.
61. Ibid., pp. 634, 252.
62. Ibid., p. 635.
63. Ibid., p. 636.
64. Ibid., p. 150.
65. Ibid., p. 632.
66. Ibid., p. 633.
67. As N. Brett puts it, 'the causal account of the mind runs afoul of the mental account of causality' ('Hume's Causal Account of the Self', *Man and Nature*, 9 (1990), pp. 23–32; p. 30).
68. Richetti, *Philosophical Writing*, pp. 200, 217.
69. A. C. Baier, *A Progress of Sentiments: Reflections on Hume's Treatise* (Cambridge, MA: Harvard University Press, 1991), p. 1. Her insights are central to my own thinking about the relations between the *Treatise*'s three books.
70. Ibid., pp. 27, 21. Also see Richetti, *Philosophical Writing*, p. 40.
71. Hume, *Treatise on Human Nature* (1978 edn), pp. 218, 269.
72. Ibid., pp. 270, 271.
73. Baier, *Progress of Sentiments*, p. 1; Richetti, *Philosophical Writing*, p. 229. Richetti earlier observes that most modern commentators 'are too concerned with narrowly defined problems to worry about the larger, cumulative effects of Hume's writing' (p. 187). Other works that read Book I as in dynamic relation with the rest of the *Treatise* include Capaldi's 'Dogmatic Slumber' and *David Hume* (Boston, MA: Twayne, 1975), and F. Wilson, 'Substance and Self in Locke and Hume', *Individuation and Identity in Early Modern Philosophy: Descartes to Kant*, ed. K. F. Barber and J. J. E. Gracia (Albany, NY: State University of New York Press, 1994), pp. 355–99.
74. Wilson, 'Substance and Self', p. 189. Wilson also writes, 'Concerning character, Hume holds, quite correctly, that our psychological dispositions, our human sentiments and passions, are dependent upon social and economic conditions, and that changes in those conditions bring about psychological transformations' (p. 190).
75. Hume, *Treatise on Human Nature* (1978 edn), p. 277. As Capaldi writes, 'the self in a public and social world is already presupposed in Hume's analysis' (*David Hume*, p. 138).
76. Hume, *Treatise on Human Nature* (1978 edn), p. 287.
77. Ibid., p. 278.
78. Ibid.

79. Ibid., p. 190.
80. Ibid., p. 191.
81. Among the finest and most detailed accounts of the complex relation between personal identity and property in the *Treatise* comes in A. Baier's 'Hume on Heaps and Bundles', *American Philosophical Quarterly*, 16:4 (1979), pp. 285–95.
82. Hume, *Treatise on Human Nature* (1978 edn), p. 288.
83. Ibid., pp. 659–60.
84. Ibid., p. 298.
85. N. K. Hayles, 'The Complexities of Seriation', *PMLA*, 117:1 (2002), pp. 117–21; pp. 117–18. Also see Hayles, 'Traumas of Code', *Critical Inquiry*, 33:1 (2006), pp. 136–57; p. 139. Hayles has in mind A. Clark's *Natural-Born Cyborgs: Minds, Technologies, and the Future of Human Intelligence* (Oxford: Oxford University Press, 2003).

    Though Hayles's work has helped me see Hume's *Treatise* with fresh eyes, it strikes me that Hume – and perhaps the eighteenth century more broadly – is a notable blind spot in her scholarship. The period serves her as the too-convenient origin ('at least since the eighteenth century') of the benighted notion that 'the literary work must be an expression of an immaterial essence' ('Translating Media', p. 280), and Hume is curiously absent in her important discussion of the 'striking originality of [Humberto] Maturana's epistemology', particularly his 'denial of causality' ('Making the Cut: The Interplay of Narrative and System, or What Systems Theory Can't See', *Cultural Critique*, 30 (1995), pp. 71–100; pp. 75–6).
86. Hume, *Treatise on Human Nature* (1978 edn), p. 303.
87. See Baier, *Progress of Sentiments*, pp. 142–3.
88. J. Locke, *Two Treatises of Government*, rev. edn (New York: Mentor, 1965), pp. 328–9. On the passage from Longinus, see N. Hertz, 'A Reading of Longinus', in *The End of the Line: Essays on Psychoanalysis and the Sublime* (New York: Columbia University Press, 1985), pp. 1–20.
89. Hume, *Treatise on Human Nature* (1978 edn), p. 309.
90. Ibid., p. 314.
91. Ibid., p. 315.
92. Ibid., p. 455.
93. Ibid., pp. 457, 103.
94. Ibid., pp. 457, 469.
95. Ibid., p. 533.
96. Ibid., p. 484.
97. Richetti, *Philosophical Writing*, pp. 228, 229.
98. Hume, *Treatise on Human Nature* (1978 edn), p. 491.
99. Ibid., p. 489.
100. Ibid., p. 488.
101. Ibid., p. 503.
102. Ibid., p. 492.
103. Ibid., p. 514.

6 Budd, 'Aesthetic Sensibility'

1. The first reader was Dorothy Bradshaigh, the second John Channing. See *Correspondence of Samuel Richardson*, ed. L. Barbauld, 6 vols (London: R. Phillips, 1804), vol. 2, p. 334; T. C. D. Eaves and B. T. Kimpel, *Samuel Richardson: A Biography* (Oxford: Oxford

University Press, 1971), p. 219. The current study examines moral and literary problems related to those I address in 'Why Clarissa Must Die: Richardson's Tragedy and Editorial Heroism' *Eighteenth Century Life*, 31 (August 2007), pp. 1–28.

2. D. Hume, *A Treatise of Human Nature*, ed. D. F. Norton and R. Norton (Oxford: Oxford University Press, 2000), p. 175.

3. "'Tis difficult for us to withhold our assent from what is painted out to us in all the colours of eloquence; and the vivacity produc'd by the fancy is in many cases greater than that which arises from custom and experience. We are hurry'd away by the lively imagination of our author or companion' (ibid., p. 84).

4. Ibid., p. 206.

5. See J. Mullan, 'The Language of Sentiment: Hume, Smith, and Henry Mackenzie', in A. Hook (ed.), *The History of Scottish Literature: Volume 2* (Aberdeen: Aberdeen University Press, 1987), pp. 273–89.

6. C. Gallagher, *Nobody's Story: The Vanishing Acts of Women Writers in the Marketplace 1670–1820* (Oxford: Clarendon Press, 1994), pp. 171–2.

7. Ibid., p. 142; P. Goring, *The Rhetoric of Sensibility in Eighteenth-Century Culture* (Cambridge: Cambridge University Press, 2004), p. 142. See also Markley, 'Sentimentality as Performance', pp. 210–30.

8. J. Richetti, The *English Novel in History: 1700–1780* (London: Routledge, 1999), p. 244. See also C. Sussman, *Consuming Anxieties: Consumer Boycott, Gender, and British Slavery, 1713–1833* (Stanford, CA: Stanford University Press, 2001); T. Keymer, 'Sentimental Fiction: Ethics, Social Critique, and Philanthropy', in J. Richetti (ed.), *The Cambridge History of English Literature, 1660–1780* (Cambridge: Cambridge University Press, 2005), pp. 572–601.

9. Major studies that exclude Hume's pre-1757 remarks on aesthetics include: D. Marshall, *The Frame of Art: Fictions of Aesthetic Experience* (Baltimore, MD: Johns Hopkins University Press, 2005); D. Townsend, *Hume's Aesthetic Theory* (New York: Routledge, 2001); P. Jones 'Hume's Aesthetic Theory', in D. F. Norton (ed.), *The Cambridge Companion to Hume* (Cambridge: Cambridge University Press, 1993), pp. 255–80; E. Mossner, 'Hume's "Of Criticism"', in H. Anderson and J. Shea (eds), *Studies in Criticism and Aesthetics 1660–1800* (Minneapolis, MN: University of Minnesota Press, 1967), pp. 232–48.

10. See M. Mothersill, 'Hume and the Paradox of Taste', in G. Dickie et al. (eds), *Aesthetics: A Critical Anthology* (New York: St Martin's Press, 1989), pp. 269–70. Original emphasis.

11. On Hume's efforts to shape his writings to suit popular tastes during the 1740s, see Christensen, *Practicing Enlightenment*; M. A. Box, *Hume's Suasive Art* (Princeton, NJ: Princeton University Press, 1990).

12. See P. Jones, *Hume's Sentiments: Their Ciceronian and French Context* (Edinburgh: Edinburgh University Press, 1982), p. 106.

13. For a strictly social interpretation of Hume's view that 'there is something weak and imperfect amidst all that seeming vehemence of thought and sentiment, which attends the fictions of poetry', see M. A. Stewart, 'Two Species of Philosophy: The Historical Significance of the First *Enquiry*', in P. Mullican (ed.), *Reading Hume on Human Understanding* (Oxford: Oxford University Press, 2002), p. 76; D. Livingston, *Philosophical Melancholy and Delusion: Hume's Pathology of Philosophy* (Chicago, IL: University of Chicago Press, 1998), p. 153.

14. Hume, *Treatise of Human Nature* (2000 edn), p. 4. See also R. Brandt, 'The Beginnings of Hume's Philosophy', in G. P. Morice (ed.), *David Hume: Bicentenary Papers* (Edin-

burgh: Edinburgh University Press, 1977), pp. 117–27; p. 119; D. Hume, *The Letters of David Hume*, ed. J. Y. T. Grieg, 2 vols (Oxford: Clarendon Press, 1932), vol. 1, pp. 12–18.

15. Hume, *Treatise of Human Nature* (2000 edn), p. 68.

16. See S. Johnson, *A Dictionary of the English Language*, 2 vols (London: W. Strahan et al., 1778), vol. 1, p. 454; J. Barnouw, 'Aesthetics', in J. Black and R. Porter (eds), *Dictionary of Eighteenth-Century History* (London: Penguin, 1996), p. 10.

17. See *A Treatise of Human Nature ... with an Appendix wherein Some Passages of the Foregoing Volumes Are Illustrated and Explain'd* (London: T. Longman, 1740). Unusually, the typeface used for 'APPENDIX' is the same size as that used for 'TREATISE', suggesting that the book was marketed on the basis of both features.

18. Norman Kemp Smith has argued persuasively that Hume drafted the first book last, and in keeping with that view, I suggest that Hume designed the insertions to the first book to clarify certain arguments in all three books. See Smith, *Philosophy of David Hume*, p. 173.

19. *Letters of David Hume*, vol. 1, p. 38.

20. See *A Treatise of Human Nature. A New Edition*, 2 vols (London: Thomas and Joseph Allman, 1817), *A Treatise of Human Nature*, ed. T. H. Green and T. H. Grose (London: Longmans, 1874) and *A Treatise of Human Nature*, ed. T. H. Green and T. H. Grose, 2nd edn (London: Longmans, 1886).

21. See *A Treatise of Human Nature*, ed. L. A. Selby-Bigge (Oxford: Clarendon Press, 1888), pp. 623–39. The title-page appearing in editions printed between 1888 and 1978 indicates that the text is 'reprinted from the original edition'; the Preface to Peter Nidditch's second edition, published in 1978 and still in print, iterates that this edition 'reproduces the original'.

22. Selby-Bigge's editions of Hume have been adopted as standard texts in D. F. Norton's *The Cambridge Companion to Hume* (Cambridge: Cambridge University Press, 1993) and in the seven–volume edition, S. Tweyman (ed.), *David Hume: Critical Assessments* (London: Routledge, 1995).

23. See R. W. Connon, Letter, in *Times Literary Supplement* (4 April 1975), p. 376; his 'Some MS Corrections by Hume in the Third Volume of his *Treatise of Human Nature*', *Long Room*, 11 (1975), pp. 14–22; and 'The Textual and Philosophical Significance of Hume's MS Alterations to *Treatise* III', in G. P. Morice (ed.), *David Hume: Bicentenary Papers* (Edinburgh: Edinburgh University Press, 1977), pp. 186–204. See also W. Nethery, 'Hume's Manuscript Corrections in a Copy of *A Treatise of Human Nature*', *Proceedings of the Bibliographical Society of America*, 57 (1963), pp. 446–7. The first speculation on Hume's full intentions was made in E. Mossner, 'A MS. Fragment of Hume's *Treatise*, 1740', *Notes and Queries*, 194 (1949), pp. 520–2.

24. For an exception, where the insertions receive useful attention, see B. Kerby, 'Hume, Sympathy, and the Theatre', *Hume Studies*, 29 (November 2003), pp. 305–25.

25. See E. Mossner, 'Hume's "Of Criticism"', p. 248.

26. See P. Kivy, *The Seventh Sense: Francis Hutcheson and Eighteenth-Century British Aesthetics* (New York: Burt Franklin, 1976), p. 198.

27. For the history of the excisions, see T. L. Beauchamp's textual notes to his critical edition of the *Enquiry Concerning Human Understanding* (Oxford: Oxford University Press, 2000), p. 237. Nidditch had planned his own edition of a 'critically established text', but died before it was published; Beauchamp cites Nidditch's notes in his edition (p. 265).

28. See T. E. Jessop, *Bibliography of David Hume and of Scottish Philosophy* (London: A. Brown & Sons, 1938), p. 7. Hume's extensive changes were noted by Green and Grose in their edition: see *David Hume: The Philosophical Works*, vol. 4, pp. 17–19.

29. Hume, *Treatise of Human Nature* (2000 edn), p. 68.

30. Ibid., p. 82.

31. Ibid., p. 67.

32. Ibid., p. 72.

33. Ibid., p. 73.

34. Sitter, *Literary Loneliness*, pp. 25, 30.

35. Ibid., p. 26; and Hume, *Treatise of Human Nature* (2000 edn), p. 172.

36. Hume, *Treatise of Human Nature* (2000 edn), p. 85.

37. *Selected Correspondence of Samuel Richardson*, ed. J. Carroll (Oxford: Oxford University Press, 1964), p. 85.

38. Hume, *Treatise of Human Nature* (2000 edn), p. 84.

39. Hume, Appendix in ibid., p. 398.

40. Hume, Abstract in ibid., p. 412.

41. Ibid., p. 85.

42. Ibid., p. 85.

43. See Sitter, *Literary Loneliness*, p. 26.

44. Hume, *Treatise of Human Nature* (2000 edn), p. 188.

45. Ibid., p. 85.

46. Ibid., p. 85.

47. Ibid., p. 85.

48. Ibid., p. 68.

49. Quoting J. P. Hunter, *Before Novels: The Cultural Contexts of Eighteenth-Century Fiction* (New York: Norton, 1990), p. 231. Samuel Johnson warned that 'If the power of example is so great as to take possession of the memory by a kind of violence, and produce effects almost without the intervention of the will, care ought to be taken that, when the choice is unrestrained, the best examples only should be exhibited; and that which is likely to operate so strongly should not be mischievous or uncertain in its effects'. See S. Johnson, *Rambler*, 4 (31 March 1750), in W. J. Bate (ed.), *Essays from the Rambler, Adventurer, and Idler* (New Haven, CT: Yale University Press, 1968), p. 12. See also I. Watt, *The Rise of the Novel* (Berkeley, CA: University of California Press, 1957), pp. 154–64; M. McKeon, *The Origins of the English Novel* (Baltimore, MD: Johns Hopkins University Press, 1987), pp. 265–271.

50. Hume, *Treatise of Human Nature* (2000 edn), p. 84.

51. Ibid.

52. Ibid.

53. Ibid., p. 85.

54. Ibid., p. 79.

55. Ibid., p. 206.

56. Ibid., p. 368.

57. Ibid., p. 368.

58. Ibid., p. 207.

59. Ibid.

60. Ibid.

61. Ibid., p. 220.

62. Ibid., p. 229.

63. Ibid., p. 75.
64. Ibid., p. 166.
65. Ibid., p. 50.
66. Ibid., pp. 85, 188.
67. Ibid., p. 394.
68. Ibid., p. 244.
69. P. Mercer, *Sympathy and Ethics: A Study of the Relationship between Sympathy and Morality with Special Reference to Hume's Treatise* (Oxford: Clarendon Press, 1972), p. 437. Gallagher ventures that 'according to Hume, human beings are generally vulnerable to this form of emotional contagion', that is, sympathetic infection through reading: see Gallagher, *Nobody's Story*, p. 169. In his essay 'Of National Characters' (1748), Hume describes 'the disposition, which gives us this propensity, [to] enter deeply into each other's sentiments ... and causes like passions and inclinations to run, as it were, by contagion', but Hume is referring to sympathy as a consequence of living in close physical contact (*Essays* (1985 edn), p. 202). Hume does not mention reading or writing in that essay.
70. Hume, Abstract, in *Treatise of Human Nature* (2000 edn), p. 417.
71. Ibid., p. 416.
72. Hume, *Treatise of Human Nature* (2000 edn), p. 85.
73. Ibid., p. 11.
74. Early in the *Treatise*, Hume made it clear that the imagination's function is to sort and merge past impressions, and then represent them, less forcefully, as ideas: 'all simple ideas may be separated by the imagination, and may be united again in what form it pleases' (ibid., p. 12). It can be considered creative only under the effect of custom: 'the imagination, when set into any train of thinking, is apt to continue, even when its object fails it, and like a galley put in motion by the oars, carries on its course without any new impulse' (ibid., p. 132).
75. Ibid., p. 206.
76. A. Pinch, *Strange Fits of Passion: Epistemologies of Emotion, Hume to Austen* (Stanford, CA: Stanford University Press, 1996), p. 24.
77. Hume, *Treatise of Human Nature* (2000 edn), pp. 234, 236.
78. Ibid., pp. 273–4.
79. Ibid., pp. 208, 210.
80. J. Warton, 'Introduction', in *Odes on Various Subjects* (London: J. Dodsley, 1746).
81. R. Wendorf, *William Collins and Eighteenth-Century Poetry* (Minneapolis, MN: University of Minnesota Press, 1981), pp. 28–9. See J. Warton, *An Essay on the Genius and Writings of Pope*, 2 vols (London: J. Dodsley, 1782), vol. 2, p. 165.
82. See S. Richardson, *Pamela, or Virtue Rewarded* (London: C. Rivington, 1740), pp. 3–4. The second instalment of the *Treatise* was published on 30 October 1740; Richardson's novel appeared on 6 November 1740. See W. B. Todd, 'David Hume: A Preliminary Bibliography', in W. B. Todd (ed.), *Hume and the Enlightenment* (Edinburgh: Edinburgh University Press, 1974), pp. 189–205; p. 191; Eaves and Kimpel, *Samuel Richardson*, p. 91.
83. Hume, *Treatise of Human Nature* (2000 edn), p. 175.
84. See [Anon.], *Review of* A Treatise of Human Nature, by D. Hume, *The History of the Works of the Learned*, 2 (December 1739), p. 402.
85. Hume, *Treatise of Human Nature* (2000 edn), p. 175.
86. While preparing the third edition of *Essays Moral and Political* (1748), Hume described this didactic process: 'I threw out some, that seem'd frivolous and finical, [and] was resolv'd to supply their Place by others, that shou'd be more instructive' (*Letters of David*

Hume, vol. 1, p. 112). On Hume's revisions to his *Essays* through the 1740s, see N. K. Smith, 'Hume's Rejected *Essays*', *Forum for Modern Language Studies*, 8 (1972), pp. 354–71. A useful table of the variable contents of the numerous editions can be found in T. Daigaku, *David Hume and the [sic] Eighteenth Century British Thought* (Tokyo: Chuo University, n.d.), pp. xvi–xvii.

87. Hume, *Treatise of Human Nature* (2000 edn), p. 5.
88. Ibid., p. 6.
89. Ibid., p. 7.
90. Ibid., pp. 206, 220, 229.
91. Ibid., p. 7.
92. D. Hume, *An Enquiry Concerning Human Understanding*, 'posthumous edition' (London: T. Cadell, 1777), p. 19.
93. Ibid., p. 19.
94. Ibid., pp. 20–1.
95. I wish to thank John Baird, Alex Dick, Noelle Gallagher, Colin Heydt, Christina Lupton and David Raynor for their helpful comments on earlier versions of this chapter.

7 Dadlez, 'David Hume and Jane Austen on Pride'

1. P. Knox-Shaw, *Jane Austen and the Enlightenment* (Cambridge: Cambridge University Press, 2004), p. 9.
2. Ibid., p. 21.
3. D. Hume, 'Of the Standard of Taste' in *Essays: Moral, Political, and Literary* (1987 edn), pp. 226–49; pp. 246–7.
4. See my work on this for a less abbreviated account: 'Spectacularly Bad: Hume and Aristotle on Tragic Spectacle', *Journal of Aesthetics and Art Criticism*, 63:4 (2005), pp. 351–8; 'Knowing Better: The Epistemic Underpinnings of Moral Criticism of Fiction', *Southwest Philosophy Review*, 21:1 (2005), pp. 35–44.
5. J. Austen, *Northanger Abbey*, in *The Novels of Jane Austen*, ed. R. W. Chapman, 3rd edn, 5 vols (Oxford: Oxford University Press, 1988), vol. 5, p. 38.
6. See S. Blackburn, 'Thought Experiment' in *The Oxford Dictionary of Philosophy* (Oxford: Oxford University Press, 1994), p. 377; R. A. Sorensen, *Thought Experiments* (New York: Oxford University Press, 1992), p. 289.
7. D. Hume, *A Treatise of Human Nature*, ed. L. A. Selby-Bigge (Oxford: Clarendon Press, 1964), p. 390.
8. Ibid., pp. 310–11.
9. Ibid., p. 332.
10. Ibid., p. 285.
11. Ibid., p. 289.
12. Ibid., p. 338.
13. J. Austen, *Mansfield Park*, in *Novels of Jane Austen*, vol. 3, p. 39.
14. Ibid., p. 42.
15. J. Austen, *Emma*, in *Novels of Jane Austen*, vol. 4, p. 17.
16. Hume, *Treatise of Human Nature* (1964 edn), pp. 278–9.
17. D. Hume, 'Idea of a Perfect Commonwealth' in *Essays: Moral, Political, and Literary* (1987 edn), pp. 512–29; p. 525.
18. D. Hume, 'Of the Dignity or Meanness of Human Nature' in *Essays: Moral, Political, and Literary* (1987 edn), pp. 80–6; p. 86.

19. Hume, *Treatise of Human Nature* (1964 edn), p. 597.
20. Ibid., p. 598.
21. Ibid., p. 599.
22. J. Austen, *Sense and Sensibility*, in *Novels of Jane Austen*, vol. 1, p. 189.
23. Austen, *Mansfield Park*, in *Novels of Jane Austen*, vol. 3, p. 201.
24. Ibid., p. 202.
25. J. Austen, *Persuasion*, in *Novels of Jane Austen*, vol. 5, p. 242.
26. Ibid.
27. Ibid., p. 247.
28. Hume, *Treatise of Human Nature* (1964 edn), p. 599.
29. Ibid.
30. J. Austen, *Pride and Prejudice*, in *Novels of Jane Austen*, vol. 2, p. 376.
31. Austen, *Persuasion*, in *Novels of Jane Austen*, vol. 5, p. 62.
32. Austen, *Emma*, in *Novels of Jane Austen*, vol. 4, p. 198.
33. Ibid., p. 285.
34. Ibid., p. 270.
35. Austen, *Persuasion*, in *Novels of Jane Austen*, vol. 5, p. 148.
36. Ibid., p. 151.
37. Austen, *Pride and Prejudice*, in *Novels of Jane Austen*, vol. 2, p. 97.
38. D. Hume, 'Of the Parties of Great Britain' in *Essays: Moral, Political, and Literary* (1987 edn), pp. 64–72; p. 66.
39. Austen, *Pride and Prejudice*, in *Novels of Jane Austen*, vol. 2, p. 173.
40. Hume, *Treatise of Human Nature* (1964 edn), pp. 389–90.
41. Ibid., p. 390.
42. Austen, *Persuasion*, in *Novels of Jane Austen*, vol. 5, p. 227.
43. Austen, *Sense and Sensibility*, in *Novels of Jane Austen*, vol. 1, p. 14.
44. Austen, *Emma*, in *Novels of Jane Austen*, vol. 4, p. 375.
45. Ibid., p. 376.
46. Hume, *Treatise of Human Nature* (1964 edn), p. 320.
47. Ibid., p. 596.
48. Austen, *Pride and Prejudice*, in *Novels of Jane Austen*, vol. 2, p. 10.
49. Ibid., p. 208.
50. Austen, *Emma*, in *Novels of Jane Austen*, vol. 4, p. 310.
51. Ibid., p. 422.
52. Austen, *Northanger Abbey*, in *Novels of Jane Austen*, vol. 5, p. 226.
53. Austen, *Sense and Sensibility*, in *Novels of Jane Austen*, vol. 1, p. 236.
54. Austen, *Emma*, in *Novels of Jane Austen*, vol. 4, pp. 412–13.
55. Hume, *Treatise of Human Nature* (1964 edn), p. 306.
56. Ibid., p. 311.
57. Ibid., p. 307.
58. Austen, *Persuasion*, in *Novels of Jane Austen*, vol. 5, pp. 157–8.
59. Austen, *Northanger Abbey*, in *Novels of Jane Austen*, vol. 5, pp. 244–5.
60. Hume, *Treatise of Human Nature* (1964 edn), p. 246.
61. Ibid., p. 323.
62. Austen, *Persuasion*, in *Novels of Jane Austen*, vol. 5, pp. 9–10.
63. Hume, *Treatise of Human Nature* (1964 edn), pp. 310–11.
64. Austen, *Persuasion*, in *Novels of Jane Austen*, vol. 5, p. 137.
65. Hume, *Treatise of Human Nature* (1964 edn), p. 587.

66. Austen, *Pride and Prejudice*, in *Novels of Jane Austen*, vol. 2, pp. 48–9.
67. Hume, *Treatise of Human Nature* (1964 edn), p. 277.

8 Richetti, 'Hume, Religion, Literary Form'

1. J. C. A. Gaskin, Introduction, in D. Hume, *Principal Writings on Religion, including Dialogues Concerning Natural Religion and The Natural History of Religion*, ed. J. C. A. Gaskin (Oxford: Oxford University Press, 1993), p. xviii. All further references to both of these works are to this edition.
2. Ibid., p. xviii.
3. Gaskin notes that in one of his last letters, 8 June 1776, Hume wrote that some of his friends who had read it told him that 'it is the best thing I ever wrote' (ibid., p. xviii).
4. 15 August 1776, in *Correspondence of Adam Smith*, ed. E. C. Mossner and I. Simpson Ross, in *Works and Correspondence of Adam Smith*, vol. 6, p. 143.
5. The letter is reprinted in Hume, *Principal Writings on Religion*, p. 25.
6. Ibid.
7. Ibid.
8. N. K. Smith, Introduction, in D. Hume, *Dialogues Concerning Natural Religion*, ed. N. K. Smith (Indianapolis, IN, and New York: Bobbs-Merrill, 1947), pp. 61–2, 64–5.
9. M. A. Box in *The Suasive Art of David Hume* puts this well when he notes that in 'arguing for the tenets of his system, Hume was acting as a philosopher; in urging empiricism as an intellectual programme he was acting as a rhetor' (p. 57). Various philosophers and philosophical commentators since Hume's day have deplored this feature of his writing, seeing it as a weakness in his thought. For a discussion of this issue, see my *Philosophical Writing: Locke, Berkeley, Hume*, pp. 187–9.
10. Hume, *Principal Writings on Religion*, pp. 25–6.
11. See W. B. Carnochan, 'The Comic Plot of Hume's "Dialogues"', *Modern Philology*, 85 (May 1988), pp. 514–22; p. 515.
12. M. B. Prince, 'Hume and the End of Religious Dialogue', *Eighteenth-Century Studies*, 25 (Spring 1992), pp. 283–308; pp. 283, 285. See also Prince's *Philosophical Dialogue in the British Enlightenment* which includes a revised version of this essay.
13. Prince, *Philosophical Dialogue in the British Enlightenment*, p. 304.
14. The two most important predecessors for Carnochan are D. Simpson, 'Hume's Intimate Voices and the Method of Dialogue', *Texas Studies in Literature and Language*, 21 (1979), pp. 68–92, and G. Shapiro, 'The Man of Letters and the Author of Nature: Hume on Philosophical Discourse', *Eighteenth Century: Theory and Interpretation*, 26 (1985), pp. 115–37.
15. Hume, *Principal Writings on Religion*, p. 29.
16. Ibid.
17. Ibid.
18. Ibid.
19. Ibid., p. 30.
20. Ibid., p. 30.
21. Ibid., p. 30.
22. Ibid., p. 30.
23. Ibid., p. 71.
24. Ibid., p. 91.
25. Ibid., p. 121.
26. Ibid., p. 32.

27. Ibid.
28. Ibid., p. 33.
29. Ibid., p. 34.
30. Carnochan, 'Comic Plot of Hume's "Dialogues"', p. 516.
31. Hume, *Principal Writings on Religion*, p. 34.
32. For one example, from Hume, *An Enquiry Concerning Human Understanding*, ed. Beauchamp:

> The sceptical objections to moral evidence, or to the reasonings concerning matter of fact, are either popular or philosophical. The popular objections are derived from the natural weakness of human understanding; the contradictory opinions, which have been entertained in different ages and nations; the variations of our judgement in sickness and health, youth and old age, prosperity and adversity; the perpetual contradiction of each particular man's opinions and sentiments; with many other topics of that kind. It is needless to insist farther on this head. These objections are but weak. For as, in common life, we reason every moment concerning fact and existence, and cannot possibly subsist, without continually employing this species of argument, any popular objections, derived from thence, must be insufficient to destroy that evidence. The great subverter of Pyrrhonism or the excessive principles of scepticism is action, and employment, and the occupations of common life. These principles may flourish and triumph in the schools; where it is, indeed, difficult, if not impossible, to refute them. But as soon as they leave the shade, and by the presence of the real objects, which actuate our passions and sentiments, are put in opposition to the more powerful principles of our nature, they vanish like smoke, and leave the most determined sceptic in the same condition as other mortals (p. 118).

33. Hume, *Principal Writings on Religion*, p. 35.
34. Ibid., p. 36.
35. Ibid., p. 37.
36. Ibid., p. 38.
37. Ibid., p. 39.
38. Ibid., p. 43.
39. Ibid., p. 42.
40. Ibid., p. 47.
41. Ibid., p. 52.
42. Ibid., p. 44.
43. Ibid., p. 33.
44. Ibid., p. 35.
45. Ibid., p. 55.
46. Ibid.
47. Ibid., p. 52.
48. Ibid.
49. Ibid., p. 53.
50. Ibid., pp. 64, 65.
51. Ibid., p. 58.
52. Ibid.
53. Ibid.
54. Ibid.
55. Ibid., p. 59.
56. Ibid.

57. Ibid.
58. Ibid., pp. 70–1.
59. Ibid., p. 84.
60. Smith, 'Introduction', in Hume, *Dialogues Concerning Natural Religion*, pp. 64–5.
61. Hume, *Principal Writings on Religion*, 90.
62. Ibid., p. 91.
63. Ibid., p. 207n. See *An Enquiry Concerning Human Understanding*:
    Whatever is may not be. No negation of a fact can involve a contradiction. The non-existence of any being, without exception, is as clear and distinct an idea as its existence. The proposition, which affirms it not to be, however false, is no less conceivable and intelligible, than that which affirms it to be (p. 122)
64. Hume, *Principal Writings on Religion*, p. 92.
65. Ibid., p. 93.
66. Ibid., pp. 93–4.
67. Ibid., p. 95.
68. Ibid.
69. Ibid.
70. Ibid., p. 96.
71. Ibid., p. 97.
72. Ibid., p. 98.
73. Ibid., p. 99.
74. Ibid., p. 100.
75. Ibid.
76. Ibid., p. 101.
77. Ibid.
78. Ibid., pp. 103, 102.
79. Ibid., p. 103.
80. Ibid., p. 104.
81. Ibid., p. 116.
82. Ibid., p. 105.
83. Ibid.
84. Ibid.
85. Ibid.
86. Ibid.
87. Ibid., p. 106.
88. Ibid.
89. Ibid., p. 107.
90. Ibid.
91. Ibid.
92. Ibid., pp. 107, 108.
93. Ibid., p. 108.
94. Ibid., pp. 108–9.
95. Ibid., pp. 109, 110.
96. Ibid., pp. 111, 112.
97. Ibid., p. 112.
98. Ibid.
99. Ibid., p. 95.

100. Alone among commentators on the *Dialogues*, Carnochan has noted the rhetorical power and importance of Philo's speech: 'Philo's oration has a dramatic and rhetorical strength rivaled only, perhaps in its time by Samuel Johnson's savage handling of Soame Jenyns. What has been lost in most accounts of the *Dialogues* is this rhetorical power' ('Comic Plot of Hume's "Dialogues"', p. 519).
101. Hume, *Principal Writings on Religion*, pp. 112–3.
102. Ibid., p. 115.
103. Ibid., p. 116.
104. Ibid.
105. Ibid., p. 119.
106. Ibid.
107. Gaskin, Introduction, in ibid., p. xxiv.
108. Hume, *Principal Writings on Religion*, p. 120.
109. Ibid.
110. Ibid. Prince argues that at this point Philo has reduced the debate to a shambles in which positions are inverted in 'a dialogue whose characters knowingly and unknowingly change sides' and in so doing 'dramatize the futility of a dialogue concerning natural religion' (*Philosophical Dialogue*, p. 303).
111. Hume, *Principal Writings on Religion*, p. 126.
112. Carnochan, 'Comic Plot of Hume's "Dialogues"', p.521.
113. Hume, *Principal Writings on Religion*, p. 126.
114. Ibid., p. 127.
115. Ibid., pp. 128, 129.

9 Sadow, 'The Epistemology of Genre'

1. P. Marivaux, *Pharsamon, ou les Nouvelles Folies romanesques. Oeuvres de jeunesse*, intro. F. Deloffre (Paris: Gallimard, 1972), p. 541. All unattributed translations are my own, with suggestions by Neil Hartlen and a debt to the 1750 English edition of *Pharsamon* (*Pharsamond, Or, The New Knight Errant*, trans. Mr Henry (repr. New York: Garland, 1974); I am unaware of any other version in English). I would also like to thank Andrew L. Blais for useful Lockean ideas, both simple and complex. I have also adopted a number of suggestions made by Christina Lupton and Alex Dick, and I wish to acknowledge their contribution.
2. Locke, *Essay Concerning Human Understanding* (1975 edn), p. 288.
3. P. de Man, 'The Epistemology of Metaphor', in S. Sacks (ed.), *On Metaphor* (Chicago, IL: Chicago University Press, 1981), pp. 11–28; p. 14.
4. Ibid., p. 28.
5. Ibid., p. 19.
6. Locke, *Essay Concerning Human Understanding* (1975 edn), p. 507.
7. de Man, 'The Epistemology of Metaphor', p. 16.
8. Locke, *Essay Concerning Human Understanding* (1975 edn), pp. 438–9.
9. It has not been *entirely* ignored: See W. Booth's 'Self-Conscious Fiction before *Tristram Shandy*' *PMLA*, 67:2 (1952), pp. 163–85, as well as F. Deloffre's introduction to Marivaux's *Oeuvres de Jeunesse*. Robert Hartwig details convincing scene-by-scene comparisons of *Joseph Andrews* and *Pharsamon* which suggest overt copying ('*Pharsamon* and *Joseph Andrews*', *Texas Studies in Literature and Language*, 14 (1972), pp. 45–52).
10. Marivaux, *Pharsamon*, pp. 8–9.

11. Lynch, *Economy of Character*, p. 29.
12. Marivaux, *Pharsamon*, p. 9.
13. Ibid., pp. 409–10.
14. Ibid., p. 457.
15. Ibid., pp. 530–1.
16. Ibid., p. 417.
17. Ibid., p. 533.
18. Ibid., pp. 520–1.
19. Ibid., p. 430.
20. de Man, 'The Epistemology of Genre' (1981 edn), pp. 21–2.
21. J. Derrida, in 'La Loi du genre', carried this argument further. Not only are genres histori-
    cally created, but genre always involves an inevitable paradox: All texts allude to genre by
    some kind of mark or symbol. And yet, no text belongs wholly to one genre, since that
    'mark' is never part of the genre itself. The 'laws' of genre, though they generate texts, fail
    to classify them. On one hand, this argument demolishes the idea of any kind of scien-
    tific or rigorous genre theory. On the other, it moves the discussion of genre back to the
    centre of any discussion of text or culture. All texts suggest categories, even as they self-
    consciously avoid conforming to a genre's platonic – yet murky and changeable – ideal
    (*Glyph*, 7 (1980), pp. 176–201).
22. H. Fielding, *The History of Tom Jones*, ed. F. Bowers (Middletown, CT: Wesleyan Univer-
    sity Press, 1975), p. 150.
23. Ibid., p. 152.
24. R. Paulson, alluding to the various modalities of the aesthetics of 'novelty', connects
    many of the figural and modal jokes to an adoption of Hogarthian aesthetics. Hog-
    arth's *Analysis of Beauty* has on the title page a quasi-religious symbol emblazoned
    with the word 'Variety'. As an offhand comment, he mentions the influence of French
    anti-romances on Fielding. Marivaux's narrator consistently employs variety as an
    explanation for shifting modes, and one might suggest that this is as much a 'source' for
    Tom Jones's theoretical orientation as anything else (R. Paulson, *The Beautiful, Novel,
    and Strange: Aesthetics and Heterodoxy* (Baltimore, MD: Johns Hopkins University
    Press, 1996)).
25. R. Cohen, 'On the Interrelations of Eighteenth Century Literary Forms', in P. Harth
    (ed.), *New Approaches to Eighteenth-Century Literature* (New York: Columbia Univer-
    sity Press, 1974), pp. 33–78; p. 76.
26. Ibid., p. 50.
27. Ibid., p. 76.
28. Ibid., p. 77.
29. Sterne, *Tristram Shandy*, vol. 1, p. 98.
30. Ibid., vol. 1, p. 100
31. Ibid., vol. 1, p. 334.
32. Ibid., vol. 1, p. 334.
33. Ibid., vol. 1, p. 443.
34. Ibid., vol. 2, p. 689.
35. See E. Davidson's 'Toward an Integrated Chronology for *Tristram Shandy*', *ELN*, 29:4
    (1992), pp. 48–56.
36. Sterne, *Tristram Shandy*, vol. 2, p. 541.
37. R. G. Collingwood, *The Idea of History* (New York: Oxford University Press, 1956).

38. D. Hume, *An Enquiry Concerning Human Understanding. Philosophical Works*, ed. T. H. Green and T. H. Gross (Aalen: Scientia, 1964), p. 139.

39. See C. Lupton, 'Tristram Shandy, David Hume, and Epistemological Fiction', *Philosophy and Literature*, 27 (2003), pp. 98–115.

40. Ibid.

10 Harkin, 'The Primitive in Adam Smith's History'

1. *Essays on Philosophical Subjects*, in *Works and Correspondence of Adam Smith*, vol. 3, p. 251.

2. See I. Simpson Ross, *The Life of Adam Smith* (Oxford: Clarendon Press, 1995), pp. 404–5.

3. *Correspondence of Adam Smith*, in *Works and Correspondence of Adam Smith*, vol. 6, pp. 286–7.

4. See Stewart's *Account of the Life and Writings of Adam Smith*, in *Essays on Philosophical Subjects*, in *Works and Correspondence of Adam Smith*, vol. 3, pp. 272–5.

5. In the closing lines of *The Theory of Moral Sentiments* Smith states: 'I shall in another discourse endeavour to give an account of the general principles of law and government, and of the different revolutions they have undergone in the different ages and periods of society ...' (*The Theory of Moral Sentiments*, ed. D. D. Raphael and A. L. Macfie, in *Works and Correspondence of Adam Smith*, vol. 1, p. 342). On Smith's teaching see Simpson Ross, *Life of Adam Smith*, pp. 121–2.

6. A particularly interesting recent approach to the problem of the missing work on history, however, is M. S. Phillips's reconstruction and interpretation of Smith's historiography based on the surviving texts. See his *Society and Sentiment* (Princeton, NJ: Princeton University Press, 2000), esp. pp. 55–6 and pp. 81–7; and 'Adam Smith and the History of Private Life: Social and Sentimental Narratives in Eighteenth-Century Historiography', in D. R. Kelley and D. H. Sacks (eds), *The Historical Imagination in Early Modern Britain: History, Rhetoric and Fiction, 1500–1800* (Cambridge: Cambridge University Press and Woodrow Wilson Press, 1997), pp. 318–42, esp. pp. 320–1.

7. *Correspondence of Adam Smith*, in *Works and Correspondence of Adam Smith*, vol. 6, p. 287.

8. Between 1786 and 1790, Smith prepared the revised and enlarged edition of the *Theory of Moral Sentiments*, which came out shortly before his death in 1790; served as Lord Rector of Glasgow University from 1787 to 1789; and from 1778 to until 1789 was also a Commissioner of Customs for Scotland, apparently taking his duties very seriously though he did not need the income from the post. Dugald Stewart blamed this last employment for Smith's failure to complete more works. See Stewart's *Account of the Life and Writings of Adam Smith*, in *Essays on Philosophical Subjects*, in *Works and Correspondence of Adam Smith*, vol. 3, p. 326, and Simpson Ross, *Life of Adam Smith*, pp. 306, 334, 403.

9. K. O'Brien, *Narratives of Enlightenment: Cosmopolitan History from Voltaire to Gibbon* (Cambridge: Cambridge University Press, 1997), esp. pp. 4–13; J. G. A. Pocock, *Barbarism and Religion, Volume Two: Narratives of Civil Government* (Cambridge: Cambridge University Press, 1999), esp. pp. 1–25.

10. Pocock. *Barbarism and Religion: Volume Two*, pp. 5–8.

11. Ibid., p. 328.

12. On the discussion of Smith's concern about verificatory notes and digressions undermining the classical supremacy of narrative in history-writing, for example, see ibid., pp. 325–6.

13. Ibid., pp. 309, 329, 333.

14. E. J. Hundert, *The Enlightenment's Fable: Bernard Mandeville and the Discovery of Society* (Cambridge: Cambridge University Press, 1994), pp. 220–1.

15. D. Hume, 'Of the Study of History', in *Essays: Moral, Political and Literary* (1987 edn), pp. 563–8; pp. 565–6.

16. See detailed chronology in R. Meek, *Smith, Marx, and After: Ten Essays in the Development of Economic Thought* (London: Chapman and Hall, 1977), pp. 22–32.

17. A. Ferguson, *Essay on the History of Civil Society* (Edinburgh: A. Millar et al., 1767); W. Robertson, *History of the Reign of the Emperor Charles V* (London: W. Strahan; T. Cadell; Edinburgh: J. Balfour, 1769); J. Millar, *The Origin of the Distinction of Ranks* (London: John Murray, 1771); H. Home and L. Kames, *Sketches of the History of Man* (Edinburgh: n.p., 1774).

18. Pocock, *Barbarism and Religion, Volume Two*, p. 322.

19. See A. Smith, *Lectures on Jurisprudence*, ed. R. L. Meek, D. D. Raphael and P. G. Stein, in *Works and Correspondence of Adam Smith*, vol. 5, pp. 14–15.

20. Ibid., p. 288, 16. See also Smith's accounts of stages of historical development in *An Inquiry into the Nature and Causes of the Wealth of Nations*, ed. R. H. Campbell and A. S. Skinner, in *Works and Correspondence of Adam Smith*, vol. 2, pp. 412–15; 689–95. The relevant sections are III.iv.4–7; and V.i.a.2–10.

21. Smith, *Lectures on Jurisprudence*, in *Works and Correspondence of Adam Smith*, vol. 5, p. 16.

22. J. Millar, *The Origin of the Distinction of Ranks*, 4th edn (Edinburgh: Blackwood, 1806), pp. 3–4.

23. Hume, *Essays: Moral, Political and Literary* (1987 edn), p. 269. Hume's essays generally give a fairly straightforward version of the notion of history as progress through stages to an age of commerce: see also 'Of the Rise and Progress of the Arts and Sciences' and 'Of National Characters' in ibid., pp. 111–37 and 197–215.

24. See J. Chandler's nuanced discussion in *England in 1819: The Politics of Literary Culture and the Case of Romantic Historicism* (Chicago, IL: University of Chicago Press, 1998), pp. 127–35.

25. Smith, *Wealth of Nations*, in *Works and Correspondence of Adam Smith*, vol. 2, p. 412.

26. Ibid., p. 413; Smith, *Lectures on Jurisprudence*, in *Works and Correspondence of Adam Smith*, vol. 5, pp. 539–41; Smith, *Wealth of Nations*, in *Works and Correspondence of Adam Smith*, vol. 2, p. 493.

27. The disjunction between the allegedly unqualified enthusiasm for capitalism and its driving force of self-interest in the *Wealth of Nations* and the concerns of the *Theory* with benevolence and social regulation produced, for an earlier generation of scholars, an idea of a career and corpus apparently split by a contradiction, the well-known 'Adam Smith problem' that turned on the assertion of these two supposedly contradictory characterizations of primary social forces. A good statement of the problem is given in R. Teichgraeber, 'Rethinking *Das Adam Smith Problem*', in J. R. A. Mason and A. Murdoch (eds), *New Perspectives on the Politics and Culture of Early Modern Scotland* (Edinburgh: John Donald, 1982), pp. 249–64. V. Brown discusses the issue in *Adam Smith's Discourse: Canonicity, Commerce and Conscience* (London: Routledge, 1994), pp. 23–54. See also A. Skinner's discussion in 'Adam Smith: Ethics and Self-Love', in P. Jones and A.

Skinner (eds), *Adam Smith Reviewed* (Edinburgh: Edinburgh University Press, 1992), pp. 142–67; and Hundert, *The Enlightenment's Fable*, pp. 234–6.

28. Here the primitive figures less as a stage in an Enlightenment narrative of the European march towards an age of capitalist freedom and prosperity, than as a category of spatial, and racial, otherness begging comparisons between the progress of Europe and the other societies it was trading with and colonizing. Chandler notes this tendency to make (invidious) comparisons between the 'rates of progress' of different societies among Scottish Enlightenment historians. Chandler, *England in 1819*, p. 128.

29. See for example O. Dickason, *The Myth of the Savage* (Edmonton, AB: University of Alberta Press, 1984). I. Simpson Ross describes the impact of specific voyage narratives and ethnographic texts on Smith in *The Life of Adam Smith*, p. 169. See the summary offered of such accounts in E. Chukwudi Eze, Introduction, in E. Chukwudi Eze (ed.), *Race and the Enlightenment* (Oxford: Blackwell, 1997), pp. 4–5.

30. Hume's discussion conflates Africans with other inhabitants of 'more southern climates'. See Hume, 'Of National Characters', and also 'Of Commerce', in *Essays: Moral, Political, and Literary* (1987 edn), pp. 253–67; pp. 207–8, 267.

31. R. Meek, *Social Science and the Ignoble Savage* (Cambridge: Cambridge University Press, 1976).

32. See Smith, *Lectures on Jurisprudence*, in *Works and Correspondence of Adam Smith*, vol. 5, pp. 107, 459.

33. J. F. Lafitau, *Moeurs des Sauvages Ameriquains, Comparees aux Moeurs des Premiers Temps* (Paris, 1724), trans. and ed. W. N. Fenton and E. L. Moore as *Customs of the American Indians Compared with the Customs of Primitive Times*, 2 vols (Toronto, ON: Champlain Society, 1974); P. François-Xavier de Charlevoix, *Histoire et Description Generale de la Nouvelle France* (Paris, 1744), trans. as *History and Description of New France*, 6 vols (Chicago, IL: Loyola University Press, 1870).

34. Smith, *Lectures on Jurisprudence*, in *Works and Correspondence of Adam Smith*, vol. 5, p. 459.

35. Pocock, *Barbarism and Religion: Volume Two*, p. 340.

36. Ibid., p. 331.

37. An earlier version of the discussion of sympathy and silence among native peoples which follows can be found in my 'Natives and Nostalgia: The Problem of the North American Savage in Adam Smith's Historiography', *Scottish Studies Review*, 3:1 (2002), pp. 25–8.

38. Smith, *Theory of Moral Sentiments*, in *Works and Correspondence of Adam Smith*, vol. 1, p. 10.

39. See especially D. Marshall's comprehensive documentation of this phenomenon in Smith, in *The Figure of Theater: Shaftesbury, Defoe, Adam Smith and George Eliot* (New York: Columbia University Press, 1986), pp. 167–92.

40. Smith, *Theory of Moral Sentiments*, in *Works and Correspondence of Adam Smith*, vol. 1, p. 182. Here Smith's evident unease with spectacle evokes Rousseau's well-known characterization of social life inseparably intertwined with and shadowed by the deluding effects of the visible in the *Second Discourse* (1755): '[As social life developed] everyone began to look at everyone else and to be wished to be looked at himself, and public esteem acquired a value;' 'to be and to appear [henceforth] became two entirely different things'. J. J. Rousseau, *Discourse on the Origin and the Foundations of Inequality Among Men (Second Discourse)*, in *The First and Second Discourses*, ed. V. Gourevitch (New York: Harper and Row), pp. 175, 180. Smith reviewed Rousseau's text in the *Edinburgh Review*

of March 1756. See Smith, *Essays on Philosophical Subjects*, in *Works and Correspondence of Adam Smith*, vol. 3, pp. 250–6.

41. Smith, *Theory of Moral Sentiments*, in *Works and Correspondence of Adam Smith*, vol. 1, pp. 204–5.

42. Ibid., p. 205.

43. See A. Smith, *Lectures on Rhetoric and Belles Lettres*, ed. J. C. Bryce, in *Works and Correspondence of Adam Smith*, vol. 4, p. 112.

44. Smith, *Theory of Moral Sentiments*, in *Works and Correspondence of Adam Smith*, vol. 1, pp. 207.

45. Ibid., p. 288.

46. Ibid., p. 283.

47. Ibid., pp. 281–2, 288. See also p. 283.

48. Ibid., p. 205.

49. Ibid., pp. 205–6.

50. Ibid., p. 208.

51. Ibid., p. 83.

52. Smith, *Lectures on Jurisprudence*, in *Works and Correspondence of Adam Smith*, vol. 5, p. 541.

53. See Rousseau, *Second Discourse*, in *First and Second Discourses*, p. 140.

54. See also Smith, *Wealth of Nations*, in *Works and Correspondence of Adam Smith*, vol. 2, pp. 782–3.

55. See, for example, Hundert, *The Enlightenment's Fable*, pp. 220, 222; Pocock, *Barbarism and Religion, Volume Two*, pp. 331, 340.

56. J. G. V. Herder, *Reflections on the Philosophy of the History of Mankind*, ed. F. E. Manuel and trans. T. O. Churchill (Chicago, IL: University of Chicago Press, 1968), pp. 58–9.

57. See discussion in C. Gallagher and S. Greenblatt, *Practicing New Historicism* (Chicago, IL: University of Chicago Press, 2000), pp. 5–8.

58. See M. Poovey's discussion of the ramifications of choice of genre in Hume, and her penetrating analysis of the larger eighteenth-century struggle of authors and genres for discursive authority, in *A History of the Modern Fact* (Chicago, IL: University of Chicago Press, 1998), esp. pp. 197–213.

59. Quoted in Simpson Ross, *Life of Adam Smith*, p. 343.

60. Smith, *Theory of Moral Sentiments*, in *Works and Correspondence of Adam Smith*, vol. 1, p. 299. Smith's account of philosophy in his *Essays* also stresses the appeal of philosophy in tidying up details or inconsistencies, sometimes at the cost of adequacy to the untidy reality it tries to explain: 'the learned easily give up the evidence of their senses to preserve the coherence of the ideas of their imagination'. Smith, *Essays on Philosophical Subjects*, in *Works and Correspondence of Adam Smith*, vol. 3, p. 77.

61. See Smith, *Lectures on Rhetoric and Belles Lettres*, in *Works and Correspondence of Adam Smith*, vol. 4, pp. 67, 80–91.

62. Ibid., p. 86.

63. See Phillips's discussion in *Society and Sentiment*, pp. 82–7.

64. W. Benjamin, 'Theses on the Philosophy of History', in *Illuminations*, ed. H. Arendt, trans. H. Zohn (New York: Schocken, 1969), pp. 253–64; p. 256.

11 Yousef, 'Can Julie be Trusted?'

1. For the most substantial treatment of this theme in Rousseau see J. Starobinski, *Transparency and Obstruction*, trans. A. Goldhammer (Chicago, IL: University of Chicago Press, 1988). This essay is dedicated to Silvia Luna Siegel-Yousef.
2. Hume, *Treatise of Human Nature* (2000 edn), pp. 332, 369–71.
3. 'Love as an inclination cannot be commanded. But beneficence from duty, even when no inclination impels it ... is practical love ... It resides in the will and not in the propensities of feeling, in principles of action and not in tender sympathy.' I. Kant, *Foundations of the Metaphysics of Morals* (1784), trans. L. White Beck (New York: Macmillan, 1990), p. 15.
4. On the role of intersubjective recognition in Kant's ethics, see C. Korsgaard, *Creating the Kingdom of Ends* (Cambridge: Cambridge University Press, 1996), pp. 188–221.
5. J. J. Rousseau, *Discourse on the Arts and Sciences*, in *The Discourse and Other Early Political Writings*, trans. V. Gourevitch (Cambridge: Cambridge University Press, 1997), pp. 3–28: p. 7.
6. J. J. Rousseau, *The Confessions*, trans. J. M. Cohen (New York: Penguin, 1953), p. 398.
7. J. J. Rousseau, *Emile, or On Education*, trans. A. Bloom (New York: Basic Books, 1979), p. 85.
8. Ibid., p. 120. Emile's virtue consists precisely in being so well known: 'Not a single movement takes place in his soul which his mouth or his eyes do not reveal', and thus he 'does not think of dissembling' (ibid., p. 319). Julie's children are raised on the same model with the same effect: 'They know not how to lie, nor to hide, and in everything they say ... they allow to be seen without constraint whatever they have in the depth of their souls' (J. J. Rousseau, *Julie, or the New Heloise*, trans. P. Stewart and J. Vaché (Hanover, NH: University Press of New England, 1997), p. 478).
9. Ibid., p. 349.
10. D. Hume, *An Enquiry Concerning the Principles of Morals* (Indianapolis, IN: Hackett Publishing, 1983), p. 93.
11. Rousseau, *Julie, or the New Heloise*, pp. 608–9.
12. Ibid., p. 406.
13. Ibid., p. 609.
14. Ibid., p. 412.
15. Ibid., pp. 406, 408.
16. Ibid., pp. 553, 548.
17. Ibid., p. 560.
18. Ibid.
19. Ibid., p. 409.
20. Ibid., p. 410.
21. Ibid., p. 551.
22. Ibid., p. 608.
23. Ibid.
24. Rousseau, *Emile*, p. 397; J. J. Rousseau, *Emilius and Sophia; or, The Solitaries*, anonymous translation (London: H. Baldwin, 1783), p. 22. J. J. Rousseau, *Émile et Sophie*, ed. B. Gagnebin and M. Raymond, in Rousseau, *Oeuvres complètes*, vol. 4, p. 890. Written largely in 1762 and left unfinished, *Émile et Sophie* was first published in 1780. On the composition and projected shape of the work, see C. Wirz, 'Note sur *Emile et*

Sophie, ou les Solitaires', *Annales de la Société Jean-Jacques-Rousseau*, 36 (1963–65), pp. 291–304.

25. Rousseau, *Emile*, pp. 360–1.
26. See Rousseau, *Emilius and Sophia*, pp. 7, [881].
27. Ibid., p. 11.
28. Ibid., p. 42.
29. Ibid., p. 36. P. Burgelin carefully traces how the novelistic sequel exposes the failure ('*échec*') of the perfect female education described in *Emile* in 'L'éducation de Sophie', *Annales de la Société Jean-Jacques-Rousseau*, 35 (1959–62), pp. 113–30. M. H. Huet takes this 'deliberate defeat of *Emile*'s most explicit goals' to be symptomatic of Rousseau's profound cultural pessimism in 'Social Entropy', *Yale French Studies*, 92 (1997), pp. 171–83. Equally important are interpretations emphasizing the connection between what A. Skillen calls the 'fatal logic of love' in Rousseau and his 'dismal dialectic of social life' more broadly conceived ('Rousseau and the Fall of Social Man', *Philosophy*, 60 (1985), pp. 105–21; p. 111). G. Besse only echoes Emile's lament when he observes that adultery is no more and no less than a negation of the social pact as such, *Jean-Jacques Rousseau: L'apprentissage de l'humanité* (Paris: Messidor, 1988), p. 381.
30. Shaftesbury, *Characteristics of Men, Manners, Opinions, Times*, pp. 287, 283.
31. Hume, *Treatise of Human Nature* (2000 edn), pp. 309, 312.
32. J. J. Rousseau, *On the Social Contract*, in *The Basic Political Writings*, trans, D. A. Cress (Indianapolis, IN: Hackett, 1987), pp. 141–227; p. 142.
33. On the conceptual discontinuities between the 'natural' and the 'social' in Rousseau, see especially V. Goldschmidt, *Anthropologie et politique: Les principes du système de Rousseau* (Paris: Librairie Philosophique J. Vrin, 1974), pp. 175–219, 261–74 and V. Gourevitch, 'Rousseau's Pure State of Nature', *Interpretation*, 16 (1988) pp. 23–59.
34. J. J. Rousseau, *Discourse on the Origins of Inequality*, in *The Discourse and Other Early Political Writings*, pp. 113–222; p. 216.
35. Ibid., pp. 164, 159. On the radical contingency of the transition from the state of nature to society in the second *Discourse*, see Gourevitch, 'Rousseau's Pure State of Nature', p. 41.
36. Rousseau, *Social Contract*, in *Basic Political Writings*, p. 142.
37. T. Hobbes, *De Cive* (1651), ed. B. Gert (Indianapolis, IN: Hackett, 1991), pp. 212–3.
38. Rousseau, *Emile*, p. 46.
39. Ibid.
40. Ibid.
41. Ibid.
42. J. J. Rousseau, 'On the Social Contract, or Essay about the Form of the Republic' (commonly called the 'Geneva manuscript'), trans. J. R. Bush, R. D. Masters and C. Kelly, in *The Collected Writings of Rousseau*, 12 vols (Hanover, NH: University Press of New England, 1990–), vol. 4, p. 90. It is worth noting that wherever Rousseau attends to legitimacy, secure transmission of property is not his principal concern. Rather emphasis is placed on the need to redress the psychological and affective vulnerabilities to which only men are subject. Because 'the wife ... has no such thing to fear', she 'does not have the same right' to oversee her husband's behaviour. The attenuation of fear is as important as deterrence of infidelity. See also *Julie, or the New Heloise*, pp. 295–6. On the relationship between sexual difference and deception in Rousseau, see I. Makus, 'The Politics of "Feminine Concealment" and "Masculine Openness"', in *Feminist Interpretations of*

Jean-Jacques Rousseau, ed. L. Lange (Philadelphia, PA: Pennsylvania State University Press, 2002), pp. 187–211.

43. J. J. Rousseau, *Letter to d'Alembert*, trans. A. Bloom et al., in *Collected Writings of Jean-Jacques Rousseau*, vol. 10, p.313. Feminist interpretation of Rousseau's articulation of sexual difference in the works of his middle career has moved beyond critical condemnation of the evident exclusion of women from the egalitarian civil societies he describes towards analysis of the interdependence and asymmetry between domestic and public spheres in Rousseau. Especially notable are recent efforts to bring the utopian failures dramatized in Rousseau's fiction to bear on systematic theoretical works such as the *Social Contract*. See, for example, L. Bradshaw, 'Rousseau on Civic Virtue, Male Autonomy and the Construction of the Divided Female' (pp. 65–88), S. M. Okin, 'The Fate of Rousseau's Heroines' (pp. 89–112), M. Morgenstern, 'Women, Power, and the Politics of Everyday Life' (pp. 113–43), and L. Marso, 'Rousseau's Subversive Women' (pp. 245–76), all in Lange (ed.), *Feminist Interpretations of Rousseau*.

44. Rousseau, 'Geneva Manuscript', p. 77.

45. Rousseau, *Julie, or the New Heloise*, p. 297.

46. Rousseau, *Emile*, p. 361.

47. Rousseau, *Letter to d'Alembert*, in *Collected Writings of Rousseau*, vol. 10, p. 345.

48. Rousseau, *Julie, or the New Heloise*, p. 279.

49. Ibid., pp. 158–9.

50. Ibid., p. 275.

51. Ibid., p. 291.

52. Ibid., pp. 294, 292.

53. Ibid., p. 306.

54. Rousseau, *Emile*, p. 430.

55. Rousseau, *Julie, or the New Heloise*, p. 307.

56. Rousseau, *Emile*, pp. 430–1.

57. Rousseau, *Letter to d'Alembert*, in *Collected Writings of Rousseau*, vol. 10, p. 292. On the imbrication of gender, romantic love and 'the aporetic nature of human relations' more generally in Rousseau's work, see R. Kukla, 'Rousseau and the Problem of Gender Relations', in Lange (ed.), *Feminist Interpretations of Rousseau*, pp. 346–81.

58. Rousseau, 'Geneva Manuscript', p. 79.

59. Rousseau, *Julie, or the New Heloise*, p. 293.

60. Rousseau, *Emile*, p. 430; Rousseau, *Discourse on the Arts and Sciences*, in *The Discourse and Other Early Political Writings* p. 8.

61. Rousseau, *Confessions*, p. 190.

62. Ibid., p. 190. See also Julie's indignant rejection of this 'sophism': 'But just look how they disculpate a secret adultery! The point is, they say, that no harm results from it, not even for the husband who is in the dark ... as if it were enough, to justify perjury and infidelity, that they harm no one else? ... How then! It is not wrong to break faith, to do everything possible to annul the force of the vow and the most inviolable contracts?' (p. 296).

63. Rousseau, *Emile*, p. 360. The same point is made by Julie on the occasion of Claire's marriage, which she marks as an entry into 'a new order of things': 'It is not enough that [a wife] be honest, she must also be honored ... were she innocent, she is in the wrong the moment she is suspected; for appearances themselves are counted among her duties' (p. 211).

64. M. Wollstonecraft, *Vindication of the Rights of Woman* (1792), in *The Works of Mary Wollstonecraft*, ed. J. Todd and M. Butler, 7 vols (New York: New York University Press, 1989), vol. 5, p. 161.
65. Rousseau, *Julie, or the New Heloise*, p. 384.
66. Rousseau, *Social Contract*, in *Basic Political Writings*, p. 203 [437] and p. 204.
67. Rousseau, *Julie, or the New Heloise*, p. 566.
68. Ibid., p. 566.
69. Rousseau, *Emile*, p. 40.
70. Rousseau, *Letter to d'Alembert*, in *Collected Writings of Rousseau*, vol. 10, pp. 347–8.
71. Ibid., p. 345. See also Rousseau, *Julie, or the New Heloise*, pp. 375–6.
72. Rousseau, *Social Contract*, in *Basic Political Writings*, pp. 162–3.
73. Rousseau, *Julie, or the New Heloise*, pp. 402–3.
74. Ibid., p. 304.
75. Ibid., p. 597.
76. For an ambitious, recent analysis of the interpretive issues at stake, see: S. G. Affeldt, 'The Force of Freedom: Rousseau on Forcing to be Free', *Political Theory*, 27:3 (1999), pp. 299–333.
77. Rousseau, *Social Contract*, in *Basic Political Writings*, p. 163; Rousseau, 'Geneva Manuscript', p. 101.
78. Rousseau, *Julie, or the New Heloise*, pp. 546, 590.
79. Rousseau, *Emilius and Sophia*, p. 42.

12 Norton, 'After the Summum Bonum'

1. J. F. Jones concurs with Paul Hazard's assessment that happiness was an 'obsession' in the period. J. F. Jones, 'Prolegomena to a History of Happiness in the Eighteenth Century', *French-American Review*, 6:2 (Fall 1982), pp. 283–95; p. 284. In Robert Mauzi's phrase, this interest 'borders on obsession'. Mauzi, *L'Idée du bonheur dans la littérature et la pensée françaises au XVIIIe siècle*, reprint (Genève: Slatkine, 1979), p. 80.
2. For treatments of happiness in Britain, see R. Porter, *The Creation of the Modern World: The Untold Story of the British Enlightenment* (New York and London: W. W. Norton and Company, 2000), esp. ch. 11, A. Potkay, *The Passion for Happiness: Samuel Johnson and David Hume* (Ithaca, NY: Cornell University Press, 2000), and A. Potkay, 'Joy and Happiness', in P. Backscheider and C. Ingrassia (eds), *A Companion to the Eighteenth-Century English and Novel and Culture* (Oxford: Blackwell Publishing, 2005), pp. 321–40.
3. J. Bethune, *Essays and Dissertations on Various Subjects Relating to Human Life and Happiness*, 2 vols (Edinburgh: Kincaid and Bell, 1771), vol. 1, p. 1.
4. Parker, *Scepticism and Literature*, p. 5.
5. Shaftesbury, *Characteristics of Men, Manners, Opinions, Times*, p. 336.
6. D. Defoe, *Robinson Crusoe* (Oxford: Oxford University Press, 1972), p. 4.
7. S. Richardson, *Pamela; or Virtue Rewarded* (Oxford: Oxford University Press, 2001), p. 20.
8. M. Hays, *Memoirs of Emma Courtney* (Oxford: Oxford University Press, 1996), pp. 26–7.
9. Taylor, *Sources of the Self*, p. 105.
10. Aristotle, *Nichomachean Ethics*, trans. T. Irwin (Indianapolis, IN: Hackett Publishing Company, 1985), p. 5.
11. Ibid.

12. R. Descartes, *The Correspondence*, trans. J. Cottingham et al., in *The Philosophical Writings of Descartes*, 3 vols (Cambridge: Cambridge University Press, 1994–91), vol. 3, p. 261.

13. P. Glover, *An Inquiry Concerning Virtue and Happiness* (London: John Whiston and Benj. White, 1751), pp. 9–14.

14. T. Hobbes, *Leviathan* (New York: Collier Books, 1962), p. 80. J. B. Schneewind points out that Hobbesian psychology amounts to a rejection of the Stoic theory of desire. 'We do not desire something because we think it good. We think it good simply because the thought of it moves us to get it.' For a fuller discussion of this issue, see J. B. Schneewind, *The Invention of Autonomy: A History of Modern Moral Philosophy* (Cambridge: Cambridge University Press, 1998), esp. ch. 5. Once again, for the moderns, desire is primary and the object secondary.

15. Locke, *An Essay Concerning Human Understanding* (1975 edn), pp. 268–9.

16. Voltaire, *Philosophical Dictionary*, ed. and trans. T. Besterman (London: Penguin Books, 1972), p. 67

17. For an interpretation of what this might mean, see Potkay, *Passion for Happiness*, pp. 70–5.

18. J. Norris, *An Idea Of Happiness*, 2nd edn (London: James Norris, 1684), p. 5.

19. Glover. *Inquiry After Happiness*, p. 174.

20. For more on 'sensationism', see J. C. O'Neal, *The Authority of Experience: Sensationist Theory in the French Enlightenment* (University Park, PA: Penn State University Press, 1996).

21. For further discussion of how 'good feeling and pleasure' informed new ideas of happiness, see D. McMahon, *Happiness: A History* (New York: Atlantic Monthly Press, 2006), pp. 209–210.

22. For a seminal study of the relation between modern happiness and ancient *eudaimonia*, see R. Kraut, 'Two Conceptions of Happiness', *Philosophical Review*, 88 (April 1979), pp. 167–97. For an example of how *eudaimonia* continues to inform psychological studies of happiness, see J. R. Averill and T. A. More, 'Happiness', in M. Lewis and J. M. Haviland-Jones (eds), *Handbook of Emotions*, 2nd edn (New York: Guilford Press, 2004), pp. 666–76.

23. Cicero, *De Finibus Bonorum et Malorum*, trans. H. Rackham (Cambridge, MA: Harvard University Press, 1983), p. 179.

24. A. A. Long, *Epictetus: A Stoic and Socratic Guide to Life* (Oxford: Clarendon Press, 2002), p. 193.

25. A. A. Long, *Stoic Studies* (Cambridge: Cambridge University Press, 1996), p. 181.

26. G. Striker, *Essays on Hellenistic Epistemology and Ethics* (Cambridge: Cambridge University Press, 1996), p. 183.

27. M. de Montaigne, *The Complete Essays of Montaigne*, trans. D. M. Frame (Stanford, CA: Stanford University Press, 1958), p. 46.

28. For a history of 'taste' in English literature and thought, see D. Gigante, *Taste: A Literary History* (New Haven, CT: Yale University Press, 2005).

29. Locke's use of the metaphor, in particular, was so extended that it becomes difficult to distinguish between the literal and the figurative, as in his claim, 'The Mind has a different relish, as well as the palate' (*Essay Concerning Human Understanding* (1975 edn), p. 269).

30. Norris, *Idea of Happiness*, p. 6.

31. T. Newman, *Sermons on Happiness* (London: J. Noon; J. Buckland; T. Field; and C. Henderson, 1760), p. 54.
32. *Gentleman's Magazine*, 5 (August 1735), p. 474.
33. Richard Lucas raises this objection, in hopes of refuting it, in his own treatise on happiness: 'The great Variety there is in the nature of Men, and consequently in their Happiness, abundantly refutes all Attempts of this nature, and demonstrates it impossible either to frame one uniform Notion of human Happiness, or prescribe any constant and general Rules for the Attainment of it' (R. Lucas, *An Enquiry after Happiness* (London: S. Smith and B. Walford, 1697), pp. 8–9).
34. Potkay, 'Joy and Happiness', p. 323.
35. Descartes, *Correspondence*, in Philosophical Writings, vol. 3, p. 261.
36. Locke, *Essay Concerning Human Understanding* (1975 edn), p. 266.
37. J. Boswell, *Life of Johnson* (Oxford: Oxford University Press, 1980), p. 825.
38. Porter defined British pragmatism as a '*philosophy* of expediency, a dedication to the art, science and duty of living well in the here and now' (*Creation of the Modern World*, p. 15).
39. J. Annas, *The Morality of Happiness* (Oxford: Oxford University Press, 1993), p. 46.
40. Ibid., p. 46.
41. S. Gott, *An Essay on the True Happiness of Man*, 2 vols (London: T. Underhill, 1650), p. 3.
42. J. Harris, *Three Treatises* (London: John Nourse and Paul Vaillant, 1744), p. 185.
43. Bethune, *Essays and Dissertations on Various Subjects*, p. 13.
44. Norris, *Idea of Happiness*, pp. 29–30.
45. Richardson, *Pamela*, p. 359.
46. Richetti, *English Novel in History, 1700–1780*, p. 1.
47. H. Fielding, *Amelia* (London: Penguin Books, 1987), p. 14. A. J. Van Sant observes of Samuel Richardson that his readers associated the moral effects of his fiction with its psychological power, and identified this with its use of 'particularity', A. J. Van Sant, 'A Dictionary of Morality: Reading for the Sentiment', in F. Stuber (ed.), *Samuel Richardson's Published Commentary on Clarissa, 1747–65*, 3 vols (London: Pickering & Chatto, 1998), vol. 3: *A Collection of the Moral and Instructive Sentiments*, pp. 411–37; p. 418.
48. M. Hays, 'On Novel Writing', *Monthly Magazine* (September 1797), pp. 180–1; p. 181.
49. According to Diderot, 'Everything that Montaigne, Charron, La Rochefoucauld and Nicole put into maxims, Richardson has put into action [mis en action]' (*Manon Lescaut*, ed. Jean Sgard (Paris: GF-Flammarion, 1995), p. 29). Prévost had earlier claimed of *Manon Lescaut* that 'The entire work is a moral treatise pleasantly put into practice [réduit agréablement en exercice]' (ibid., p. 49).
50. G. Justice has observed that *Rasselas* 'is relentlessly suspicious of "treatises"' ('Imlac's Pedagogy', *Age of Johnson: A Scholarly Annual*, 13 (2002), pp. 1–29; p. 17).
51. N. Hudson, 'Three Steps to Perfection: *Rasselas* and the Philosophy of Richard Hooker', *Eighteenth-Century Life*, 14:3 (November 1990), pp. 29–39. Such sensualism, as we have seen, is built into emerging ideas of happiness. Johnson's description of the Happy Valley, in fact, comes very close to the *Encylopédie*'s assertion that 'the most perfect happiness in this life ... is nothing but a tranquil state sprinkled here and there with enlivening pleasures.'
52. Norris, *Idea of Happiness*, p. 10.
53. Glover, *Inquiry Concerning Virtue and Justice*, p. 174.

54. D. A. Miller, *Narrative and its Discontents: Problems of Closure in the Traditional Novel* (Princeton, NJ: Princeton University Press, 1981), p. 3.

55. Johnson, *Rasselas*, p. 8.

56. Adam Potkay has pointed out that for Johnson, as for the empiricists, happiness is not so much an *end* as a never-ending 'dialectic' between desire and gratification. See *Passion for Happiness*, pp. 65–70. Mauzi too speaks of happiness as a 'dialectic of desire and possession' (*L'Idée du bonheur*, p. 101). One Mme de Puisieux illustrates this dialectic in a memorable image: 'Happiness is a ball we chase wherever it rolls and we push with our foot whenever it stops' [le bonheur est une boule après laquelle nous courons tant qu'elle roule et que nous poussons du pied quand elle s'arrête], quoted in *L'Idée du bonheur*, p. 85.

57. For insightful discussions of the practical emphasis of Johnson's thought, see Van Sant, 'Dictionary of Morality'; L. Damrosch, Jr., 'Johnson's *Rasselas*: Limits of Wisdom, Limits of Art', in D. L. Patey and T. Keegan (eds), *Augustan Studies; Essays in Honour of Irvin Ehrenpreis* (Newark: University of Delaware Press, 1985), pp. 205–14; P. Davis, 'Extraordinarily Ordinary: The Life of Samuel Johnson', in G. Clingham (ed.), *The Cambridge Companion to Samuel Johnson* (Cambridge: Cambridge University Press, 1997), pp. 4–17, L. Lipking, 'Johnson and the Meaning of Life', in J. Engell (ed.), *Johnson and his Age* (Cambridge, MA: Harvard University Press, 1984), pp. 1–28.

58. Damrosch Jr, 'Johnson's *Rasselas*', p. 207.

59. A. L. Barbauld, *The British Novelists*, in J. T. Boulton (ed.), *Johnson: The Critical Heritage* (London: Routledge & Kegan Paul, 1971), pp. 149–54; p. 151.

60. Ibid., p. 151.

61. See S. Haines, 'Deepening the Self: The Language of Ethics and the Language of Literature', in J. Adamson, R. Freadman and D. Parker (eds), *Renegotiating Ethics in Literature, Philosophy, and Theory* (Cambridge: Cambridge University Press, 1998), pp. 21–38, and A. MacIntyre, *After Virtue* (Notre Dame, IN: University of Notre Dame Press, 1984). Even defenders of the Enlightenment, such as Selya Benhabib, refer to its 'metaphysical illusions', such as 'the illusion of a self-transparent and self-grounding reason, the illusion of a disembedded and disembodied subject, and the illusion of having found an Archimedean standpoint, situated beyond historical and cultural contingency.' S. Benhabib, *Situating the Self: Gender, Community and Postmodernism in Contemporary Ethics* (New York: Routledge, 1992), p. 4.

62. For an excellent rethinking of Enlightenment 'autonomy', see N. Yousef, *Isolated Cases: The Anxieties of Autonomy in Enlightenment Philosophy and Romantic Literature* (Ithaca, NY: Cornell University Press, 2004).

13 Potkay, 'Music vs Conscience'

1. A. Gerard, *An Essay on Taste* (London: A. Millar, A. Kincaid and J. Bell, 1759), p. 64 (part I, section V: 'Of the Sense or Taste of Harmony')).

2. See, e.g. Romans 2:14–15.

3. 'Conscience', in F. L. Cross and E. A. Livingstone (eds), *The Oxford Dictionary of the Christian Church*, 2nd rev. edn (Oxford: Oxford University Press, 1983), p. 335.

4. See R. Javelet's monumental study of commentary on Genesis 1:26, *Image et Resemblance au douziéme siècle de Saint Anselm à Alain de Lille*, 2 vols (Paris: Letouzey & Ané, 1967).

5. M. de Montaigne, *The Essays of Michael Seigneur de Montaigne, Translated into English*, 7th rev. edn, 3 vols (London: S. and E. Ballard, J. Clarke, D. Browne, C. Hitch and L. Hawes et al., 1759), vol. 2, pp. 45–51.

6. F. Atterbury, D. D., *Sermons and Discourses on Several Subjects and Occasions*, 8th edn, 4 vols (London: L. Davis and C. Reymers, J. Rivington, W. Johnston, R. Baldwin et al., 1766), vol. 4, p. 91.

7. H. Blair, D.D., Sermon 13, 'On the Power of Conscience', in *Sermons* (Edinburgh: William Creech, 1777), p. 379.

8. 'The Children of the Wood' appears in Bishop T. Percy, *Reliques of Ancient English Poetry* (1765), 3rd series, book II, no. 18; Wordsworth quotes another stanza from this poem, in defence of ballad art, in the 1800 *Preface* to *Lyrical Ballads*. On the hell of conscience, see also F. Holcroft's ballad 'Conscience the Worst of Tortures' (*Monthly Magazine* (April 1798)), reprinted in W. Wordsworth and S. T. Coleridge, *Lyrical Ballads and Related Writings*, ed. W. Richey and D. Robinson (Boston, MA: Houghton Mifflin/Riverside, 2002), pp. 270–1.

9. J. Butler, Sermon 3, 'Upon Human Nature', from *Fifteen Sermons Preached at the Rolls Chapel* (1726), reprinted in J. Butler, *The Analogy of Religion ... to which Are Added, Two Brief Dissertations ... and Fifteen Sermons* (London: George Bell and Sons, 1878), pp. 410–1.

10. Alluding to 1 Corinthians 13:1; see W. Cowper, *The Task*, book 5, 'The Winter Morning Walk', ll. 681–5.

11. W. Wilberforce, *A Practical View of the Prevailing Religious System of Professed Christians in the Higher and Middle Classes of this Country, contrasted with Real Christianity*, 2nd edn (London: T. Cadell, jun. and W. Davies, 1797), p. 235.

12. V. Knox, Essay 146, 'On the Weight and Efficacy which Morality may Derive from the Influence and Example of Those Who are Called the Great', in *Essays Moral and Literary*, 2 vols (London: Charles Dilly, 1795), vol. 2, p. 259.

13. W. Crowe, *Lewesdon Hill: A Poem* (Oxford: Clarendon Press, 1788), pp. 4–5. Wordsworth read *Lewesdon Hill* in 1795 according to D. Wu, *Wordsworth's Reading 1770–1799* (Cambridge: Cambridge University Press, 1993), p. 42.

14. On Wordsworth as a poet of guilt and mourning, see especially D. Wu, *Wordsworth: An Inner Life* (Oxford Blackwell, 2002), p. x and *passim*.

15. W. Wordsworth, *The Borderers* (1797–9), ed. R. Osborn (Ithaca, NY: Cornell University Press, 1982), ll. 145–6.

16. Wordsworth, 'The Convict', ll. 29–32, cited from *Lyrical Ballads, and Other Poems, 1797–1800*, ed. J. Butler and K. Green (Ithaca, NY: Cornell University Press, 1992), pp. 114–15.

17. Ibid., ll. 50–1.

18. W. Wordsworth, *An Evening Walk* (1793 version), l. 436; cited from *An Evening Walk*, ed. J. Averill (Ithaca, NY: Cornell University Press, 1984).

19. W. Wordsworth, *The Ruined Cottage*, ll. 15, 531–3; cited from *The Ruined Cottage* and *The Pedlar*, ed. J. Butler (Ithaca, NY: Cornell University Press, 1979).

20. W. Wordsworth, Fragment, 'There is an Active Principle Alive in All Things', l. 73; cited from *Lyrical Ballads, and Other Poems, 1797–1800*, p. 310.

21. P. Kivy, *Sound Sentiment: An Essay on the Musical Emotions* (Philadelphia, PA: Temple University Press, 1989), pp. 2–15, 46–52. Kivy establishes his crucial distinction between expression and looks/sounds that are 'expressive of' through a critical reading of J. Mattheson's 1739 treatise *Der Vollkommene Capellmeister*, concluding, 'what we

see as, and say is, *expressive* of φ is parasitic on what we see as, and say is, *expressing* φ'; 'Mattheson's legacy ... is the notion that *music, in many respects, resembles our expressive behavior*' (pp. 50–2). I would suggest that this legacy may ultimately derive from Aristotle's *Poetics*, which holds that the 'motions' of music (its rhythms and arrangements of sound) resemble human actions and manners: T. Twining grapples with this aspect of Aristotle's musical theory in *Aristotle's Treatise of Poetry, Translated ... With Notes ... and Two Dissertations, on Poetical, and Musical, Imitation* (London: Payne and son, 1789), pp. 55–61. A. Ridley's recent survey, *The Philosophy of Music: Themes and Variations* (Edinburgh: Edinburgh University Press, 2004), notes that Kivy's (eighteenth-century) linkage between music and expressive human behaviour now has 'widespread acceptance' (p. 73), arguing that Kivy's only weak spot is that he does not show that or how music is or should be *valued* for its expressive properties.

22. S. T. Coleridge, *Philosophical Lectures*, ed. K. Coburn (London: Pilot Press, 1949), p. 168.

23. P. Kivy, *Introduction to a Philosophy of Music* (Oxford: Oxford University Press, 2002), pp. 132–4.

24. F. Nietzsche, *The Birth of Tragedy and The Case of Wagner*, trans. W. Kaufman (New York: Vintage/Random House, 1967), p. 104.

25. W. Wordsworth, 'Prospectus to *The Recluse*', ll. 20–2; cited from *The Excursion*, in *William Wordsworth: The Poems*, 2 vols, ed. J. O. Hayden (New Haven, CT: Yale University Press, 1981), vol. 2, pp. 35–289.

26. Wordsworth, *Home at Grasmere*, ll. 959–72; cited from *Home at Grasmere: Part First, Book First of 'The Recluse'*, ed. B. Darlington (Ithaca, NY: Cornell University Press, 1977).

27. Quoted in J. Butler's editorial Introduction to *The Ruined Cottage*, p. 15.

28. W. Wordsworth, 'O Nightingale!', ll. 11–12; cited from *Poems, in Two Volumes, and Other Poems, 1800–1807*, ed. J. Curtis (Ithaca, NY: Cornell University Press, 1983), p. 205.

29. Wordsworth, *Evening Walk*, ll. 349–50.

30. Ibid., ll. 435–6. G. Hartman admires *An Evening Walk* for 'its renderings of tranquility in which undercurrents of sound emerge', and notes the absence of anthropocentrism in the poem relative to Thomson's *Seasons*, in which 'one continues to feel the baton of Man Superior leading the chorus of glad creation' (*Wordsworth's Poetry 1787–1814* (New Haven, CT: Yale University Press, 1971), pp. 96–7).

31. W. Wordsworth, *Descriptive Sketches* (1793), ll. 424–49.

32. Wordsworth, *Descriptive Sketches* (1836), ll. 377–8.

33. Wordsworth, *The Prelude* (1799 version), II:358; cited from *The Prelude 1788, 1805, 1850*.

34. Wordsworth, *The Prelude* (1805 version), I.348.

35. Ibid., VI 408–9.

36. Ibid., VI 562–4.

37. A. J. Dick, 'Poverty, Charity, Poetry: The Unproductive Labors of "The Old Cumberland Beggar"', *Studies in Romanticism*, 39 (2000), pp. 365–96.

38. J. Thomson, 'Spring', l. 615; cited from *The Seasons and Castle of Indolence*, ed. J. Sambrook (Oxford: Clarendon Press, 1987), p. 20.

39. I allude here to S. Benso, *The Face of Things: A Different Side of Ethics* (Albany, NY: State University of New York Press, 2000):

The prevailing economy of exchange within which things have been inserted condemns them to the status of faceless entities to be offered in payment, compensation and reward, as if they were quantified and quantifiable currency to be tendered among humans. Beyond such an economical meaning of 'tendered', *The Face of Things* aims at restoring things to a preeconomical horizon of festive appreciation and celebration within which things can be encountered in their facialities and tendered – that is, treated with tenderness – because of the generosity of their self-giving as if their alterity were a gift. (p. xxxi)

For a fuller exposition of Benso's ethics in relation to Wordsworth, see my article 'Wordsworth and the Ethics of Things,' forthcoming in *PMLA* (2008).

40. Wordsworth, *The Prelude* (1805 version), XII.171–3, 225–9.
41. Ibid., XII.266–71.
42. Ibid., XII.245–7.
43. This phrase, offered as an insight into Wordsworth's style, is originally from J. Jones, *The Egotistical Sublime: A History of Wordsworth's Imagination* (London: Chatto & Windus, 1954), p. 206; C. Ricks more thoroughly analyses Wordsworth's 'busy prepositions', in *The Force of Poetry* (Oxford: Clarendon, 1984), pp. 110–34.
44. Wordsworth, *The Prelude* (1805 version), II.431–4.
45. D. Bromwich, *Disowned by Memory: Wordsworth's Poetry of the 1790s* (Chicago, IL: University of Chicago Press, 1998), p. 88.
46. Ibid., p. 89.
47. Ibid., p. 89, n. 15.
48. Virgil, *Georgics*, IV.464–527; cited from Virgil, *Eclogues, Georgics, Aeneid I–VI*, ed. H. R. Fairclough (Cambridge, MA: Harvard University Press, 1916).
49. Ibid., IV.510. W. Wordsworth, *Georgics Translations*, in *Early Poems and Fragments, 1785–1797*, ed. C. Landon and J. Curtis (Ithaca, NY: Cornell University Press, 1997), p. 642. Dryden renders Virgil's lines more faithfully: 'Trees bent their heads to hear him sing his Wrongs, / Fierce Tygers couch'd around, and loll'd their fawning Tongues' (IV.740–1); cited from Dryden, *The Works of Virgil in English*, ed. W. Frost and V. Dearing, in *The Works of John Dryden*, 20 vols (Berkeley, CA: University of California Press, 1956–2002), vol. 5 (1987), p. 263. Landon and Curtis (*Early Poems and Fragments*, pp. 508–9) note that behind Wordsworth's rendition of Virgil's lines lie Milton's from *Paradise Lost* VII.34–6: 'that wild Rout that tore the *Thracian* Bard / In *Rhodope*, where Woods and Rocks had Ears / To rapture'; however, in Milton the rapture of the woods and rocks is not, as it is in Wordsworth, specifically a response to a song of sorrow.
50. On Wordsworth's 1807 ballad 'The Power of Music', see my essay 'Captivation and Liberty in Wordsworth's Poems on Music', *Romantic Circles, Praxis Series: 'Soundings of Things Done': The Poetry and Poetics of Sound in the Romantic Era*, http://romantic.arhu. umd.edu/praxis/soundings/potkay/potkay.html (accessed 4 April 2008). K. Fosso writes engagingly of Wordsworth himself as an Orpheus figure, the pastoral-elegist who mourns incessantly: see *Buried Communities: Wordsworth and the Bonds of Mourning* (Albany, NY: State University of New York Press, 2004), pp. 31–2, 164–9. My only qualification is to note that in Wordsworth, Orphic-mourning has or ought to produce joy in its auditors.
51. This line is not in Virgil, *Georgics*, IV.526–7.
52. W. Pater, 'The School of Giorgione', from *The Renaissance: Studies in Art and Poetry*, in *Selected Writings of Walter Pater*, ed. H. Bloom (New York: New American Library, 1974), p. 55.
53. [Anon.], 'William Wordsworth', *Southern Literary Messenger* 3:12 (December, 1837), pp. 705–11; p. 706.

54. [E. P. Whipple], Review of Wordsworth's *Complete Poetical Works, North American Review*, 59:125 (October 1844), pp. 352–84; p. 365.

55. Wordsworth claimed that each of his poems had 'a worthy *purpose*', in the 1800 Preface to *Lyrical Ballads* (1992 edn, p. 744).

56. A. Brooks, 'Wordsworth and Human Suffering: Notes on Two Early Poems', in *From Sensibility to Romanticism: Essays Presented to Frederick A. Pottle* (New York: Oxford University Press, 1965), pp. 373–87; pp. 385–6. Jonathan Wordsworth accepts Brooks's observation, without qualification, as explaining *The Ruined Cottage*: see *The Music of Humanity: A Critical Study of Wordsworth's Ruined Cottage* (New York: Harper & Row, 1969), pp. 146–7. On Stoic acquiescence in suffering, see also J. Averill, *Wordsworth and the Poetry of Human Suffering* (Ithaca, NY: Cornell University Press, 1980), pp. 128–35.

57. On Schopenhauer and Nietzsche, see my book *The Story of Joy from the Bible to Late Romanticism* (Cambridge: Cambridge University Press, 2007), ch. 8, 'Tragic Joy in Wagner, Nietzsche, and Yeats', pp. 196–8, 206–9.

58. Wordsworth, 'Prospectus to *The Recluse*', ll. 21–2.

59. See B. Graver, 'The Oratorical Pedlar', in D. H. Bialostosky and L. D. Needham (eds), *Rhetorical Traditions and British Romantic Literature* (Bloomington, IN: Indiana University Press, 1995), pp. 94–107.

60. Wordsworth, '*The Excursion*', III:844–50.

61. Ibid., VI.109–111.

62. Ibid., II.887–8.

63. J. Alleine, *An Alarme to Unconverted Sinners* (London: Nevil Simmons, 1673), p. 8.

64. Wordsworth, '*The Excursion*', IV.222–7.

65. Ibid., IV.634–5.

66. Ibid., VIII.596–7.

67. Wordsworth's verse becomes more euphemistic as well, as K. Goodman shows in her reading of *The Excursion*: for Goodman, the 'noise' of unwelcome sounds (e.g., the facts of death and frustration; a raven's knell), only half-silenced in the poem's euphemisms, threaten to engross the 'ear of Faith' praised by the Wanderer (*Georgic Modernity and British Romanticism: Poetry and the Mediation of History* (Cambridge: Cambridge University Press, 2004), pp. 137–9, p. 142).

68. Wordsworth, *The Excursion*, IV.10–2, IX.554–5.

69. Wordsworth, *The Borderers*, ll.2217–19.

70. W. Wordsworth, *Guilt and Sorrow*, ll. 655–7; cited from *William Wordsworth: The Poems*, vol. 1, pp. 118–41.

71. W. Wordworth, 'On the Power of Sound', ll. 97–106; cited from *William Wordsworth: The Poems*, vol. 2, pp. 664–71.

72. Ibid., ll.204–8.

73. On 'On the Power of Sound' in relation to the 'Ode', see J. Chandler, 'The Sound of Power', *Romantic Circles, Praxis Series: 'Soundings of Things Done': The Poetry and Poetics of Sound in the Romantic Era*, http://romantic.arhu.umd.edu/praxis/soundings/chandler/chandler.html (accessed 4 April 2008).

74. Wordsworth, 'On the Power of Sound', ll. 217–24.

75. E. Gaskell, *Mary Barton, A Tale of Manchester Life*, ed. S. Gill (Harmondsworth: Penguin, 1970), p. 422.

76. Ibid., p. 303.

WORKS CITED

Primary Sources

Alleine, J., *An Admonition to Unconverted Sinners* (London: Nevil Simmons, 1673).

[Anon.], Review of *A Treatise of Human Nature*, by D. Hume, *History of the Works of the Learned*, 2 (December 1739), p. 402.

—, 'William Wordsworth', *Southern Literary Messenger* 3:12 (December, 1837), pp. 705–11.

Aristotle, *Nichomachean Ethics*, trans. T. Irwin (Indianapolis, IN: Hackett Publishing Company, 1985).

Atterbury, F., *Sermons and Discourses on Several Subjects and Occasions*, 8th edn, 4 vols (London: L. Davis and C. Reymers, J. Rivington, W. Johnston, R. Baldwin, et al., 1766).

Austen, J., *Emma*, in *The Novels of Jane Austen*, ed. R. W. Chapman, 3rd edn, 5 vols (Oxford: Oxford University Press, 1988), vol. 4.

—, *Mansfield Park*, in *The Novels of Jane Austen*, ed. R. W. Chapman, 3rd edn, 5 vols (Oxford: Oxford University Press, 1988), vol. 3.

—, *Northanger Abbey*, in *The Novels of Jane Austen*, ed. R. W. Chapman, 3rd edn, 5 vols (Oxford: Oxford University Press, 1988), vol. 5.

—, *Persuasion*, in *The Novels of Jane Austen*, ed. R. W. Chapman, 3rd edn, 5 vols (Oxford: Oxford University Press, 1988), vol. 5.

—, *Pride and Prejudice*, in *The Novels of Jane Austen*, ed. R. W. Chapman, 3rd edn, 5 vols (Oxford: Oxford University Press, 1988), vol. 2.

—, *Sense and Sensibility*, in *The Novels of Jane Austen*, ed. R. W. Chapman, 3rd edn, 5 vols (Oxford: Oxford University Press, 1988), vol. 1.

Bailey, N., *An Universal Etymological English Dictionary*, 3rd edn (London: J. Darby. A. Bettesworth, F. Fayram, J. Pemberton, J. Hooke et al., 1726).

Barbauld, A. L., *The British Novelists*, in J. T. Boulton (ed.), *Johnson: The Critical Heritage* (London: Routledge & Kegan Paul, 1971), pp. 149–54.

Berkeley, G., *A Treatise Concerning the Principles of Human Understanding*, in *Works of George Berkeley*, ed. A. C. Fraser, 4 vols (Oxford: Clarendon Press, 1901), vol. 1, pp. 211–374.

—, *A New Theory of Vision*, in *Works of George Berkeley*, ed. A. C. Fraser, 4 vols (Oxford: Clarendon Press, 1901), vol. 1, pp. 93–210.

Bethune, J., *Essays and Dissertations on Various Subjects Relating to Human Life and Happiness*, 2 vols (Edinburgh: Kincaid and Bell, 1771).

Blair, H., *Sermons* (Edinburgh: William Creech, 1777).

Boswell, J., *Life of Johnson* (Oxford: Oxford University Press, 1980).

Burke, E., *A Philosophical Enquiry into the Origin of our Ideas of the Sublime and Beautiful* (London: R. and J. Dodsley, 1757).

Butler, J., Sermon 3, 'Upon Human Nature', from *Fifteen Sermons Preached at the Rolls Chapel* (1726), repr. in *The Analogy of Religion ... to which Are Added, Two Brief Dissertations ... and Fifteen Sermons* (London: George Bell and Sons, 1878), pp. 410–11.

Cicero, *De Finibus Bonorum et Malorum*, trans. H. Rackham (Cambridge, MA: Harvard University Press, 1983).

Clarke, H., *Practical Perspective* (London: for the author, 1781).

Coleridge, S. T., *Philosophical Lectures*, ed. K. Coburn (London: Pilot Press, 1949).

Condillac, E. B. de, *An Essay on the Origin of Human Knowledge*, trans. T. Nugent (London, 1756;. repr. Gainesville, FL: Scholars' Facsmilies & Reprints, 1971).

—, *Grammaire*, in *Œuvres philosophiques*, ed. G. le Rou (Paris: Presses Universitaires de France, 1947).

—, *Cours d'études pour l'instruction du prince de Parme*, in *Œuvres philosophiques*, ed. G. le Rou (Paris: Presses Universitaires de France, 1947).

Court de Gébelin, A., *Monde primtif, analysé et comparé avec le monde moderne*, 9 vols (Paris, 1771–83).

Crowe, W., *Lewesdon Hill: A Poem* (Oxford: Clarendon Press, 1788).

Cudworth, R., *True Intellectual System of the Universe* (London: Richard Royston, 1678).

de Charlevoix, P. F. X., *Histoire et Description Generale de la Nouvelle France* (Paris, 1744); trans. as *History and Description of New France*, 6 vols (Chicago, IL: Loyola University Press, 1870).

de Condillac, E. B., *An Essay on the Origin of Human Knowledge*, trans. T. Nugent (London, 1756;. repr. Gainesville, FL: Scholars' Facsmilies & Reprints, 1971).

—, *Grammaire*, in *Œuvres philosophiques*, ed. G. le Rou (Paris: Presses Universitaires de France, 1947).

Defoe, D., *Robinson Crusoe* (Oxford: Oxford University Press, 1972).

Descartes, R., *The Correspondence*, trans. J. Cottingham et al., in *The Philosophical Writings of Descartes*, 3 vols (Cambridge: Cambridge University Press, 1994–91), vol. 3.

Diderot, D., *Lettre sur les sourds et muets* (Paris: n.p., 1751).

—, *Manon Lescaut*, ed. Jean Sgard (Paris: G. F-Flammarion, 1995).

Ditton, H., *A Treatise of Perspective Demonstrative and Practical* (London: B. Tooke, 1712).

Dryden, J., *The Works of Virgil in English*, ed. W. Frost and V. Dearing, in *The Works of John Dryden*, 20 vols (Berkeley, CA: University of California Press, 1956–2002).

Ferguson, A., *Essay on the History of Civil Society* (Edinburgh: A. Millar et al., 1767).

Fielding, H., *The History of Tom Jones*, ed. F. Bowers (Middletown, CT: Wesleyan University Press, 1975).

—, *Amelia* (London: Penguin Books, 1987).

Gaskell, E., *Mary Barton, A Tale of Manchester Life*, ed. S. Gill (Harmondsworth: Penguin, 1970).

Gerard, A, *An Essay on Taste* (London: A. Millar, A. Kincaid and J. Bell, 1759).

Glover, P., *An Inquiry Concerning Virtue and Happiness* (London: John Whiston and Benj. White 1751).

Gott, S., *An Essay on the True Happiness of Man*, 2 vols (London: Thomas Underhill, 1650).

Halfpenny, W., *Perspective Made Easy, or a New Method of Practical Perspective* (London: John Oswald, 1731).

Hartley, D., *Observations on Man* (London: James Leake and Wm. Frederick, 1749).

Harris, J., *Three Treatises* (London: John Nourse and Paul Vaillant, 1744).

Hays, M., 'On Novel Writing', *Monthly Magazine* (September 1797), pp. 180–1.

—, *Memoirs of Emma Courtney* (Oxford: Oxford University Press, 1996).

Herder, J. G. V., *Reflections on the Philosophy of the History of Mankind*, ed. F. E. Manuel and trans. T. O. Churchill (Chicago, IL: University of Chicago Press, 1968).

Hobbes, T., *Leviathan* (New York: Collier Books, 1962).

—, *De Cive* (1651), ed. B. Gert (Indianapolis, IN: Hackett, 1991).

Holcroft, F., 'Conscience the Worst of Tortures' (*Monthly Magazine*, April 1798), repr. in W. Wordsworth and S. T. Coleridge, *Lyrical Ballads and Related Writings*, ed. W. Richey and D. Robinson (Boston, MA: Houghton Mifflin/Riverside, 2002), pp. 270–1.

Home, H., and L. Kames, *Sketches of the History of Man* (Edinburgh: n.p., 1774).

Hume, D., *A Treatise of Human Nature ... with an Appendix wherein Some Passages of the Foregoing Volumes Are Illustrated and Explain'd* (London: Thomas Longman, 1740).

—, *An Enquiry Concerning Human Understanding*, 'posthumous edition' (London: T. Cadell, 1777).

—, *A Treatise of Human Nature. A New Edition*, 2 vols (London: Thomas and Joseph Allman, 1817).

—, *A Treatise of Human Nature*, ed. T. H. Green and T. H. Grose (London: Longmans, 1874).

—, *A Treatise of Human Nature*, ed. T. H. Green and T. H. Grose, 2nd edn (London: Longmans, 1886)

—, *Letters of David Hume to William Strahan*, ed. B. Hill (Oxford: Clarendon Press, 1888).

—, *A Treatise of Human Nature*, ed. L. A. Selby-Bigge (Oxford: Clarendon Press, 1888).

—, *An Enquiry Concerning Human Understanding*, ed. L. A. Selby-Bigge (Oxford: Clarendon Press, 1902).

—, *The Letters of David Hume*, ed. J. Y. T. Grieg, 2 vols (Oxford: Clarendon Press, 1932).

—, *Dialogues Concerning Natural Religion*, ed. N. K. Smith (Indianapolis, IN, and New York: Bobbs-Merrill, 1947).

—, *An Enquiry Concerning Human Understanding. Philosophical Works*, ed. T. H. Green and T. H. Gross (Aalen: Scientia, 1964).

—, *A Treatise of Human Nature*, ed. L. A. Selby-Bigge (Oxford: Clarendon Press, 1964).

—, *A Treatise of Human Nature*, ed. L. A. Selby-Bigge and P. H. Nidditch, 2nd edn (Oxford: Clarendon Press, 1978).

—, *An Enquiry Concerning the Principles of Morals* (Indianapolis, IN: Hackett Publishing, 1983).

—, 'Of Essay Writing', in *Essays: Moral, Political, and Literary*, ed. E. F. Miller (Indianapolis, IN: Liberty Classics, 1985), pp. 533–7.

—, 'Idea of a Perfect Commonwealth', in, *Essays: Moral, Political, and Literary*, ed. E. F. Miller, rev. edn (Indianapolis, IN: Liberty Classics, 1987), pp. 512–29.

—, 'Of Commerce', in *Essays: Moral, Political, and Literary*, ed. E. F. Miller, rev. edn (Indianapolis, IN: Liberty Classics, 1987), pp. 253–67.

—, 'Of Eloquence', in *Essays: Moral, Political, and Literary*, ed. E. F. Miller, rev. edn (Indianapolis, IN: Liberty Classics, 1987), pp. 97–110.

—, 'Of the Dignity or Meanness of Human Nature', in E. F. Miller (ed.), *Essays: Moral, Political, and Literary*, rev. edn (Indianapolis, IN: Liberty Classics, 1987), pp. 80–6.

—, 'Of National Characters', in *Essays: Moral, Political, and Literary*, ed. E. F. Miller, rev. edn (Indianapolis, IN: Liberty Classics, 1987), pp. 197–215.

—, 'Of the Parties of Great Britain', in *Essays: Moral, Political, and Literary*, ed. E. F. Miller, rev. edn (Indianapolis, IN: Liberty Classics, 1987), pp. 64–72.

—, 'Of the Rise and Progress of the Arts and Sciences', in *Essays: Moral, Political, and Literary*, ed. E. F. Miller, rev. edn (Indianapolis, IN: Liberty Classics, 1987), pp. 111–37.

—, 'Of the Standard of Taste', in *Essays: Moral, Political, and Literary*, ed. E. F. Miller, rev. edn (Indianapolis, IN: Liberty Classics, 1987), pp. 226–49.

—, 'Of the Study of History', in E. F. Miller (ed.), *Essays: Moral, Political and Literary*, rev. edn (Indianapolis, IN: Liberty Classics, 1987), pp. 563–8.

—, *Principal Writings on Religion, Including Dialogues Concerning Natural Religion and The Natural History of Religion*, ed. J. C. A. Gaskin (Oxford: Oxford University Press, 1993).

—, *An Enquiry Concerning Human Understanding: A Critical Edition*, ed. T. L. Beauchamp (Oxford: Oxford University Press, 2000).

—, *A Treatise of Human Nature*, ed. D. F. Norton and M. J. Norton (Oxford: Oxford University Press, 2000).

Hutcheson, F., *An Inquiry into the Original of our Ideas of Beauty and Virtue in Two Treatises*, ed. W. Leidhold (Indianapolis, IN: Liberty Fund, 2004).

Johnson, S., *A Dictionary of the English Language*, 2 vols (London: J. and P. Knapton, 1755).

—, *A Dictionary of the English Language*, 2 vols (London: W. Strahan et al., 1778).

—, *Rambler*, 4 (31 March 1750), in *Essays from the Rambler, Adventurer, and Idler*, ed. W. J. Bate (New Haven, CT: Yale University Press, 1968).

Jones, R., *Hieroglyphic: or, A Grammatical Introduction to an Universal Hieroglyphic Language* (London: John Hughs, 1768).

Kant, I., *Foundations of the Metaphysics of Morals*, trans. L. W. Beck (New York: Macmillan, 1990).

—, *Prolegomena to Any Future Metaphysics*, trans. P. G. Lucas and G. Zöller (Oxford: Oxford University Press, 2004).

Knox, V., *Essays Moral and Literary*, 2 vols (London: Charles Dilly, 1795).

Lafitau, J. F., *Moeurs des Sauvages Ameriquains, Comparees aux Moeurs des Premiers Temps* (Paris, 1724), trans. and ed. W. N. Fenton and E. L. Moore as *Customs of the American Indians Compared with the Customs of Primitive Times*, 2 vols (Toronto, ON: Champlain Society, 1974).

Locke, J., *An Essay Concerning Human Understanding*, 1st edn (London: T. Basset, 1690).

—, *An Essay Concerning Human Understanding*, 2nd edn (London: Awnsham and John Churchil; and Samuel Manship, 1694).

—, *An Essay Concerning Human Understanding*, 5th edn (London: Awnsham and John Churchil; and Samuel Manship, 1706).

—, *Some Familiar Letters Between Mr. Locke and His Friends* (London: A. and J. Churchill, 1708).

—, *Two Treatises of Government*, rev. edn (New York: Mentor, 1965).

—, *An Essay Concerning Human Understanding*, ed. P. H. Nidditch (Oxford: Clarendon Press, 1975).

—, *The Correspondence of John Locke*, ed. E. S. De Beer, 7 vols (Oxford: Clarendon, 1979).

Longinus, D., *Dionysius Longinus on the Sublime*, trans. W. Smith (London: W. Innys and R. Manby, 1739).

Lucas, R., *An Enquiry after Happiness* (London: S. Smith and B. Walford, 1697).

Mandeville, B., *The Fable of the Bees: or, Private Vices, Publick Benefits* and *The Fable of the Bees, Part II*, ed. F. B. Kaye, 2 vols (Oxford: Clarendon Press, 1924).

—, *The Fable of the Bees*, ed. F. B. Kaye, 2 vols (Indianapolis, IN: Liberty Classics, 1988).

Marivaux, P., *Pharsamon, ou les Nouvelles Folies romanesques. Oeuvres de jeunesse*, intro. F. Deloffre (Paris: Gallimard, 1972).

—, *Pharsamond, or The New Knight Errant*, trans. Mr Henry, repr. of the1750 edn (New York: Garland, 1974).

Masham, L. D., *A Discourse Concerning the Love of God* (London: Awnsham and John Churchil, 1696).

Maupertuis, P. L. M. de, *Réflexions philosophiques sur l'origine des langues et la signification des mots*, in *Œuvres de Maupertuis*, 2nd edn, 4 vols (Lyons: Jean Marie Bruyset, 1768), vol. 1, pp. 259–309.

Millar, J., *The Origin of the Distinction of Ranks* (London: John Murray, 1771).

—, *The Origin of the Distinction of Ranks*, 4th edn (Edinburgh: Blackwood, 1816).

Montaigne, M. de, *The Complete Essays of Montaigne*, trans. D. M. Frame (Stanford, CA: Stanford University Press, 1958).

—, *The Essays of Michael Seigneur de Montaigne, Translated into English*, 7th rev. edn, 3 vols (London: S. and E. Ballard, J. Clarke, D. Browne, C. Hitch and L. Hawes et al., 1759).

More, H., *The Immortality of the Soul* (London: William Morden, 1659).

Newman, T., *Sermons on Happiness* (London: J. Noon; J. Buckland; T. Field; and C. Henderson, 1760).

Norris, J., *An Idea Of Happiness*, 2nd edn (London: James Norris, 1684).

—, *The Theory and Regulation of Love: A Moral Essay* (Oxford, 1688).

—, *Cursory Reflections on a Book Call'd An Essay Concerning Human Understanding* (London, 1690).

Priestley, J., *An Examination of Dr. Reid's Inquiry into the Human Mind on the Principles of Common Sense, Dr. Beattie's Essay on the Nature and Immutability of Truth, and Dr. Oswald's Appeal to Common Sense in Behalf of Religion* (London: J. Johnson, 1774).

Puttenham, G., *The Arte of English Poesie*, ed. G. D. Willcock and A. Walker (Cambridge: Cambridge University Press, 1936).

Reid, T., 'An Essay on Quantity, Occasioned by Reading a Treatise in which Simple and Compound Ratio's Are Applied to Virtue and Merit', *Philosophical Transactions*, 45 (1748), pp. 505–20.

—, *An Inquiry into the Human Mind, on the Principles of Common Sense* (London: A. Millar; Edinburgh: A. Kincaid & J. Bell, 1764).

—, *Essays on the Intellectual Powers of Man* (London: G. G. J. and J. Robinson, 1785).

—, *Essays on the Active Powers of Man* (London: G. G. J. and J. Robinson, 1788).

—, *Philosophical Orations of Thomas Reid: Delivered at Graduation Ceremonies at King's College, Aberdeen in 1753, 1756, 1759, 1762*, trans. S. Darcus Sullivan, ed. D. D. Todd (Carbondale, IL: Southern Illinois University Press, 1989).

—, 'An Essay by Thomas Reid on the Conception of Power', *Philosophical Quarterly*, 51 (2001), pp. 1–12.

—, *The Correspondence of Thomas Reid*, ed. P. Wood (University Park, PA: Pennsylvania State University Press, 2002).

Richardson, S., *Pamela, or Virtue Rewarded* (London: C. Rivington, 1740).

—, *Correspondence of Samuel Richardson*, ed. L. Barbauld, 6 vols (London: R. Phillips, 1804).

—, *Pamela; or Virtue Rewarded* (Oxford: Oxford University Press, 2001).

—, *Selected Correspondence of Samuel Richardson*, ed. J. Carroll (Oxford: Oxford University Press, 1964).

Robertson, W., *History of the Reign of the Emperor Charles V* (London: W. Strahan; T. Cadell; Edinburgh: J. Balfour, 1769).

Rousseau, J. J., *Emilius and Sophia; or, The Solitaries*, anonymous translation (London: H. Baldwin, 1783).

—, *The Confessions*, trans. J. M. Cohen (New York: Penguin, 1953).

—, *Émile et Sophie*, ed. B. Gagnebin and M. Raymond, in in J. J. Rousseau, *Oeuvres complètes* 5 vols (Paris: Gallimard, 1959–95), vol. 4.

—, *Essay on the Origin of Languages*, in *On the Origin of Language*, trans. J. H. Moran and A. Gode (Chicago, IL, and London: University of Chicago Press, 1966).

—, *Emile, or On Education*, trans. A. Bloom (New York: Basic Books, 1979).

—, *A Discourse on Inequality*, trans. M. Cranston (Harmondsworth: Penguin, 1984).

—, *Discourse on the Origin and the Foundations of Inequality among Men* (*Second Discourse*), in *The First and Second Discourses*, ed. V. Gourevitch (New York: Harper and Row, 1986).

—, *On the Social Contract*, in *The Basic Political Writings*, trans, D. A. Cress (Indianapolis, IN: Hackett, 1987), pp. 141–227.

—, *Letter to d'Alembert*, trans. A. Bloom et al., in *The Collected Writings of Rousseau*, 12 vols (Hanover, NH: University Press of New England, 1990–), vol. 10.

—, 'On the Social Contract, or Essay about the Form of the Republic' (commonly called the 'Geneva Manuscript'), trans. J. R. Bush, R. D. Masters and C. Kelly, in *The Collected Writings of Rousseau*, 12 vols (Hanover, NH: University Press of New England, 1990–), vol. 4.

—, *Discourse on the Arts and Sciences*, in *The Discourse and Other Early Political Writings*, trans. V. Gourevitch (Cambridge: Cambridge University Press, 1997), pp. 3–28.

—, *Discourse on the Origins of Inequality*, in *The Discourse and Other Early Political Writings*, trans. V. Gourevitch (Cambridge: Cambridge University Press, 1997), pp. 113–222.

—, *Julie, or the New Heloise*, trans. P. Stewart and J. Vaché (Hanover, NH: University Press of New England, 1997).

Shaftesbury, A. A. Cooper, Earl of, *Characteristics of Men, Manners, Opinions, Times*, ed. L. E. Klein (Cambridge and New York: Cambridge University Press, 1999).

Sherlock, W., *A Practical Discourse Concerning a Future Judgment* (London: W. Rogers, 1692).

Smith, A., *Considerations Concerning the First Formation of Languages* (Edinburgh, 1767).

—, *Correspondence of Adam Smith*, ed. E. C. Mossner and I. Simpson Ross, in *The Glasgow Edition of the Works and Correspondence of Adam Smith*, 6 vols (Oxford: Oxford University Press, 1976–83), vol. 6.

—, *Essays on Philosophical Subjects*, ed. W. P. D. Wightman, J. C. Bryce and I. S. Ross, in *The Glasgow Edition of the Works and Correspondence of Adam Smith*, 6 vols (Oxford: Clarendon Press, 1976–83), vol. 3.

—, *An Inquiry into the Nature and Causes of the Wealth of Nations*, ed. R. H. Campbell and A.S. Skinner, in *The Glasgow Edition of the Works and Correspondence of Adam Smith*, 6 vols (Oxford: Oxford University Press, 1976–83), vol. 2.

—, *Lectures on Rhetoric and Belles Lettres*, ed. J. C. Bryce, in *The Glasgow Edition of the Works and Correspondence of Adam Smith*, 6 vols (Oxford: Oxford University Press, 1976–83), vol. 4.

—, *Lectures on Jurisprudence*, ed. R. L. Meek, D. D. Raphael and P. G. Stein, in *The Glasgow Edition of the Works and Correspondence of Adam Smith*, 6 vols (Oxford: Oxford University Press, 1976–83), vol. 5.

—, *The Theory of Moral Sentiments*, ed. D. D. Raphael and A. L. Macfie, in *The Glasgow Edition of the Works and Correspondence of Adam Smith*, 6 vols (Oxford: Oxford University Press, 1976–83), vol. 1.

Sterne, L., *The Life and Opinions of Tristram Shandy, Gentleman* (1759–67), ed. M. New and J. New, in *The Florida Edition of the Works of Laurence Sterne* (Gainesville, FL: University Presses of Florida, 1978–84), vols 1–3.

Stewart, D., *An Account of the Life and Writings of Adam Smith*, in A. Smith, *Essays on Philosophical Subjects*, ed. W. P. D. Wightman, J. C. Bryce and I. S. Ross, in *The Glasgow Edition of the Works and Correspondence of Adam Smith*, 6 vols (Oxford: Clarendon Press, 1976–83), vol. 3.

Taylor, B., *Principles in Linear Perspective* (London: R. Knaplock, 1715).

Thomson, J., 'Spring', in *The Seasons* and *Castle of Indolence*, ed. J. Sambrook (Oxford: Clarendon Press, 1987), p. 20.

Twining, T., *Aristotle's Treatise of Poetry, Translated ... With Notes ... and Two Dissertations, on Poetical, and Musical, Imitation* (London: Payne and son, 1789).

Van Sant, A. J., 'A Dictionary of Morality: Reading for the Sentiment', in F. Stuber (ed.), *Samuel Richardson's Published Commentary on Clarissa, 1747–65*, 3 vols (London: Pickering & Chatto, 1998), vol. 3: *A Collection of the Moral and Instructive Sentiments*, pp. 411–37.

Vico, G., *La scienza nuova* (Naples, 1725–44).

Virgil, *Eclogues, Georgics, Aeneid I–VI*, ed. H. R. Fairclough (Cambridge, MA: Harvard University Press, 1916).

Voltaire, *Philosophical Dictionary*, ed. and trans. T. Besterman (London: Penguin Books, 1972).

Wachter, J., *Naturæ et scripturæ concordia* (Lipsiæ et Hafniæ, 1752).

Warburton, W., *The Divine Legation of Moses*, 4 vols (London: Fletcher Gyles, 1738–41).

Warton, J., *Odes on Various Subjects* (London: J. Dodsley, 1746).

—, *An Essay on the Genius and Writings of Pope*, 2 vols (London: J. Dodsley, 1782).

Whipple, E. P., Unsigned Review of Wordsworth's *Complete Poetical Works*, *North American Review*, 59:125 (October 1844), pp. 352–84.

Wilberforce, W., *A Practical View of the Prevailing Religious System of Professed Christians in the Higher and Middle Classes of this Country, contrasted with Real Christianity*, 2nd edn (London: T. Cadell, jun. and W. Davies, 1797).

Wollstonecraft, M., *Vindication of the Rights of Woman* (1792), in *The Works of Mary Woll-stonecraft*, ed. J. Todd and M. Butler, 7 vols (New York: New York University Press, 1989), vol. 5.

Wordsworth, W., *The Borderers* (1797–9), ed. R. Osborn (Ithaca, NY: Cornell University Press, 1982).

—, *Home at Grasmere: Part First, Book First of 'The Recluse'*, ed. B. Darlington (Ithaca, NY: Cornell University Press, 1977).

—, *The Prelude 1799, 1805, 1850*, ed. J. Wordsworth, M. H. Abrams and S. Gill (New York: Norton, 1979).

—, *The Ruined Cottage* and *The Pedlar*, ed. J. Butler (Ithaca, NY: Cornell University Press, 1979).

—, *The Excursion*, in William *Wordsworth: The Poems*, ed. J. O. Hayden, 2 vols (New Haven, CT: Yale University Press, 1981), vol. 2, pp. 35–289.

—, *Guilt and Sorrow*, in William *Wordsworth: The Poems*, ed. J. O. Hayden, 2 vols (New Haven, CT: Yale University Press, 1981).

—, 'O Nightingale!', in *Poems, in Two Volumes, and Other Poems, 1800–1807*, ed. J. Curtis (Ithaca, NY: Cornell University Press, 1983).

—, *An Evening Walk*, ed. J. Averill (Ithaca, NY: Cornell University Press, 1984).

—, *Descriptive Sketches*, ed. E. Birdsall (Ithaca, NY: Cornell University Press, 1984).

—, *Lyrical Ballads, and Other Poems, 1797–1800*, ed. J. Butler and K. Green (Ithaca, NY: Cornell University Press, 1992).

—, *Georgics Translations*, in *Early Poems and Fragments, 1785–1797*, ed. C. Landon and J. Curtis (Ithaca, NY: Cornell University Press, 1997).

—, 'Steamboat, Viaducts, and Railways', in G. Jackson (ed.), *Sonnet Series and Itinerary Poems 1820–1845* (Ithaca, NY: Cornell University Press, 2004), p. 604.

Secondary Sources

Aarsleff, H., *From Locke to Saussure: Essays on the Study of Language and Intellectual History* (Minneapolis, MN: University of Minnesota Press, 1982).

Affeldt, S. G., 'The Force of Freedom: Rousseau on Forcing to be Free', *Political Theory*, 27:3 (1999), pp. 299–333.

Altman, J., '"Preposterous Conclusions": Eros, *Enargeia*, and the Composition of *Othello*', *Representations*, 18 (1987), pp. 129–57.

Anderson, B., *Imagined Communities: Reflections on the Origin and Spread of Nationalism*, rev. edn (London: Verso, 1991).

Annas, J., *The Morality of Happiness* (Oxford: Oxford University Press, 1993).

Armstrong, I., *The Radical Aesthetic* (Oxford: Blackwell, 2000).

Averill, J., *Wordsworth and the Poetry of Human Suffering* (Ithaca, NY: Cornell University Press, 1980).

Averill J. R., and T. A. More, 'Happiness', in M. Lewis and J. M. Haviland-Jones (eds), *Handbook of Emotions*, 2nd edn (New York: Guilford Press, 2004), pp. 666–76.

Ayers, M., *Locke: Epistemology and Ontology*, 2 vols (New York: Routledge, 1991).

Baier, A. C., 'Hume on Heaps and Bundles', *American Philosophical Quarterly*, 16:4 (1979), pp. 285–95.

—, *A Progress of Sentiments: Reflections on Hume's Treatise* (Cambridge, MA: Harvard University Press, 1991).

Bal, M., *Narratology: Introduction to the Theory of Narrative*, 2nd edn (Toronto, ON: University of Toronto Press, 1997).

Barker-Benfield, G. J., *The Culture of Sensibility: Sex and Society in Eighteenth-Century Britain* (Chicago, IL: University of Chicago Press, 1992).

Barnouw, J., 'Peirce and Derrida: "Natural Signs" Empiricism versus "Originary Trace" Deconstruction', *Poetics Today*, 7 (1986), pp. 73–94.

—, 'Aesthetics', in J. Black and R. Porter (eds), *Dictionary of Eighteenth-Century History* (London: Penguin, 1996), p. 10.

Barrell, J., *English Literature in History 1730–80: An Equal, Wide Survey* (London: Hutchinson, 1983).

Benedict, B., *Curiosity: A Cultural History of Early Modern Inquiry* (Chicago, IL: University of Chicago Press, 2001).

Benhabib, S., *Situating the Self: Gender, Community and Postmodernism in Contemporary Ethics* (New York: Routledge, 1992).

Benjamin, W., 'Theses on the Philosophy of History', in *Illuminations*, ed. H. Arendt, trans. H. Zohn (New York: Schocken, 1969), pp. 253–64.

Bennington, G., 'Derrida's "Eighteenth Century"', *Eighteenth-Century Studies*, 40:3 (2007), pp. 381–93.

Benso, S., *The Face of Things: A Different Side of Ethics* (Albany, NY: State University of New York Press, 2000).

Besse, G., *Jean-Jacques Rousseau: L'apprentissage de l'humanité* (Paris: Messidor, 1988).

Blackburn, S., 'Thought Experiment', in *The Oxford Dictionary of Philosophy* (Oxford: Oxford University Press, 1994), p. 377.

Bolter, J., *Writing Space: The Computer, Hypertext, and the History of Writing* (Hillsdale, NJ: Lawrence Erlbaum Associates, 1991).

Booth, W., 'The Self-Conscious Narrator in Comic Fiction before *Tristram Shandy*', *PMLA*, 67:2 (1952), pp. 163–85.

Bolter, J. D., and R. Grusin, *Remediation: Understanding New Media* (Cambridge: MIT Press, 2002).

Box, M. A., *The Suasive Art of David Hume* (Princeton, NJ: Princeton University Press, 1990).

Bradshaw, L., 'Rousseau on Civic Virtue, Male Autonomy and the Construction of the Divided Female', in L. Lange (ed.), *Feminist Interpretations of Jean-Jacques Rousseau* (Philadelphia, PA: Pennsylvania State University Press, 2002), pp. 65–88.

Brandt, R., 'The Beginnings of Hume's Philosophy', in G. P. Morice (ed.), *David Hume: Bicentenary Papers* (Edinburgh: Edinburgh University Press, 1977), pp. 117–27.

Bray, A., 'Homosexuality and the Signs of Male Friendship in Elizabethan England', in J. Goldberg (ed.), *Queering the Renaissance* (Durham, NC: Duke University Press, 1993), pp. 40–61.

Brett, N., 'Hume's Causal Account of the Self', *Man and Nature*, 9 (1990), pp. 23–32.

Broadie, A., 'George Campbell, Thomas Reid, and Universals of Language', in P. Wood (ed.), *The Scottish Enlightenment: Essays in Reinterpretation* (Rochester, NY: University of Rochester Press, 2000), pp. 351–71.

Bromwich, D., *Disowned by Memory: Wordsworth's Poetry of the 1790s* (Chicago, IL: University of Chicago Press, 1998).

Brooks, C., 'Wordsworth and Human Suffering: Notes on Two Early Poems', in *From Sensibility to Romanticism: Essays Presented to Frederick A. Pottle* (New York: Oxford University Press, 1965), pp. 373–87.

Brown, L., *Fables of Modernity: Literature and Culture in the English Eighteenth Century* (Ithaca, NY: Cornell University Press, 2001).

Brown, V., *Adam Smith's Discourse: Canonicity, Commerce and Conscience* (London: Routledge, 1994).

Budd, A., 'Why Clarissa Must Die: Richardson's Tragedy and Editorial Heroism', *Eighteenth Century Life*, 31 (August 2007), pp. 1–28.

Burgelin, P. 'L'éducation de Sophie', *Annales de la Société Jean-Jacques-Rousseau*, 35 (1959–62), pp. 113–30.

Butler, J., *The Psychic Life of Power* (Stanford, CA: Stanford University Press, 1997).

Candler Hayes, J., 'Unconditional Translation: Derrida's Enlightenment-To-Come', *Eighteenth-Century Studies*, 40 (2007), pp. 443–55.

Capaldi, N., *David Hume* (Boston, MA: Twayne, 1975)

—, 'The Dogmatic Slumber of Hume Scholarship', *Hume Studies*, 18:2 (1992), pp. 117–35.

Carnochan, W. B., 'The Comic Plot of Hume's "Dialogues"', *Modern Philology*, 85 (May 1988), pp. 514–22.

Caygill, H., *Art of Judgment* (Oxford: Blackwell, 1989).

Chandler, J., *England in 1819: The Politics of Literary Culture and the Case of Romantic Historicism* (Chicago, IL: University of Chicago Press, 1998).

—, 'The Sound of Power', *Romantic Circles, Praxis Series: 'Soundings of Things Done'. The Poetry and Poetics of Sound in the Romantic Era*, http://romantic.arhu.umd.edu/praxis/soundings/chandler/chandler.html (accessed 4 April 2008).

Chappel, V., 'Locke on Freedom of the Will', in G. A. J. Rogers (ed.), *Locke's Philosophy: Content and Context* (Oxford: Clarendon Press, 1994), pp. 101–21.

Christensen, J., *Practicing Enlightenment: Hume and the Formation of a Literary Career* (Madison, WI: University of Wisconsin Press, 1987).

Chukwudi Eze, E., Introduction, in E. Chukwudi Eze (ed.), *Race and the Enlightenment* (Oxford: Blackwell, 1997), pp. 4–5.

Clark, A., *Natural-Born Cyborgs: Minds, Technologies, and the Future of Human Intelligence* (Oxford: Oxford University Press, 2003).

Cohen, R., 'On the Interrelations of Eighteenth Century Literary Forms', in P. Harth (ed.), *New Approaches to Eighteenth-Century Literature* (New York: Columbia University Press, 1974), pp. 33–78.

Collingwood, R. G., *The Idea of History* (New York: Oxford University Press, 1956).

Connon, R. W., Letter, in *Times Literary Supplement* (4 April 1975), p. 376.

—, 'Some MS Corrections by Hume in the Third Volume of his *Treatise of Human Nature*', *Long Room*, 11 (1975), pp. 14–22.

—, 'The Textual and Philosophical Significance of Hume's MS Alterations to *Treatise* III', in G. P. Morice (ed.), *David Hume: Bicentenary Papers* (Edinburgh: Edinburgh University Press, 1977), pp. 186–204.

Copenhaver, R., 'A Realism for Reid: Mediated But Direct', *British Journal for the History of Philosophy*, 12 (2004), pp. 61–74.

Cragg, G., *Reason and Authority in the Eighteenth Century* (Cambridge: Cambridge University Press, 1964).

Cranston, M., *John Locke, a Biography* (London: Longmans, 1957).

Cross, F. L., and E. A. Livingstone (eds), *The Oxford Dictionary of the Christian Church*, 2nd rev. edn (Oxford: Oxford University Press, 1983).

Dadlez, E., 'Knowing Better: The Epistemic Underpinnings of Moral Criticism of Fiction', *Southwest Philosophy Review*, 21:1 (2005), pp. 35–44.

—, 'Spectacularly Bad: Hume and Aristotle on Tragic Spectacle', *Journal of Aesthetics and Art Criticism*, 63:4 (2005), pp. 351–8.

Daigaku, T., *David Hume and the [sic] Eighteenth Century British Thought* (Tokyo: Chuo University, n.d.).

Damrosch, Jr., L., 'Johnson's *Rasselas*: Limits of Wisdom, Limits of Art', in D. L. Patey and T. Keegan (eds), *Augustan Studies; Essays in Honour of Irvin Ehrenpreis* (Newark, DE: University of Delaware Press, 1985), pp. 205–14.

—, *Fictions of Reality in the Age of Hume and Johnson* (Madison, WI: University of Wisconsin Press, 1989).

Darnwall, S., *The British Moralists and the Internal 'Ought'* (Cambridge: Cambridge University Press, 1995).

Davidson, E., 'Toward an Integrated Chronology for *Tristram Shandy*', *ELN*, 29:4 (1992), pp. 48–56.

Davis, P., 'Extraordinarily Ordinary: The Life of Samuel Johnson', in G. Clingham (ed.), *The Cambridge Companion to Samuel Johnson* (Cambridge: Cambridge University Press, 1997), pp. 4–17.

de Man, P., 'The Epistemology of Metaphor', *Critical Inquiry*, 5:1 (1978), pp. 13–30.

—, 'The Epistemology of Metaphor', in S. Sacks (ed.), *On Metaphor* (Chicago, IL: Chicago University Press, 1981), pp. 11–28.

Deleuze, G., *Empiricism and Subjectivity: An Essay on Hume's Theory of Human Nature*, trans. C. V. Boundas (New York: Columbia University Press, 1991).

Derrida, J., *Speech and Phenomena and the Essay on Husserl's Theory of Signs*, trans. D. B. Allison (Evanston, IL: Northwestern University Press, 1973).

—, *Of Grammatology*, trans. G. C. Spivak (London and Baltimore, MD: Johns Hopkins University Press, 1974).

—, 'Violence and Metaphysics: An Essay on the Thought of Emmanuel Levinas', in *Writing and Difference*, trans. A. Bass (London, Melbourne and Henley: Routledge & Kegan Paul, 1978), pp. 79–153.

—, 'Scribble (Writing-Power)', trans. C. Plotkin, *Yale French Studies*, 58 (1979), pp. 116–47.

—, *The Archeology of the Frivolous*, trans. J. P. Leavey, Jr (Lincoln, NE, and London: University of Nebraska Press, 1980).

—, 'La loi du genre', *Glyph*, 7 (1980), pp. 176–201.

—, 'Signature, Event, Context', in *Margins of Philosophy*, ed. A. Bass (Chicago, IL: University of Chicago Press, 1982), pp. 308–30.

Dick, A. J., 'Poverty, Charity, Poetry: The Unproductive Labors of "The Old Cumberland Beggar"', *Studies in Romanticism*, 39 (2000), pp. 365–96.

Dickason, O., *The Myth of the Savage* (Edmonton, AB: University of Alberta Press, 1984).

Eaves, T. C. D., and B. T. Kimpel, *Samuel Richardson: A Biography* (Oxford: Oxford University Press, 1971).

Esterhammer, A., *The Romantic Performative: Language and Action in British and German Romanticism* (Stanford, CA: Stanford University Press, 2000).

Formigari, L., *Signs, Science and Politics: Philosophies of Language in Europe 1700–1830*, trans. W. Dodd (Amsterdam and Philadelphia, PA: John Benjamins, 1993).

Fosso, K., *Buried Communities: Wordsworth and the Bonds of Mourning* (Albany, NY: State University of New York Press, 2004).

Foucault, M., *The Order of Things* (London: Tavistock Publications, 1970).

—, 'What is Critique?', in *What is Enlightenment?*, ed. S. Schmidt (Berkeley, CA: University of California Press, 1995), pp. 182–204.

Freud, S., 'Mourning and Melancholia', in *The Standard Edition of the Complete Psychological Works of Sigmund Freud*, ed. and trans. J. Strachey et al., 24 vols (London: Hogarth, 1953–74), vol. 14.

Gadamer, H.-G., *Truth and Method*, trans. J. Weinsheimer and D. G. Marshall (New York: Crossroad, 1989).

Gallagher, C., *Nobody's Story: The Vanishing Acts of Women Writers in the Marketplace 1670–1820* (Oxford: Clarendon Press, 1994).

Gallagher, C., and S. Greenblatt. *Practicing New Historicism* (Chicago, IL: University of Chicago Press, 2000).

Gaskin, J. C. A., *Hume's Philosophy of Religion* (New York: Barnes & Noble, 1978).

Giddens, A., *The Consequences of Modernity* (Stanford, CA: Stanford University Press, 1990).

Gigante, D., *Taste: A Literary History* (New Haven, CT: Yale University Press, 2005).

Goldschmidt, V., *Anthropologie et politique: Les principes du système de Rousseau* (Paris: Librairie Philosophique J. Vrin, 1974).

Goldsmith, E., *Exclusive Conversations: The Art of Interaction in Seventeenth-Century France* (Philadelphia, PA University of Philadelphia Press, 1989).

Goodman, K., *Georgic Modernity and British Romanticism: Poetry and the Mediation of History* (Cambridge: Cambridge University Press, 2004).

Goring, P., *The Rhetoric of Sensibility in Eighteenth-Century Culture* (Cambridge: Cambridge University Press, 2004).

Gourevitch, V., 'Rousseau's Pure State of Nature', *Interpretation*, 16 (1988) pp. 23–59.

Graver, B., 'The Oratorical Pedlar', in D. H. Bialostosky and L. D. Needham (eds), *Rhetorical Traditions and British Romantic Literature* (Bloomington, IN: Indiana University Press, 1995), pp. 94–107.

Greene, J., 'Hors D'Œuvre', *Eighteenth-Century Studies*, 40 (2007), pp. 367–79.

Guillory, J., *Cultural Capital: The Problem of Literary Canon Formation* (Chicago, IL Chicago University Press, 1993).

Habermas, J., *The Philosophical Discourse of Modernity* (Cambridge, MA: MIT Press, 1987).

—, *The Structural Transformation of the Public Sphere*, trans. T. Burger (Cambridge: MIT Press, 1989).

Haines, S., 'Deepening the Self: The Language of Ethics and the Language of Literature', in J. Adamson, R. Freadman and D. Parker (eds), *Renegotiating Ethics in Literature, Philosophy, and Theory* (Cambridge: Cambridge University Press, 1998), pp. 21–38.

Harkin, M., 'Natives and Nostalgia: The Problem of the North American Savage in Adam Smith's Historiography', *Scottish Studies Review*, 3:1 (2002), pp. 25–8.

Hartman, G., *Wordsworth's Poetry 1787–1814* (New Haven, CT: Yale University Press, 1971).

Hartwig, R. J., '*Pharsamon* and *Joseph Andrews*', *Texas Studies in Literature and Language*, 14 (1972), pp. 45–52.

Hayles, N. K., 'Making the Cut: The Interplay of Narrative and System, or What Systems Theory Can't See', *Cultural Critique*, 30 (1995), pp. 71–100.

—, 'The Complexities of Seriation', *PMLA*, 117:1 (2002), pp. 117–21.

—, *Writing Machines* (Cambridge, MA: MIT Press, 2002).

—, 'Translating Media: Why We Should Rethink Textuality', *Yale Journal of Criticism*, 16:2 (2003), pp. 263–90.

—, 'Traumas of Code', *Critical Inquiry*, 33:1 (2006), pp. 136–57.

Hertz, N., 'A Reading of Longinus', in *The End of the Line: Essays on Psychoanalysis and the Sublime* (New York: Columbia University Press, 1985), pp. 1–20.

Horkheimer, M., and T. W. Adorno, *The Dialectic of Enlightenment*, trans. J. Cumming (New York: Continuum, 1972).

Houston, J., 'Reading Reid', in J. Houston (ed.), *Thomas Reid: Context, Influence, and Significance* (Edinburgh: Dunedin Academic Press, 2004), pp. 1–7.

Hudson, N., 'Three Steps to Perfection: *Rasselas* and the Philosophy of Richard Hooker', *Eighteenth-Century Life*, 14:3 (November 1990), pp. 29–39.

—, *Writing and European Thought, 1600–1830* (Cambridge: Cambridge University Press, 1994).

—, 'John Locke and the Tradition of Nominalism', in H. Keiper, C. Bode and R. J. Utz (eds), *Nominalism and Literary Discourse: New Perspectives* (Amsterdam: Rodopi, 1997), pp. 283–300.

—, 'Theories of Language', in *The Cambridge History of Literary Criticism: Vol. 4, The Eighteenth Century*, eds H. B. Nisbet and C. Rawson (Cambridge: Cambridge University Press, 1997), pp. 335–48.

Huet, M. H., 'Social Entropy', *Yale French Studies*, 92 (1997), pp. 171–83.

Hundert, E. J., *The Enlightenment's Fable: Bernard Mandeville and the Discovery of Society* (Cambridge: Cambridge University Press, 1994).

Hunter, J. P., *Before Novels: The Cultural Contexts of Eighteenth-Century Fiction* (New York Norton, 1990).

Javelet, R., *Image et Resemblance au douziéme siécle de Saint Anselm à Alain de Lille*, 2 vols (Paris: Letouzey & Ané, 1967).

Jessop, T. E., *Bibliography of David Hume and of Scottish Philosophy* (London: A. Brown & Sons, 1938).

Jones, J., *The Egotistical Sublime: A History of Wordsworth's Imagination* (London: Chatto & Windus, 1954).

Jones, J. F., 'Prolegomena to a History of Happiness in the Eighteenth Century', *French-American Review*, 6:2 (Fall 1982), pp. 283–95.

Jones, P., 'Hume's Aesthetic Theory', in D. F. Norton (ed.), *The Cambridge Companion to Hume* (Cambridge: Cambridge University Press, 1993), pp. 255–80.

—, *Hume's Sentiments: Their Ciceronian and French Context* (Edinburgh: Edinburgh University Press, 1982).

Justice, G., 'Imlac's Pedagogy', *Age of Johnson: A Scholarly Annual*, 13 (2002), pp. 1–29.

Keen, P., 'The "Balloonomania": Science and Spectacle in 1780s England', *Eighteenth-Century Studies*, 39 (2006), pp. 507–35.

Kerby, B., 'Hume, Sympathy, and the Theatre', *Hume Studies*, 29 (November 2003), pp. 305–25.

Keymer, T., 'Sentimental Fiction: Ethics, Social Critique, and Philanthropy', in J. Richetti (ed.), *The Cambridge History of English Literature, 1660–1780* (Cambridge: Cambridge University Press, 2005), pp. 572–601.

Kivy, P., '"Lectures on the Fine Arts": An Unpublished Manuscript of Thomas Reid's', *Journal of the History of Ideas*, 31 (1970), pp. 17–31.

—, *The Seventh Sense: Francis Hutcheson and Eighteenth-Century British Aesthetics* (New York: Burt Franklin, 1976).

—, *Sound Sentiment: An Essay on the Musical Emotions* (Philadelphia, PA: Temple University Press, 1989).

—, *Introduction to a Philosophy of Music* (Oxford: Oxford University Press, 2002).

Klein, L. E., 'The Third Earl of Shaftesbury and the Progress of Politeness', *Eighteenth-Century Studies*, 18:2 (1984–5), pp. 185–214.

—, *Shaftesbury and the Culture of Politeness: Moral Discourse and the Cultural Politics of Early Eighteenth-Century England* (New York: Cambridge University Press, 1994).

—, 'Enlightenment as Conversation', in K. M. Baker and P. Hanns Reill (eds), *What's Left of Enlightenment? A Postmodern Question* (Stanford, CA: Stanford University Press, 2001), pp. 148–66.

Knox-Shaw, P., *Jane Austen and the Enlightenment* (Cambridge: Cambridge University Press, 2004).

Korsgaard, C., *Creating the Kingdom of Ends* (Cambridge: Cambridge University Press, 1996).

Kramnick, J., *Making the English Canon* (Cambridge: Cambridge University Press, 1999).

Kraut, R., 'Two Conceptions of Happiness', *Philosophical Review*, 88:2 (April 1979), pp. 167–97.

Kukla, R., 'Rousseau and the Problem of Gender Relations', in L. Lange (ed.), *Feminist Interpretations of Jean-Jacques Rousseau* (Philadelphia, PA: Pennsylvania State University Press, 2002), pp. 346–81.

Lehrer, K., *Thomas Reid* (London: Routledge, 1989).

Levinas, E., *Totality and Infinity: An Essay on Exteriority*, trans. A. Lingis (The Hague, Boston, MA, and London: Martinus Nijhoff, 1979).

Lipking, L., 'Johnson and the Meaning of Life', in J. Engell (ed.), *Johnson and his Age* (Cambridge, MA: Harvard University Press, 1984), pp. 1–28.

Livingston, D., *Philosophical Melancholy and Delusion: Hume's Pathology of Philosophy* (Chicago, IL: University of Chicago Press, 1998).

Long, A. A., *Studies* (Cambridge: Cambridge University Press, 1996).

—, *Epictetus: A Stoic and Socratic Guide to Life* (Oxford: Clarendon Press, 2002).

Luhmann, N., *Love as Passion: The Codification of Intimacy*, trans. J. Gaines and D. Jones (Cambridge, MA: Harvard University Press, 1988).

Lupton, C., '*Tristram Shandy*, David Hume, and Epistemological Fiction', *Philosophy and Literature*, 27 (2003), pp. 98–115.

Lynch, D. S., *The Economy of Character: Novels, Market Culture, and the Business of Inner Meaning* (Chicago, IL: University of Chicago Press, 1998).

Lyotard, J. F., *The Postmodern Condition: A Report on Knowledge* (Minneapolis, MN: University of Minnesota Press, 1984).

—, 'The Sublime and the Avant-Garde', in *The Lyotard Reader*, ed. A. Benjamin (New York: Blackwell, 1989).

Maas, H., 'Where Mechanism Ends: Thomas Reid on the Moral and the Animal Oeconomy', *History of Political Economy*, 35 (2003), pp. 338–60.

MacIntyre, A., *After Virtue* (Notre Dame, IN: University of Notre Dame Press, 1984).

Makus, I. 'The Politics of "Feminine Concealment" and "Masculine Openness"', in L. Lange (ed.), *Feminist Interpretations of Jean-Jacques Rousseau* (Philadelphia, PA: Pennsylvania State University Press, 2002), pp. 187–211.

Markley, R., 'Sentimentality as Performance: Shaftesbury, Sterne, and the Theatrics of Virtue', in F. Nussbaum and L. Brown (eds), *The New Eighteeth Century* (London: Methuen, 1987), pp. 210–30.

Marsh, R., 'Shaftesbury's Theory of Poetry: The Importance of the Inward Colloquy', *English Literary History*, 28 (1961), pp. 54–69.

Marshall, D., *The Figure of Theater: Shaftesbury, Defoe, Adam Smith and George Eliot* (New York: Columbia University Press, 1986).

—, *The Frame of Art: Fictions of Aesthetic Experience* (Baltimore, MD: Johns Hopkins University Press, 2005).

Marso, L. J., 'Rousseau's Subversive Women', in L. Lange (ed.), *Feminist Interpretations of Jean-Jacques Rousseau* (Philadelphia, PA: Pennsylvania State University Press, 2002), pp. 245–76

Mauzi, R., *L'Idée du bonheur dans la littérature et la pensée françaises au XVIIIe siècle* (Genève: Slatkine, 1979).

Mayr, O., *Authority, Liberty and Automatic Machinery in Early Modern Europe* (Baltimore, MD, and London: Johns Hopkins University Press, 1986).

McCracken, C., *Malebranche and the British Philosophy* (Oxford: Oxford University Press, 1983).

McFarlane, C., *The Sodomite in Fiction and Satire, 1660–1750* (New York: Columbia University Press, 1997).

McIntosh, C., *The Evolution of English Prose, 1700–1800: Style, Politeness and Print Culture* (Cambridge: Cambridge University Press, 1998).

McKeon, M., *The Origins of the English Novel* (Baltimore, MD: Johns Hopkins University Press, 1987).

McMahon, D., *Happiness: A History* (New York: Atlantic Monthly Press, 2006).

Meek, R., *Social Science and the Ignoble Savage* (Cambridge: Cambridge University Press, 1976).

—, *Smith, Marx, and After: Ten Essays in the Development of Economic Thought* (London: Chapman and Hall, 1977).

Mellanby, A., *James Watt: Mathematical Instrument Maker to the University of Glasgow* (Glasgow: Jackson and Son, 1936).

Mercer, P., *Sympathy and Ethics: A Study of the Relationship between Sympathy and Morality with Special Reference to Hume's Treatise* (Oxford: Clarendon Press, 1972).

Miller, D. A., *Narrative and its Discontents: Problems of Closure in the Traditional Novel* (Princeton, NJ: Princeton University Press, 1981).

Mooney, T., 'Derrida's Empirical Realism', *Philosophy & Social Criticism*, 25 (1999), pp. 33–56.

Morgenstrern, M., 'Women, Power and the Politics of Everyday Life', in L. Lange (ed.), *Feminist Interpretations of Jean-Jacques Rousseau* (Philadelphia, PA: Pennsylvania State University Press, 2002), pp. 113–43.

Mossner, E. C., 'A MS. Fragment of Hume's *Treatise*, 1740', *Notes and Queries*, 194 (1949), pp. 520–2.

—, 'Hume's "Of Criticism"', in H. Anderson and J. Shea (eds), *Studies in Criticism and Aesthetics 1660–1800* (Minneapolis, MN: University of Minnesota Press, 1967), pp. 232–48.

—, *The Life of David Hume*, 2nd edn (Oxford: Clarendon Press, 1980).

Mothersill, M., 'Hume and the Paradox of Taste', in G. Dickie et al. (eds), *Aesthetics: A Critical Anthology* (New York: St Martin's Press, 1989), pp. 269–86.

Mullan, J., 'The Language of Sentiment: Hume, Smith, and Henry Mackenzie', in A. Hook (ed.), *The History of Scottish Literature: Volume 2* (Aberdeen: Aberdeen University Press, 1987), pp. 273–89.

Nethery, W., 'Hume's Manuscript Corrections in a Copy of *A Treatise of Human Nature*', *Proceedings of the Bibliographical Society of America*, 57 (1963), pp. 446–7.

Nietzsche, F., *The Birth of Tragedy and The Case of Wagner*, trans. W. Kaufman (New York: Vintage/Random House, 1967).

Norton, D. F. (ed.), *The Cambridge Companion to Hume* (Cambridge: Cambridge University Press, 1993).

O'Brien, K., *Narratives of Enlightenment: Cosmopolitan History from Voltaire to Gibbon* (Cambridge: Cambridge University Press, 1997).

Okin, S. M. 'The Fate of Rousseau's Heroines', in L. Lange (ed.), *Feminist Interpretations of Jean-Jacques Rousseau* (Philadelphia, PA: Pennsylvania State University Press, 2002), pp. 89–112.

O'Neal, J. C., *The Authority of Experience: Sensationist Theory in the French Enlightenment* (University Park, PA: Penn State University Press, 1996).

Park, J., 'Pains and Pleasures of the Automaton: Frances Burney's Mechanics of Coming Out', *Eighteenth-Century Studies*, 40 (2006), pp. 23–49.

Parker, F., *Scepticism and Literature: An Essay on Pope, Hume, Sterne, and Johnson* (Oxford: Oxford University Press, 2003).

Pater, W., *The Renaissance: Studies in Art and Poetry*, in *Selected Writings of Walter Pater*, ed. H. Bloom (New York: New American Library, 1974).

Paulson, R., *The Beautiful, Novel, and Strange: Aesthetics and Heterodoxy* (Baltimore, MD: Johns Hopkins University Press, 1996).

Paulson, R., *Breaking and Remaking: Aesthetic Practice in England, 1700–1820* (New Brunswick, NJ: Rutgers University Press, 1989).

Phillips, M. S, 'Adam Smith and the History of Private Life: Social and Sentimental Narratives in Eighteenth-Century Historiography', in D. R. Kelley and D. H. Sacks (eds), *The Historical Imagination in Early Modern Britain: History, Rhetoric and Fiction, 1500–1800* (Cambridge: Cambridge University Press and Woodrow Wilson Press, 1997), pp. 318–42.

—, *Society and Sentiment* (Princeton, NJ: Princeton University Press, 2000).

Pinch, A., *Strange Fits of Passion: Epistemologies of Emotion, Hume to Austen* (Stanford, CA: Stanford University Press, 1996).

Pocock, J. G., A. *Barbarism and Religion, Volume Two: Narratives of Civil Government* (Cambridge: Cambridge University Press, 1999).

Polin, R., 'John Locke's Conception of Freedom', in J. Yolton (ed.), *John Locke: Problems and Perspectives* (Cambridge: Cambridge University Press, 1969), pp. 1–18.

Poovey, M., *A History of the Modern Fact* (Chicago, IL: University of Chicago Press, 1998).

Porter, R., *The Creation of the Modern World: The Untold Story of the British Enlightenment* (New York and London: W. W. Norton and Company, 2000).

Potkay, A., *The Passion for Happiness: Samuel Johnson and David Hume* (Ithaca, NY: Cornell University Press, 2000).

—, 'Joy and Happiness', in P. Backsheider and C. Ingrassia (eds), *A Companion to the Eighteenth-Century English and Novel and Culture* (Oxford: Blackwell Publishing, 2005), pp. 321–40.

—, *The Story of Joy from the Bible to Late Romanticism* (Cambridge: Cambridge University Press, 2007).

—, 'Captivation and Liberty in Wordsworth's Poems on Music', *Romantic Circles, Praxis Series. 'Soundings of Things Done': The Poetry and Poetics of Sound in the Romantic Era,* http://romantic.arhu.umd.edu/praxis/soundings/potkay/potkay.html (accessed 4 April 2008)

—, 'Wordsworth and the Ethics of Things', *PMLA* (2008), forthcoming.

Preminger, A., and T. V. F. Brogan (eds), *The New Princeton Encyclopedia of Poetry and Poetics* (New York: MJF Books, 1993).

Price, M., *To the Palace of Wisdom: Studies in Order and Energy from Dryden to Blake* (New York: Doubleday & Co., 1964).

Prince, M. B., 'Hume and the End of Religious Dialogue', *Eighteenth-Century Studies*, 25 (Spring 1992), pp. 283–308.

—, *Philosophical Dialogue in the British Enlightenment: Theology, Aesthetics, and the Novel* (Cambridge: Cambridge University Press, 1996).

Richetti, J., *Philosophical Writing: Locke, Berkeley, Hume* (Cambridge, MA: Harvard University Press, 1983).

—, *The English Novel in History: 1700–1780* (London: Routledge, 1999).

Ricken, U., *Linguistics, Anthropology and Philosophy in the French Enlightenment*, trans. R. W. Norton (London and New York: Routledge, 1994).

Ricks, C., *The Force of Poetry* (Oxford: Clarendon Press, 1984).

Ridley, A., *The Philosophy of Music: Themes and Variations* (Edinburgh: Edinburgh University Press, 2004).

Rorty, R., 'Remarks on Deconstruction and Pragmatism', in C. Mouffe (ed.), *Deconstruction and Pragmatism* (London and New York: Routledge, 1996), pp. 13–18.

Rotman, B., *Signifying Nothing: The Semiotics of Zero* (Stanford, CA: Stanford University Press, 1987).

Ruthven, K. K., 'Preposterous Chatterton', *ELH*, 71:2 (2004), pp. 345–75.

Schaffer, S., 'Enlightened Automata', in W. Clark, J. Golinski and S. Schaffer (eds), *The Sciences in Enlightened Europe* (Chicago, IL: University of Chicago Press, 1999), pp. 126–65.

Schneewind, J. B., *The Invention of Autonomy: A History of Modern Moral Philosophy* (Cambridge: Cambridge University Press, 1998).

Schouls, P., *Reasoned Freedom: John Locke and Enlightenment* (Ithaca, NY: Cornell University Press, 1992).

Searle, J. R, 'Reiterating the Differences: A Reply to Derrida', *Glyph*, 1 (1977), pp. 198–208.

Shapin, S., *The Social History of Truth: Civility and Science in Seventeenth-Century England* (Chicago, IL, and London: University of Chicago Press, 1994).

Shapiro, G., 'The Man of Letters and the Author of Nature: Hume on Philosophical Discourse', *The Eighteenth Century: Theory and Interpretation*, 26 (1985), pp. 115–37.

Simpson, D., 'Hume's Intimate Voices and the Method of Dialogue', *Texas Studies in Literature and Language*, 21 (1979), pp. 68–92.

Simpson Ross, I., *The Life of Adam Smith* (Oxford: Clarendon Press, 1995).

Siskin, C., *Work of Writing: Literature and Social Change in Britain 1700–1830* (Baltimore, MD, and London: Johns Hopkins University Press).

Sitter, J., *Literary Loneliness in Mid-Eighteenth Century England* (Ithaca, NY: Cornell University Press, 1982).

Skillin, A., 'Rousseau and the Fall of Social Man', *Philosophy*, 60 (1985), pp. 105–21.

Skinner, A., 'Adam Smith: Ethics and Self-Love', in P. Jones and A. Skinner (eds), *Adam Smith Reviewed* (Edinburgh: Edinburgh University Press, 1992), pp. 142–67.

Smith, N. K., *The Philosophy of David Hume: A Critical Study of its Origins and Central Doctrines* (London: Macmillan, 1940).

—, 'Hume's Rejected *Essays*', *Forum for Modern Language Studies*, 8 (1972), pp. 354–71.

Sorensen, R. A., *Thought Experiments* (New York: Oxford University Press, 1992).

Stafford, B., *Artful Science: Enlightenment Education and the Eclipse of Visual Entertainment* (Cambridge, MA: MIT Press, 1994).

Starobinski, J., *Transparency and Obstruction*, trans. A. Goldhammer (Chicago, IL: University of Chicago Press, 1988).

Stewart, L., *The Rise of Public Science: Rhetoric, Technology, and Natural Philosophy in Newtonian Britain, 1660–1750* (Cambridge: Cambridge University Press, 1992).

Stewart, M. A., 'Two Species of Philosophy: The Historical Significance of the First *Enquiry*', in P. Mullican (ed.), *Reading Hume on Human Understanding* (Oxford: Oxford University Press, 2002), pp. 67–95.

Straub, K., *Sexual Suspects: Eighteenth-Century Players and Sexual Ideology* (Princeton, NJ: Princeton University Press, 1992).

Striker, G., *Essays on Hellenistic Epistemology and Ethics* (Cambridge: Cambridge University Press, 1996).

Sussman, C., *Consuming Anxieties: Consumer Boycott, Gender, and British Slavery, 1713–1833* (Stanford, CA: Stanford University Press, 2001).

Taylor, C., *Sources of the Self: The Making of Modern Identity* (Cambridge, MA: Harvard University Press, 1989).

—, *Modern Social Imaginaries* (Durham, NC: Duke University Press, 2004).

Teichgraeber, R., 'Rethinking *Das Adam Smith Problem*', in J. R. A. Mason and A. Murdoch (eds), *New Perspectives on the Politics and Culture of Early Modern Scotland* (Edinburgh: John Donald, 1982), pp. 249–64.

Tierney-Hynes, R., 'Shaftesbury's Soliloquy: Authorship and the Psychology of Romance', *Eighteenth-Century Studies*, 38:4 (2005), pp. 605–21.

Todd, W., B., 'David Hume: A Preliminary Bibliography', in W. B. Todd (ed.), *Hume and the Enlightenment* (Edinburgh: Edinburgh University Press, 1974), pp. 189–205.

Townsend, D., *Hume's Aesthetic Theory* (New York: Routledge, 2001).

—, 'Thomas Reid and the Theory of Taste', *Journal of Aesthetics and Art Criticism*, 61 (2003), pp. 341–51.

Trumbach, R., *Sex and the Gender Revolution 1: Heterosexuality and the Third Gender in Enlightenment London* (Chicago, IL: University of Chicago Press, 1998).

Tweyman, S. (ed.), *David Hume: Critical Assessments* (London: Routledge, 1995).

Voitle, R., *The Third Earl of Shaftesbury, 1671–1713* (Baton Rouge, LA, and London: Louisiana State University Press, 1984).

Watt, I., *The Rise of the Novel* (Berkeley, CA: University of California Press, 1957).

Wendorf, R. *William Collins and Eighteenth-Century Poetry* (Minneapolis, MN: University of Minnesota Press, 1981).

Wilson, F., 'Substance and Self in Locke and Hume', in K. F. Barber and J. J. E. Gracia (eds), *Individuation and Identity in Early Modern Philosophy: Descartes to Kant* (Albany, NY: State University of New York Press, 1994), pp. 355–99.

Wirz, C., 'Note sur *Emile et Sophie, ou les Solitaires*', *Annales de la Société Jean-Jacques-Rousseau*, 36 (1963–65), pp. 291–304.

Wolterstorff, N., 'God and Darkness in Reid', in ed. J. Houston (ed.), *Thomas Reid: Context, Influence, and Significance* (Edinburgh: Dunedin Academic Press, 2004), pp. 77–102.

Wood, P. (ed.), *Thomas Reid on the Animate Creation: Papers Related to the Life Science* (Edinburgh: Edinburgh University Press, 1995).

Wordsworth, J., *The Music of Humanity: A Critical Study of Wordsworth's Ruined Cottage* (New York: Harper & Row, 1969).

Wu, D., *Wordsworth: An Inner Life* (Oxford: Blackwell, 2002).

—, *Wordsworth's Reading 1770–1799* (Cambridge: Cambridge University Press, 1993).

Yousef, N., *Isolated Cases: The Anxieties of Autonomy in Enlightenment Philosophy and Romantic Literature* (Ithaca, NY: Cornell University Press, 2004).

INDEX